D1798167

Foreigners and Englishmen

Foreigners and Englishmen

The Controversy over Immigration and Population, 1660–1760

Daniel Statt

DELAWARE

Newark: University of Delaware Press
London and Toronto: Associated University Presses

© 1995 by Associated University Presses

All rights reserved. Authorization to photocopy items for internal or personal use, or the internal or personal use of specific clients, is granted by the copyright owner, provided that a base fee of $10.00, plus eight cents per page, per copy is paid directly to the Copyright Clearance Center, 222 Rosewood Drive, Danvers, Massachusetts 01923. [0-87413-531-1/95 $10.00 + 8¢ pp, pc.]

Associated University Presses
440 Forsgate Drive
Cranbury, NJ 08512

Associated University Presses
25 Sicilian Avenue
London WC1A 2QH, England

Associated University Presses
P.O. Box 338, Port Credit
Mississauga, Ontario
Canada L5G 4L8

The paper used in this publication meets the requirements
of the American National Standard for Permanence of Paper
for Printed Library Materials Z39.48-1984.

Library of Congress Cataloging-in-Publication Data

Statt, Daniel, 1956–
    Foreigners and Englishmen : the controversy over immigration and
population, 1660–1760 / Daniel Statt.
        p.   cm.
    Includes bibliographical references and indexes.
    ISBN 0-87413-531-1 (alk. paper)
    1. England—Emigration and immigration—Government policy—
History—17th century.   2. Immigrants—England—History.
3. Refugees—England—History.   4. England—Population—History.
[1. England—Emigration and immigration—Government policy—
History—18th century.]   I. Title.
JV7622.S7   1995
325.41—dc20   94-28898
                                                             CIP

PRINTED IN THE UNITED STATES OF AMERICA

To My Mother and Father

Contents

Preface

This book is a study of the debate over population and immigration to England in the late seventeenth and eighteenth centuries. It examines the ideas of those who advocated the admission of foreigners, the evolving government policy with respect to immigrants, and the consequences of their arrival and reception in England. The origins of the book lie in a Cambridge Ph.D. thesis that I embarked on in 1984. Since then I have incurred many debts, only some of which can be acknowledged here. The work embodied in this book has in many respects involved the investigation of, if not terra incognita, at least some of the less well-known historical terrain of early modern Britain. Immigration before the nineteenth century has been little studied, and the paths that I have followed have been traveled by few recent historians. As a result, the discussions that I have had with colleagues, and the comments and criticisms that I have received from them, have been doubly helpful to me in integrating my research into the body of scholarship on the seventeenth and eighteenth centuries, and it is a pleasure to have this opportunity to acknowledge my gratitude. I owe my greatest thanks to Brian Outhwaite, my Ph.D. thesis supervisor, whose guidance and encouragement were invaluable, and whose patience was seemingly inexhaustible. I received many acute comments and helpful suggestions from D. C. Coleman, and Henry Roseveare and Barry Supple provided great assistance. John Morrill offered direction in the early stages of research, as did Maarten Ultee and Irene Scouloudi. I benefited greatly from the kind criticism of Jack Crowley, who faithfully read the entire manuscript. Others whose help along the way made this book possible are John Fair, Dan Henderson, Daniel Woolf, Greg Hanlon, Monika Küster, and Dean Worcester.

I should like as well to thank the staffs of the many libraries and archives where I pursued the research embodied here. The help I received from the staff of the Corporation of London Record Office was especially valuable. I am also indebted to the staffs of the British Library, the Public Record Office, the Guildhall Library, St. Paul's Library, the Goldsmiths' Library, the House of Lords Record Office, and the Huntington Library.

Research grants from Gonville & Caius College, Cambridge, and from Magdalene College, Cambridge, were of help in the early stages of research. A research fellowship at the Huntington Library in the academic year 1989–90 allowed me to examine many rare printed works that I could other-

9

wise not have seen. The bulk of the writing of the book was completed during my tenure as a Killam postdoctoral fellow at Dalhousie University, and I wish to extend special thanks to the Killam Trust and to the Department of History at Dalhousie University for the support that allowed me the luxury of devoting myself full time to research and writing. I am also grateful to Auburn University at Montgomery for the leaves of absence that allowed me to take up research fellowships and for generous grants in aid of research that helped to bring the work to fruition.

Some of the arguments and evidence presented in chapters 1, 4, and 7 first appeared in journal articles, and I thank the following publications for permission to adapt or reprint small parts of those materials: the *Historical Journal, Eighteenth-Century Studies*, and the *Proceedings of the Huguenot Society of Great Britain and Ireland.*

List Of Tables

Conventions and Abbreviations

During this period two calendars were used in England. The Julian or Old Style calendar continued in use until 31 December 1751. By that time, it was eleven days behind the Gregorian or New Style calendar in use elsewhere in Europe. Under the Old Style calendar the year was taken to begin on 25 March, not 1 January. Unless otherwise indicated, all dates in this book are Old Style until 1752, but the year is taken to begin on 1 January. The place of publication is London unless otherwise stated. Likewise, letters for which no place is stated were written from London. Spelling and punctuation have been largely, though not uniformly, modernized.

BIHR	*Bulletin of the Institute of Historical Research*
BL	British Library
BM, OPL	British Museum, Official Publications Library
BSHPF	*Bulletin Historique et Littéraire de la Société de l'Histoire de la Protestantisme Française*
BTJ	*Journal of the Commissioners for Trade and Plantations*
Cal. Tr. Bks.	*Calendar of Treasury Books*
Cal. Tr. Papers	*Calendar of Treasury Papers*
Canaan	*Das Verlangte, nicht Erlangte Canaan* (Frankfurt and Leipzig: 1711).
CJ	*Journals of the House of Commons*
CLRO	Corporation of London Record Office
CSPA	*Calendar of State Papers Colonial Series: America and the West Indies*

CSPD   *Calendar of State Papers Domestic*

CSPV   *Calendar of State Papers Venetian*

DNB   *Dictionary of National Biography*

EcHR   *Economic History Review*

Grey's *Debates*   Anchitell Grey, ed., *Debates of the House of Commons from the Year 1667 to the Year 1694*, 10 vols. (1763).

Harl. Misc.   *The Harleian Miscellany*, 12 vols. (1808–11).

HMC Reports   *Historical Manuscripts Commission Reports.*

HSQS   *Huguenot Society of Great Britain and Ireland Quarto Series*

LJ   *Journals of the House of Lords*

McCulloch, *Tracts*   J.R. McCulloch, ed., *Early English Tracts on Commerce* (1856; Cambridge, 1970).

P & P   *Past & Present*

Parl. Hist.   *The Parliamentary History of England from the Earliest Period to the Year 1803*, 36 vols. (1806–20).

Petty Papers   Marquis of Lansdowne, ed., *The Petty Papers: Some Unpublished Writings of Sir William Petty*, 2 vols. (1927).

PHSL   *Proceedings of the Huguenot Society of London/Great Britain and Ireland*

PRO   Public Record Office

Review   A. W. Secord, ed., *Defoe's Review*, 22 vols. (New York, 1938).

Shaw, *1603–1700*   W. A. Shaw, ed., *Letters of Denization and Acts of Naturalization for Aliens in England and Ireland, 1603–1700, HSQS,* vol. 17 (Lymington, 1911).

Shaw, *1701–1800*   W. A. Shaw, ed., *Letters of Denization and Acts of Naturalization for Aliens in England and Ireland, 1701–1800, HSQS*, vol. 27 (Manchester, 1923).

Somer's Tracts   Walter Scott, ed., *Somer's Tracts: A Collection of Scarce and Valuable Tracts, on the Most Interesting and Entertaining Subjects*, 2nd. ed., 13 vols. (London, 1809–15).

TRHS   *Transactions of the Royal Historical Society*

Foreigners and Englishmen

1

Introduction

Jacques Fontaine was a French Protestant who fled for refuge to England in the 1680s at the time of the Revocation of the Edict of Nantes. His life in England, as he recorded it in his memoirs, provides an illuminating example of the kind of reception that most immigrants to England in that age faced. He landed with a group of fellow refugees at Barnstable, in north Devon, where the English inhabitants, as he wrote, "took us into their houses and treated us with the greatest kindness; God raised up for us fathers and mothers, and brothers and sisters in a strange land." As a refugee from the persecution of Protestants then at its height in France, Fontaine was received with open sympathy by the English as a victim of absolutism and Popish intolerance. But the generosity that he marveled at was not to last for long.

Fontaine was a model of the industriousness for which the French immigrants were both cherished and resented. In the years after his arrival in England, he worked as a merchant, a teacher of French, a shopkeeper, a woollen manufacturer, and a fisherman. He settled in Taunton where he opened a shop and sold many of the commodities traded by his fellow French refugees in England and Holland, from brandy to beaver hats. But his success provoked the anger of the native English tradesmen. Fontaine's absence from services at the Anglican parish church excited suspicion, and led some townspeople to think that he was a Jesuit spy, perhaps an instrument of the hated Louis XIV. "Those who knew better," he wrote, "studiously kept up the false impression in order to injure me with the community at large" and undermine the economic competition that he presented. The resentful inhabitants of Taunton finally took action. Fontaine was brought before the town's Mayor and Court of Aldermen, accused of not having served his seven years' apprenticeship, of destroying the trade of other shopkeepers, and of being a disguised Jesuit. "One word would describe him as well as a thousand," his accusers declared, "he was a French dog, taking the bread out of the mouths of the English." The prosecution was dropped after the intervention of the town's sympathetic Recorder, but Fontaine continued to be harrassed and over-taxed, and eventually he was forced to leave Taunton and settle elsewhere, though he remained in England and never again saw his native France.[1]

Jacques Fontaine's story accords with the experiences of many late seventeenth and eighteenth-century immigrants to England. It reveals the sympathy that newcomers, and particularly religious refugees, could usually expect on their first arrival, as well as the economic contribution that they often made to their adopted homeland; but it also suggests the antagonism that could make settlement in England a trial of fortitude and endurance. Immigrants nevertheless came in large numbers during this period, and the questions of whether foreigners should be received in England, what their legal and economic rights should be, and how they were to be acculturated within English society came to play a prominent role in the public discourse of the age. Nor did this discourse develop solely in passive reaction to the arrival of immigrants propelled by outside forces. On the contrary, from the Restoration of Charles II in 1660 to the middle of the eighteenth century a protracted controversy unfolded over whether a positive policy ought to be adopted to actively encourage foreigners to come to settle in England. The debate was usually phrased in terms of whether aliens should be granted naturalization in England, that is, whether a cheap and convenient way should be offered for an immigrant to acquire the rights of a native-born subject. All parties to this lively exchange, which formed one branch of a burgeoning discourse on economic principles and policies after the Restoration, believed that a general naturalization act would inspire a large influx of foreign Protestants seeking to leave behind them the religious and political turmoil of the continent.

The book falls into three parts. Chapters 2, 3, and 4 treat the controversy over immigration from the Restoration to the reign of Queen Anne. A striking evolution in the economic discourse can be seen over the course of these fifty years, and the political character of the debate became more and more intense. Promoters of immigration in Parliament, eager to increase the number of England's people in order to stimulate trade, made over a dozen attempts from the 1660s onward to pass a liberal naturalization act, and their efforts finally bore fruit in the General Naturalization Act of 1709. The Act of 1709 represented the great experiment in immigration policy during this century of debate, as well as a monument to the intense partisan struggle of Queen Anne's reign.

The test of the policy came only months after the passage of the Act of 1709 with the immigration to England in the space of a few months of roughly 13,000 Germans from the Rhenish Palatinate and other parts of the Rhine Valley, the "Poor Palatines," encouraged to migrate by English agents. The Palatines probably represented the largest number of people to enter England in a single year in either the seventeenth or eighteenth centuries, though the migration has received little attention from historians. Chapters 5 and 6 place the debate over immigration in a very concrete context by recounting the Palatine migration and the futile struggle of the British government to settle the Germans in England. Both the act and the Germans themselves rapidly became pawns in the partisan frenzy of the last years of Queen Anne's reign, and the naturalization policy that had been promoted by the Whig ministry was discredited along with the party that had supported it.

The third part of the book traces the immigration and population controversy to the middle of the eighteenth century. Many observers attributed the disastrous failure of the Palatine migration to the hostility of the native English to the arrival of foreigners, and chapter 7 examines the attitudes of the English to foreign settlers throughout this period. The measure of hospitality or hostility that immigrants confronted represented one of the great mediating factors in the success or failure of their settlement, and the English reaction reflected not only an ambivalent mixture of popular sympathy and xenophobia but the consequences of clashing political ideologies. Even a brief examination of the attitudes of the English towards foreigners, a subject that would require another work of this length to do full justice to, puts the intellectual and political side of the story in a broader context, and casts grave doubts on the practicability of the pleas for the admission of large numbers of foreigners. The chapter also explores the apparent detachment and indeed incongruity between the economic controversy over naturalization and the cultural discourse on the reception of foreigners.

The liberalized immigration policy created by the Act of 1709, realized only after a long campaign, seemed in its first test a failure. The name of Palatine became a stigma for a policy reproved as catastrophic, and the ascendant Tory administration repealed the act only three years after its passage. The unfortunate events of 1709, however, did not bring the naturalization movement to an end. The contentious discourse on immigration continued, and its supporters in Parliament introduced several more bills for a naturalization statute in the 1740s and 1750s, when agitation over the admission of foreigners flared up again. Chapter 8 follows the evolution of the debate to the accession of George III. Over the course of those fifty years, the complexion of economic thought, views on population, and economic conditions all underwent profound change as English society became increasingly commercialized. The discourse over immigration evolved as well, and proponents of naturalization became much more sophisticated in both their rhetorical terms and in their definition of their objectives in admitting foreigners. By the end of the period, however, the fears that England had too few people had subsided or had been redirected away from immigration schemes. It even seemed to some that the population was too large. Concern over depopulation had provoked and fueled the immigration debate, but by 1760 that foundation of the controversy had crumbled, or rather shifted, as the discourse on population embarked on new paths. The pleas for the encouragement of immigration came to an end. Population became the subject of an intense debate on several occasions during the latter half of the eighteenth century, but the proposition that the nation should, or indeed could, increase its population by encouraging large-scale immigration was discredited if not forgotten. A body of opinion in England was already anticipating fears of Malthusian overpopulation, and only in the nineteenth century would the immigration question again be squarely faced.[2] Throughout the period, and to a large degree indifferent to the ebb and flow of the immigration controversy in England, a formidable influx of foreign immigrants continued to arrive, mostly from Western Europe, in numbers that would not be surpassed until the late nineteenth century. The century after 1660 marks one of the great ages of immigration to England, and the challenge and promise presented by foreign settlers helped to shape the fundamental changes that in these years transformed England into a commercial society.[3]

Although the immigration issue was intensely political, the controversy unfolded itself most fully not in Parliament but in the pages of the hundreds of economic tracts, pamphlets, treatises, and broadsides that tumbled from the presses throughout the period. The fates of French, German, and other foreigners in England, as well as those intending to immigrate, became pledges in wars of words and ideas as England's early economic writers debated immigration policy and expounded their theories of population. In the forge of topical controversy over immigration the disputants gradually wrought an economic discourse and a vocabulary for demographic enquiry that strove to explain and justify a progressive commercialization of England's economy and society and the role of population and immigration within that process. In this discourse population and immigration were inextricably intertwined. The advocates of encouraging immigration argued that the number of England's people was dwindling, and that it must at all costs be increased. A spectre of depopulation haunted England, and a fragile consensus emerged amongst writers on trade, at least in the last decades of the seventeenth century, that the only immediate means to stem the apparent hemorrhaging was the admission of foreigners. The story of the immigration question, and of the fluctuating policies of the English government toward foreign newcomers, therefore forms in large part a chapter in the history of economic and social thought. The movement for the repopulation of England, for so it was conceived at the time, found expression through a great development of thought about population: what it was, what it ought to be, what determined it. It is not too much to say that these years witnessed the birth of an ideology of population, or more precisely, the integration of a growing body of thought on population into broader political, social, and economic ideologies and discourses.

Historical demographers have in recent years invested enormous amounts of scholarly energy into mapping the contours of the population history of early modern England. They have achieved a great deal. Much has been learned about population size and the factors that influenced demographic change. Scant attention has been paid, however, to what contemporaries thought about England's population. No systematic history of the theories of population current in England before Malthus exists,[4] nor has any major attempt been made to relate demographic change to the evolution of ideas about population. The immigration controversy invites such questions to be asked. The proposals for a general naturalization emerged directly from the fears that crystalized after the Restoration that England's population was dwindling in size. The debate over naturalization, actuated by the desire to increase the number of England's people, was limited almost precisely to the century from 1660 to 1760, a period that witnessed demographic stability and at times even stagnation. What was the relation between the fears of depopulation and actual changes in England's population in this period? The evolution in the discourse on population expressed in the polemical literature corresponded remarkably well with the actual demographic changes now charted by historical demographers.[5] As population stagnated, fears of depopulation became more acute. The difficult question to answer is why such a relationship should have existed. The authors of economic tracts and those active in the political disputes over immigration certainly possessed no reliable information on England's population. Despite abortive attempts to undertake a numbering of the people in the 1750s, the first census awaited the opening of the nineteenth century.[6] Observers had a variety of indirect evidence to judge from, however, and such putative reflections of population change as low agricultural prices or difficulties in finding laborers or tenants seem to have been enough to galvanize opinion on the need for an accession of foreign immigrants. The volume of emigration was also perceived as a sobering warning of the trend of England's population, especially as many observers saw little immigration to balance it. In any event, as the naturalization controversy is examined the question must be addressed of why the immigration debate paralleled actual changes in population growth, however tentative the answers to that question may be.

As demographic history has tended to neglect the factor of international migration, so general histories of economic thought have largely ignored the issues of population and immigration. Both historians and economists have tended to search in the early economic discourse for evidence that casts light on the economic questions that engage the attention of economic inquiry today, such as theories of value and price mechanisms, rather than those that absorbed early modern thinkers, such as population and poverty. In the arena of political thought, historians have learned to attend more closely to the preoccupations and the language peculiar to the historical context of the Stuart and Hanoverian periods. It is time that the same sensitivity to the language and the contours of discourse be extended to the social and economic thought of the age. One must also guard against a Whig interpretation of economic history that sees early economic thought as struggling towards the doctrines of the classical economists. The titles of two important studies in this area, E. A. J. Johnson's *Predecessors of Adam Smith: The Growth of British Economic Thought* (1937), and Terence Hutchison's *Before Adam Smith: The Emergence of Political Economy, 1662–1776* (1988), reflect the traditional tendency to see early economic ideas as culminating in *The Wealth of Nations*, a teleological view that has caused considerable distortion, as well as a denigration of pre-Smithian economic discourse. Adam Smith himself pushed questions of population and immigration to the periphery of economic discourse. It is hardly surprising, then, that no study has been undertaken of the immigration issue that loomed so large in the economic publications of the seventeenth and eighteenth centuries. The rise of demographic history in recent years has made it all the more necessary for us to seek to recover how contemporaries understood population questions, how they struggled to integrate such views into larger ideological frameworks, and how the discourse on population influenced public policy and in turn altered the lives of foreigners coming to England. This book then seeks to put our newly accumulated wealth of quantitative demographic data in their historical context by examining theories of population and immigration in the crucial years during which English writings on social and trade issues coalesced into a coherent economic discourse.

This study undertakes an examination of a question that falls under the head of economic thought traditionally called *mercantilist*. Denoting in its broadest sense the body of economic ideas and state economic regulations of early modern Europe, the idea of mercantilism has suffered a good deal of abuse, some of it deserved, at the hands of historians who doubt the value of the term as an analytic category.[7] Part of the difficulty lies in confusion over the application of the term mercantilism to the economic theories of writers on trade as opposed to the economic policies of early modern states. The distinction between policy and theory is crucial in most economic matters, and is certainly so in the case of immigration and population issues.

On the whole, however, the vexed question of the meaning of mercantilism need not be tackled in order to examine the immigration controversy. The object of this book is to analyze and interpret a branch of economic discourse, rather than to attach a label to it. The discord over the meaning of the term *mercantilism* nevertheless betrays more than a semantic quibble. It reveals a fundamental flaw in many studies of early economic issues that must be guarded against: the failure to explore the relation between economic thought, economic conditions, and economic policy. There are numerous studies of the history of economic doctrine, but few of them make more than a token bow towards the economic conditions in which the theories were formulated, or the way in which they were—or more often were not— put into effect by governments. Some historians have dismissed early modern economic ideas as merely mechanically conditioned by the economic circumstances in which they were articulated, spasms of intellectual interest brought about by a slump in the woollen trade or a rise in the price of pig iron.[8] Others grant overriding importance to the political circumstances that led to the implementation of particular policies, as, for example in the case of the economic policies of the Cromwellian commonwealth.[9] None of these approaches provides a complete picture of a historical context. This book seeks to explore the complex relations and discontinuities between the ideas expressed in the discourse on immigration, the policies that governed immigration and their implementation, the economic and political circumstances that conditioned the controversy, and the human consequences for immigrants and natives when the policy of encouraging immigration in order to increase England's population was put to the test.[10]

The subject of this study is not immigrants so much as their reception by the English, the experience of immigration from the point of view of the host culture. The book's object is to reconstruct the controversy over immigration and its social and intellectual bases rather than to attempt a reconstitution of any particular foreign communities. The equally interesting and important question of the experiences of immigrants, their gradual acculturation and assimilation, is one that has received relatively little attention. Although it would be difficult to name a subject more topical today than immigration, historians have had relatively little to say about foreign immigrants to Britain, and the early modern period has suffered particular neglect.[11] The second half of the nineteenth century was the heyday of immigrant histories, mostly of the Protestants who came to England from France. The histories produced by Samuel Smiles, R. L. Poole, William Cunningham, and others are still valuable for their wealth of detail. They are, however, largely biographical in character, and their concentration on church history and their inspirational tone reflect their flavor of Protestant piety.[12] Even very recent work has tended to concentrate on particular religious groups of immigrants.[13] Bernard Cottret's book on the Huguenot immigration, based on French Protestant consistory registers, makes by far the most important contribution to date to our understanding of the process of acculturation in England. Much work on individual immigrant communities remains to be undertaken.[14] The present study, however, takes a broader view, approaching the phenomenon of immigration through a different facet of the historian's prism. It explores the arrival of foreigners in England not through the study of individual communities but within the context of the political and economic discourse on population and public policy.

The scene must nevertheless be set and the dramatis personae introduced by a brief account of those who migrated to England in the period. An alien presence had of course existed in England for centuries. Before the sixteenth century most aliens had probably been merchants whose stays were often temporary. The number of immigrants had never been large. In the early modern period, however, religious persecution following the Reformation and the clash of expanding nation-states added a new dimension to the potential for large-scale immigration.

The movement of peoples in Europe in the early modern period owing to religious persecution and the disruptions of dynastic war rivaled the displacements that would occur in the twentieth century. Europe had witnessed its share of religious intolerance in the Middle Ages: heretics had been burned, crusades had been staged, infidels had been put to the sword. But religious intolerance had seldom caused large-scale movements of people; and persecution, limited in its scope by the physical and economic constraints of the age and the decentralization of political power, had more often than not been a localized and desultory affair, dependent upon the fervor of local churchmen and the energies of magistrates and secular rulers. The religious dissection of Europe in the sixteenth century, however, joined with the expanding powers—military and fiscal—of the dynastic nation-states to greatly increase the compass and the devastation of religious persecution. Wars and persecutions, pursued with zealous rivalry by Protestants and Catholics alike, uprooted large numbers of people and drove many into exile. Indeed, the persecutions and the migrations that they provoked had begun before Luther's break with Rome: the Inquisition had begun operations in Spain against the Jews and *conversos* from 1480, and the consequent expulsions culminated in the final and general expulsion order of 1492, which cast out perhaps 35,000 families from Castile alone.[15] In the years after the Reformation, the French Wars of Religion, the Thirty Years' War, and the wars of Louis XIV contributed to the flow of migrants within Europe, many of them the miserable victims of religious hatred, wartime destruction, or both. The importance of war in bringing about large-scale movements of people in the early modern period must not be overshadowed by the sensational cruelties of religious persecution, in which Spain continued to distinguish itself: some 275,000 Moriscos suffered deportation between 1609 and 1614. In fact, the two forces of persecution and war often acted in concert to uproot peoples.

Even in the ostensibly enlightened eighteenth century massive expulsions on religious grounds continued to occur, for example the exile of some 20,000 or more Protestants from the archbishopric of Salzburg in the 1730s.[16] And of course the transoceanic movement of peoples brought about by new discoveries and colonial expansion paralleled the massive migrations within Europe, as soldiers and debtors, deserters and uprooted sectarians, displaced peasants and penniless vagabonds joined the flow of people on the move. Nor does this picture include the migrations of Eastern Europe, where the movement of Southern Serbs into Hungary, the flight of Old Believers from the new Russia of Peter the Great, and the less familiar displacements within the Ottoman empire rivaled and perhaps surpassed the movements of peoples further west.[17]

In this drama of large movements of people over the face of Europe England played a prominent though not a central part. The Marian exiles earned a place in the hagiography of English Protestantism, but England received more in religious refugees than it gave. From 1550, when the first "stranger" churches were established with the permission of Edward VI, England became a place of refuge for displaced Protestants.[18] The two largest waves of newcomers to England in the early modern period were composed of victims, or professed victims, of religious persecution on the continent. In the second half of the sixteenth century Protestants from the Spanish Netherlands sought in England a refuge from the depredations of the Duke of Alva. In addition, the St. Bartholomew's Day Massacre in 1572 led to an influx of Huguenots from France and the foundation of a considerable number of French Protestant churches in England. The second great influx of Protestant refugees arrived in the latter half of the seventeenth century as a result of the devastation caused by Louis XIV's ambitious wars and of the persecutions that culminated in that king's revocation of the Edict of Nantes in 1685. Perhaps a quarter of the 200,000 or so Huguenots who left France in the late seventeenth century came to England.[19] The paucity of sources, however, makes reliable statements on the numbers of foreign settlers and the reasons for their migration exceedingly difficult.

Before the nineteenth century no general, or at least permanent, restrictions on the entry of immigrants to England existed, and almost no records were kept of comings and goings. During time of war (especially in the 1690s) it is true that passes were required of those going to or returning from the continent. Limited in duration and political in purpose, sources of this sort contribute little to the attempt to discern patterns in the movements of people in and out of the country, much less to quantify those movements.[20] With no restrictions on entry and few records of arrivals and departures, it is difficult to determine how many immigrants came to England and how long they stayed. Some foreigners arrived as temporary visitors or merchants intending to sojourn for a limited time. Others at first glance appear to have been more than sojourners, but many of the French Protestants who came to England in the 1680s passed back and forth to Holland in a way that makes it hard to tell where they were settled. The shadow figure of those who reemigrated, to Ireland, to North America, or back to the continent, was probably large. The difficulty of measuring immigration is especially marked in the case of the Scots and the Irish, who were often merely temporary residents, working for a season, traveling as itinerant peddlers, or coming only for the harvest. Despite these obstacles, the difficulty of quantifying immigration should not lead us to underestimate its importance. Demographic historians have generally had little to say about immigrants, and have often ignored the limited historical sources that do provide narrow windows on foreign settlement in England. The authors of the most important recent work on England's population history remark laconically of immigrants that "their numbers are uncertain in the absence of adequate records."[21] Can more be said about the volume of immigration to England in a period when immigration policy loomed so large in the minds of publicists and politicians?

One possible source on the volume of immigration is the figures for denizations and naturalizations, the two legal procedures by which foreigners could shed their alien status. These records offer scant help, since for reasons that will be explained presently they represent only a fraction of those who immigrated. There were "Returns" of strangers living in London in 1593, 1627, 1635, and 1639, undertaken in part out of suspicion of the foreign churches, but no such surveys were taken after the Restoration.[22] In the absence of formal censuses, by far the most fruitful sources of information about immigrants are the records of the foreign churches to which they belonged. The ecclesiastical records of the French churches in England in particular contain considerable information about the size of the refugee migration from France. Such records are flawed, however, by the transitory nature of the foreign congregations, whose members entered sometimes late in life, had their children baptized in the Anglican parish church, or moved from one to another of the foreign congregations. Family reconstitution of the sort undertaken through Anglican parish records is impossible, and the foreign church registers provide only fragmentary information on place of origin, age structure, or occupations.[23] A portrait can be painted, but only in broad brush strokes, and for the most part only the largest groups of foreign settlers can be delineated with any certainty.

The figures to be drawn from the registers and other records of the French churches in England have been variously published. Dr. Robin Gwynn has produced the most authoritative recent estimates of the size of the French immigrant community. He concludes that between 40,000 and 50,000 French arrived in England after 1680, a figure that agrees with the estimates of contemporaries. Recent work on the French immigrant community in the Netherlands suggests a somewhat lower figure for England;[24] but Gwynn's estimate that 8,000 to 10,000 Huguenot immigrants arrived in England between the middle of the century and 1680 seems if anything to be an underestimate in view of the turmoil in London aroused by the arrival of immigrant French artisans in the 1660s and early 1670s, and the complaints in France of a burgeoning emigration of skilled Protestants in the late 1660s.[25] One acute observer claimed in 1668 that England had "drained" France of its artisans; however much an exaggeration that remark may have been, the French authorities were eager to prevent the loss of skilled artisans, especially to their occasional enemy across the channel.[26] In any case, the records of the foreign churches provide not only a measure of the number of immigrants but an outline of the pace of religious assimilation, if relatively little information about how that assimilation occurred. The story of the foreign churches is one of decline over the course of the eighteenth century: the congregations steadily dwindled, bereft of large infusions of fresh refugee members in the calmer religious climate of the eighteenth century. By the end of the century many of the foreign congregations had disappeared.[27] However, religious conformity to the Church of England, as indicated by the contraction of the foreign churches, should not be equated with the loss of a distinctive culture, since social and cultural assimilation probably proceeded at a slower tempo.[28]

The records of the French churches permit a fuller reconstruction of the Huguenot immigrant community than can be made of any other group, and in the century after 1660 more immigrants came from France than from any other country. But the French were far from the only foreigners to settle in England. Immigration from outside Europe, it is true, was negligible. Africans, such as Dr. Johnson's black servant, were treated as curiosities; and no substantial numbers of South Asians arrived until toward the end of the eighteenth century.[29] But Europe contributed a diversity of people to enrich England's ethnic and cultural complexion. Probably second in numbers to the French were the Germans, especially in view of the large migration from the Rhine Valley to England in 1709. There were three German churches in London: the German, Hamburg Lutheran Church, the Lutheran Church in the Savoy district, established in 1694, and also in the Savoy the High German Reformed Protestant Church, established in 1697. None of the German congregations was large: the Hamburg Church, the largest, had perhaps two hundred members in the 1670s and three hundred by the 1690s, but its membership was declining by the middle of the eighteenth century.[30]

A similar decline in membership afflicted the Dutch Church of Austin Friars in London, the most important of the several Dutch Calvinist churches established in England.[31] The Dutch Church, like other foreign churches, lost members to the Anglican parish churches; but, unlike the other foreign churches, it received few new recruits by way of immigration in the eighteenth century. The largest immigration from the Low Countries had occurred in the sixteenth century, when it was said that every third inhabitant of Norwich was Dutch, and immigration continued in the first half of the seventeenth century; however, only a very modest flow of newcomers arrived after the Restoration. The records of the Austin Friars church include lists of attestations from those arriving from abroad and wishing to join the congregation, and these records bear witness to the withering away of Dutch immigration. The largest number of attestations came in the 1670s and 1680s, when they averaged roughly thirty-seven each year. In the 1690s the stream began to dry up, and by the second decade of the eighteenth century the number of attestations, and presumably of immigrants, had declined to only a half-dozen or so each year. The number of baptisms dropped from forty-two in 1680 to one in 1766.[32] Other foreign communities were similarly small. In London could be found a Danish-Norwegian church and a Swedish church, the latter of which had around one hundred members in the 1720s. A Greek church was established in London in 1674, but the size of its congregation was tiny.[33] Other groups, if they existed, were too small to justify a formally established church.

Jewish immigration in this period, made possible after the informal readmission of the Jews in 1655, has been more thoroughly studied than that of any other group. Cromwell took the initiative in promoting the readmission by putting the question before the Council of State for debate. Although no formal legal steps were taken for a readmission, and the expulsion of the Jews from England by Edward I in 1290 remained technically the law of the land, a few Sephardim from Holland took the risk of settling in England, and in 1656 the first synagogue opened in London. The laws remained unaltered, but the return of the Jews became a fait accompli, and Charles II ensured that they enjoyed de facto toleration.[34] The volume of Jewish immigration was very small. Almost all of those who came to England in the first few decades after the Restoration were Sephardim from the Low Countries, themselves exiles of the Marrano diaspora from the Iberian peninsula. Their numbers did not exceed 500 until the mid-1680s at the earliest. In 1690 an Ashkenazic synagogue was established, but a census in 1695 still revealed fewer than a thousand Jews in London, and there were no Jewish communities outside the metropolis until the second half of the eighteenth century. Jewish settlement in England was very different from that in contemporary Germany and Italy, however, where segregation and special regulations set the Jews apart in enclaves; nor did the advent of large numbers of Ashkenazim from the ghettos of Germany and Poland in the eighteenth century change the nature of the English settlement. The Sephardim and Ashkenazim, separated by language, culture, and social standing, numbered together perhaps 6,000 to 8,000 by the middle of the eighteenth century.[35]

The Scots and Irish began to arrive in England in substantial numbers only in the eighteenth century, but it is extremely difficult to trace these "domestic foreigners." The Irish came, often at first as seasonal laborers for the hay harvest, and settled in fairly close-knit communities, the largest of which was in the parish of St. Giles in the Fields in London. Many were unskilled laborers who found work in the building trade or in the port of London, usually at wages considerably lower than those paid to English laborers, a fact that—combined with their Catholicism and poverty—made the welcome they received from the English less than cordial. Scots peddlers had long been a common sight on the roads of England, but larger numbers of Scots began to come south as permanent or semipermanent settlers in the mid-eighteenth century. Of course, after the Act of Union of 1707, they were British subjects, but their distinctive customs and language ensured that they would be treated by the English as foreigners. In contrast to the

Irish, many Scots—physicians, lawyers, men of letters—managed to make their entry into English society at a level high enough to arouse a good deal of jealousy amongst the natives, and they were often depicted in melodramatic eruptions from Grub Street as descending like rapacious locusts to batten on the greater wealth of the southern kingdom.[36]

The great majority of these diverse immigrants—religious refugees, adventurers, uprooted victims of war, artisans in search of new markets—congregated in the foreigners' mecca of London. The capital's cosmopolitan social structure, perhaps more fluid than in the provinces, and containing a strong element of migrants from within England, was probably more congenial to newcomers than smaller communities. Immigrant communities, then as now, tended to grow like crystals, with established communities attracting new arrivals; those already settled in London attracted relations and acquaintances from abroad. Even the relative anonymity of the largest city in Europe may have acted an an inducement to those from an alien culture. Quarters like Spitalfields in the east and Soho in the west had such large French populations that it was said that the stubbornly insular could learn colloquial French there without setting foot outside England. Foreign artisans, like the French silk-weavers, congregated in the East End outside the jurisdiction of the City of London, while immigrants who traded in luxury goods tended to settle in the West End near the Court and the elegant new neighborhoods where they found their best customers. Germans clustered in Suffolk Street, and Jews settled near the synagogue established in Bevis Marks. Merchants and financiers, not an insignificant segment of the immigrant population, lived in or near the City. Coffeehouses served as gathering places for resident foreigners in the same way that London inns acted as rendezvous for those from various corners of the English provinces; some catered to a French clientele, some to Germans, others to foreigners in general. London possessed the bulk of the foreign churches, a network of patronage and connections amongst immigrants, and probably a greater promise of employment than elsewhere. Perhaps a quarter of the French refugees of the late seventeenth century settled in towns outside London, but an observer writing in 1751 came close to the truth when he maintained that foreign immigrants "have been wholly possessed by London."[37]

One reason for the concentration of immigrants in London at this time was the absence of economic projects or planned settlements of the kind that William Cecil and the Commonwealthmen of Elizabeth's reign had orchestrated, many of them in the country towns of England.[38] The only substantial public project for the settlement of immigrants after the Restoration was one for the establishment of a linen manufacture at Ipswich. Even in this case there was a difference from the sixteenth-century schemes sponsored by the government, as the project was a private one, financed by almost seventy entrepreneurs who raised the capital for the scheme early in 1681. Among them were Josiah Child, Thomas Papillon, and John Pollexfen, all outspoken advocates of the naturalization of foreigners. The town of Ipswich agreed to receive the French artisans, offered them a church, and made them free from town and parish charges. The project was not a great success, as the linen manufacture was not at first profitable, though the settlement did survive.[39]

The importance of the Ipswich project, however, lies in its uniqueness. Most immigrants to England after the Restoration came on their own initiative, as individuals and families, to escape religious persecution or to better their circumstances, without any direct invitation from the English government. They settled where they could, mostly where foreign communities were already established, and sought to earn their livings in England. Some of them managed to do very well. Foreign settlers made an important contribution to the development of England's commerce, through their overseas trading connections, and to English manufactures by their superior skills in such trades as glassmaking, gold and silversmithing, papermaking, and silkweaving.[40] The potential economic contribution of immigrants of course played a crucial part in the controversy over their admission. But planned government projects like those of earlier years were never seriously considered as a substantial part of a naturalization scheme after the Restoration. For the champions of naturalization, the role of the English government would not be orchestrating planned settlements of groups of artisans, but rather extending legal privileges that would attract large numbers of immigrants and realize the cherished hope that such foreign settlers could help to propel the English economy to a superiority over all rivals.

The character of those legal privileges must now be briefly sketched.[41] Since the debate over immigration usually expressed itself in terms of whether Parliament should pass a general naturalization act, the broader issues of population and immigration revolved around the narrower question of the legal status of aliens in England. The English law of nationality, which conditioned the traditional means by which an alien immigrant could change his status, was laid down in *Calvin's Case* in 1608. The Court of Exchequer was presented with the question whether those born in Scotland after James I's accession and the union of the Crowns in 1603, the *postnati*, were to be considered subjects in England. The court held that the *postnati* Scots were indeed subjects in England, and in so doing the court articulated a common law of nationality that survived into the nineteenth century. The place of birth determined nationality: those born in England or in countries under the dominion of the king were subjects; all others were aliens. Such a simply-stated doctrine proved to be far from simple in its application, and the apparent clarity of the decision in *Calvin's Case* became woefully opaque outside the rarified air of the Exchequer Chamber. Thus by law the *postnati*

Scots—and by the Restoration very nearly all Scots immigrants had been born after 1603—and the Irish were subjects in England, but in practice they were often not treated as such. Lawyers and jurists found ample room for contention over the meaning and application of the principle of nationality based on place of birth. On a popular level, the doctrine laid down in *Calvin's Case* seems to have been overpowered, as such legal rules tend to be, by the feeling that the Scots and Irish were simply not Englishmen. Even after the Union with Scotland in 1707 the legal equality of the Scots could not be taken for granted.[42]

Yet much hung in the balance in the determination of an immigrant's legal status, for an alien lay under a number of disabilities: he could own no real property in England; he could not hold a lease; he could have no heir, nor could he himself inherit; he could not have the benefit of curtesy, dower, or guardianship; he could bring no legal action that related to real property; he was subject to the customs duties imposed upon aliens by king and Parliament and by the corporate cities; he had no political rights and could not vote or hold office; nor could he own an English ship, trade in the plantations, or otherwise qualify as English under the Navigation Act.[43] He was, moreover, subject to a variety of restrictions contained in old statute law—such as the prohibition on employing fellow-aliens—most of which lay in the unmourned oblivion of fusty statute books, but some of which were from time to time dusted off and enforced against immigrants to their considerable hardship.[44]

Despite these disabilities, and the weight that English champions of immigration attributed to them, the advantages of formally renouncing the status of alien seem to have been far from compelling for most foreign settlers. There were two procedures available to immigrants: denization by a grant from the Crown in the form of a Letter Patent, and naturalization by a private act of Parliament. Both were time-consuming and expensive, and few immigrants bothered to become either denizens or naturalized subjects under the customary procedures in either the seventeenth or eighteenth centuries. The distinction between a denizen and a naturalized subject was by no means clear as a point of legal doctrine and had scarcely existed prior to *Calvin's Case*, but the difference as a practical matter is not difficult to define. In effect, a denizen enjoyed only some of the privileges of a natural-born subject, whereas a naturalized alien enjoyed virtually all of them. The principal disability of aliens, the inability to hold real property, was removed by both denization and naturalization. The other important disability, the liability to pay alien customs and duties, was sometimes removed by a grant of denization, but not always: as an exercise of the Crown's prerogative power, the grant of denization conferred rights that varied depending upon the wording of the particular instrument. The parliamentary acts of naturalization, however, were of a fixed form, and they granted all the privileges of a subject, with the exception that after 1700 naturalized aliens could not hold office or receive grants of land from the Crown.[45]

The promotion of a private bill of naturalization in Parliament was slow, expensive, and risky. It began with a petition to either house. Bills commonly named a dozen or more petitioners, but each paid as if for a separate bill, and it was necessary to retain a lawyer to steer the bill through Parliament. Petitioners were required to take oaths in the Lords, and to prove that they had received the sacrament within one month before the introduction of the bill. In the normal course of parliamentary business naturalization bills seldom encountered opposition, but they ran the great risk, especially before the establishment of more regular sessions of Parliment after 1689, of being lost at the sudden prorogation of Parliament, an event that happened with alarming regularity—but not predictability—before the Revolution. There were, moreover, long periods during which Parliament did not sit; the Cavalier Parliament was in session for only sixty months of its eighteen year life. An ample supply of both money and stamina were required to obtain a parliamentary grant, and the exasperated complaint of 1685 from a petitioner who had already paid his fees three times and lost them by the delay of bills that never passed must have expressed the frustration of many aspiring English subjects. Even if the bill was not lost, naturalization was a lengthy process. Its precise cost is not known and has been a subject of considerable debate and speculation. Several sources mention the figure of one hundred pounds, but even the lower, and probably more accurate, figure of sixty-three pounds cited by a Commons committee report of 1732 was an enormous sum for the period, one that put naturalization outside the reach of all but the richest of immigrants.[46]

Becoming a denizen was rather easier. Unlike petitioners for naturalization, those seeking denization did not have to present proof of having received the sacrament, nor were they required to take any oaths. Denization was therefore the only alternative for Jewish immigrants. The cost of becoming a denizen remains, like that of naturalization, uncertain. A source of 1798 gives the figure of twenty-five pounds, though the cost was probably less in the late seventeenth century when the largest number of denizations were issued, and in any event the Crown frequently remitted the fees.[47] Denization, then, was cheaper and surer than a private act of naturalization, though it conveyed only the lesser privileges of a status between that of alien and naturalized subject.[48]

In view of the obstacles, it is hardly surprising that most foreign settlers resigned themselves to remaining legal aliens. Why did some choose to become denizens or to be naturalized? The two principal advantages were economic: the right to hold real property and the exemption from aliens' customs duties. Clearly these gains would have been attractive only to those of substantial wealth, and most particularly to merchants. The majority of immigrants probably suffered little hardship on account of the legal disabilities of alien status—their exclusion from the trading and craft companies caused them more grief. There may have been less tangible motives, such as the desire to solemnize a new allegiance to England. But otherwise, the sample we have of naturalized immigrants is likely biased very heavily toward merchants and the wealthy.

During two brief periods, however, an alien could change his or her status cheaply and without delay. The two exceptions to the procedures described above were, first, the period from 1681 to 1688 during which an Order in Council allowed denizations free of charge by a special process, and second, the period of three years during which the General Naturalization Act of 1709 provided for speedy naturalization for a fee of one shilling.[49] While in effect, both procedures were used by an enormously larger number of aliens than usually sought to change their legal status by the customary procedures. Table 1 summarizes the number of naturalizations and denizations from 1660 to 1759, Table 2 gives the number of denizations under the Order in Council of 1681, and Table 3 lists the number of naturalizations known to have been granted under the Act of 1709.[50]

Table 1

Five-year averages of Denizations and Naturalizations, 1660–1759

Year	Denizations	Naturalizations
1660–64	34	54
1665–69	14	14
1670–74	12	7
1675–79	42	21
1680–84	337	0
1685–89	372	27
1690–94	119	14
1695–99	145	112
1700–04	20	135
1705–09	11	307
1710–14	2	322
1715–19	6	11
1720–24	9	65
1725–29	4	10
1730–34	5	9
1735–39	0	18
1740–44	6	14
1745–49	0	10
1750–54	4	16
1755–59	11	10

Sources: The figures are derived from the lists in Shaw, ed., *Letters, 1603–1700*, and *Letters, 1701–1800*.

Table 2

Letters Patent of Denization Granted 1681–1688

Year	Entry Book Denizations	Entry Book Denizations Later Duplicated	Patent Roll Denizations	Total Denizations	New Denizens
1681	178	165	131	309	188
1682	97	97	1289	1386	1285
1683	98	98	148	246	109
1684	78	78	20	98	97
1685	104	104	211	315	134
1686	153	153	161	314	161
1687	1036	1033	543	1579	1070
1688	421	421	991	1412	466
Totals:	2165	2149	3494	5659	3510

Sources: Shaw, ed., *Letters, 1603–1700,* and *Letters, 1701–1800.* The raw lists compiled by Shaw misrepresent the total number of grants, as there was a considerable duplication of grants recorded either in the Entry Books or on the Patent Rolls. The nominally separate methods of denization seem to have been utterly confused by those administering the Order. The table therefore offers in the final column, "New Denizens," the total number of persons receiving a grant for the first time during the years that the Order was in effect.

Table 3

Naturalizations from 1709 to 1712 under 7 Anne c. 5.

Year	Queen's Bench	Middlesex	Exchequer	Total
1709	698	34	201	933
1710	521	58	26	605
1711	562	19	93	674
1712	33	84	0	117

Grand Total: 2329

Sources: Figures compiled from Shaw, ed., *Letters, 1701–1800,* and W. & S. Minet, *A Supplement.*

The most striking feature of the tabulated figures is the vastly larger numbers of grants under the exceptions of 1681 to 1688 and 1709 to 1712, when they were available at nominal cost through relatively quick and simple administrative procedures. The much higher numbers of those receiving grants during those two periods leaves little doubt that an important reason for the otherwise low proportion of immigrants obtaining a change in their legal status was the usual difficulty and expense involved. The cost and trouble of using the customary procedures ensured that only the wealthy, the powerful, or those who had a special incentive to escape from the disabilities of alien status, such as merchants, would seek denization or naturalization.

On the whole, however, the proportion of immigrants in this period who obtained naturalization or denization was still very low. Roughly 50,000 French Protestants came to England between 1660 and 1700 alone, with smaller numbers of French, Dutch, German, and Jewish settlers arriving throughout the period, as well as the sudden influx of 13,000 Germans from the Palatinate in 1709 when the General Naturalization Act was in effect. Few of these tens of thousands of settlers ever became denizens or naturalized subjects. Many immigrants scorned even free denization. Of the 3,419 French refugees who received monetary or other relief from the French Church of London in Threadneedle Street from 1681 to 1687, the years during which the Order in Council provided for free denization, only 546, about one in six, obtained a grant.[51] By choice or necessity, most immigrants who settled in England bore not only the social stigma of "foreigner" but the legal stigma of "alien" for the rest of their lives. The assumption shared by both the advocates of general naturalization and its opponents that such an act's grant of legal privileges would act as a magnet to draw to England large numbers of immigrants and thus increase the nation's population seems to have been wholly unfounded. Immigrants came in order to escape persecution or to better themselves economically, not in order to obtain legal privileges. But the political debate posed the question whether immigration ought to be actively encouraged, not simply tolerated, and naturalization seemed to be a plausible way to entice foreigners to leave their native lands. This was the basic premise of the controversy to which we now turn.

2

The Foundations of the Debate

The Restoration of the monarchy in 1660 marks a watershed in England's history in many respects. The intense religious fervor of the preceding decades gradually subsided, and a more secular spirit began to infuse English society. Religion retained a central social role in what it has become fashionable to call the "confessional state" of late seventeenth- and eighteenth-century England.[1] But the movement towards more worldly and rationalist patterns of thought, traditionally associated with the early stages of the Enlightenment, was no less conspicuous in Charles II's regained realm than in the continental states that few would demur at calling ancien régime societies. One expression of the more secular outlook perceptible after 1660 was the transformation in thinking about trade matters as a new economic and commercial ethos began to dawn in England. The change represents not only an alteration in the understanding of the proper working of the economy, but more importantly a heightened interest in the material rather than spiritual dimension of statesmanship and social policy.

The Restoration marks the end of the period in which the state, seeking to fill the vacuum left by the dwindling powers of the traditional medieval system of urban economic regulation, attempted to fashion industry and trade in accordance with paternalistic principles. Many of the Tudor and early Stuart economic statutes were abandoned or openly flouted after 1660 as attitudes towards the proper role of the state in economic development changed. In the place of the traditional approach to comprehensive regulation with the king as the fountainhead of central direction, an approach more paternalistic and moralistic than commercial in inspiration, there grew up a regime of regulation whose inspiration was essentially commercial. The Navigation Acts stand as a monument to the new economic policy, for they represent, as Adam Smith observed, the epitome of the mercantilist approach to trade (which was economic rather than social in intent) and imposed as a uniform regulatory regime applicable to all.[2] The new tack in government economic policy as England's trade grew was paralleled by a burgeoning intellectual interest in economic questions, for as a commercial transformation imbued the English economy after 1660 and gradually trans-

38

formed English society, a new economic discourse emerged that betrayed a process of commercialization in the realm of social thought. The "commercial revolution" that transformed English trade in the years 1660 to 1760 was mirrored by a revolution in economic discourse.[3]

The years after the Restoration witnessed a great blossoming of economic literature, and the new wealth of trade publications that issued from the presses became the principal forum in which the polemical give and take of the controversy over immigration played itself out. The immigration issue occupied one corner of a developing space of public discourse that had emerged during the intense religious and constitutional ferment of the 1640s and 1650s. Newsletters and pamphlets had been in existence in England from the late sixteenth century, if not earlier, and their circulation was accelerated by the hunger for international news during the period of the Thirty Years' War,[4] but the mid-seventeenth century witnessed a dramatic increase in their volume. With censorship in abeyance during the civil war, a rising tide of polemical and speculative pamphlets, books, and tracts, and newssheets created a heady sense of a public dialogue in the medium of print. After 1660 the number of chapbooks, tracts, and broadsides increased rapidly,[5] and while much of this literature was devotional or popular in character, there was also a virtual explosion in the number of publications that treated public policy questions generally and economic issues in particular. Some at least of the rhetorical energy that had gone into religious and political disputation during the Interregnum was now channeled into more measured disputes over trade policy. More measured, but no less apparently vital to the well-being of English society, for after the Restoration an assumption lay behind the growing corpus of trade literature that the path to England's greatness lay through commercial expansion. An intense curiosity, nourished by commercial and economic change, developed about the causes of national wealth, and writers filled their pamphlets with proposals for the expansion of the nation's trade in an accumulating body of exchanges that coalesced into a public discourse on economic questions.

Works on trade found an eager and eclectic audience amongst merchants, tradesmen, Members of Parliament, and the increasingly broad group, some of them quite humble, who took an active interest in public affairs. Literacy rates in England were high by European standards and reading had come to be an integral part of the public culture in which economic discourse defined itself.[6] Yet literacy was not strictly necessary for participation in the accelerating exchange of economic ideas, for the arguments of the tracts on trade echoed especially loudly in the forums of popular intellectual and political discussion, the coffeehouses, where oral and written cultures overlapped and merged. The range of the coffeehouses' clientele stretched nearly to the antipodes of the English urban social hierarchy, embracing the broad spectrum of peoples that an essentially commercial ethos brought together. Joseph Addison's much-quoted paean to the cosmopolitanism of trade that mingled Muslim with Christian and Irishman with Indian might be applied as well to the coffeehouses as to the Royal Exchange, and to the public discourse on trade as to trade itself. The origins of the coffeehouses lay in trade, and they retained their commercial and mercantile associations throughout this period of increasing commercialization; they echoed with a lively discourse on economic questions, both printed and oral; and they multiplied the influence of economic discussion by their circulation of pamphlets, broadsides, and other vehicles of trade talk. As the *Craftsman* remarked ironically in 1729, "we are become a nation of statesmen. Our Coffee-houses and taverns are full of them".[7]

The volume of publications on economic questions multipled greatly after the Restoration, but mere numbers of press runs grossly underrepresent the impact of such works. Defoe's news-sheet, the *Review* (1704–1713), for example, a publication typical of the period in its preoccupation with economic matters within a broader discourse of public policy issues, probably never exceeded a circulation of one thousand, yet its readership may have been ten, twenty, or more times that number, as it circulated from hand to hand and was read aloud to groups at the coffeehouses and other gathering places of those interested in trade.[8] The growing economic discourse that developed after the Restoration, and within which immigration policy was debated, embraced a broad spectrum of participants and enjoyed a very considerable currency, and even—curious to say of matters economic—a measure of social fashionableness.

To speak of an emerging economic discourse after the Restoration is not to suggest that the literature on trade questions was monolithic. On the contrary, the forms of economic discourse were varied and experimental, undergoing a continual flux as genres appeared, developed, and gradually defined themselves, or were supplanted by newer forms. Some economic works assumed the guise of dialogues, others of letters, still others of satire. The query form was used from the beginning to the end of the period, by writers as diverse as the political arithmetician William Petty, the Quaker philanthropist John Bellers, the philosopher George Berkeley, and the churchman Josiah Tucker. Perhaps the most typical form was the *discourse*, wide-ranging and topical in its treatment and prescriptive in tone. There was great flexibility in the length of pamphlets and tracts. The different forms could accommodate a short rebuttal or an attack on a particular proposal, or a longer disquisition of more general scope. Many shorter works, and particularly broadsides, addressed themselves to Parliament, often in titles that began with the formulaic words "The Case of" or "Reasons for."[9] Such appeals to Parliament were sometimes merely a matter of form, but often the doorkeepers of the Houses received stacks of copies and douceurs to secure their help in distribution. The prevalence of this sort of special pleading, sometimes paid for by the ministry itself, is hardly surprising in view of the cheapness of printing such short sheets.[10] Indeed, printed pleas were sometimes given away in large numbers, thrust into the hands of passersby on the street or even thrown in the windows of coaches as they passed.[11] Such publications, usually addressing particular economic policy questions, seem to have enjoyed a very wide circulation outside Parliament: the tendency apparent from the Revolution, and especially from the 1730s, for publications to explicitly address themselves to the wider audience of the political nation should not be taken to mean that earlier political and economic discourse confined itself to a narrow political elite. A title addressing a tract or broadside to Parliament served as often to identify a genre and a mode of argumentation as to designate an audience.

The variety of rhetorical methods, patterns of argument, and vocabulary to be found in the economic literature that blossomed after the Restoration rivaled the diversity of its forms. Groping to define their unique subject, authors whose uncertainty is betrayed by the definitions of trade with which they often began their works[12] gradually over the course of the latter half of the seventeenth century marked out the parameters of economic discourse and its structure and language. Such definitions were in part a gesture of self-justification: by the middle of the eighteenth century such exercises had petered out, as the need for writing on trade became self-evident. This process of maturation can be traced in the immigration debate perhaps as clearly as in any other facet of the literature, as economic discourse gradually defined itself as an area of inquiry and as explanations and recommendations on economic policy refined themselves.

The circumstances of their production casts a good deal of light on the character of early economic works. The great majority of publications treating trade matters were published in London; literacy rates there were probably much higher than in the provinces, and the capital was the dominant market for the writings of the proto-economists of the late seventeenth century.[13] London had no monopoly on print, however. In the eighteenth century distribution systems for printed matter became more extensive and faster; but even at the beginning of the period a network of carriers, peddlers, coffeemen, and booksellers conveyed a large volume of books and other printed matter to the country.[14]

Censorship restrictions still applied during the first part of the period, but the Licensing Act probably had no great effect on trade publications with political content that expressed itself only indirectly.[15] Most were published anonymously, perhaps from the hope of creating the appearance of disinterestedness, and many remain anonymous. Some were the work of active merchants or men eminent in public affairs, such as Joshua Gee and Charles Davenant, and scholars and clergymen such as John Locke and Josiah Tucker occasionally applied their pens to economic matters. Professional writers also produced their share of such publications, either from the promise of lively sales or because they were engaged by someone with a stake in a particular economic issue that must be defeated or promoted. Daniel

Defoe was the archetype of such hack writers, and the greatest of them, but he had many predecessors and heirs, trade specialists in the Grub Street fraternity. The most characteristic author of trade publications, however, was the gentleman-writer who wished to express his pet theories, the results of his research, or his indignation at particular policy proposals. Often lawyers or public servants, such dilettante publicists had usually been to university, and some had personal experience of trade, as either merchants or government officials. Finally, there were the partisan polemicists who entered the fray over economic issues within the framework of a broader political dialectic. The varied backgrounds of its authors contributed to the diversity of the economic literature and its tremendous variety in literary quality, adding to the rich texture of the debate over immigration and population.

One feature binds together the diverse publications on trade: a polemical tone is a common thread through nearly all early economic discourse. Objectivity was scarcely dreamt of, much less striven for. The very absence of a received canon of mercantilist orthodoxy encouraged a polemical approach to economic issues like immigration. Writers on trade were intensely practical, and so were the ideas that they developed. These authors were so often merchants, minor political figures, or men of affairs, as to be the actors in their own dramas. Bathed in the tides of the trade whose features they described and whose benefits they praised, the early economic writers were enthusiasts for their new subject, eager for converts to their own commercial perspective on social and political questions. Their practical bent contrasts with the more theoretical tone of the political economists who followed them, and one of the striking features of the economic literature in this century is its seeming evolution towards a more disinterested and analytic approach, a process of divorce from directly political questions that proves upon closer examination to be more apparent than real. Weighty economic questions after all must always be political. The inconsistencies for which the mercantilists are often reproached[16] were the natural result of their pragmatic, topical, and often polemical treatment of economic questions. The temptation to cast into the rhetoric of argument every point conceivably in their favor was one that few mercantilist writers could resist, and inconsistency was the unavoidable result. Their works were more often than not *pieces d'occasion*, ephemeral, to one degree or another, in conception as well as in the event.[17] Creating a unified and internally consistent system was of little importance to them in comparison with the mustering of the fullest argument on any particular issue. The early writers on trade cannot be dismissed as either stupid or insincere for having failed to achieve a goal that they never set for themselves. Nothing could illustrate this pattern better than the heterogeneous arguments employed by the proponents and adversaries alike of the policy of admitting foreign immigrants to England.

The authors of the economic works that multiplied after the Restoration generally employed a rhetorical language of polemics rather than that of objective analysis; their approach and the forms in which they wrote were far from uniform; and they addressed an audience whose diversity bordered on incongruence, from the student of William Petty's speculative tracts to the casual reader of the declamations of a broadside pinned on the coffee-house wall. In spite of the variety of this literature, however, a coherent discourse on economic questions coalesced in the course of the second half of the seventeenth century. Gradually, more consistent and clearer modes of expression developed, as patterns of seeing economic issues and languages for describing them became settled. A commonly understood vocabulary of terms to denote economic relations grew up. A structure of discourse emerged in which the set of issues in play and the manner of addressing those issues came to be, if not canonically stipulated, at least generally agreed upon.

Some historians, for example Keith Tribe in *Land, Labour, and Economic Discourse* (1978), refuse to find in late seventeenth-and early eighteenth-century English publications on trade a body of economic discourse. Such scholars argue that economic questions in this period were embedded too integrally in the discourse of the polity and of civil society to have enjoyed an existence as a separate field of thought and discussion; that a specifically economic set of assumptions and arguments, independent from questions of state administration, had not evolved; that the preoccupation with circulation rather than production in this period betrays a lack of interest in the central question of economic discourse; and that a genuine economic discourse could only come about from the challenge of truly capitalist economic relations that had not yet established themselves. It will come as no surprise that the conclusion of such reasoning identifies Smith's *Wealth of Nations* as the fountainhead of economic discourse properly so called.[18]

Yet as a close reading of the immigration and population controversy will demonstrate, an economic discourse had indeed developed before the annus mirabilis of 1776. That discourse was not the intellectual handmaiden of capitalism, whenever that system is imagined to have made its momentous triumph—a question that in any case has proved so perplexing that it has occupied whole generations of scholars. Rather, the economic discourse of our period responded naturally to the process of commercialization that gradually transformed the English economy and society in the seventeenth and eighteenth centuries. The economic thought of this period in fact can perhaps be more aptly described as commercial in its concerns than as mercantile or mercantilist, since it sought not only to nurture commerce but to guide the commercialization of society as well. As commerce deals with circulation and exchange rather than with production, it is to be expected that economic discourse should reveal a corresponding preoccupation with circulation in its strictly economic sense. Indeed, that preoccupation, in terms of the circulation of people, led to the overriding concern of thinkers with population size and distribution, from Josiah Child in the 1660s to Josiah Tucker in the 1750s.

The suggestion that economic questions were entirely subordinated to matters of state, and that the language of economics failed to separate itself from the language of politics, while it may fairly describe the treatment of economic questions in the century before 1660, misconstrues the blossoming of economic discourse in the century after 1660. True, tracts on trade were seldom without a strong political content and very often betrayed an undisguised partisan bias. Many works did profess to be written for the commendably civic end of increasing the royal revenue. But the expression of such ends relating to the polity were more often than not in the nature of conventional maxims rather than essential substance. The classical economists' professions of political neutrality and their claims to have established a positive rather than normative discipline of economics may have lent weight to their pronouncements, but they can hardly be accepted at face value. While it remained concerned with the political ends of economic policy, economic discourse in the century after the Restoration did not, as some have suggested, remain unchanged: essentially premodern, paternalistic, and without coherent structure. On the contrary, economic discourse answered the need of an evolving commercial society for an intellectual structure within which economic issues, such as those of immigration and population policy, could be analyzed, discussed, and questioned.

Despite the dangers of speaking of early economic theory in the abstract, one can distill from the economic writings of this century some general assumptions and beliefs that underlay the proposals for the admission of foreigners. Prominent amongst these was the balance of trade doctrine. The earliest English economic writers, such as Gerald Malynes, associated wealth with precious metal, and advocated the accumulation of bullion.[19] By the latter half of the seventeenth century, however, bullionism had been superseded as received dogma by the doctrine that a favorable balance of foreign trade (that is, a surplus of the value of exports over the value of imports) was the only way to increase national wealth. Without an export surplus, as Richard Haines wrote in 1674, "out goes money and in comes poverty." The balance of trade doctrine became, in Ephraim Lipson's words, "the accepted dogma of English economic opinion and the touchstone of national prosperity." The most implacable opponents in questions of economic affairs could agree that the balance of trade would determine the power and prosperity of the nation.[20]

The doctrine rested upon the premise that only foreign trade could create national wealth, a proposition exemplified by the title of Thomas Mun's celebrated work, *England's Treasure by Foreign Trade, or, The Balance of our Foreign Trade is the Rule of our Treasure* (1664). *England's Treasure* became the canonical text on the balance of trade doctrine. Only international exchange could make England prosper, Mun held: internal trade was a sterile necessity. Commerce within a nation represented merely a circulation of wealth, a fabric of exchange like Penelope's shroud for Laertes, woven by day, unraveled by night, in which one person's loss always balanced another's gain. Foreign trade was thought to provide the only means for a nation to increase its wealth, and few questioned the proposition that one nation could grow wealthier only at the expense of another. The doctrine encouraged fierce international competition, and one of the factors of production over which nations fought was labor, embodied in their people and measured by the idea of "populousness."[21] The assumption that the wealth of nations was a fixed sum to be fought over thus formed the most fundamental assumption behind the immigration controversy.

The balance of trade doctrine contributed to a preoccupation with labor as an instrument of production and exchange. The application of labor to a raw material to enhance its value, to make it a finished product, was considered the best means to ensure that England's exports were of the highest possible value. The more finished that exported commodities were, the greater the national gain by their sale abroad. Without the manufacture of materials into finished goods by the application of labor, many of the early economic writers argued, the balance of trade was meaningless. "The Dutch we see import all," wrote Roger Coke in 1670, "yet thrive upon trade, and the Irish export eight times more than they import, yet grow poorer." As Daniel Defoe declared in the *Review* in 1709, "whatever value we can put upon labour, which we can make our neighbours pay, must be clearly our gain." The process of acquiring national wealth was conceived as falling into three stages: the existence of a pool of labor, the application of that labor to raw materials, and the sale of the resulting manufactured goods in foreign markets. The gains from the export surplus reflected the increase in national wealth from this three-step process.[22] The proposals for the admission of foreign settlers sought to nurture the first of these stages by topping up the reservoir of labor in the nation.

The central role of labor in the early economic writers' formula for wealth contributed to their absorbing concern with populousness, and consequently to their pleas for the encouragement of immigration. Economic thinkers exalted labor as the essential creative force in the formation of national wealth. "Labour is the father and active principle of wealth, as lands are the mother," proclaimed William Petty in 1662, defining wealth simply as "the effect of . . . past labour." The same sentiments continued to be expressed throughout the period.[23] Indeed, William Hay wrote in 1735 that "the proposition . . . [that] labour is the great principle of all riches [is] as capable of demonstration as any mathematical problem."[24] And in 1751 Josiah Tucker, writing in favor of a general naturalization bill, asked "is not that country richest which has the most labour?" and answered his question with others:

What are the riches of a country?—Land? Money? Or labour? What is the value of land but in proportion to the numbers of people? What is money, but a common measure, tally, or counter, to set forth or denominate the price of labour in the several transfers of it? . . . Is not that country wealthiest which has the most labour? And hath not that country the most labour which hath the most people to create mutual employment for each other? Was a country thinly inhabited ever rich? Was a populous country ever poor?[25]

Laborers, the indispensable instruments of England's greatness, would bring both power and plenty.[26] As William Petyt wrote in *Britannia Languens* (1680), "people are in truth the chiefest, most fundamental and precious commodity . . . and the labours of the people bestowed on manufactures must necessarily glomerate the riches of the world and make any nation a prodigy of wealth."[27]

Nor were such forcefully expressed views simply theoretical suppositions. The belief in the preeminence of labor mirrored its importance as the principal productive resource of England's economy. In this respect, economic theory merely acknowledged the facts of production in the preindustrial economy in which muscle-power was the chief source of energy and *manufacture* literally meant "to make by hand." The multiplication of manufacturing and consumer industries in the seventeenth and eighteenth centuries only served to underscore the vital need for laborers in the process of commercial expansion.[28] The growth in manufacture also contributed to the dawning realization over the course of this century, and to the gradual integration into the economic discourse, of the need for skilled laborers, who represented valuable human capital.

The potency of labor as simply an abstract idea in this period nevertheless cannot be ignored. John Locke, it will be recalled, placed labor at the heart of his theory of the state, theorizing that civil government was constituted primarily to protect private property, which was created by the application of labor to resources in the state of nature. Indeed, thought about labor could become so abstract as to lose sight of the humanity of the men, women, and children who embodied this "active principle." The facile identification of a nation's wealth with its labor led some economic writers into callous reckonings in which people counted for little more than commodities. Thomas Sheridan wrote in 1677 that "though an individuum of mankind be reckoned [in value] but about eight years purchase, the species is as valuable as land, being, in its own nature, perhaps as durable, and as improveable, too, if not more." William Petty at various times gave figures of from sixty-nine pounds to as much as ninety pounds for the value of "a head of labour." Such calculations bear witness not only to the elite perspective from which much of the early economic discourse viewed labor—the implicit question was how much work could be got out of the laboring classes—but to a fallacy that was only painfully exposed and excised from the economic discourse: the assumption that each "unit of labor" is equal to every other.[29] That fallacy played a crucial role in the immigration debate. For the most part, however, the productive powers of labor entranced the writers on trade, and their fascination reinforced their belief that national wealth and strength depended upon a large and growing population. There was, at least until near the middle of the eighteenth century, a remarkable harmony of opinion on the importance of a large and growing population. It seemed an almost self-evident proposition that the more hands in the field, the richer would be England's harvest of wealth.[30]

A faith in the productive powers of labor contributed to the preoccupation with population that arose in the middle of the seventeenth century. That preoccupation, and the crescendo of pleas after 1660 to increase population, were new. In the late sixteenth and the first half of the seventeenth century it was not a lack of people in England but overpopulation that excited fear. Opinion had in fact come full circle in the century and a half before the Restoration, for in the early sixteenth century too there had been much talk of depopulation.[31] By the latter half of Elizabeth's reign, however, complaints were being voiced, as William Harrison observed in 1587, that "the increase of the people" was increasing poverty, and that "the land was never so full" of people. Thomas Smith at the same time declared that "England was never . . . fuller of people than it is at this day." The fears of overpopulation reflected the growing problems of poverty, unemployment, and "masterless men" in the late sixteenth and early seventeenth centuries, all of which seemed to threaten social order.[32] Nor were such problems imaginary: they betrayed the strain upon traditional customary arrangements and upon an essentially static economic order of a formidable increase in population. In the period from 1550 to 1650 England's population increased from under three million to over five million; suffering increased and social disorder threatened as real wages declined; and despite the devastations of repeated outbreaks of plague, the country seemed overburdened with people.[33] In a tract published in 1609 under the title *A Good Speed to Virginia*, Robert Gray wrote that:

> There is nothing more dangerous for the estate of commonwealths than when the people do increase to a greater multitude and number than may justly parallel with the largeness of the place and country. When this multitude of people increaseth to over great a number, the commonwealth stands subject to many perilous inconveniences. . . . Our multitudes, like too much blood in the body, do infect our country with plague and poverty.[34]

Gray proposed that the superfluous members of the population leave England for America. Nor did complaints of overpopulation, as has sometimes been suggested, come solely from those urging emigration to the plantations: Raleigh, Bacon, and Hobbes all expressed depopulationist sentiments on more disinterested grounds.[35]

Emigration was a controversial issue before 1660, as immigration was thereafter. Yet like immigration after the Restoration, no consistent records were kept of those leaving England before, or for that matter after, 1660. Technically, anyone emigrating had to have a license from the Crown, but the regulation of emigration was mostly intended to protect commercial monopolies in the plantations and was seldom enforced. Only in the mid-1630s did the volume of emigration and the settlements in the plantations come to be issues in government policy, and then almost wholly on religious grounds. Regulations severe enough to discourage emigration were in effect for only a few years, and even then presented little hindrance to religious dissidents leaving for the continent or for New England. In any case, the volume of emigration dropped off substantially around the middle of the seventeenth century.[36]

Although their departure was largely unhindered, emigrants were not numerous enough to quell the fears of overpopulation shared by many before the middle of the seventeenth century. Just a year before the Restoration John Bland could still urge that England disburden itself of its "supernumerary people" by sending them to Virginia.[37] Only at the very juncture of the Restoration, and with a surprising abruptness, did the polarity of fears shift from overpopulation to underpopulation. Only then did the encouragement of immigration to increase population, to achieve the new desideratum of populousness, become a prominent issue in the economic literature and in political discourse within and outside Parliament.

Proposals for the encouragement of immigration were almost unknown before the Restoration, though an economic discourse of a rudimentary sort had certainly appeared by then. Thomas Mun's celebrated *England's Treasure*, written about 1630 in response to the trade crisis of the 1620s, for example, made no mention of population, and its only reference to immigration consisted of an invidious diatribe against Dutch settlers in England. Mun's tract presents a striking illustration of the temporal bounds of the immigration controversy, since no economic tract of the latter half of the seventeenth century treating the same general subjects as *England's Treasure* would have omitted at least a passing comment on the nation's populousness and the gains to be enjoyed from the admission of foreigners.

Yet when the potential gains from a larger population seized the imagination of English economic writers around 1660, their zeal was that of the newly converted. "Fewness of people is real poverty," William Petty declared a short time after the Restoration, summarizing in that pregnant phrase a conviction that would begin to erode only well into the eighteenth century. Populationism, the virtually unquenchable craving for a large and growing population, found expression in a multitude of forms and contexts. The most honored economic writer of the age, Josiah Child, wrote in the years after the Restoration that "it is multitudes of people [that] principally enrich any country"; that "whatever doth increase the stock of people must be a procuring cause of riches"; and again, that "most nations in the civilized parts of the world are more or less rich or poor, proportionable to the paucity or plenty of their people." Others echoed Child that "to hope for a vast trade where people are wanting is not only to expect [that] brick can be made without straw, but without hands"; that "the people are the riches and strength of the country"; and even that the improvement to trade brought about by great numbers of people "is necessary in the nature of man."[38] "People are indeed the essential of commerce," Defoe declared in the *Review*,

and the more people the more trade; the more trade, the more money, the more money, the more strength; and the more strength, the greater the nation. . . . All temporal felicities, I mean national, spring from the number of people.[39]

Since populousness would bring England wealth and power, it was a national concern, calling for a national—and indeed international—policy of augmenting population by encouraging immigration. The economic discourse on immigration then rested on the twin beliefs that a larger population would bring prosperity and that active government policies, especially offers of easy naturalization, could be employed to immediately expand the nation's population. The road to Damascus, however, is perhaps not the best path to follow for those who seek to establish practicable state policy; the faith of the advocates of naturalization would suffer many trials and only modest successes in the century following their conversion to the dogma of populationism.

Far from being confined to England, the preoccupation with population was common intellectual currency in early modern of Europe, especially from the middle years of the seventeenth century. Many countries had laws that encouraged early marriage, energetic procreation, and immigration. Although military motives played a larger role on the continent than in England, economic rationales nevertheless predominated.[40] In France, Colbert sought to increase population by government policies that encouraged large families and immigration, and discouraged emigration. The exodus of Huguenots provoked by the persecution that ended in the revocation of the Edict of Nantes in 1685 was witnessed with consternation by those who, lacking the Sun King's zeal for religious uniformity, deplored the loss of so many valuable subjects.[41] Other states, Holland, Brandenburg, and England, received the French refugees with the comforting conviction that such immigrants would not only benefit them but hurt France, tilting the balance of population in their favor. After 1685 the French government even relaxed its scruples enough to attempt to entice back to France some of the most valuable craftsmen who had fled.[42]

The bulk of French economic opinion agreed with Colbert's populationist strategy. Vauban exalted population as the source of wealth in *An Essay for a General Tax* (1710), produced an abstract of a census in 1707, and declared that depopulation was the greatest evil that could befall a kingdom. Writing at the same time, Belesbat analyzed the causes of depopulation and the ways to stimulate population growth. Fénelon held populousness to be an unmitigated good, and advocated the naturalization of immigrants. The best known of France's economic thinkers before the Physiocrats, Boisguillebert, praised a large population as a means to national wealth, and as late as the 1760s some of the Physiocrats continued to insist that more laborers applied to the land would create more national wealth.[43] In Germany such writers on trade as Johann Joachim Becher and Wilhelm Freiherr von Schroeder espoused the policy of *Volksvermehrung* (population-increase). Becher defined a nation as quite simply "a populous productive community," and counted a large population as not only an aspiration but as the principal goal of state policy. Theodor Ludwig Lau echoed those sentiments in 1719, declaring that "multitudes of people are the power and wealth of the state." In Habsburg Austria, Philipp von Hornick—writing in the flush of optimism after the raising of the Turkish siege of Vienna—urged in his mercantilist classic, *Österreich über Alles, wann es nur Will* (1684), that population should be as large as a country could support. In a similar vein, the Russian Possochkov in his *Poverty and Wealth* (1724) argued that a rising population, by increasing the number of laborers, would increase national wealth.[44] In the wake of the mid-seventeenth century turmoil of economic crisis, social unrest, and political upheaval that touched nearly every corner of Europe, populationism was far from an insular preoccupation of the English.

The fascination with increasing population was international, and might seem to be an expression of a common development in economic thought.[45] That explanation would offer only a partial picture of developments in economic thought, as populationist strivings also reflected altered economic and demographic circumstances. France needed manpower to carry forward the dynastic and expansionist ambitions of Louis XIV, and all the more so after the exodus of the Huguenots; Germany had been horribly devastated and depopulated by the Thirty Years' War, losing perhaps as much as one-third of its people through disease, battle, and emigration; and Russia possessed a vast territory whose economic exploitation depended on more people. Densely populated and urbanized Italy, the European country in the early modern period that perhaps had the least cause to worry about a lack of people, produced few calls for an active policy of population expansion.[46] Moreover, statesmen as well as economic and political writers recognized that the benefit to one nation from immigrants would be balanced by the loss suffered by the countries from which migrants came. The issues of population and immigration became another element in the intense rivalry amongst the nation-states of early modern Europe. Populationism partook not only of a hopeful attempt at demographic and economic engineering but of reasons of state.

The differences between English and continental motives for population growth, however, are at least as important as the similarities. It is noteworthy that in England the preoccupation with population in the period 1660 to 1760, and especially in the period to 1688, arose overwhelmingly from economic considerations. Tudor policies and proposals to increase the number of people and reverse the decay of villages may have been primarily military rather than economic in motivation, seeking to ensure a supply of soldiers,[47] but by the second half of the seventeenth century military incentives for a large population had receded into the shadows. The period from the Restoration to the Revolution was a time of relative peace, dominated by the opportunistic equivocations and reversals of Charles II's foreign policy, and England only emerged as a major international power in the 1690s. That is not to say that military considerations had been totally eclipsed; but the surging national ambition of the age sought out the channels of trade through which an England of growing wealth and power could dominate Europe economically. To that end men were sought for the workshop, not the battlefield, and their weapon was to be not the sword, but the clothier's shears.

Although they were few, some pleas for the admission of immigrants, based not on a hunger for population but on more traditional grounds, were heard before the 1660s. These pleas echoed in the economic discourse and political debate well after the Restoration, and represented what may be called the traditionalist school of those who advocated the encouragement of immigration. The traditionalist perspective, exemplified (until his death in 1662) by the publications of the goldsmith and alderman of London Thomas Violet, continued to inform the writings of not only some of the advocates but most of the opponents of naturalization well into the eighteenth century. Neither Violet nor his contemporary, the merchant and trade writer Henry Robinson, made any reference to population in their proposals for the admission of foreign settlers. Like the traditionalists who followed them, these pre-Restoration controversialists must be distinguished from the progressive advocates of immigration, who sought a naturalization scheme as a facet of state demographic policy. The language, the rhetoric, and the assumptions of the traditionalists were fundamentally at odds with those of the populationist school that arose in the 1660s. Envisioning an essentially static and paternalistic traditional social order, the traditionalists sought an accession of foreigners on quite different grounds from the more forward-looking advocates of a general naturalization, whose pleas reflected a conception of a commercial society of essentially dynamic economic, rather than personal, relations. The progressives addressed the issues of immigration and population from a commercial perspective that conceived of society in essentially aggregate terms. The traditionalists, though eager to stimulate English trade by an influx of settlers, laid more stress, if only implicitly, on the integrity of the social fabric and the cultural, rather than strictly economic, dimension of a policy to encourage immigration. The conflicting visions of the nature of English society held by the progressive commercial advocates of immigration and their traditionalist allies seems seldom to have been recognized. Yet this internal division within the ranks of the promoters of naturalization perhaps contributed to the overall inefficacy of their pleas during the century of the naturalization controversy. Their opponents revealed more solidarity in their concern for the cultural impact upon an English society that indeed proved to be limited in the measure of pluralism that it could tolerate.

The traditionalists looked to the precedents of the past in advocating the admission of foreigners, to the attempts—most of them successful— of sixteenth-century governments to establish immigrant communities in England. There were also more recent precedents: the policy of admitting foreign artisans adopted by Cromwell and the Council of State was definitely of the traditional sort, contemplating an essentially stable hierarchical social structure within which small groups of newcomers could find a niche of their own, or rather be placed in a niche by central government.[48] The traditionalists proposed the admission of two types of immigrants: skilled artisans and wealthy foreign merchants. Thomas Violet, writing a few years before the Restoration, in *The Advancement of Merchandize* (1651), argued that foreign mariners and artisans ought to be encouraged to immigrate, both to introduce skills unknown in England and to enforce the industriousness of the native English laborers by a healthy dose of competition. Artisans who could introduce or perfect a particular trade or manufacture seemed an especially promising catch, and indeed they were. In an age when manufacturing and trading skills were learned through the training provided by a master, technology was essentially personal. Skills were transmitted not by books or formal training but by personal instruction; indeed one of the striking innovations of Diderot's *Encyclopédie* published at the end of our period was its minute descriptions and analyses of the manufacturing processes that up to that time were as a rule known only to their practitioners. To transplant a manufacturing technology by the reception of a foreign artisan was a very real means to economic progress in preindustrial Europe.[49]

The importance of personal skills held true not only of manufacturing technology but of competence in banking, finance, and commerce as well, and foreign merchants represented the second category of immigrants sought by traditionalists like Violet. Wealthy merchants would not only lend England the weight of their trading connections and their expertise, but would buy land in England and, as Violet bluntly put it, "bring over their banks of money." Their naturalization, he argued, would raise land values and lower the rate of interest, and they would assimilate quickly; the Dutch, for example, had married natives and had "all turned English." Violet's eagerness to entice wealthy merchants to England was by no means unique on the eve of the Restoration.[50] Such thinking inspired the controversy over the readmission of the Jews in these years, an episode that bears further witness to how tangential raw numbers of settlers were to the frame of reference of the traditionalist school.

The issue of Jewish immigration remained beneath the surface of politics and played only a minor role in the economic discourse during most of the period, though Cromwell's interest in a readmission inspired a brief flurry of polemical exchanges in the 1650s. Manasseh ben Israel, a prominent figure in the Jewish community in Holland, published a pamphlet in 1655 advocating the legal readmission of the Jews, pleading for the liberty to establish a synagogue in England, and stressing the profit to England in admitting the Jews. They excelled at trade and could offer England the most profitable of commercial connections.[51]

Manasseh's claims deserved credence, but the obstacles to a substantial concession to the Jews were religious rather than economic. No better proof of the religious character of the Jewish question could be offered than the identity of the author who replied to Manasseh and denounced the readmission: William Prynne. Prynne's *A Short Demurrer to the Jews' Long-Discontinued Remitter into England* (1656), was typical of the polemical literature concerning the Jews, almost all of it religious in motivation and character. But Jewish immigration was in any event peripheral to the interests of most economic writers and political supporters of the admission of foreigners by the 1660s, since the volume of Jewish immigration could never be great. As populationism came to dominate traditional motives for naturalization, the issue of the Jews moved to the margin of the discourse on immigration. On all sides it was acknowledged that the people in question were a relatively small number of substantial merchants, in particular Sephardim from the United Provinces of the Netherlands. Because of its prominently religious (rather than commercial) dimension, and its irrelevance to the central issue of population, the exchange over the readmission of the Jews, and later the issue of Jewish naturalization, will not play a prominent part in this story. The debate over the Jews, moreover, often strayed far from the issue of immigration and the status of foreign settlers to become a question of the disabilities of Jews, not as aliens, but as Dissenters from the established religion who were unable to take the oaths required for the exercise of many civil privileges. After the spate of writings occasioned by the readmission, however, the debate over Jewish naturalization subsided into occasional byplay to the central controversy over the admission of foreign Protestants.

An increasing proportion of the pleas for naturalization that multiplied after the Restoration employed the language and expressed the interests not of traditionalists like Thomas Violet, who sought skilled artisans and wealthy merchants, but of the participants in an emerging economic discourse who craved foreign immigrants of all sorts. The reason for the difference is apparent. The naturalization movement was inspired by fears that England's population was too small in absolute terms, and indeed that it was shrinking.

Merchants and skilled artisans would never add up to large numbers of people, and the traditionalists' proposals could never answer the newly-felt need for more people. The arguments of Thomas Violet and the potential offered by the admission of the Jews typify the traditionalists' shrewd stress on selectivity in the admission of foreigners; but that selectivity was for a considerable time eclipsed by the promiscuous hunger for large numbers of people.

No sooner had political stability been restored after the Restoration than immigration policy emerged as an important social, political, and economic issue. Within a year of Charles II's return the newly-established Committee of Trade was proposing that foreign artificers be encouraged to settle in England,[52] and general naturalization bills were being debated in Parliament. Moreover, circumstances soon conspired to bring about a political and more especially economic crisis that stimulated the quest for policy solutions like naturalization. The 1660s witnessed the last and perhaps most devastating outbreak of plague to strike London in the early modern period, the destruction of much of the capital by the Great Fire, and a severe trade crisis. A wealth of economic tracts appeared in response to these disasters, many of them lamenting the decay of trade and proposing ways to remedy it. These years produced the first proposals to encourage a large-scale immigration that would expand the nation's population and stimulate trade. Fears of depopulation spawned the new school of immigration proponents, whose pleas continued till past the middle of the following century.

The years from the Restoration to the Revolution are treated here and in the next chapter as an internally coherent period. Theories of population and proposals for naturalization in the Restoration period, whether expressed in economic discourse or in political debate, shared features that make them distinguishable from the controversy as it developed after the Revolution of 1688–89. Of course it is impossible to obtain a statistically significant sample of ideas about an economic and political policy question such as immigration, or otherwise to quantify such matters. An impression of the numbers of publications in a particular decade, say, can be gained from short-title catalogues. But ideas cannot be expressed statistically. For the historian of economic discourse to strive to do so would be as naive as the proposal of one early political arithmetician to cast up a "balance of opinion" by using "all our English pamphlets and books about trade stated so, in a way of debitor and creditor, in an alphabetical manner on all heads, that whatsoever has been said on any head may stand on one side and what against it on the other."[53]

Periodization always involves compromise, but the more common mistake has been to treat the economic literature in too long rather than in too short units of time. This is a conspicuous weakness in Edgar Furniss's otherwise superb book, *The Position of the Laborer in a System of Nationalism* (1920), which treats as homogeneous the economic thought of the entire period from 1660 to 1776. The problem with such an approach is that it tends to neglect the economic, political, and social circumstances in which the economic discourse developed. The century during which the immigration debate unfolded was one that witnessed dramatic changes in English society, and many of those changes found expression in the economic discourse. The chronological divisions adopted here, like all such temporal compartments, are far from watertight. Unless one wishes, however, to stereotype as "preclassical" and unchanging the whole of the economic discourse in the period before the publication of the *The Wealth of Nations*—rather as the eighteenth century dismissed anything medieval as "gothic"—a more nuanced periodization must be adopted than has generally been used heretofore. The justification for a more differentiated chronology of economic discourse will become apparent as the story of the immigration controversy unfolds itself.

The Restoration marked the threshold to the immigration controversy, and one of the developments visible from the early 1660s was a growing interest in population. The publication in 1662 of John Graunt's *Natural and Political Observations Made upon the Bills of Mortality* signaled the beginnings of a science of population statistics and an awakening interest in the study of demography. England's first census would not be taken until 1801, but the first tentative steps towards the numbering of the people and in the study of population dynamics began at this point. Graunt, a haberdasher and member of the Common Council of the City of London, was no pure theorist; but the influences upon him were of a higher sphere than one would expect of a practical shopkeeper. He drew inspiration from Bacon's method of empirical observation, experiment, and inductive reasoning, and he made the practical object of his inquiries a "more certain and regular" understanding of trade and government. Practical utility was one of the chief objects of the seventeenth-century scientists, in economic questions as in other areas.[54] Graunt was in fact among the first writers on economic matters to be strongly influenced by the philosophical and scientific developments of the first half of the seventeenth century. He was by no means unique, however: the ideas of Bacon, Hobbes, and Descartes increasingly gave direction to and stimulated the study of economic matters, although admittedly the philosophic influence was often at several removes and seldom betrayed itself at any but the more rarified levels of economic discourse.[55] With the founding of the Royal Society, science became an institutionalized feature of English society. One of the central concerns of the new body was economic matters. As early as 1664 a committee of the Society was established to study "histories of trade."[56]

Yet the necessary vocabulary for a science of demography developed only slowly. Even the word *population* was absent from the vocabulary of economic works until around the middle of the eighteenth century. Instead, commentators used the words *people, inhabitants, heads, hands,* and especially the word *populousness*. *Populousness* describes a quality rather than an abstract quantity, and its use instead of *population*[57] in the discourse on demographic and immigration issues betrays not only the lack of a strong quantitative sense, but the profoundly normative mentality of the early economic writers. Nevertheless, the growing scientific spirit of the years after the Restoration contributed to the study of population, since it encouraged a view of society as more a generalized body of persons operating within a common commercial economic framework than a miscellany of diverse communities forged together by strong personal, religious, and cultural links. Because of its aggregative perspective, the new science was allied to the vision of society cherished by the proponents of naturalization. Moreover, scientific studies were twinned with trade inquiries as fashionable pursuits for the virtuosi and gentlemen scholars of the John Evelyn type, who contributed more than they are sometimes given credit for to both the growth of science and the development of economic discourse.

Although the interest that he inspired in England's population touched the immigration debate, Graunt did not himself write on the subject. His friend William Petty, however, painted on a much larger canvas and in bolder brush strokes. The question of immigration was one of the many that he addressed in his wide-ranging writings, and his remarks will be examined presently. More important for present purposes was Petty's symbolic prominence as one of the founders of the study of the economics of population. Called by Marx the "founder of political economy," William Petty was a physician, a professor of anatomy and of music, and—as an administrator of the resettlement of Ireland in the 1650s—a man with personal experience in the acquisition of riches. His friendship with Hobbes, his latitudinarian religious views, his long residence abroad, and his close ties with the English Crown all contributed to the formation of his political and economic ideas. Like Graunt's, Petty's studies reflect the dawning empirical approach to economic and political questions, and he is best known for his famous methodology of "political arithmetic."[58] His writings, nevertheless, were topical, often inconsistent, and he formulated no systematic body of general doctrine. He more often wrote as an advocate than as an objective observer. His remarks on the immigration issue form a pastiche of statements and allusions that appear in publications whose composition was separated by as much as thirty years. In this Petty was, despite his unique genius, typical of his time. The bulk of his writings date from the 1670s and 1680s, and will be treated in the next chapter, but it should be observed here that even his first economic tract, *A Treatise of Taxes and Contributions* (1662), expressed both the importance that he attributed to labor and his belief that England suffered from acute underpopulation. The *Treatise* did not address the naturalization issue directly; but Petty's observation that England's population should be doubled was amongst the earliest of the many complaints, which reached a sustained crescendo by the end of the decade, of England's lack of people.[59] The most eminent of the political arithmeticians, then, was amongst the first to issue a plea for a larger population; but Petty's lone voice would soon be joined by others to form a populationist chorus.

The earliest notable proposal for the admission of foreigners on grounds of population appeared in Samuel Fortrey's *England's Interest and Improvement* (1663). Fortrey, a merchant and the great-grandson of a refugee from Lille, made the naturalization of immigrants one of the principal themes of his tract. Fortrey declared that populousness was equal to riches themselves in making a nation great and powerful: other nations would grow at England's expense unless active policies were adopted to increase both population and wealth. Like Petty, Fortrey thought that England, to some degree drained of people by emigration to the plantations, had space enough to double the number of its people, so long as they were rightly employed.[60] The means to increase the number of the people was to permit "all people of foreign countries, under such restrictions as the state shall think fit, freely to inhabit and reside within this kingdom . . . with the like privilege and freedom that English men have." Such an offer of full legal privileges, Fortrey insisted, would act as a magnet to bring foreigners to England, expanding the population and multiplying wealth. Wealthy immigrants would use the money they brought with them to buy land or advance trade, and foreign artisans would introduce or perfect manufactures that England now had to import. But even without these benefits, Fortrey urged, the potential population increase offered by immigration was crucial. In this new view, quite different from traditional pleas for the reception of foreigners, sheer numbers of immigrants, not simply the wealth of merchants or the skills of artisans, would contribute to England's power and plenty. Although he clung to the older idea that foreigners with large estates should be attracted, Fortrey took a great step beyond the pre-Restoration proposals for encouraging immigration, for now the object was population engineering.[61]

Fortrey identified four reasons why foreigners would leave their native lands to settle in England: first, England was simply more pleasant and healthful than any other country; second, English law and government offered peace and security; third, the potential for prosperity of England's trade and manufactures would offer industrious people a wonderful chance to grow rich; and fourth, and most important, England could become the asylum of all the oppressed Protestants of Europe if free liberty of conscience were established. Fortrey's stress on the need of religious toleration, underlined by lengthy warnings against popery that were no doubt intended to lessen and redirect fears of Dissent, whether foreign or native, introduced from the beginning of the controversy what would be its axial issue until the Revolution. The policies of toleration and of encouraging immigration were intimately related, both in the sphere of politics and in the economic and political literature, and that connection became abundantly obvious within a handful of years after the publication of Fortrey's tract.[62] The fourth and last of Fortrey's reasons proved to be not only the most controversial facet of the immigration debate, but the most potent factor in attracting immigrants to England in the following several decades.

Fortrey admitted that the proposal had its detractors. In view of the number of England's poor, some complained, could it be said that there were too few people? Should not natives be employed before foreigners were brought in? It was true, Fortrey conceded, that a decline in trade had reduced employment; but if manufactures and other trades were properly encouraged, he argued, people and riches would multiply together, as "the begetters the one of the other." From the outset of the controversy, then, a paradox haunted the proponents of immigration. Why encourage immigration when poverty was such a conspicuous problem? The embarassment of this apparent contradiction became much more acute when the problem of poverty worsened near the end of the century. Fortrey's optimism, however, rested on a foundation of tacit premises that he shared with most of the others who promoted immigration for the following century. The most important of those premises, at least until the early eighteenth century, was that laborers must be kept poor, and their wages low, in order to stimulate their appetite for work.[63] To top up the pool of labor with immigrants, even to the point of overflowing, ensured that English laborers would not slacken in their industry on account of a too generous wage. So far from being a misfortune, an accession of foreign laborers would bring a benefit beyond their numbers by prodding English workers out of their sluggishness.

Some observers complained that foreigners would "undo the natives" by their foreign connections and their frugality. But Fortrey scoffed that "any Englishman of the like ingenuity as a stranger, will have the like advantage of trade." The race belonged to the swiftest, and the edge of competition could only be honed by the admission of industrious foreigners—the increment of wealth would strengthen England in any case. Moreover, immigrants would provide English natives with foreign goods at better prices and increase the demand for English manufactures.[64] At base, Fortrey's immigration proposal, like those that would follow, rested on an abiding faith in the vitality, adaptability, and powers of growth of the English economy. Fortrey's later claim that he had foretold in *England's Interest* many of the coming developments in economic policy and debate was not an empty boast.[65] On the issue of immigration, at least, Fortrey was remarkably ahead of his time.

Just as the speculations on population dynamics of Graunt and Petty, and the proposals such as Fortrey's for a populationist immigration scheme, appeared shortly after 1660, so did the opponents of naturalization first make their voices heard soon after the return of Charles II from exile. Although relatively few aliens had been naturalized during the Interregnum, several broadsides and pamphlets appeared immediately after the Restoration to denounce the naturalization in 1657 of a group of Dutch merchants and the policy of naturalization more generally. Their authors, who claimed to write on behalf of the City of London and of English merchants, seem to have hoped that the reestablished monarchy would prove a regime more congenial to paternalist protection than that of Cromwell. That hope was frustrated, but publications of this sort were not without effect in proclaiming the perils of a liberal immigration policy.

The publications rehearsed arguments that became the common currency of adversaries of naturalization, faithfully repeated at every opportunity. The most substantial alien merchants, it was argued, had procured naturalization by declaring their affection for England and promising that they could import commodities more cheaply than English merchants; although the new subjects might undersell the English in order to ruin them, however, they would treacherously raise their prices once their design had been accomplished. In any case, English merchants had "stock enough to drive the whole trade." If Parliament had to naturalize aliens, the new subjects should at least be required to pay alien duties.[66] Naturalized aliens had saved enormous sums in alien duties, a great loss to the City of London and other ports. Invoking historical precedent, the publications cited statutes of the reigns of Henry VII and Henry VIII that imposed high alien duties and customs, a tradition now abandoned. Naturalized aliens might, it was said, appear in the guise of skilled craftsmen, but all were in reality unscrupulous merchants, who only kept chambers, had the advantage of funds at low interest rates and of foreign connections, and contributed nothing to taxes. They usurped the foreign commissions of English merchants and evaded the king's customs by their ability to color or cover[67] the goods of foreign correspondents.

Moreover, the publications warned, important political considerations were in play, as the admission of foreigners posed dangers from rival nations. Naturalizations "transplanted" English trade from natives to aliens, who would make it "but a drudge and stalking-horse" to the trade of their own countries. Naturalization would not change the affections or allegiance of aliens; they would remain aloof, perhaps spies, staying in England only long enough to accumulate estates. Naturalizing aliens was only "a design of the enemies of England" to undermine English trade.[68]

The publications' thinly veiled preoccupation with the exemption from alien duties and customs conferred by naturalization betrays their origin. Two interests were at stake in regard to alien duties and tolls: those of English merchants and those of the corporate cities themselves, particularly the corporation of London, which because of its enormous volume of trade had far more to lose than the other cities. Higher alien customs duties under the Act of Tonnage and Poundage blunted the edge of alien competition.[69] In addition, the City lost revenue from its own alien duties each time a foreign merchant was naturalized. Of these two interests, those of the corporations, especially London, predominated. Throughout the century of the naturalization controversy, the corporate cities presented the most vigorous opposition to the admission of foreigners. The broadsides and pamphlets alleged that the alien duties were as much a burden to the City as an advantage. This was patently false. The corporation of London was keenly interested in its duties, and most of the City's vehement opposition to naturalization throughout the century after the Restoration arose not from mercantile interests, but from the fear that those cherished privileges would be lost, or their value diminished. The arguments rehearsed above became the rhetorical staples of the pamphlets, broadsides, and petitions in which the City of London publicized its antagonism to the naturalization of foreigners. But the City's opposition, after this group of publications at the time of the Restoration, remained muted until the 1680s, when it expanded into a vigorous campaign against foreign settlements and naturalizations.

It may seem incongruous to juxtapose the polemics of the City of London's broadsides and pamphlets against naturalization and the apparently disinterested and theoretical writings of men such as Samuel Fortrey, John Graunt, and William Petty. But the contrast reveals the curiously asymmetrical contours of the immigration controversy, especially in its early years. Most of the proponents of naturalization schemes belonged to no distinct group whose interests hung in the balance of the success or failure of their proposals. That is not to say that they were strictly impartial. Many of them wrote in order to promote projects and policies in which they had some personal stake. But in most cases, the naturalization of foreigners represented only one instrument in an ensemble—and in some cases an entire orchestra—of economic and political proposals that they offered, at least ostensibly, to promote the prosperity and power of England. Few publications until well into the eighteenth century were devoted wholly to advocating naturalization. The controversy over immigration unfolded as an integral part of the expanding discourse on trade. The opponents of naturalization, however—conservatives fearful of the cultural effect of an influx of foreigners, manufacturers and merchants menaced by the competition of naturalized aliens, and more importantly the corporations, intent upon preserving their privileges—could form a phalanx of opposition that the sustained but diffuse favor of the writers of economic tracts and the proponents of naturalization inside and outside Parliament could resist only with difficulty.

Not all the adversaries of naturalization, however, betrayed the partiality of the spokesmen for the corporate cities. The eminent jurist Sir Matthew Hale joined the exchange over immigration policy that blossomed shortly after the Restoration, presenting arguments that distinguished him as perhaps the most articulate opponent of immigration schemes in the period up to the Revolution. While the publications of the City of London sought to protect the special interests of the corporation, Hale's manuscript tract, entitled *Sundry Considerations against a General Naturalization of Aliens* [1664] represents a more disinterested and thoughtful expression of distrust in naturalization proposals. The undated tract, occasioned by a general naturalization bill introduced in Parliament, probably that of 1664, is a monument to a conservative and traditional view of immigration that was then under attack by the growing camp of populationists, who represented a progressive and dynamic vision of England's social order.[70] Hale, an eminent barrister before the civil war, and a judge of the Court of Common Pleas under the Commonwealth, was created Chief Justice of the King's Bench in 1671. A friend to the principle of religious toleration, as a member of the Convention Parliament he introduced an unsuccessful bill for the comprehension of Presbyterians. On the bench he acquired a reputation for leniency in the enforcement of the penal laws against Dissenters.[71] Yet unlike most of those who espoused the cause of toleration Hale opposed a free admission of foreigners.

Although Hale shared with the new breed of economic writers a conviction that religious liberty should form a cornerstone of the English polity, he expressed a hostility to trade that betrayed his conservatively paternalistic understanding of English society. While progressive economic writers sought a religious policy that would provide a climate congenial to the growth of a dynamic commercial order, and that would prove attractive to prospective immigrants, Hale saw toleration as part of a hierarchical and essentially static social and religious dispensation. Far from conceiving toleration as progressive or reformist, Hale and many fellow conservatives viewed a comprehension of the heterodoxy that had blossomed in the preceding two decades as a means to restore English religious unity. Economic motives inspired the pleas for the admission of foreigners to expand population and stimulate commercial growth, as they inspired many of the pleas for religious toleration; yet Hale rejected the economic and demographic approach to these vexing issues in favor of cultural, political, and moral arguments. Indeed, the refusal of Hale and many of the other opponents of naturalization to address immigration as an economic issue makes it perhaps more proper to consider their contentions not as part of Restoration economic discourse but as a discourse of opposition to the growing commercial ethos and the conception of the market as the ordering principle of English society.

The absence of any references to population in the *Sundry Considerations* bears silent witness to Hale's traditionalist perspective on the immigration question. This silence is all the more surprising as he had a keen interest in the subject. Indeed, some scholars, impressed with Hale's *Primitive Origination of Mankind* (1677), in which he articulated at considerable length his views on population, have even classed him with Graunt and Petty as one of the founders of demographic studies.[72] Ranging Hale with the political arithmeticians, however, loses sight of the fundamental differences between his and their views of the nature of English society. While Graunt and Petty shared Hale's concern with the social order, they recognized the irreversible changes that had by the middle of the seventeenth century permanently altered the traditional, paternalistic, hierarchical bases of social structure. Acknowledging the dynamic nature of English society, they sought in the quantifying spirit of political arithmetic a means to a new understanding of social order, an understanding that accepted conflict and change as inevitable.[73] Population change, guided by state policy, could in their view form one facet of a new pattern of political and social order. To Hale, however, change posed a threat rather than a promise, and the question of population arose within the conception of a traditional social order to which he clung.

On a first examination Hale's speculations on population might seem forward-looking, for he was interested in the dynamics of growth and sought to prove that human population was capable of very rapid expansion "in a kind of geometrical progression." According to his calculations, a human population had the potential to double in thirty-five years. Only natural "correctives"—plagues, famines, wars, floods, and fires—established a "certain due stay and equability" (the similarity to Malthus's notion of positive checks on population is obvious). Yet Hale discovered no natural movement towards equilibrium in the number of people. On the contrary, he declared that the population of England was rising, and that the number of the poor in particular was increasing at a formidable rate.[74] It is no wonder then that he saw no need to encourage immigration, for his belief in the potential for rapid growth of population would make nonsense of the populationists' fears that England had too few people. Even Hale's population studies, however, were not written as, and cannot be considered, economic or scientific inquiries. Their inspiration partook of traditional religious preoccupations with numbers of people rather than with the new spirit of natural philosophy. Hale was an intimate friend of Archbishop Ussher, known for his Biblical chronological researches that dated the Creation to the year 4004 b.c., and the two men eagerly compared notes on questions of creationist chronology and population size that they viewed as inseparable. Hale's demographic speculations savor of orthodox attempts to prove the age of humanity by "curious searches into antiquity," and bore the stamp of exegetical piety rather than of political arithmetic.[75] Deriving from Biblical roots that by 1660 found no place in the economic discourse,[76] Hale's writings offer a warning against a facile equation of Restoration demographic inquiry with a progressive view of the social order or with the primarily secular interests of the new natural philosophy and economic discourse.

Although Hale ignored the question of population that soon assumed the central place in the naturalization debate, he admitted that some of the arguments for the encouragement of immigration seemed plausible. Its advocates argued that rents and the value of land would increase; that foreign merchants would be attracted; that foreign artisans would come as well, and teach new skills to English laborers; and that England would become "the commune and mobile emporium of the world" to the benefit of shipping and mariners. But such a splendid picture, Hale warned, would prove no more substantial than a mirage if put to the test. He minced no words in condemning the authors of naturalization proposals, the new school of economic writers and political arithmeticians, as "speculative and notional men" with no grounding in public affairs and no sense of the social and cultural consequences of their projects. The only object of such airy economic theorists, he charged, was to "strike sail for profit," by inviting foreigners to bring their wealth, manufactures, and stocks to England, no matter the damage to the fabric of English society and state. The more extensive the privilege granted to immigrants, he reasoned ironically, the greater the advantage, "if trade be the saint that is adored." Naturalization must therefore be universal, he declared, adopting the lawyerly device of the *reductio ad absurdum*, and comprehend all persons of all nations and religions indiscriminately: Protestants, papists, Jews, Turks, and pagans should enjoy every privilege possessed by a native. More forthright than most participants in the controversy, Hale proclaimed in the plainest possible terms his fundamental opposition to the new commercial order in England and his disdain for the reasonings of its intellectual defenders.

In any case the economic consequences of naturalization would be disastrous. If immigrants were wealthy, Hale declared, they would be a "canker to eat the natives out of their possessions" keeping estates in their countries of origin, to which they would drain English wealth. Foreign artisans would refuse to instruct their English counterparts in the mysteries of their trades. If immigrants were poor, they would be an intolerable burden. Both rich and poor would continue to be strangers in a strange land, keeping apart from the English and acting as spies and enemies in England's bosom if war arose. The laws of apprenticeship and the restrictions and privileges of the corporate cities presented further problems. If subject to such laws, foreigners would be discouraged from coming to England; if they were exempted from them, they would enjoy more privileges than the natives themselves. As for alien merchants, Hale complained that those already naturalized covered the goods of their relations overseas in order to evade customs rates. By reason of their commercial connections the legal equality granted by naturalization gave them a competitive superiority over English merchants. On this point Hale's complaints rang true: immigrant merchants and financiers often did enjoy an extensive network of commercial correspondents,[77] and the complaints about covering goods arose from very real abuses of the law.[78]

In history and tradition Hale found ample warning of the egregious error that England would make by admitting large numbers of foreigners. Aliens had never been deemed beneficial in the past, he wrote, and had been forbidden to own houses or enjoy hereditary succession. They had paid higher customs rates since the time of Edward I. Parliament had always exercised care in its naturalizations, and grants had not been given in shoals, as had occurred recently. Foreign merchants were in any event fully free except as to land ownership, customs rates, and the restrictions of the Act of Navigation. The right to own land was only "collateral to trade," and the higher customs rates represented no great discouragement. Again Hale's terms of reference look to the past, and the ancient laws and decrees that he cited dealt almost exclusively with "merchant strangers" rather than immigrant settlers. In fact few if any historical precedents existed to shed light on the practicability of immigration schemes to increase population of the sort floated after 1660.

Hale drew one crucial lesson from the historical experience of immigration to England, however, that proved prophetic: the perils posed by the hostility to foreigners of the native English, especially the laboring people. The arrival of foreign settlers, he warned, "would presently give an universal disgust to the whole kingdom," and immigrants would be greeted by "animosities and heart burnings" that would make their successful settlement nearly impossible. English tradesmen were "a numerous, indigent, querulous company," Hale observed, and if oppressed by aliens their discontent would lead to public disorder. They caused unrest on account of the few alien artisans in England already; what would happen if Parliament allowed "a deluge to overflow and destroy" them? The English stood not a chance. Foreign workers would undersell and underwork them, and make the English "hewers of wood and drawers of water to strangers." Naturalization would exchange the birthright of Englishmen for an economic mess of potage, betraying "our countrymen, [and] exterminating them that we might increase trade for strangers."[79] Hale's stress on the invidious hostility that foreigners would face in England proved exaggerated but not entirely misplaced.[80] By exposing, indeed almost brandishing, the resentment that foreigners would face in England, he contributed to the debate what should have been a central issue. Yet the dangers of popular hostility to immigrants were largely ignored in Parliament and in the discourse over immigration and population until its potency was made all too apparent after the passage of the General Naturalization Act of 1709.

What would befall England should "speculative men" press through their naturalization schemes? Infinite numbers of foreigners would wash up on England's shores, an "inundation" of millions of people. In time, Hale warned, a naturalized foreigner would inhabit every second house in the country. Such dire scenarios betray Hale's tacit acceptance of one key assumption of the proimmigration camp: that naturalization privileges would inspire colossal numbers of aliens to uproot themselves in order to settle in England. Having surcharged the kingdom with aliens, Hale proclaimed, naturalization would conspire to "consume or quite blot out the English nation." The economic and commercial objections to the admission of foreigners counted for him as mere addenda to the corrosive danger of a cultural pollution that would rend the fabric of English society and destroy the cohesive ties that preserved social order. Moreover, the accession of foreigners would transform English law and poison the very roots of English government and religion. Hale viewed social and economic change as necessarily disruptive and destructive, and his concern with the risk of social disorder and cultural ferment from the admission of foreign settlers betrays his paternalistic vision of a static and morally defined social order. That vision of the right ordering of English society represented in the decades after the Restoration a legacy from the past, though one that continued to enjoy considerable vitality and widespread support. Such a traditional view clashed irreconcilably, however, with the mental terrain being mapped out in the economic discourse. That terrain described a dynamic commercial society held together not by traditional bonds of personal obligation and a communal moral order—acutely vulnerable to foreign cultural dissolution—but by the cement of a growing commercial ethos.

Although Hales's *Sundry Considerations* did not appear in print until several decades after it was composed, it apparently circulated in manuscript form, and represented an important early statement of the opposition to immigration schemes.[81] Hale's legalistic turn of mind directed his gaze to the past rather than to the future. He failed to foresee the importance of the emerging fears of depopulation that fueled the pleas for naturalization. Yet he saw more clearly than most observers the barrier of popular hostility that contributed to the failure of schemes for the admission and settlement of foreigners when they were put into effect. In reflecting on such impediments, Hale and some of the other opponents of immigration demonstrated perhaps a more realistic understanding of the cultural inertia of English society than the economic writers, for the lengthy processes of commercialization and social change advanced only by increments. The *Sundry Considerations*, however, presented as a reply to the general naturalization bill of 1664, testifies to the entry of the issue into the political arena at the same time that it appeared in the pamphlet literature. The development of the political side of the controversy must now be addressed.

3

Populationism, Religion, and Immigration

With the Restoration, the immigration issue became not only an element in the emerging economic discourse but a feature of political life as well. Those eager to promote immigration introduced general naturalization bills in Parliament, the Crown issued proclamations to encourage foreign settlers, and petitions and official recommendations regarding alien newcomers flowed in the channels of extraparliamentary politics. Charles II in the 1660s and 1670s set a model of Crown support for immigrants that lasted through the next century. Parliament on the other hand, though it repeatedly addressed the issue of a naturalization scheme, achieved no tangible results. Both Lords and Commons treated the establishment of an active immigration policy as a distinctly secondary political priority, and as one pregnant with potential dangers. Broader religious and constitutional questions tended to shape the debate over the admission of foreigners during the reigns of Charles II and James II. Indeed, it would not be an exaggeration to say that the controversy over immigration formed a byplay to the divisive politics of the Restoration religious settlement.

From the outset of Charles II's reign the Crown acted as the champion of immigrants, and supported immigration schemes. Less than a year after the triumphal return of the king, a petition against aliens in England elicited a thorough official inquiry into the issue by the recently established Council of Trade, a body whose existence itself bears testimony to the concern of the new regime with economic policy. The shopkeepers, tradesmen, and artificers of London complained in the petition, dated November 1660, that multitudes of aliens had taken up trades in the capital and its liberties in violation of the privileges of the City and of a variety of older statutes. The aliens carried on their trades so secretively, the petition charged, that it was impossible to bring informations against them according to the law—yet native tradesmen would be ruined if the abuse continued. The petitioners ambitiously prayed for a royal proclamation forbidding aliens from exercising their trades and crafts in England, a prohibition that would have virtually sealed the country off from immigrants. The Council of Trade proved unsympathetic. After deliberating over the question at several meetings, it issued an opinion in March 1661 acknowledging a measure of truth in the tradesmen's petition, but concluding that the Council could not consider any reform that would act as a restraint upon alien immigrants. To forbid foreigners from practicing their trades would cause great hardship to people who had mostly come to England to escape religious persecution, the Council declared; immigrants were mostly laboring people who would soon be incorporated into the fabric of English society; and if they were expelled they would carry their skills to rival countries. Indeed, so far from agreeing with the complaints of the London tradesmen, the Council praised the policy of encouraging immigration as a way of gaining a multitude of people, and refused the petition with the dismissive suggestion that the petitioners could have recourse to the laws already in force.[1]

The recommendations of the Council of Trade represent the first modest episode of a recurring pattern in which royal officials or the Crown itself extended protection to immigrants. Subsequent events proved that the Crown was much more inclined than Parliament to grant foreigners the privileges of natives, or to otherwise assist them to establish themselves in England. The scepticism of Caroline Robbins on this point in her brief account of naturalization under the Stuarts seems unfounded.[2] Charles II does not enjoy a reputation for either strong personal compassion or sincerity of sentiment, but he seems to have felt a genuine sympathy for foreign immigrants. Such sympathy also complemented the king's vision of monarchy. The reception of immigrants could be considered not only a point of mercantilist orthodoxy but a precept of absolutism. The Crown betrayed an especial eagerness to encourage the settlement of skilled artisans along the lines of traditional economic thinking, for the doctrine of the rivalry of nations for personal skills must have seemed particularly convincing from the perspective of the throne. But the Crown also aspired to realize the threadbare Biblical axiom that the honor and glory of the king consisted in the number and multitude of his people, a precept invoked with liturgical repetitiveness by the defenders of royal power, and not only in England—Bishop Bossuet reiterated the truism in his great defense of absolutism, the *Politique tireé des Propres Paroles de l'Écriture Sainte* of 1709.[3] Economic and political motives conspired with a measure of sympathy to make the Crown the most consistent defender of the foreign immigrant.

Charles II supported traditional proposals to attract skilled artisans to England, and the first attempt by the Cavalier Parliament to address immigration policy followed similarly traditional lines. An act was passed in 1663 that sought to introduce new skills into England by providing for the naturalization of any foreigners who carried on the manufacture of linen cloth or tapestries in England for three years. Openly mercantilist in its attempt to improve the balance of trade by diminishing the import of foreign goods and the export of money, the act obviously envisioned only a very selective policy of admission.[4] Only in the following year did Parliament first debate

the novel scheme of a general naturalization that sought to influence population trends by encouraging large-scale immigration.

On 2 May 1664 the Commons Committee on Trade proposed the introduction of a bill that would allow the naturalization of all foreigners, except
Jews, who took the oaths of allegiance and supremacy. A precedent existed
for such a measure, though not in England, for a similar act had been passed
in Ireland only two years earlier. The Irish naturalization act of 1662 bore
almost no fruit, but the lesson of its failure went unheeded in Westminster,
both in 1664 and thereafter.[5] The session of 1664 had already seen the passage of a number of measures favorable to the Court, and initial debate on
the bill seems to have been promising. On 4 May, however, Sir John Holland,
an avowed opponent of the complementary policy of religious toleration,
spoke forcefully against what he called the "great business of General Naturalization." Holland, member for Aldborough in Suffolk, reminded the Commons of the discontent already palpable amongst native tradesmen at the
coming of foreigners, and warned against inflaming it. The customs rates
had just been settled, he reminded the House, and the exemption of aliens
would undermine the king's revenues. Moreover, the measure would flout
the Act of Uniformity and the just-passed Conventicle Act, for without a
provision for religious toleration, he argued, few foreigners would come to
England. The incorporated cities and their merchants would be injured by
the measure, arousing discontentment and disturbing the peace of the
Church and state. Holland concluded that since hostilities with the Dutch
loomed ominously, so controversial a measure should be set aside for the
time being; the parliamentary session, he urged, would in any case end
before a full debate could be had and the bill could pass. Holland's arguments seem to have persuaded the House, which set aside consideration of
the proposal on the same day by a division of 118 to 63.[6]

The partisan or factional alignments involved in discussion of the 1664
bill remain elusive. Precise and consistent political orientations on the immigration question are difficult to discern for the period before the Revolution.
The legislative history of the issue forms only a fragmentary picture in the
early years, but there does not appear to have existed a clear party split
before 1689.[7] Courtiers, falling in line with the proimmigration stance of the
Crown, tended to support, as Country Members of Parliament opposed, the
admission of foreigners. But religion formed the most decisive factor in
the politics of the immigration question during the Restoration era.

The uneasy religious settlement, which made permanent the division of
the country that it had been intended to end, shaped English political culture
in the reigns of Charles II and James II. The failure of the Savoy Conference
to achieve a comprehension that would have reconciled religious differences, the emptiness of Charles's promises of liberty for tender consciences,
and the Act of Uniformity and the Clarendon code of penal laws, all fixed
the key in which religious and political dissonances would resound until the

Revolution. The failure to recognize and tolerate Dissent, and the opportunistic alliance of the gentry and the High Churchmen, hardened into features of English social and political life that formed the backdrop to the controversy over immigration, not only in the reigns of the later Stuarts, but virtually to the end of our period. The High Church party opposed naturalization as consistently as did one other group: the corporate towns and the interests that they represented. Fears that immigrants of openly Nonconformist or unknown belief would undermine the religious settlement in England, so conspicuously precarious in itself, played a decisive role in the debate over immigration from the Restoration to the Revolution. In the early years after the Restoration, proposals for the admission of immigrants excited fears that the newcomers would swell the ranks of Dissent. By the 1670s, however, those fears had been augmented by suspicions that a liberal immigration policy could also bring in a cadre of papists. Religious arguments proved the most persuasive of those mustered by the opponents of naturalization. Its proponents, on the other hand, saw toleration and the admission of foreigners as complementary policies for the increase of England's wealth and power. Members of both camps recognized that any decision on immigration policy required grappling with the problems inherent in the religious settlement, the most fundamental and vexing constitutional question of the later Stuart polity. It is hardly surprising then that a consensus on immigration policy proved so elusive.

That the religious turmoil of Restoration England colored the immigration debate and defined its dialectic can be very clearly seen in the case of the second broaching of the issue in Parliament, in 1667. The Second Dutch War had ended in an inconclusive peace in July of that year after the humiliating destruction of the English fleet at Chatham in June. The now odious Earl of Clarendon had been dismissed in August as a scapegoat, but discontent and confusion at the mismanagement of the war and financial difficulties contributed to the formation of a coherent opposition. When Parliament met in October 1667 the impeachment of Clarendon became its most pressing care. In spite of the confusion of the time, many inside and outside Parliament felt the moment to be auspicious for an improvement in the legal status of Dissent.[8]

The toleration question posed two separate but interrelated issues: a comprehension would have admitted to the Church of England moderate Nonconformists, mostly Presbyterians; a relaxation of the penal laws would have provided relief for the more extreme Dissenting sects, such as the Independents. Some of the unpopularity of Clarendon reflected on the code that bore his name, however unfairly, and the Lord Chancellor's fall in 1667 seemed to many to have cleared the air and created a new political climate. Dissenters greeted the appointment of Sir Orlando Bridgeman as Lord Keeper with delight as the signal for a change. Those sympathetic to Nonconformity soon put afoot a proposal for moderating the terms of the Act of Uniformity and for a comprehension, and their draft bill was prepared before Parliament met on 10 October 1667. Colonel John Birch, a Presbyterian and placeman, made some overtures toward introducing the bill, but the time was not ripe. Conferences ensued between Hezekiah Burton (Bridgeman's chaplain), John Wilkins, later Bishop of Chester, and several Presbyterian leaders. Two new and separate proposals resulted, one for comprehension inside the Church of England and the other for indulgence outside it. Sir Matthew Hale, always sympathetic to the principle of freedom of conscience, cast the Wilkins proposals into the form of a bill. The Duke of Buckingham, in the ascendancy since the fall of Clarendon, hurriedly put together a proposal for toleration as well; and so did the Independents, under the direction of Dr. John Owen. Their supporters were to present these proposals after the Christmas recess.

In the meantime, and under the same auspices, a general naturalization bill was introduced. Debate took place on 3 and 4 December 1667, when the bill was championed by Colonel Birch, who urged that such a measure would fill the kingdom with people. The courtier John Milward and others held that the measure would endanger the Established Church, and suspected that it had been sponsored by Dissenters as an indirect movement towards a toleration. Those suspicions were amply justified, though overdrawn, for the proponents of the two proposals were to a large degree the same men, the exception of Hale only proving how hazy remained party lines on the issue. But the naturalization bill, which some members attacked on the ground that it would attract unneeded merchants instead of the desired artisans, met with no more success than had the 1664 bill. The excitement and confusion occasioned by the news that Clarendon had fled to France interrupted the debate, and consideration of the bill was not resumed.[9] The corollary proposals for toleration fared no better. When Parliament reconvened early in February the king spoke in support of the proposals; but even before Charles's address, the Commons had voted against the introduction of any such bill and called for a stricter enforcement of the penal laws. Richard Baxter's lament that "so it died" might equally have been applied to the companion naturalization bill lost two months earlier.[10]

Three years later Parliament broached the immigration issue again, when in November 1670 a general naturalization bill was introduced in the Lords. It passed rapidly, with the firm support of the king, who was said to have attended the debates. The bill applied to "any foreigners, being Christians," required the taking of the oath of allegiance and the declaration against transubstantiation, and contained a proviso that it would not affect the provisions of the Navigation Act. But the Commons resolved to delay debate for three weeks, and the bill lapsed.[11] Its ignominious end typified the fate of naturalization proposals: of the more than half dozen such measures introduced in Parliament before 1689, none was defeated in a vote on its merit.

In the 1670s pleas for a liberty of conscience echoed still more loudly than they had in the preceding decade, and the proposals for a religious toleration and for a liberal immigration policy came to be forged together ever more securely. It had become clear to the political nation that Charles II supported a general toleration as a way of obtaining relief for Catholics, and by the early 1670s the prospects of a toleration outside the Established Church grew as hopes for a comprehension faded. Hostility towards Dissenters gradually subsided as the Interregnum receded further into the past, and in Parliament an opposition sympathetic to Nonconformity grew in strength.[12] Charles's Declaration of Indulgence in March 1672 contributed to these developments, although its flavor of absolutism and its transparent favoritism to Catholics ensured that it would not survive the reconvening of Parliament in February of the next year. With the prospect of a Catholic succession, and the alliance with absolutist and Catholic France, fears of popery became acute. By 1673, and most certainly by the time of the Popish Plot and the Exclusion Crisis at the end of the decade, the dread of Catholicism had surpassed, though it had certainly not supplanted, that of Dissent. Charles was forced to withdraw the Declaration, and Parliament passed the Test Act, which effectively disabled Catholics from holding office. At the same time a bill was introduced in the Commons for the ease of Protestant Dissenters, but that bill was lost at the adjournment, a victim of the anxious religious climate. Fears of papist conspiracies had scuttled the attempts to relieve Nonconformists; they also indirectly dealt a formidable blow to hopes for the admission of large numbers of foreign Protestants, so inseparable had the two policies become in English politics.[13]

Rising fears of a pro-Catholic royal policy aroused deep suspicions of toleration proposals. At the same time, however, many saw a policy of encouraging the immigration of continental Protestants as a way to buttress the Protestant interest in England. Indeed, Caroline Robbins identifies this aspiration as the strongest argument in favor of the proposals to encourage immigration.[14] Yet a general naturalization act would be a dead letter without an assurance of religious freedom. As a consequence of this quandary, proposals for a more liberal immigration policy were almost hopelessly compromised by the religious divisions within and outside Parliament. Despite the rising chorus of pleas from economic and political publicists, Parliament proved a dead hand in altering immigration policy until after 1689. However opportunistic the motives involved, as the immigration question became part of the byzantine politics of royal religious policy, only the Crown offered concrete concessions to foreign settlers before the Revolution; indeed, such concessions became a staple of royal religious policy.

Charles II's attempts to establish a toleration were not wholly self-serving—certainly they corresponded with the eagerness to encourage and protect immigrants that he demonstrated on numerous occasions—but the political aspect of the issue could not be escaped. Indeed, domestic politics, the religious settlement, and foreign policy frequently converged. In the declaration of war against the Dutch issued two days after the Declaration of Indulgence, for example, the king offered protection to French and Dutch subjects who wished to immigrate to or remain in England. A similar provision had appeared in the declaration of war issued in February 1666 at the opening of the Second Dutch War.[15] In June 1672, some months before the issuance of the ill-fated Declaration of Indulgence, Charles had issued a declaration to encourage the subjects of the United Provinces of the Netherlands to settle in England, printed in parallel columns in English, French, and Dutch, and promising full liberty of conscience and all the rights of natural-born subjects. Charles also promised in the declaration to pass a bill at the next session of Parliament for naturalizing those who came.[16]

Some foreigners, perhaps ill-informed of the political circumstances in England, immigrated in reliance on the Declaration of 1672, as had some in 1666, but their numbers do not seem to have been large; nor is it possible to say for how long the terms of the Declaration were honored.[17] The Declaration of Indulgence itself cited as one of the advantages of religious toleration the advance of trade and the "inviting strangers . . . to come and live with us," although such expressions can hardly be accepted at face value.[18] Nevertheless, in the 1680s Charles—by then much freer to pursue his own interests—betrayed a sincere concern in the reception and relief of the French refugees. The 1681 Order in Council providing for free denization also ordered a brief for the collection of money to assist those arriving. Throughout the period, the Crown played an instrumental role in collecting charity for needy immigrants, and the protection it extended to foreign settlers presents a stark contrast with the relative indifference, or at least ineffectualness, of Parliament. The *Journals* of the two Houses are strewn with references to abortive general naturalization bills, almost all of them lost through neglect or by lapse at prorogations. In Parliament the immigration issue could neither overcome the obstacle presented by an ambivalent religious settlement nor compete with matters that were felt to be of more political urgency.

The events of the heady session of February 1673 demonstrated once again the political difficulties of immigration schemes, for bills for a general naturalization were introduced in both the Lords and Commons. The Lords bill was passed on 27 March. It was apparently a revival of the bill considered in the Lords three years earlier, with the same requirements of the oath and declaration, and the exception in favor of the Navigation Act. In the Commons the courtiers Henry Coventry and John Duncombe spoke in favor of the bill, as did Colonel Birch and Edmund Waller, the last two both stressing its connection with religious toleration. The Commons never acted on the Lords bill, and their own bill was committed only a few days before prorogation. When Parliament met again at the end of October, Colonel Birch's motion for reconsideration of the bill preceded another prorogation by only one day. Like the complementary toleration proposal at the same juncture, the naturalization proposal lapsed once again, a victim of the apparently insoluble issues of religious politics.[19]

After the session of 1673 the situation for Dissent definitely worsened. The dismissal of Shaftesbury as Lord Chancellor in 1674 and the appointment as Lord Treasurer of Sir Thomas Osborne, later Earl of Danby, symbolized the change of climate. The period of Danby's ascendancy witnessed renewed enforcement of the penal laws, and the economic discourse reflected the change by its fervid pleas for liberty of conscience in order to ensure the efficacy of a naturalization policy, and indeed, the very preservation of English trade.[20] Economic writers of all political leanings urged religious toleration. Slingsby Bethel, a republican and later Whig politician denounced religious intolerance in his tract *The Present Interest of England Stated* (1671) as a "mischief unto trade transcending all others whatsoever" that discouraged vital immigration.[21] At the other end of the political spectrum, toleration was also urged by Thomas Sheridan, a fellow of the Royal Society, a protégé of the Duke of York, and a Jacobite who followed James into exile. In his *A Discourse of the Rise and Power of Parliaments* (1677) Sheridan lamented the decline of England's population and proposed such measures as a tax on celibacy to encourage natural increase. England's need, he argued could be met by a variety of encouragements to immigration:

> Naturalization without charge, plain laws, and speedy justice, freedom in all corporations, immunities from taxes and tolls for seven years, and lastly, liberty of conscience; the restraint of which has been the greatest cause at first of unpeopling England, and of its not being since repeopled.[22]

Since High Churchmen and Tories after the Revolution took the initiative in focusing the naturalization debate on religion, it is noteworthy that Sheridan dismissed religious fears as irrelevant to what he saw as a matter of political and economic policy.[23] Indeed, he painted immigration policy as a matter of international political gamesmanship in which the Dutch held the most formidable hand and England was rapidly discarding itself into poverty.

Beyond the ferment over the religious settlement, changed economic conditions in the 1660s and 1670s contributed another dimension to the controversy over immigration. The advocates of a naturalization scheme in Parliament stressed the need for an influx of foreign settlers to counteract the severe trade depression that had seized England. The crisis began in 1664 and lasted until late in 1667, when a tentative recovery dawned. The series of discouraging and costly defeats in the Second Dutch War crippled English trade and nourished the sentiments of commercial rivalry with Holland. The plague ravaged the kingdom in 1665, and in the following year the Fire of London left much of the capital in smoldering ruins. In 1663 customs revenues were the largest source of the Crown's income, yet the losses in the two years from September 1665 to 1667 amounted to almost £320,000.

Crown debts became unmanageable; prices fell sharply; and a financial panic led to a run on the bankers in June 1667, contributing to a scene of general economic chaos.[24]

The land market languished more perhaps than the economy as a whole. Laments resounded at the collapse in the value of land, and Pepys wrote of the dramatic fall in rents and the frequent surrender of tenancies. The anxieties at the decay of rents reached a zenith at the end of the decade, when tracts such as *An Essay Concerning the Decay of Rents* (1670) warned of a general catastrophe, and makeshift remedies were bruited about every coffeehouse and parish vestry. From the mid-1660s until at least 1690 agricultural prices sank and rents fell. From the Restoration until the turn of the century land generally sold at less than twenty-years' purchase, sometimes for as little as fourteen-years', whereas in the eighteenth century the years of purchase were generally in the mid-twenties. The economic ills of those years were far from imaginary.[25]

In the 1670s an economic malaise followed the crisis of the late 1660s, keeping alive fears of depopulation and stimulating proposals for the admission of foreigners in order to promote England's trade. A feeble recovery ended in 1672 with the "Stop of the Exchequer," when payments on the government debt were suspended, and the declaration of the Third Dutch War. The state of public finance was ruinous, and the "Stop" precipitated a financial crisis that left five of the largest bankers ruined. After the conclusion of peace in 1674, the nation enjoyed a modest improvement in its trade by exploiting its neutrality while France and Holland, its greatest commercial rivals, battled on. Yet foreign trade, as reflected in the gross annual value of the customs, expanded very little in the 1670s, and a full economic and financial recovery awaited the end of the decade. The complaints in the economic literature of the decay of trade and the pervasive tone of deep pessimism continued through the 1670s, Thomas Overbury bemoaning a "sinking if not ruined and undone nation." Sir Richard Haines grieved that "a general poverty seems to have invaded the whole nation, leases being continually thrown up in the country, and tradesmen daily breaking in the City."[26] The discontent expressed in the 1660s at the stagnation of the land market extended in the 1670s to every branch of trade.

With this acute economic slump there appeared a problem of a much more chronic nature. The Great Plague crystalized fears, until then mostly latent, that England's population was stagnant or declining. Perhaps 100,000 victims fell in greater London alone to this last great outbreak of bubonic plague, but the psychological effect of the plague visitation loomed larger than the number of the dead may suggest. The Great Plague represented a wrenching one-act tragedy that dramatized for its horrified audience the vulnerability of England's population and warned of a feebleness of population growth that would, as events proved, persist until the middle of the eighteenth century. According to the estimates of E. A. Wrigley and R. S.

Schofield, in the century from 1661 to 1761 England's population increased by only about one million, in contrast to an increase from fewer than three million in 1561 to over five million in 1661. The five-year period from 1656 to 1661 was the first in over a century in which the population actually shrank. The gross reproduction rate, a measure of fertility, fell to very low levels in the late seventeenth century: the rate of 1.8 in the five-year period centering on 1661 was the lowest of the entire period from 1541 to 1871. The decline in population continued until the mid-1680s, after which a very tentative recovery occurred. Not until about 1720, however, did England's total population rise again to the level of five and a quarter million that Wrigley and Schofield have estimated for the year 1656.[27]

Without the benefit of such tools of modern historical demography as we have, those who lived through the plague were convinced that England faced a severe population problem. The plague of 1665, unlike earlier outbreaks, received thorough coverage in the growing English press, and weekly totals of burials in London were published for all to read. Lurid accounts of the horrors of the plague multiplied, and the publication of its effects and the large number of its victims amplified the impact of the visitation on the mentality of the age. Occasional cases of plague continued to be reported in the bills of mortality until 1679, and the threat and fear of plague persisted, as the panic of the 1720s bears witness. Moreover, the plague killed mostly the poor, whose labor counted most in the English economy and in the minds of those who interested themselves in economic affairs. Fears of depopulation continued to be expressed until nearly the end of our period, though their passion and frequency diminished. Those fears, heightened by the intense international rivalry of the age, harmonize with the conclusions of modern scholars that population growth remained torpid until after the middle of the eighteenth century.[28] The plague of 1665 acted as a crucial catalyst of anxieties that nourished the populationist calls for a liberal immigration policy.

The dislocations caused by the plague, fire, and trade crisis of the 1660s contributed to the searching thought about the economic basis of English society that characterized the Restoration. Barry Supple has identified economic crisis as one of the chief stimulants to commercial change and to developments in economic thought.[29] Whether economic crises such as that in the 1660s molded economic ideas, and economic discourse faithfully reflected the peculiar circumstances in which it developed, may well be doubted; but there is little doubt that such periods of hardship excited curiosity about the economic order and invited the exploration of new fields of inquiry. Economic crisis tended to foster the development of new explanations of how the economy worked, or failed to work. If the volume of economic publications provides any measure of the vitality of thought on trade matters, then the period from the mid-1660s to about 1680 represents the most dynamic period in this century of commercialization and evolving economic speculation. Joyce Appleby has argued that the seventeenth century witnessed the development of an economic ideology that sought to explain the commercial changes in England's economy and society. New values and a new vision of the ties that bind society together emerged as the participants in public discourse articulated an essentially economic ethic that looked to the market as an ordering principle for English society. The changes in mental outlook that formed the necessary prelude to the transformation of England into a fully commercial and then industrial nation, Appleby argues, arose not from the emergence of a new ruling class—for England's old elite proved remarkably tenacious and resilient—but from the working out in economic discourse of a secular commercial ideology.[30]

Appleby presents a cogent argument for the emergence of an economic ideology in England as a response to the forces of commercial growth. A dynamic commercial system came to be seen as providing a principle of social order that could supersede the traditional norms of a hierarchical, paternalistic, and essentially static community. The evidence of the economic discourse suggests, however, that the appearance of a vision of England as a commercial society rather than as a traditional, tightly-knit community, should be dated only to the period after the Restoration. Only then did England become identified preeminently as a trading nation; only then were traditional state policies of a paternalistic stamp largely abandoned; only then did the volume and sophistication of economic discourse respond to the forces of commercialization at work in English society. Perhaps ironically, the trade crisis of the 1660s nurtured the development of a commercial economic ideology; and the immigration controversy exemplifies the changes in the understanding of the economic order that Appleby identifies, and that became conspicuous after the Restoration.

The economic crisis and the devastations of the plague galvanized opinion that England must increase its population. Josiah Child, the most respected economic expert of the day and a substantial merchant, proclaimed more clearly and cogently than anyone to that time that a large population was the foundation of national wealth.[31] "It is multitudes of people," Child wrote, "which principally enrich any country," for "whatever tends to the populating of a kingdom, tends to the improvement of it." He placed the greatest priority for enlarging trade and raising the value of land on the increase in the number of "hands."[32] In his faith in the productive power of population, and in his insistence that the people must be considered in gross and not in particular, Child reflected the economic mentality that saw people as units within a market system rather than as integral members of a cohesive social fabric. The aggregative view of population reflected the growth of a vision that saw as essentially economic in character problems that previously had been treated as social. Such a conception of population naturally suggested the possibility of expanding the number of people by encouraging immigration, and Child was to distinguish himself as a prominent advocate of a general naturalization of foreigners.

Most economic writers shared Child's belief that an expansion of population would revive England's beleaguered economy. As the anonymous author of *The Grand Concern of England* (1673) proclaimed, there was "nothing so much wanting in England as people."[33] The relation between wealth and population was reciprocal: "the more populous, the more trade; the more trade, the more populous," declared Carew Reynell in *The True English Interest* (1674)—the two qualities mutually reinforced one another.[34] Those lamenting depopulation identified various reasons for England's lack of people. The Tory MP Sir William Coventry blamed the civil war, the resettlement of Ireland, and the peopling of the plantations for draining England of population.[35] Reynell, a Hampshire gentleman eager to promote England's manufactures, echoed Coventry's complaints, but stressed the depredations of plague that robbed England of people.[36] Other observers named the wars on the continent, religious intolerance, the laws against debtors, and poverty itself as conspiring to draw people out of the country.[37] An anonymous pamphlet of 1677, *An Humble Address with Some Proposals for the Future Preventing of the Decrease of the Inhabitants of this Realm*, complained that farmers had fled England, and great expanses of unoccupied land had opened up like mute wounds in the nation's flesh. Artisans and seamen had departed as well, carrying their skills with them. Another tract, *The Royal Fishing Revived* (1670), blamed the decline of the fishery on the fewness of laborers generally and mariners and fishermen in particular.[38] Everywhere complaints resounded of the fewness of people.

Many commentators, such as the Tory political publicist Roger Coke, grew passionate in their denunciations of emigration to the plantations as drawing off able-bodied men who might otherwise have contributed to the home economy.[39] While the authorities now discarded the regulation of emigration on religious grounds, a policy desultorily pursued in the reign of Charles I, economic concerns came to the fore. Emigration to the plantations and to Ireland had "wasted" hundreds of thousands, Reynell complained in 1674, and drained England of people. They were "decoyed away to New England and Virginia . . . unprofitable countries [that] help us not, but hinder us, are chargeable, and waste our people." The plantations themselves grew because of their abundant variety of employments for all people, and emigration could be stopped "by raising of employments, professions, and trade" in England.[40] In fact, the volume of emigration had declined, and the fervor of the economic writers was largely misplaced, but those who advocated immigration schemes often envisaged such measures as compensating for a steady drain of people leaving England for the colonies.

Lord Ashley, later Shaftesbury, in a 1669 Memorial to the King praised populousness and condemned emigration as preventing it; the solution to the loss from emigration, he suggested, lay in admitting foreigners to England and ensuring religious toleration. Such arguments were then becoming almost commonplace. Yet Ashley, as one of the proprietors of the Carolinas, had reason to wish for foreign immigration not to England but to the plantations and to connive at the departure of the English for America. The colonies manifestly had a greater relative need of people than the mother country. As the Committee of the Council of Plantations stated in 1662, it was "universally agreed that people are the foundation and improvement of all plantations" as much as of the home country.[41] But the relative benefit of settlement in America or in England remained far less clear than the absolute need.

A subtle competition for immigrant settlers between the home country and the colonies took place during the Restoration period—certainly the plantations offered more liberal legal privileges to newcomers.[42] Yet until the eighteenth century both English lawmakers and economic writers generally viewed the colonies as an economic burden and as a vortex of people. They looked askance at the shunting of settlers to transatlantic destinations. Only in the more imperialistic environment that developed after 1689 did the tremendous potential of the colonies as a market for English manufactures begin to be recognized, and only then did the economic discourse acknowledge the potential gains from colonial immigration.[43] Josiah Child, writing in the 1670s, argued forcefully that the plantations had not reduced England's population—but he had to concede that his view was that of the minority. The kind of people who emigrated, he argued, would not contribute to the wealth of England if they stayed at home. Child maintained that Spain, the archetype of a languishing economy and state, had been depopulated by religious persecution, not by emigration to its colonies.[44] But the orthodox view after the Restoration held that the colonies depopulated England with no offsetting economic gain, and emigration struck most observers as a dead loss.

The fears of depopulation that burgeoned in the late 1660s, whether they blamed emigration or other causes for the lack of people, added urgency to the study of demography that had begun a few years earlier. Most of William Petty's important works on economic and demographic questions date from the 1670s and early 1680s,[45] but it would be misleading to suggest that Petty's thought simply responded to the current of economic and political events. On the contrary, Petty's writings often seem to have little to do with the general patterns of thought in his day. At times a brilliant shaft of penetrating light seems to sear through the vagueness of volumes of other works on trade and illuminate in a few sentences a field of inquiry that had been cloaked in obscurity. But his writings were essentially sui generis and they therefore resist historical treatment. That is not to say that Petty could not be topical and even brutally pragmatic as well as intellectually incisive. He wrote his *Political Arithmetic* (1690), for example, to refute in quantitative terms the unending stream of complaints at the decay of English trade.

Although Petty epitomized those whom Matthew Hale scoffed at as "speculative and notional men," he was not immune from partisanship, and clearly knew where his interests lay.[46] Whatever the limitations of his vision, however, Petty had powers of insight denied to most of the participants in the Restoration economic discourse, and he concentrated those powers on matters of population.

Nothing speaks more eloquently of Petty's preoccupation with demographic issues than the titles of his essays: "About the Increase of Mankind," "On Doubling the People," "Cogitata de Connubiis," "Concerning Marriages," "Of Marriages," "California Marriages with the Reasons thereof." Such titles attest as well to Petty's conviction that procreation offered the best means of increasing population. He proposed rewards for early marriage and fecundity, fines for celibacy or infertility, and praised what he called "married teeming women" and "married teemers." In these studies Petty directed his ambitions towards a doubling of England's population, which he thought could be achieved "by soft and practicable means" in the space of twenty-five years.[47] For even the analysis of Petty—whom scholars remember as a brilliant theoretician—like those of virtually all his contemporaries, aimed towards specific policy objectives. In the 1660s and 1670s that meant repopulation, and few were more optimistic than he about how quickly the end could be achieved.

Petty was particularly interested in the population of London. He calculated from the bills of mortality that the number of inhabitants in the capital had doubled in forty years while the population of the nation in the same period had stagnated. Not only did this conclusion hold the promise of a potential growth in national population, but Petty counted the expansion of the capital itself as no disadvantage. The nation would gain by having people cramped closely together, he argued, since manufactures would be improved by the narrower division of labor that such density promoted. Some observers, of course, such as the author of *The Trade of England Revived* (1681) deplored the growth of London, and complained that depopulation and the "statute against naturalization" were to blame for the lack of people beyond fifty or sixty miles from London. An abundance of wasteland lay at hand in the countryside, the pamphleteer declared, on which multitudes of immigrants could be employed.[48] But the complaints of London's being a head too large for the body had become stereotyped by this time, and the question of the relative populations of town and country formed no more than occasional byplay to the debate over national population.[49] Again, the aggregative conception of the Restoration economic discourse tended to redirect the channels of debate. That is not to say that contemporaries ignored the demographic impact of urban growth. Most observers recognized that a great influx of migrants from the countryside, perhaps 8,000 per year by modern estimates, was necessary to compensate for the natural decrease of the capital's population.[50] Nevertheless, the creators of economic discourse generally treated England's demographic situation as the product of an integrated system, and left denunciations of the city to moralists. They viewed urban growth as part of the process of commercialization that would expand population, not as corruption in the body of the polity. In this respect as in others, the economic discourse of the Restoration betrayed a remarkable detachment from traditional moral criteria.

Petty praised the demographic vitality of London; but other observers, so far from expressing worry at the size of the capital, bemoaned the capital's lack of inhabitants. John Houghton in 1681 recalled that after the plague and fire, London had so few people that grass grew between the Exchange and Drapers' Hall. A tract of 1672 complained that whole streets of new-built houses within the City stood uninhabited, its author arguing that restrictions on acquiring the freedom of the City and trading there kept people out. A relaxation would refill the City, and the resulting vast expansion in population would reinvigorate trade. Foreigners would settle in London if the City's rulers did not discourage them by raising protectionist barriers to preserve their own profit.[51] Thus encouraging immigration figured as a panacea for both urban and rural woes, economic and demographic.

While Petty explored the population growth of the capital, others worried at the depopulation of the countryside, especially in view of the severe slump in the land market from the mid-1660s. Sir William Coventry in *An Essay Concerning the Decay of Rents* (c. 1670) blamed the lack of people on the land as one of the primary reasons for depressed rents and land values, and the consequent diminution of domestic market and the general contraction in trade. Depopulation resulted in a lack of demand for goods and caused what Coventry called the "evil of abundance." The solutions were either to naturalize foreigners, or to encourage marriage and banish idleness through the creation of workhouses. Coventry's fear of underconsumption perhaps reflected his preoccupation with the plight of landholders who faced a lean market for agricultural products. In any case, the encouragement of immigration promised to bring in many potential new tenants and stimulate demand for the commodities that threatened, he wrote, to choke the market.[52] In the economically difficult 1660s and 1670s, then, immigration offered hope not only to those interested in commercial growth but to the landed interests that saw their chief asset drastically reduced in value. Landed and mercantile interests, at odds over many questions in this period, could agree on the policy of increasing population. In any event, however, few of the immigrants that came to England after the Restoration actually settled on the land, and the rural laborers who did come found a niche for themselves only with difficulty. Whatever benefit foreign settlers brought to the land can have been only indirect, by augmenting the number of consumers in the way that Coventry envisioned.

The trade depression of the late 1660s elicited not only a flush of speculation in the economic discourse but a mobilization of the government in an attempt to put trade back on a firm footing. As in the economic literature, the necessity of expanding population and the potential gains from a measure to encourage immigration figured prominently in the deliberations of parliamentarians and civil servants. The crisis provoked the kind of proliferation of government bodies typical of such junctures: at the end of 1667 the House of Commons appointed a large Select Committee on the State of Trade; in the following year the king established a Council of Trade whose members included eminent merchants and important figures in politics; and the House of Lords, true to the preoccupation of its members with landed wealth, appointed in 1669 a Committee "to consider of the causes and grounds of the fall of rents and decay of trade."[53] The Lords Committee first met on 28 October 1669, when its members agreed on several causes of the slump in trade, including the nation's lack of people. Yet the members of the Committee remained uncertain of their own expertise, and resolved that five members of the king's Council of Trade, including Josiah Child, should attend to testify before it. The deliberations of the Committee drew together into one thread the ideas of acknowledged experts on trade, the insights of the developing economic discourse, and the concerted efforts of practicing merchants and lawmakers to formulate and implement a government economic policy.[54]

The presentations to the Committee offered great scope for the articulation of novel economic ideas in a very public forum. No one was better suited to exploit such an opportunity than Josiah Child. Child, never parsimonious with words, spoke more extensively before the Committee than the other witnesses, and on several occasions. He began with the startling avowal that in gross the trade of England had not decayed but had increased. A national economic policy could nevertheless foster prosperity, and to succeed such a policy required a close study and strict emulation of the Dutch. Liberal standards for admission to the freedom of their cities, combined with low interest rates, made the trade of Holland thrive. More important was their religious liberty, Child urged, for Holland now surpassed England as the asylum of refugees. In addition, the apprenticeship laws and the bylaws of artisanal companies hindered English trade, and contributed to the want of hands that represented a principal cause of feeble trade. Child mentioned the fire, the plague, and the pressures on land. He dilated upon his pet panacea of a low rate of interest, and parried the sardonic remark of one member of the Committee that "if a low interest would do all this, it were easy to be rich." He concluded his remarks before the Committee, so similar to his tracts, by affirming that "whatever tends to the increase of hands and stocks doth increase the trade of a nation."[55]

The French Protestant merchant Thomas Papillon told the Committee that the plague had consumed several hundred thousand souls and deprived the nation of hands to improve manufactures, and mouths to consume provisions. A naturalization of foreigners would be advantageous so long as they were foreigners that would incorporate with the natives and become English, otherwise they would accumulate English riches and carry them away to other countries. Protestant immigrants were desirable, but the Jews, Papillon warned, would never be assimilated. Sir Thomas Culpeper also spoke before the Committee, arguing that easier money would increase the number of people, especially artisans, by affording them more subsistence, and that immigrants would be attracted by the additional employment available in England.[56]

The Committee showed especial interest in the policy of encouraging immigration, and on 13 November its members had a "long and serious debate" over the admission of foreigners. They resolved that the want of people in England was one of the causes of the decay of rents, and that a bill of naturalization would be an important remedy. The Committee stipulated that those who would settle on the land as tenants and revive flagging rents in particular ought to be encouraged, rather than the artisans who were traditionally sought. The Committee's report to the Lords omitted the language regarding the kind of immigrant desired, but added a vaguely-worded recommendation that "some ease and relaxation in ecclesiastical matters" should be introduced. Parliament was prorogued on 11 December, a few days after the Committee's report, and although the Committee was reappointed in the next session, nothing further came of its naturalization proposal until a year later, when the bill of 1670 passed the Lords and then died a lingering procedural death.[57] The meetings of the Committee succeeded in publicizing the desirability of an immigration policy to increase population, but the Committee proved no more effectual than Parliament itself in putting such a measure into effect.

As the deliberations of the Lords Committee bear witness, by 1670 a consensus had crystallized amongst economic experts that population must be expanded in order to achieve prosperity, and that the admission of foreign settlers should be the principal means to achieve that end. Some observers suggested other means to increase population. Carew Reynell, for example, offered several positive proposals for correcting the population problem in addition to immigration: encouraging marriage and a settled life as well as providing incentives for having many children could stimulate natural increase; the imposition of a tax on those not married by the age of twenty-five would penalize such "vicious persons"; and the practice in many country parishes of hindering the poor from marrying must be stopped. On the whole, however, population schemes focused on encouraging immigration. Roger Coke, for example, writing in the early 1670s, thought that a scheme for the admission of foreigners should crown a general program for stimulating English trade, which he believed had declined steeply.[58] A general naturalization would infuse English trade with new vitality by improving manufactures, by increasing the number of purchasers, and by raising the value of lands on account of the general expansion of trade.[59] For the following several decades the naturalization of foreigners became practically a point of dogma in the creed of the economic writers.

Many of the calls for immigration betrayed the undiscriminating zeal of new converts to this supposed key to prosperity and power. Reynell, for example, gushed that foreign merchants would "bring over millions of money," and tradesmen would cross the Channel like a flotilla, bringing with them "all the arts, manufactures, and ingenuity of Europe." Soberer observers recognized, however, that facile calls for the admission of foreign settlers must contain some measure of selectivity to be successful, and that a bare offer of naturalization might not be enough to stimulate large-scale immigration. The old notion that immigrants should be sought to introduce new manufacturing skills had not disappeared in the flush of enthusiasm for population. Coke argued that immigrants could instruct the native English in skills imperfectly known in England, as had earlier groups in the reigns of Edward III and Elizabeth, if the exclusive privileges of the corporations were curtailed. Without such a freeing up of corporate and guild restrictions, he warned, artisans would find it difficult or impossible to practice a trade.[60]

Josiah Child elaborated on Coke's point, insisting that foreign settlers had to be free to earn a livelihood in order for a naturalization scheme to work. Like Coke, Child counted it a necessity to allow for the admission of foreigners to the freedom of the chartered cities, and to lessen the exclusive privileges of the urban craft guilds, whose jurisdiction he thought was far too extensive. The provision of the Statute of Artificers that required a seven-years' apprenticeship to practice a trade, he wrote, presented a further impediment, and jealous English tradesmen exploited the statute to harass foreigners even in the suburbs. Child very rightly stressed the need to liberalize these restrictions as a necessary complement to a naturalization, a qualification that too seldom found expression in the economic discourse. Yet foreign settlers themselves demonstrated a keener preoccupation with corporate restrictions than with the disabilities of alien status under English nationality law. When in 1669 the Committee of Trade requested a statement from the French and Dutch Churches of London of what privileges foreign artisans sought, the reply petitioned for freedom to practice trades, liberty of conscience, and an end to the disturbances, arrests, and molestations carried on by companies of English tradesmen. No mention was made of naturalization, a silence that confirms the lesson of the naturalization rolls: few immigrants came for the sake of legal privileges alone. The problem was an intractable one. Foreign artisans would have been discouraged from settling in England if they had been required to bind themselves as apprentices to English tradesmen, perhaps less skilled than they were. To handicap them in that way would have been economic waste, and the frustration of one of the motives for their naturalization. Yet English artisans complained with considerable justice that to exempt aliens from the apprenticeship laws would give them a privileged status. In any event, English tradesmen and the craft guilds employed the apprenticeship laws as the main instrument of their harassment of immigrants, and Child's warnings went unheeded.[61]

A dangerous optimism lurked also in the tacit assumption behind the pleas for naturalization that foreign settlers would quickly and painlessly be assimilated into English society. Reynell buoyantly declared that immigrants would marry English women, and would "in half an age" be perfectly English—even the English who had abandoned their homeland might be drawn back by an active policy of encouraging immigration. Detractors grumbled that the admission of foreigners would "breed a mixed nation," he conceded, but the numbers of immigrants would not be great enough to rival the natives, since they would come in by degrees—and several nations of people could live peaceably and prosperously under one government, as in Holland. The Dutch and French already in England had been assimilated quickly. "Whatever they are before," he declared, "when once they come here . . . they are soon all one with us."[62] Reynell believed, as all proponents of naturalization sought to argue, that assimilation and acculturation would be swift and frictionless. That belief represented a fatal blemish in the reasoning of the advocates of naturalization, for it ignored both the cultural axis of immigration and the resolution of native English laborers and tradesmen to defend themselves against what they saw as the encroachments of aliens. The reception that immigrant settlers met with will be addressed presently; but it must be stressed here that in their eagerness to construct an essentially economic vision of English society and policy, most of the participants in the discourse blinded themselves to the very real cultural dimensions of their schemes.

The silence of the advocates of naturalization on the question of what sort of immigrants should be sought could be seen as a symptom of sloppy thinking, a lax indifference, or an attempt to gloss over the risks of the policy. In another light, however, naturalization could be presented as an inherently selective policy of repopulation, as the author of *The Grand Concern of England* (1673) made plain. The men lost in recent years, he noted, whether victims of plague or casualties of war or emigration, were "in the prime of their years, in perfect strength." It had been better, the tract's author argued, if 100,000 children had been lost than that the same number of adult men had perished, for in three years men in their prime could have had as many children. Instead the loss had deprived England of skilled adult laborers. A general naturalization would fill the country with adult men and women ready to contribute their productive powers to England's economy and take the places of those that had been lost. In this lay the great advantage of immigration over what *The Grand Concern* confessed would be preferable, the expansion of the native population by natural generation.[63] The only solution in the circumstances, the tract concluded with an attitude of resignation, was to get "a supply of people from some place or other."[64]. The policy of admitting foreigners, however *faute de mieux*, had the advantage of introducing at once a body of adults ready to enter in one step the ranks of consumers and producers of the nation's wealth. The author of *The Grand Concern* here made explicit a constant undercurrent in the discourse. The advocates of immigration were not xenophiles. They simply wanted more people—and the admission of foreigners seemed the fastest way to get them. The author of *The Grand Concern* distinguished himself only by acknowledging candidly that encouraging immigration was a second-best measure calculated to answer an immediate exigency.

In addition to making their own contribution to the English economy, however, adult immigrant laborers and tradesmen would by their competition force native workers to be more industrious as well. It has been noted that the early economic writers believed that labor drove the engine of economic growth—but their admiration attached to labor in the abstract, not laborers as a class. The counterpoint to the songs of praise of labor as a productive principle was the cadence of complaints about the indolence of laborers. The workman's propensity to cast down his tools when he had earned enough to buy himself a few days' bread and beer led Petty, Thomas Manley, and other economic writers to advocate a subsistence wage as the necessary stimulant to industry in what Petty called the "vile and brutish part of mankind."[65] The laborer, Petty wrote, should be allowed "just wherewithal to live; for if you allow double, then he works but half so much as he could have done." Petty exemplified to an exceptional degree the angry indignation felt at such idleness. He believed that the productive powers of English laborers had to be forcibly increased, and he condemned "fallacious tenderness" to the poor. Next in importance to doubling the population, he vowed, was making the present population do double the work. The English worker, neither born to industry, nor having achieved industry, must have industry thrust upon him. Petty insisted that the idle should be put to work even if only in acts of futility, such as bringing the monoliths of Stonehenge to Tower Hill: the habit of hard work must suffer no dilution. At times Petty's obsession with laziness seemed to border on paranoia, as when he complained agitatedly of "strange wrongs from paupers set up on purpose to plague me," and when he grumbled that the Irish lived in too much ease since the introduction of the potato.[66]

Most of the early economic thinkers believed that low wages were necessary to force laborers to work, and that despair was a stronger stimulus than hope. To many, unemployment was the result of too-high wages, and of course, moral weakness. The notorious remark of Arthur Young that "every one but an idiot knows that the lower classes must be kept poor or they will never be industrious" expressed sentiments far more typical of the late seventeenth than of the late eighteenth century.[67] A large and growing population, augmented by immigrants, would compel workers to be industrious. Roger Coke, on most issues an antagonist of William Petty,[68] concurred that a denser population would reduce wages and encourage industry.[69] Josiah Child agreed that an accession of foreigners would enforce industrious habits upon the natives. In contrast to most of the promoters of naturalization before the 1690s, Child took care to refer to the increase of England's "hands" rather than to the increase of its "people," or simply to "numbers." To increase the hands busy in production, rather than simply the number of bodies in England, was his object.[70] The participants in the early economic discourse saw the enforcing of industry as one of the cornerstones of prosperity, and they believed that the admission of foreign settlers could materially advance that purpose.

The voluntary unemployment or underemployment that so incensed economic writers has been admirably described by D. C. Coleman, as has the debate surrounding unemployment in the economic literature by E. S. Furniss.[71] As they have demonstrated, periods of idleness, seasonality of employment, holidays, and trade fluctuations were all integral features of the preindustrial economy. No sharp division existed for most artisans and laborers between work and leisure, either spatially or temporally.[72] The admission of industrious foreigners would not change these basic structural features of the English economy. But Petty and most of his contemporaries took a moral view of unemployment as voluntary, the result of a "debauched indolence." It remains a largely unexplored question to what extent the tone of moral indignation in the economic discourse was colored by the close connections between the rising commercial ideology and Nonconformist cultural traditions of a work ethic.[73] In any case, in spite of structural unemployment, resentment was directed towards the leisure preference of laborers, the backward-bending supply curve of labor in the terminology of the economists. In the age of the Restoration, observers still took an essentially moral stance towards the question of labor, industriousness, and unemployment. Many still do. But even in the day of Charles II doubts could be expressed about what "voluntary unemployment" actually meant. As Sir Matthew Hale remarked in a moment of humanistic good sense that does him much credit, "it is a difficult thing to determine who shall be said an idle person."[74]

Those who viewed immigration as a turn of the screw to enforce industriousness focused on the supply side of the economic equation. Other observers, more progressive in their perspective, lauded naturalization schemes as a way to expand aggregate demand. The admission of foreign settlers, argued the author of *The Grand Concern of England*, would increase the consumption of the provisions and manufactures of the kingdom, employ the poor, and improve the rents and value of land by supplying more tenants. Of these benefits, however, the greatest would be the immigrants' expansion of demand, for England needed more consumers more urgently than it needed more producers. Unless foreigners came in, he warned, echoing the earlier words of Sir William Coventry, there would not be people enough to consume English commodities, which would accumulate and clog the circulation of the nation's trade.[75] The stress on immigrants as providing a fulcrum for demand, however, remained muted until the early eighteenth century.

The arrival of frugal and industrious foreigners was said to be a way to prod the natives to work harder. Immigrants would set a good example, and their ability to subsist on a lower wage would compel English laborers to apply themselves to their work. In addition, they would increase total demand and stimulate the expansion of manufacturing and commerce. But did England possess the power to attract desirable immigrants? What could best attract them? These questions usually received short shrift in the economic discourse, since the efficacy of an offer of easy naturalization was seldom called into question. Perhaps predictably, William Petty provided the most iconoclastic answers to those questions. Petty distrusted naturalization schemes. He conceded that "selling lands to foreigners for gold and silver would enlarge the stock of the kingdom . . . and increase both money and people, and consequently trade." He agreed that the laws denying foreigners the right to purchase land or to trade without paying exceptional duties were inimical to trade. He championed religious toleration as promoting trade and expanding population. He even proposed in a paper to James II an alliance with France providing that 100,000 French Protestants be settled half in England and half in Ireland, the latter presumably destined for Petty's estates in Kerry.[76] But he refused to endorse a general naturalization act. The general naturalization act in Ireland, he noted nearly twenty years after its passage, had attracted few foreign settlers and had certainly failed to increase the number of people. Could an offer of naturalization really encourage immigration? In *Political Arithmetic* Petty emphatically answered the question in the negative. He praised the United Provinces for hiring foreigners as common soldiers; their children were natural-born Dutch, and the population of the country multiplied indefinitely. Holland's policy had achieved

> what others have in vain attempted by laws for naturalizing of strangers, as if men could be charmed to transplant themselves from their own native, in to a foreign country merely by words, and for the bare leave of being called by a new name.[77]

The schemes for a general naturalization upon which nearly all economic writers had staked their dreams of repopulation would achieve nothing. The populous and pluralistic England of Child's and Coke's dreams would vanish even before the sleepers awoke; in fact, declared Petty, it could never have existed. By calling into question the unspoken assumption of almost every proposal for the admission of foreigners, Petty challenged the very foundation of the populationist movement. Remarkably, in view of subsequent events, Petty's was a lone voice in dismissing naturalization schemes, not, as their detractors argued, because they would bring about disaster, but because they would bring about nothing at all. His criticisms of naturalization schemes went unrebutted and apparently unheeded even well into the next century.[78]

Despite Petty's arguments to the contrary, in one quarter naturalization seemed to have proved a resounding success. Holland offered writers on trade the best example of the fruits of religious freedom and an open immigration policy. No country in that age greeted immigrants of all religions with more charity or more legal privileges than did the United Provinces of the Netherlands. Some Englishmen, particularly those with High Church predilections, dismissed Holland as a hotbed of religious extremists and radical republicans; even Andrew Marvell, an ardent defender of the principle of religious toleration, could refer to the United Provinces as the "staple of sects and the mint of schism."[79] Marvell's commercial imagery is telling. Both its admirers and its detractors saw Dutch society as fundamentally dynamic and commercial, a place where most traditional social bonds had been broken down by the solvent of trade. For English economic writers who sought after the Restoration to construct an intellectual framework for a society organized essentially by market relations rather than personal and paternalistic ties, the Netherlands presented not only a national challenge but a model for emulation.

English observers enviously marveled at the power of the Dutch to attract desirable settlers. The allure of the United Provinces revealed itself especially in the Dutch cities, which were more cosmopolitan than any in Western Europe, for in the Netherlands as elsewhere migrants gravitated toward urban areas. The component state and town governments of the decentralized federal system of the United Provinces exercised an independence that made the imposition of autocratic precepts in religion most unlikely, and the resulting security proved magnetic in attracting immigrants. Indeed, the mosaic of authorities in Holland competed amongst one another in the privileges they offered in order to attract foreigners of the better sort.[80] Amsterdam took the lead in seeking to win over desirable settlers, employing offers of legal privileges, tax exemptions, and publicly-provided assistance to encourage immigration. The drive to encourage settlements amounted to a Dutch publicity campaign that involved the placing of newspaper advertisements, the use of agents to spread the word, and the publication of a multiplicity of brochures, leaflets, and pamphlets puffing the unique charms of Holland.[81] The inducements were not lost on potential immigrants. The Huguenot minister Jean Tirel, for example, declared plainly in his pastoral letters in the 1680s that the Dutch Republic offered more to French Protestant refugees than England.[82]

English economic writers wished to win the advantage from the Dutch. The success of Holland in gaining settlers only confirmed English observers in their conviction that a positive government policy could indeed increase immigration and reverse the trend of depopulation. Some thought as well that the liberal Dutch policies towards foreigners accelerated their assimilation once in Holland—and there may have been some truth in this observation. But the success of the Dutch model lay not so much in any eagerness to absorb and acculturate newcomers as in the acceptance of the essentially pluralistic character of a commercial society. The Restoration economic writers shared a vision of an England that possessed a similarly commercial social order. They proclaimed that the joint policies of toleration and naturalization that had made Holland the preferred asylum of the most economically desirable immigrants of Europe would prove a comparable boon to the economy of England.[83] In their view the contrast of the densely-peopled cities and fields of Holland with the depopulation of Spain illustrated the tangible results of the seemingly antithetical government policies of those two countries. Religious freedom and the encouragement of immigration had made the Netherlands wealthy and strong, while intolerance, colonial emigration, and aversion to manufacture and trade conspired with a more general entrepreneurial lethargy to draw Spain into an eddy from which it could not escape. The two nations stood in English economic discourse as totems of good and evil trade policy. Joyce Appleby has remarked that Dutch commercial success figured more prominently in the English imagination than any other economic fact of the seventeenth century.[84] In no sphere can that influence be seen more clearly than in thought about population.

Perhaps the greatest English expert on the Netherlands was Sir William Temple, architect of the Triple Alliance, friend of John De Witt and later of the Prince of Orange, and often the official representative of England in Holland.[85] In his acclaimed *Observations upon the United Provinces of the Netherlands* (1673), Temple praised the Dutch policy of liberty of conscience that offered refuge to oppressed foreigners and multiplied people and trade. Temple named safety from invasion, a constitution that secured property, and opportunities for safe investment (for example, in the Bank of Amsterdam) as other attractions of Holland. Most important, however, was the general "liberty and ease," not only in religion but in all points that served to secure "the commodiousness and quiet of life."[86] In the view of Temple the liberty of Holland's government represented the most important of the country's assets in attracting immigrants. Political liberty, or as he wrote, "safety and ease under the government," created the circumstances in which population would multiply indefinitely.[87] The specter of absolutism that hung over England, Temple implied, acted as a brake upon both population growth and economic expansion.

Temple stressed a theme that enjoyed a prominent place in economic discourse by the 1670s: that Holland throve because of the density rather than merely the size of its population. Most of the English writers on trade, indeed, most mercantilist thinkers, believed that nations should be as densely peopled as some of the more exuberant baroque paintings of the day. A *horror vacui* in terms of national populations haunted the seventeenth-century conscience. Where population was dense, Temple wrote, people "naturally break out into trade." He contrasted Holland's dense ranks of people with the sparseness of Ireland's population, and concluded that

> the true original and ground of trade [is] great multitudes of people crowded into small compass of land, whereby all things necessary to life become dear, and all men who have possessions are induced to parsimony; but those who have none, are forced to industry and labor.[88]

Thomas Sheridan expressed the same views: "where many are cooped into a narrow spot of ground, they are under a necessity of labouring." Slingsby Bethel also remarked upon the density of the Dutch population, where, he claimed, six persons inhabited one acre of land, in contrast with England's one to each ten acres. One of the chief themes of Petty's *Political Arithmetic* was that a small country could be as powerful as a large one. A dense population meant not only numbers of people, but the assurance that they would be industrious. "Better that a people should want country than a country should want people," wrote Charles Davenant in 1699, for few inhabitants meant nothing but sloth and poverty. When large numbers were "confined to a narrow compass of ground, necessity puts them upon invention, frugality, and industry." Roger Coke declared with characteristic bluntness that "wherever people are thin or few, they are poor, lazy, rude and of little use to the public."[89] Density would ensure the industriousness that nearly all agreed was necessary for national economic expansion, and indeed for national survival—it represented another goad to force laborers to work.[90]

Perhaps the chief lesson to be drawn from the Dutch experience was the relation between naturalization schemes and the policy of religious toleration. *The Grand Concern of England* (1673), perhaps the best-written and clearest-reasoned economic work of the Restoration period, insisted on the intimate connection between religious toleration and the encouragement of immigration, treating the two policies as virtually inseparable. Liberty of conscience for not only foreign settlers but native Englishmen must accompany an act for a general naturalization of all foreign Protestants.[91] Owing to the acute lack of people in England, naturalization was "absolutely necessary," the tract asserted. Those who would most benefit England, however, would never come to be accounted aliens, nor would most have the fifty or sixty pounds to spare to procure private acts of naturalization from Parliament. Conscience and interest alike demanded the passage of an act of general naturalization; but legal privileges would not be enough. Without religious toleration, the door remained closed to immigrants: population would dwindle and trade would languish. Josiah Child expressed the same sentiments, calling for religious toleration as necessary to encourage immigration and to keep Englishmen at home. At present England offered a "bare connivance" at Dissenters that stifled trade. A full legal toleration, he urged, would allay fears and remove "the sword that hangs over their heads."[92]

Child naturally praised the Dutch policy of toleration as a model for England. Yet Dutch religious freedom seemed to many observers to invite social disorder and even disintegration. The author of *The Brief Observations Examined* (1668), a rebuttal of Child's first important tract, rejected the proposition that toleration was a means to improve trade. "Union in religion," he wrote, "rather begets correspondency, the mother of commerce, which toleration destroys." The sentiment, though alien to the values implicit in the economic discourse, represented a very considerable body of opinion in Restoration England. Religious unity formed perhaps the most central feature of a traditional vision of the social polity that conceived of order as imposed through a hierarchical and paternalistic community. Each person occupied an identifiable place within a settled social matrix, or formed a link in the Great Chain of Being.[93] Religious pluralism corroded, as commercial change twisted and tangled, that chain. Where would a foreign immigrant fit within such a concatenation of traditional dependency?

It is too easy to forget that more than malicious bigotry actuated those in Restoration England who advocated an imposition of religious uniformity by compulsion. Mark Goldie has identifed three strands in the theory of religious intolerance after the Restoration, which he calls the political, the ecclesiological, and the theological arguments.[94] Religious uniformity, it was said, would ensure against the seditious political tendencies inherent in Dissent, secure order and decency through a publically regulated Established Church, and uphold the truth of theological orthodoxy by the force of persuasion. All three strands of argument conceived of a structured and ordered society, essentially homogeneous and static. Nothing could have been further from the ideas of the economic theorists. In the dynamic society envisaged in their discourse, commercial growth would emerge from a continual circulation of people, commodities, and wealth. An enforced religious unity would irretrievably undermine that process of wealth creation. The ordering principle of society would be created by the forces of the market rather than be imposed by civil society.

The reasoning of orthodox churchmen failed to excite more than dismissive denials from the economic writers, most of whom disdained to even seriously address the cultural and religious concerns of their adversaries. An accession of foreign Protestants, Roger Coke ironically remarked, would increase ecclesiastical revenues based on the returns to land and provide potential new members for the Church of England.[95] The predominant view amongst merchants and writers on trade accounted toleration as an economic necessity, the very foundation stone of prosperity in a commercial society.[96] Their view, often naive in its disregard of historical and cultural circumstances, represented a developing conception of English society that embraced commercial growth and change. How thoroughly the liberal economic ideology, with its free-trade ambitions, carried the day in the late seventeenth century may be questioned. Joyce Appleby perhaps exaggerates its triumph in the Restoration period.[97] Its importance as an alternative ideology to traditional conceptions of English society nevertheless justifies the attention lavished upon it by historians. The pleas for a policy to encourage immigration represented one of the natural fruits of such a new social vision.

In the 1680s the rising crescendo of religious and constitutional controversy that culminated in political revolution tended to distract attention from the economic side of the immigration question. Religious issues had from the beginning dominated the debate over population and naturalization. Now the furor over the politics of religion almost wholly absorbed the immigration issue within broader ideological confrontations. Yet the economic depression that had oppressed England to a greater or lesser degree since the Restoration finally gave way to a period of vigorous trade. The last years of Charles II's reign saw the firmer establishment of the Crown's finances, and a lightening of taxation. Despite a brief economic collapse in 1682, the 1680s witnessed remarkable growth, both in domestic and overseas trade. Customs receipts, the best measure of foreign trade, expanded greatly. Despite the constitutional crisis, the last two years before James II's fall marked the most active years for trade of the late seventeenth century.[98] Indeed, for half a century after the Revolution, Jacobites could linger nostalgically over the legendary prosperity of James II's brief reign. While the protagonists of high politics acted out their parts at Whitehall, Westminster, and the Hague, English merchants pressed on with the business of making money.

In the more prosperous environment of the 1680s, the economic discourse developed at a slower pace, as fewer works on trade appeared, and the energies of publicists shifted to constitutional controversy. Preoccupation with political and religious issues, and contentment with the expansion of trade, seem to have dampened interest in economic matters. In any case, the 1680s in no way augured the explosion of economic literature in the turbulent 1690s.

The persecution of Protestants in France culminating in the revocation of the Edict of Nantes in 1685 naturally influenced thinking about immigration policy in England. The oppressions carried out by the minions of Louis XIV seemed to confirm the staggering costs of religious intolerance, in terms of population and prosperity. The expulsion of the Huguenots heightened the urgency of the debate in England over the admission of foreigners, as the exodus of scores of thousands of Protestants from France offered new hopes for a repopulation with foreign settlers. Many economic writers rejoiced at the coming of the French refugees. Sir Peter Pett exclaimed that French families had filled hundreds of the empty new-built houses of London, and had "given us an occasion of entertaining angels." The author of *England's Wants* (1685) urged an act of Parliament to naturalize the French Protestants, especially artisans and craftsmen who were willing to conform to the Church of England. If encouraged to take English apprentices, he declared, the refugees would instruct the natives in the manufacture of paper, hats, canvas, laid silk, scissors, and goldsmiths' wares, and England would save the vast sums of money sent to France for those goods.[99]

Many of these prophecies were fulfilled. There is no reason to doubt the conventional wisdom that France's loss was England's gain—and the gain of Holland, Brandenburg-Prussia, and other refugee destinations. French artisans introduced new trades and manufactures, and improved many that already existed in England in a rudimentary state.[100] Yet the promise offered by the Huguenot exodus remained largely unrealized—not least because the "angels" who arrived in England proved reluctant to trade their Calvinism for a set of Anglican wings.

In any event, the reception of the Huguenots became hopelessly compromised by the religious and political crisis brought about by James II's policies regarding England's Dissenters: first persecution, then toleration. The pronouncements of parliamentarians and the published sermons of High and Low Churchmen alike used the refugees as counters in their ideological exchanges.[101] James II himself distrusted the Huguenots as antimonarchical, and sought to impose conformity to the Anglican rite upon them.[102] The question of how the French Protestants were to be treated figured prominently in the debate over James's Declaration of Indulgence. By then, the king's about-face had caused him to seek allies in the refugees. Some observers considered it scandalous that a group of the refugees had sent a letter of thanks to the king for the declaration. Others defended the declaration, arguing that it was folly to try to reduce the nation to a strict conformity in religion, a policy that destroyed trade, depopulated the country, and discouraged foreigners from settling.[103] Thus the issues raised in the religious and political controversy of the 1680s came to dominate, for a handful of years, the debate over population and the admission of immigrants. It is not necessary to treat these events here, as Robin Gwynn has provided an admirable account of them.[104] In consequence of the entanglement of the immigration issue with constitutional politics, however, the encouragement and reception of the French Protestants in England betrayed a striking ineptitude. As John Evelyn remarked, the treatment of the immigrants suffered by the "fatality of the times we were fallen into."[105]

The severity of the persecution in France and the arrival of large numbers of refugees elicited a response from Parliament, though to no more effect than in earlier years. As early as March 1677 a bill was read in the Lords to allow foreigners who were householders, who conformed to the Church of England, and who had served their apprenticeship abroad and exercised their trade for at least seven years, to freely practice those trades in Westminster, the suburbs of London, Middlesex, Surrey, and Essex. The French Church in the Savoy, London, a congregation that conformed to the Anglican litrugy (translated into French) proposed and apparently modeled the bill. Promoted by those who would benefit from its terms, the bill took a very different tack from the proposals for a general naturalization: it addressed the problem of trading freedom rather than legal privileges. Passed by the Lords on 9 April 1677, the bill languished in the Commons, which added a clause that would offer naturalization to artificers in the manufacture of woollen goods and tapestries.[106]

An almost identical bill was considered in the Lords again in June of the following year. The committee for the bill heard arguments against it by the Recorder for the City of London and by the counsel for the Weavers' Company of London, for such a proposal represented a far more immediate threat to English corporate and trading interests than naturalization schemes. The counsel for the Dutch Church and the French Church in Threadneedle Street, which had sponsored this second bill, informed the committee that those who had petitioned for it had come to England in reliance on the king's proclamation (of 1672), were devout Protestants, and wished to practice their trades without molestation. The bill passed, but Parliament was prorogued two days later on 15 July 1678.[107] A similar bill introduced in the Commons in 1685 elicited an instant response from the City of Westminster. Aliens, the corporation argued, would engross English trade, promote the sale of only foreign goods, leave the younger sons of the gentry with no occupations, turn spies in time of war, and even abandon their children to be maintained by English parishes.[108] The proposals from the immigrants themselves for lessening the restrictions on trade within the corporations, and the prompt opposition that they provoked, reveal the centrality of this issue and the misdirection of immigration schemes that focused on offers of naturalization.

Dogged in their persistence, however, the supporters of the policy again put bills on the table in both Houses in December 1680. The Lords bill, the last of the many to be introduced in that House, was remarkably liberal: it provided for naturalization, free exercise of trades in all corporations, and free admission to the trade guilds. The bill was committed, but received only one reading before the prorogation on 10 January 1681. Lord Halifax wrote to his disappointed brother Henry Savile, envoy in Paris, that he had supported the bill, "but greater matters depending, it could not be dispatched."[109] The Commons bill, which was apparently as broad as that considered in the Lords, was debated on 31 December. Opposition now came from within as well as without Parliament. Hugh Boscowen, a leading Dissenter, argued that the bill would undermine English tradesmen and the corporations, and Sir John Knight, Tory MP for Bristol, argued that foreign artisans would have more privileges than those enjoyed by natives. Other MPs expressed similar reservations, and the bill received no further consideration after the debate.[110]

Two short-lived attempts at a naturalization bill were made during the brief sessions of James II's Parliament. A bill was introduced in the Commons in June 1685 on the petition of "divers poor French Protestants," and a lengthy debate took place on 1 July. Sir John Reresby, Tory Member for York, spoke in favor of committing the bill provided that it include a requirement that foreigners conform to the Church of England. The Tory Roger North, who opposed the bill as an open invitation to the scum of Europe, wrote that the proposed requirement of conformity to the Anglican rite was a tactic intended to force the king to confirm the Anglican liturgy by act of Parliament. The courtiers argued against the amendment, but the country gentlemen were won over by its proponents, and the committee for the bill was instructed to insert a clause requiring not only that those naturalized conform to the Anglican liturgy but also that all French congregations already established in England be required to conform. The next day Parliament was adjourned, and no further action was taken when the committee was revived in the following November.[111] The issue had become a pawn in the constitutional struggle that culminated in the Revolution, the economic motives for encouraging immigration had been lost sight of, and the pleas of the French Protestants and other immigrants for legal privileges went unanswered.

The arrival of perhaps 40,000 French also made the degree of hostility to immigrants, of which Matthew Hale had warned twenty years earlier, much more apparent. The author of *The Present State of England* (1683) wrote cautiously that to admit the French Protestants would successfully repeople England only if it could be managed so as to provoke the least possible repugnance amongst the natives. The tract warned of the risk of discontent—and worse—from the tradesmen of London who grumbled of "French dogs" who ate the bread from their mouths.[112] Strong animosities seem to have surfaced as soon as the volume of immigration began to rise substantially in the early 1680s. Whatever the opinions of the tract-writers, the proponents of naturalization in Parliament, or the communities where the foreigners settled, the French did arrive in their tens of thousands, and they found it necessary, or at least useful, to defend themselves in print.

In 1682 the French Church of the Savoy in London published a pamphlet advocating a general naturalization and professing the loyalty of the French refugees to their new homeland. Strategically praising a large population, the pamphlet declared as "a truth clear and unquestionable" that populousness stimulated prosperity. The French refugees came to England with the intention of settling permanently, the pamphleteer vowed, and brought with them their arts and estates. The refugees' children born in England were already completely English. Yet despite the contribution the French made to their new homeland, the English met immigrants with envy and animosity. The enemies of the refugees, the tract complained, were the masters of the trading companies (who accused them of not having served their seven years' apprenticeship), religious bigots, atheists, and papists. The "hard usage" of the refugees in England, the pamphlet stated, could not be believed by Huguenots abroad who envisioned England as a sanctuary and refuge of Protestants.[113]

An Apology for the Protestants of France (1683) struck a similarly defensive note. Its English author denied that the French refugees were enemies to England's religious establishment, and dismissed as absurd the complaints that they appeared as a mixed multitude, part Protestant, part papist. Their partisan adversaries incited the common people with whisperings that foreigners came to take the bread out of their mouths and usurp their employment. Yet England, the pamphlet argued, needed a million more inhabitants, and the French Protestants could fill the nation with hands. They had already introduced many new manufactures, and improved others. Above all, Christian charity demanded that they be given a kind reception as the victims of persecution and absolutism.[114] Neither pleas for religious sympathy nor the recitation of populationist shibboleths could quell the popular resentment of such a large wave of foreign arrivals. In any event, however, the Huguenot immigration proved a success and as economic assimilation proceeded, hostility died out.

In one quarter nevertheless, the opposition to naturalization positively gained strength over the several decades after the 1680s. Beginning in the mid-1680s, a spate of broadsides and pamphlets appeared denouncing the naturalization of aliens in terms that were so similar as to betray a systematic offensive. Their titles and arguments suggest only subtle variations on a continually reiterated theme. The publications condemned both general naturalization proposals and the private naturalizations of particular aliens.[115] Like their handful of very similar predecessors of the early 1660s, the broadsides give the appearance of a concerted campaign by the corporate towns to stop naturalizations that threatened the merchants and tradesmen of those cities with foreign competitors. Yet the barrage of tracts and broadsides came from the City of London alone, and was motivated solely by a desire to preserve the City's alien duties. For almost forty years a single determined man fought the City of London's campaign against naturalization. That man was Richard Pierce, officer in the king's Custom House, freeman of the City of London, member of the Grocers' Company, and the City's Collector of Alien Duties from 1684 until his death in 1722. During those years the Corporation farmed the collection of the duties to Pierce for an annual rent of £1,200. His fear that the admission of foreigners would diminish the revenues from the Corporation's alien duties impelled him to his perseverant struggle against naturalizations.[116] Pierce used every means at his disposal to mount a successful opposition to immigration. He made regular appearances before the City governors to urge them to be vigilant, petitioned Parliament, appeared before parliamentary naturalization committees, and brought suit against those who either refused to pay or evaded the alien duties. The Corporation was all the more willing to resist any erosion of the duties because of its dire financial circumstances. Its debts were enormous, and the consolidation of those debts by the Orphans Act of 1694 did not improve the City's financial circumstances materially. Only well into the eighteenth century, as the Corporation's revenues from its duty on coal increased rapidly, did it recover its solvency.[117]

The stream of broadsides began to appear immediately after Pierce assumed the office of Collector in 1684. Their common arguments can be treated synoptically. Nothing disturbed the minds of the nation's tradesmen, the publications argued, as the encroachments made by foreigners upon their native birthright. Sometimes aliens like the French Protestants were received on religious grounds, but most came for profit. History demonstrated the wisdom of excluding foreigners; indeed, few aliens had been naturalized in the ages when English trade had thrived. Naturalization ruined English trade and English merchants, as natives lost foreign commissions to aliens who had relations and friends abroad. Naturalized foreigners had devastated the English factories in Europe and drained the capital stock of the kingdom. Foreigner merchants, able to live frugally in chambers, frustrated the training of the younger sons of the gentry in trade, and refused to instruct the English in foreign manufacturing skills. The argument that naturalization would increase the import of commodities and thereby the king's customs revenues had proved illusory. Alien merchants traded in foreign baubles, not solid English manufactures, and thus contributed nothing to the balance of trade. Since the nation could not consume the additional goods, prices would fall, and imports cease. The Act of Navigation would be frustrated, and native mariners discouraged and driven into foreign countries to work. Even in Holland, where aliens were admitted freely, they still paid duties to the towns or ports through which they exported or imported goods.

Naturalization undermined religion as well, the City publications insisted. *A Brief and Summary Narrative of the Many Mischiefs and Inconveniences . . . Occasioned by Naturalizing of Aliens* (c. 1689) argued that naturalized foreigners had "been a great cause of our division in religion." Errors of doctrine and discipline had crept into the Established Church, and papists in particular had greatly strengthened their hands, spreading their doctrines "boldly and barefaced." Naturalized foreigners, the publications argued, would never assimilate but continue "a distinct body," as would their children. Moreover, the object of expanding population would be frustrated by the admission of foreigners: aliens were "like summer birds who when they have filled their pockets" returned into their native lands.[118]

The efficacy of the City's arguments in discouraging naturalization cannot easily be assessed. Certainly the broadsides and tracts took few pains to conceal their special pleading, arguing at times, for example, that the nation's greatest interest lay in "keeping up the magistracy in all corporations in its due honour and reputation" and preserving corporate tolls and duties.[119] Nothing could be more convincing than this current of publications that the center of organized opposition to naturalization lay in the Guildhall of London, and that its sponsor and protagonist was the Collector of the City's Alien Duties. The evidence of these publications more than amply bears out the accusations of the French Protestants in the 1680s that harassment and opposition emanated from the corporations. Yet this strand of opposition to immigration schemes could not be said to have had a powerful influence on the course of the economic discourse or on the discussion of naturalization in Parliament.

Aside from the vocal opposition of the City of London, the discourse over immigration in the years leading up to the Revolution took their primary resonances from the prolonged religious and constitutional uncertainties that came to a head in the crisis of James II's reign. The measures that followed the arrival of William III, particularly but not solely the establishment of the principle of religious toleration, permanently shifted the foundation of the discourse of population and immigration. The debate over immigration in the 1690s, almost entirely in the context of the acute and probing economic inquiries stimulated by rapid financial change brought about by years of war, contrasts sharply with the earlier religious and constitutional tone of the controversy. The 1690s marked perhaps the most dynamic years in the discourse of population and naturalization, as opinions were reformulated and expectations matured. The last years of the seventeenth century, a time when commercial change and discursive change advanced pari passu, witnessed both the apogee of the discourse over immigration and the first omens of its eventual demise.

4

Revolution and Economic Ferment

The Revolution of 1689 brought about fundamental changes in the public discourse over population policy and immigration schemes. The two decades from the Revolution to the passage of the Whig General Naturalization Act of 1709 witnessed the permanent fracturing of the political nation along party lines, as Whigs and Tories coalesced into increasingly polarized partisan camps. Proposals for the encouragement of immigration became amongst the most divisive of party issues. As England entered into the prodigious contest to defeat the ambitions of Louis XIV, the demands of war began to figure more prominently in the controversy over population. The financial exigencies of war also accelerated the commercialization of England's economy, and consequently stimulated a probing examination of the government policies proper to a commercial social order. The imperial consciousness that gradually dawned in Britain during these years cast a different light on the question of immigration, as a growing sense of the value of the colonies added a new dimension to populationist ambitions. The reigns of William and Mary, and that of Queen Anne, however, witnessed more tumultuous economic change than actual prosperity, and the problems of poverty and unemployment nagged the consciences of the economic writers more insistently than in earlier years. Moreover, a rising chorus of hostility to immigrants—in part partisan, in part economic, in part cultural—found voice in the 1690s.

It might be expected that a more concerted political effort to encourage immigration would be mounted after the Revolution. Certainly William III supported a liberal policy of admitting foreign settlers. In April 1689, the same month as his coronation, the new king issued a declaration to encourage French Protestants to settle in England, offering them protection and assistance in their trades.[1] Throughout his reign William continued to be vigilant in seeing that officers of the Crown promptly suppressed any harassment of foreign artisans.[2] But the increasingly bitter opposition to immigration schemes from Tory and High Church interests widened the partisan split on the issue and made the price of strong support from the Crown too high in terms of political capital. As a consequence, no strong pressure came from the Court for a major alteration in immigration policy: the king's overriding concern for the national unity necessary to carry on the war against France, was deemed—no doubt properly—more important than a change in naturalization law.[3] After two abortive attempts in Parliament to introduce a general naturalization bill, in April 1689 and April 1690, the influential Whig William Palmes succeeded in putting such a bill on the table in December 1693. The subsequent debate provoked a notorious speech against naturalization schemes by the Tory Sir John Knight, Member for Bristol, that exemplified the rising partisan bile at such proposals. The bill was lost, and a motion to bring in a similar bill was defeated in January 1696.[4]

In February of the next year a new bill was introduced, debated, and finally defeated in a division of 168 to 127 on a motion for its committment, the only one of the many bills for a general naturalization in the seventeenth century to be rejected outright. After a failed motion to introduce another bill in January 1698, no new attempt was forthcoming for over a decade.[5] Opinion turned against the proposals as jealousy of William's Dutch and Huguenot followers, alloyed with the mental climate of war, increased the general level of xenophobic sentiment. Partisan adversaries of naturalization in Parliament exploited the mounting popular resentment of foreigners, although their opposition expressed broad ideological and religious concerns rather than simple cultural chauvinism.

The religious side of the immigration controversy had been changed once and for all by the Revolution and the Toleration Act. No longer was it necessary to weld arguments for toleration of Nonconformists to pleas for the admission of foreigners. True, some complaints after 1689 echoed those of earlier years. The custom of reordaining their ministers was said to discourage French Protestants from settling in England. The disabilities imposed on Quakers troubled the more scrupulous.[6] The Deist Matthew Tindal, a vehement opponent of the High Church party, argued in 1697 for a general freedom of religion and a further liberty for Dissenters: a "universal, impartial, inviolable liberty of conscience," and the naturalization of foreigners, he wrote, would quickly repopulate the nation.[7] These complaints represented more than the carping of idealists. The Revolution religious settlement left much undone. Indeed, the Toleration Act, a product of political compromise, and perhaps the best measure that could be achieved in the circumstances of 1689, sought neither to proclaim nor to enforce a general freedom of religion.[8]

The Revolution Settlement had nevertheless transformed the religious issues involved in the immigration controversy, and made them essentially political. Henceforth the naturalization of aliens formed a plank, though a removable one, in the policies of Whig political interests. The admission of foreign settlers as a measure favorable to trade corresponded with the Whig party's ideological alliance with commercial interests, and with their willingness to embrace a more dynamic social order. The Tory and High Church camp opposed naturalization schemes for fear that they would erode the social fabric and undermine the Established Church. Tory controversialists regularly employed the perennial Tory cry of "the Church in danger" as a riposte against naturalization proposals. Such religious arguments had long been heard. But after 1689 the religious side of the immigration question became a facet of the ideological and party fissures of English society. Many observers harbored sincere fears for the integrity of England's settlement in Church and state; but others used religious arguments to cloak cultural animosities, economic self-interest, and political partisanship.

The deepened political dimension of the immigration question conditioned the published debate, but perhaps equally important in molding the changing contours of economic discourse were the profound changes in England's economic conditions. A great confidence in the possibility of progress suffused English society after the heady events of 1689, as those ambitious for their country and for themselves thrust forward a thousand projects and schemes for the nation's improvement. Yet the frenetic speculations of the "projecting age" proclaim not contentment but hope. The inexorable war against France caused formidable dislocations in English trade, and every resource felt the strain of the long contest against French hegemony. The old complaints of the decay of trade, largely silent in the 1680s, revived in new forms.[9] The 1690s witnessed a transformation in England's economy rather than either absolute decline or unambiguous growth. The war severely disrupted foreign trade, especially from 1692 to 1695, and a domestic trade crisis in 1696 only subsided as negotations for peace progressed. Yet at the same time the home and colonial trades expanded.[10] Thrust back upon its own resources by the prohibition of trade with France and the difficulties of wartime shipping, England nurtured its own industries and improved the variety and quality of its manufactures, thus laying the foundations for the vigorous inland trade of the eighteenth century. The burden of debt and taxation resulting from the war led to sweeping changes in public finance. The Bank of England was founded and joint-stock companies proliferated. The reform of the coinage in 1693 resolved a chronic problem that had provoked endless and acrimonious debate. By the turn of the century England's economy had been remodeled by the pressures of fiscal necessity created by the war.[11] Still, these structural changes brought about no sustained improvement in economic conditions until the peace of 1713. Trade, especially the export trade, throve during the brief intermission in the war, but a more settled economic climate awaited the second decade of the new century. The years from 1704 to 1709 witnessed a long depression and trade crisis, with severe weather contributing to food shortages, exceptionally high prices, and widespread unemployment.[12]

The strains of the war and the dramatic economic changes of the time caused an intense ferment of economic inquiry and brought forth in the 1690s a flood of economic tracts and broadsides. The two most discussed policy issues were interest rates and the recoinage, but the treatment of these two issues embraced the most far-reaching theoretical and ideological questions. Moreover, a growing number of economic writers treated matters of trade comprehensively, and their relatively unimpassioned tone contrasts with the boisterous polemical style that characterized the Restoration discourse.[13] The expiration in 1695 of the Licensing Act of 1663 made England unique in Europe for the freedom of its press, and the volume of printed matter rose steeply, though libel laws still imposed an important restriction.[14] The increase in published tracts on economic issues followed this general blossoming of print culture, but more fundamental forces were in play. The economic turmoil of the financial revolution demanded examination in economic discourse. Perhaps more importantly, as economic policy was absorbed into the political divisions of English society, economic discourse took on a stronger ideological color. With the entry of England into the Nine Years' War the commercial basis of military rivalry and national power became more conspicuous than they had been for generations, and trade became a more integral part of the language of politics.[15]

Concern over England's population continued to inspire schemes for increasing the number of people, and the naturalization issue retained its prominence in the economic literature. The national, and sometimes expressly military, advantages of admitting immigrants received more stress as the rigors of the war heightened the sense of international economic and political competition of which population was a part.[16] This nationalist strain can be seen in the writings of John Locke, Nicholas Barbon, and Sir William Harris, all advocates of naturalization on traditional grounds. All three sought immigrants who would purchase lands in England with money brought from abroad, reviving the wistful yearning for an easy injection of foreign cash. Barbon, a high-flying entrepreneur who made his fortune in property development and fire insurance, urged in 1696 that the nation's wealth would expand as the number of people grew and as cities and towns were rebuilt.[17] Harris wanted foreign artisans who lived and worked cheaper than the natives, and who could introduce new manufactures. They would not usurp employment, he asserted, since their trades would be novel ones, and their arrival would raise rents, increase home consumption, and improve the balance of trade.[18] None of these arguments were new. Both Barbon and Locke, however, made much of the efficacy of naturalization as one means for England to achieve superiority over its enemies. There was a competition amongst nations over the number of their people and the skills of particular artisans, the argument ran, and immigrants weakened their own country by leaving as much as they strengthened England by settling there.[19] This reasoning was hardly novel either, but in the changed circumstances of the 1690s it took on a weightier meaning. The example of the Huguenots, whose departure was thought to have weakened the kingdom of France, was fresh in memory.[20] Indeed, many of the officers in the armies of William III were

French Protestant exiles, and the Nine Years' War saw more than one battle in which French faced French across the battlefield. The confrontation could also be less direct. As Roger Coke wrote, "by permitting foreigners the freedom of English natives, we conquer without a war, run no hazard, and enrich and strengthen the nation."[21] Military motives persistently thrust themselves into a discourse upon which they had scarcely intruded before 1689.

That observers should dwell on the military advantages of populationist policies in the reigns of William and Mary and of Queen Anne is hardly cause for surprise; the wonder is that those advantages so seldom received attention before. The lack of concern with military motives attests to the faith of the early economic writers that international power ultimately rested on the foundation of a prosperous economy—that power and plenty must be sought simultaneously. The military reputation of England during the Restoration in any case could hardly be called a distinguished one. It is true that in the middle years of the seventeenth century the navy became a buttress to commercial expansion and a token at least of future British supremacy at sea. Commentators recognized the importance of naval power, and that recognition was magnified after 1689. Many observers thought it especially necessary to receive foreign seamen in order to relieve natives from the press and ensure England's naval power.[22] Barbon urged repopulation policies in order to supply a larger number of ships and promote naval strength. The subjects of absolutist nations would come to England for political freedom, he argued, and the resulting populousness would empower England to seize dominion of the seas and ensure its hegemony over France. Nevertheless, seamen must possess skills, so immigrants—unless they were already seamen—could only contribute to English military potential indirectly.

Only when William III propelled England into the role of combatant in the continental struggle, and only as the nation transformed itself into a major power and as imperial ambitions began to emerge, did military considerations acquire a substantial resonance in the immigration controversy. By the end of the seventeenth century the English government was spending on the military a proportion of its total government expenditures comparable to that of continental powers, and military men represented a substantial presence in the Commons.[23] England embarked on a rapid mobilization that formed part of the second phase of the early modern military revolution whose most conspicuous token was the huge armies put in the field by Louis XIV. The pattern of warfare at this time involved large numbers of forces, strategies of attrition, and high rates of wastage of men. In these circumstances, manpower was essential, and pleas for immigrants to fill the ranks grew accordingly.[24] Geoffrey Parker has suggested that perhaps one of every four or five soldiers died in each year of service. This annual wastage rate of roughly 20 percent represents death from all causes, but casualties in battle alone could be very heavy. The battle of Malplaquet in 1709 cost the allies 24,000 dead, or one-quarter of their men in the field.[25] Extended marches, sieges, skirmishes, prolonged manoeuvering, and other strategies of attrition perhaps reduced the rate of loss. But such strategies cost a great deal, and presented secondary economic needs for a large population. In view of the military conditions of the time, war would naturally excite anxieties about population size, and immigration schemes seemed to answer the need for more men. Recruitment for the army presented fewer technical obstacles than recruitment for the navy, so an accession of foreigners might make a direct contribution to the war effort.

The stress on military motives raises the issue of the relationship between economic and political discourse in the altered climate after 1689, and the ideas of Locke can be used as a fulcrum to examine this question. John Locke's views on economic issues were traditional, and were probably formulated much earlier, before 1680.[26] He was not a pathfinder in the development of ideas about trade, although his voice carried a great deal of weight in the 1690s. His writings on economic matters were polemical, and as one of the Commissioners for Trade from 1696 to 1700 he seems to have toed a conservative mercantilist line.[27] Indeed, Joyce Appleby has identified Locke as the chief architect of the revived mercantilist balance of trade policies that dominated the eighteenth century.[28] Locke's traditionalism can be seen in his 1693 unpublished tract on naturalization. Hands were essential, he argued, to both manufacture and navigation. Immigrants who worked cheaply would allow English manufactures to prevail in foreign markets. If they ate the bread out of English mouths it meant only that they would bring down the unreasonably high wages of English laborers. Population density would compel laborers to work harder, and England could not receive too many foreign settlers. Locke's arguments echoed those of earlier economic theorists, and his remarks on the importance of the the woollen manufacture might as easily have been written in the 1670s as in the 1690s.[29] The stress on stimulating and protecting English manufactures typifies the concerns of the 1690s and further identifies Locke's views as assuming the rhetorical stance of more traditional mercantilist than of progressive free-trade advocates of naturalization. No stark division emerged in the controversy over immigration between the manufacturers—represented in the economic discourse especially by the spokesmen for the clothiers—and the merchants.[30] Both groups advocated the admission of foreign settlers, though on different grounds. However, it is safe to say that those who, like Locke, were concerned with manufactures and with broader national interest (such as the treatment of the plantations) took a more cautious stance on the issue of naturalization.

It is ironic that Locke—the greatest of the English liberal political philosophers of the period and a man who has often been singled out as one of the founders of the ideology of individualism—should have voiced economic ideas that had been common currency amongst trade writers for decades and that looked backward rather than forward. The example of Locke warns against a too facile association of liberalism with a commercial mentality. Like the Whigs whose darling he became, Locke tempered his vision of a progressive commercial society founded on individualism with the conviction that English economic policy served larger political ends than simply the enshrinement of market forces as the ordering principle of society. He represented a middle ground between the free-trade notions of mercantile apologists such as Josiah Child and Barbon, and the conservatives who distrusted commercialization in any guise. Locke's arguments for government economic regulation lay the foundations for a Whig commercial order that rejected both the Scylla of free-trade articulated by some economic writers and the Charybdis of anticommercial nostalgia expressed by the spokesmen of Country values. Riches lay not in land but in trade, Locke argued, as shown by the comparison of populous Holland and depopulated Spain. But trade must be regulated in the interests of the emerging Whig oligarchy, of England's growing manufacturing sector, and of the proper economic exploitation of colonial possessions. That Locke played a central role in the creation of the Board of Trade, which fashioned the old colonial system of the eighteenth century, bears witness to the triumph of his understanding of the role of state economic policy in England's new political circumstances after 1689.

Locke must always play a prominent role in the history of seventeenth and eighteenth century political thought, but another tradition of political discourse counterbalanced his Whig liberalism. Much recent historical work on English political thought has been influenced by the writings of J. G. A. Pocock and his model of the civic humanist tradition that descended from the ancient political philosophers through Macchiavelli and James Harrington to Lord Bolingbroke and others in the eighteenth century.[31] How does the immigration debate fit into the categories of civic humanist as opposed to new commercial and liberal political languages? The Tory enemies of naturalization favored the language of civic virtue at the same time that Whig apologists of immigration schemes tended to rely on the rhetoric of liberal commercialism. As the immigration issue split so cleanly along party lines, and as the Tory–Whig division continued to condition British politics until the middle of the eighteenth century,[32] these ideological confrontations cannot be ignored. The models developed by Pocock and other historians of political thought must be employed with caution in studying economic discourse and the controversy over population and immigration that evolved within that discourse. Ideological alignments are more often implicit than explicit in the economic discourse. Moreover, political and economic discourse were by no means perfectly congruent. Indeed, disturbing ideological ambiguities and discontinuites marbled the discussion of the economics of population and immigration.

It can be said, in rough terms, that the advocates of naturalization are best seen as spokesmen for the new commercial liberalism that is associated in these years with the Whig party,[33] and that the civic humanist tradition, on the other hand, offered a rhetoric more serviceable to the Tory and High Church opponents of schemes to encourage immigration, since they could argue that the admission of immigrants would undermine the integrity of the civic community and replace the value of virtue with a narrow striving after wealth. Those generalizations must, however, be qualified by recalling the backgrounds of these two ideologies.

Macchiavelli, one of the chief (though unacknowledged) inspirations, particularly in the *Discourses*, for the notion of civic virtue, praised the Roman methods of naturalizing peoples to expand the population and power of the state. But that expansion was military in nature, effected by military means to achieve military ends. Naturalization followed conquest by the sword. Trade was not an important part of the equation, except as an aftereffect. James Harrington's mid-seventeenth-century vision of Oceana, a society of virtue grounded in the class of rural gentry, proposed "a commonwealth for increase," a dynamic state that would employ various encouragements to population growth. But Oceana, like Rome, was to expand by conquest, not by commerce. New people were needed for its army of citizen soldiers. Yet this aspect of the ideology of civic virtue clashed with the position of the Tory party. Such militarism was alien to the Tory vision of the English state, and it implied to many the creation of a paid standing army, anathema to the Tory and Country interests that tended to adopt both the rhetoric and the perspective of civic humanism and to oppose naturalization.[34] The conflict between the ideal of civic virtue and the peace policy of the Tory party represents a vexing contradiction. Nor did the Tory adversaries of immigration schemes seek to conceal this somewhat embarrassing root of their polemics. John Knight's vituperative denunciation of foreigners and of naturalization proposals in Parliament in 1693 fairly reveled in references to ancient Roman virtue.

Another, less martial, tradition from Rome that economic writers and policy makers often praised was the encouragement of procreation associated with the laws passed by Augustus. Whether advocates or opponents of the admission of foreigners, those urging population growth, Locke amongst them, often cited Augustus's laws with approval, for this aspect at least of the model of the public-minded citizen or subject could be employed by all participants in the controversy over population, irrespective of ideological orientation.[35] Of course there was another facet to the classical tradition, almost wholly ignored in the age of mercantilist populationism, that found nothing to praise in growth for its own sake. Both Aristotle and Plato had held that the size of a state had definite limits and that the polis of Athens had already far exceeded those limits to its grievous cost. In the English canon, Thomas More had relied on this tradition in arguing that there was a right and proper number of people for every nation, and that the correct population could be achieved by state regulation.[36] Giovanni Botero, one of the most important of the early modern thinkers on population, had also perceived a limit to desirable growth.[37] The intellectual traditions on which the controversialists in the English debate could call were by no means one-sided. Yet in the late seventeenth century notions of an equilibrium in population enjoyed very little currency. The quest for a vast population, an intellectual product of the seventeenth century, was in fact a very baroque idea. Numbers of people were to expand without limit just as a wide baroque avenue extended to the vanishing point of a seeming infinity. All limits were to be transcended, or rather ignored, in the drive for populousness.

The traditionalists who opposed naturalization schemes and argued in the language of civic humanism seldom called into question such fundamental assumptions of the day, but they had an array of more mundane dialectic weapons to hand. Tories claimed the legacy of the arguments that Matthew Hale had articulated in the 1660s: an influx of foreigners would corrupt the "ancient constitution," undermine civic virtue, and betray the sacred birthright of Englishmen. They denounced the advocates of naturalization as opportunists who would sacrifice civic virtues for the new commercial society's individualist interests. To disciples of the vision of a homogeneous civic body of shared values and culture, immigration schemes threatened a moral corrosion of social and national integrity in order to exalt commercial principles.

Locke and other writers on trade, eager to promote English commercial expansion, advocated not the Roman brand of militarism that served as a model in the civic humanist tradition—however compromising to its Tory adherents—but the kind expressed by Defoe when he declared that the longest purse, not the longest sword, would conquer. Whig war was based on Whig finance and commerce. The champions of the new commercial ethos envisioned England as a trading nation rather than an empire based on military power, though prosperity would buttress an imperial economic order. Like Locke in his tract on naturalization, defenders of a Whig commercial order cited the model of Holland, a liberal, commercial state, and contrasted it to Spain,[38] the largest empire created by Europeans since Rome. Populousness and the free admission of foreign settlers would contribute to England's commercial, and consequently military, supremacy. The commercial school nevertheless contained its own internal contradictions. If a commercial order could achieve so much, could it not achieve a proper rate of population growth without the intervention of the state to increase population by the naturalization of foreigners? Faith in the powers of market forces might undermine the grounds for an active immigration policy. These questions only began to be raised in the 1690s, however, and this period marks perhaps the sharpest partisan and ideological division between the proponents and the enemies of the policy of encouraging immigration.

Ideological and partisan motives, however, tell only part of the story of the immigration controversy in the years after the Revolution. Intellectual interest in population and fears of its decline persisted and even increased after 1689. Modern estimates indicate modest increases in population in the 1690s, but contemporaries perceived no improvement in the problem of underpopulation. Continuing economic turmoil fueled calls for an admission of foreigners to infuse new blood in a seemingly anemic English economy. This was more true after 1700 than before, and the first years of the new century witnessed hardships that earned them the name the "seven ill years,"[39] as the losses of war conspired with poor harvests and low employment. Practical motives then continued to inspire the growth of the infant science of vital statistics. The astronomer Edmund Halley advanced the work of Petty and Graunt in the field of population studies in his *Estimate of the Degrees of Mortality of Mankind* (1693). Halley's work, based on detailed figures compiled for the city of Breslau, represented the most sophisticated attempt to analyze population dynamics around the turn of the eighteenth century.[40] Far better publicized, however, was Gregory King's *Natural and Political Observations*, written in 1696, though in King's lifetime known only through quotations in the publications of Charles Davenant.

A divine-right Tory who saw the war on the continent as reducing England's wealth and population,[41] King declared that the economic crisis brought about by the war made knowledge of the number of people of the highest concern. He estimated the total population of England at five and a half million people, and thought that England's "populousness" (its density) was exceeded only by that of China and Holland, the latter having less than four acres to the head compared with England's seven. The natural increase in England's people, King calculated, proceeded at the rate of nine thousand a year in the longer term. In his view, then, England possessed considerable potential for demographic growth. Yet, he argued, the nation had suffered a net loss amounting to 50,000 people during the period from 1688 to 1696, a setback occasioned by war and economic dislocation. Almost half the population consisted of children under the age of sixteen, King observed, meaning that even in an age when work began very early in life a large proportion of the people had to be supported by the labor of others: England suffered from what demographers now call a high dependency ratio. King estimated in his much-quoted "scheme of income and expense of families" that less than half the people of the kingdom were increasing its wealth while more than half were decreasing it.[42] King's conclusions certainly lent support to the case for admitting adult laboring foreigners who would immediately augment the pool of adult laborers, although he never addressed the issue of immigration himself.[43]

In another light, however, Gregory King's theories indirectly conflicted with the premises of the immigration schemes. In stressing the potential for strong natural growth of the native population, King expressed a growing sense at the end of the seventeenth century that encouraging procreation might be the more efficacious state population policy. Proposals to increase the number of natives by pronatal measures multiplied in the 1690s. Of course this had always been the conservative position of those who saw the population question in essentially moral terms. A tract from the hand of Samuel Dugard, Rector of Fornton, Staffordshire, entitled *A Discourse Concerning the Having Many Children* (1695) exemplified this line of argument in its laments over the general disrespect for marriage. The neglect of marriage and child-bearing had brought upon England a lack of people that made laborers difficult to find in many places, Dugard insisted, and land values had consequently fallen. The state, he suggested, should impose fines upon the unmarried to encourage procreation.[44] Dugard wrote from the country, and his complaints perhaps bear witness to a poor distribution of population as well as a poverty of absolute numbers. As a clergyman, he looked to the fertility of the marital state for a larger population. It was a godly thing for a Christian to proceate, and the conviction of the churchmen that moral virtue lay in natural generation meshed well with the detestation of their Tory allies for immigrants and foreign influence.

Political arithmeticians as well as moralists praised pronatal policies, however. The physician and scientist Nehemiah Grew, writing in 1707,[45] argued that women should be encouraged to marry while young, that taxes should be levied on bachelors, and that inducements to celibacy, such as fellowships at colleges, should be reduced. In addition, Grew urged that the wisest public policy would husband the people England already had by reducing the loss from death and disease: suitable regulations could be enacted to ensure medical treatment to those in need.[46] The pleas of Grew and others for measures to encourage marriage and procreation did not go wholly unheeded. In 1695 Parliament passed an act that imposed duties on bachelors and widowers. The immediate object of the act, however, like much of the economic legislation of the 1690s, was to raise revenue to carry on the war.[47] The measure cannot be considered as evidence of either an active populationist policy or a turning away from the prolonged flirtation with naturalization projects.

Yet the heightened interest in pronatal measures betrayed a subtle erosion of enthusiasm for immigration schemes. In spite of the support of such prominent public figures as Locke, increasingly after 1689 the proponents of immigration approached the subject with more caution and often qualified their proposals in ways that the Restoration economic writers seldom had. Economic writers tended to shift their stress to the necessity of making the existing population of England more productive, urging the creation of employment as a chief object of economic policy. Those who faithfully pleaded for increased population often insisted that additional inhabitants must be industrious and skilled, whether they were immigrants with proven trade skills, or English-born children trained in some art. In 1694 Sir Humphrey Mackworth scoffed at the suggestion that England had a large enough population already, but he insisted that mere numbers were not enough: "I propose employment," he proclaimed pointedly.[48] Nehemiah Grew expressed similar sentiments, acknowledging that populousness was necessary for the improvement of all manufactures and trades, but cautiously using the formula "a multitude of hands well employed" rather than earlier vague references to "heads." Grew argued that the object of economic policy should be to increase productive labor, and the first step to that end was to banish idleness and beggary and to compel the poor to work. Those engaged in useless work must also be shifted into productive occupations. In this way England's stock of human capital would be redistributed to ensure that employment was productive.[49]

The paradox implicit in actively striving to increase the population while deploring unemployment grew more vexing. As Sir Francis Brewster exclaimed in exasperation, "it is unaccountable that we should, as in truth we do, want people, yet know not how to employ those we have." Despite the anomaly, he argued eloquently for the reception of foreign settlers who could fill wastelands, increase consumption, raise the value of land, and add their estates to the wealth of natives. Yet he thought that full employment of the present population was the only way to get more people.[50] The paradox that nagged the adherents of naturalization became more irksome as laments about unemployment and the poor multiplied. The simultaneous complaints of unemployment and pleas for a larger population caused grief to contemporaries, and they are no easier for the historian to reconcile.[51] Some scholars have stressed the early economic writers' rhapsodic vision of the potential growth of England's trade and strength.[52] Merchants and civil servants, parliamentarians, pamphleteers, and theorists embraced this vision of the vital forces of growth at work in the economy of England. Yet the optimism of this dream, vision, or fancy[53] of a larger population that would be fully employed began to wane as the eighteenth century wore on, and with it ebbed the pleas for the encouragement of immigration. That is not to say that the eighteenth century did not possess a powerful vision of the superiority and the promise of commercial society; quite the contrary was the case, for the eighteenth-century economic vision was in many respects more acute than what had gone before. Indeed, the late-seventeenth-century eagerness to artificially stimulate population growth, and the economic vision from which it sprang, contained a strain of euphoria that betokened more hope than solid confidence.

Francis Brewster recognized the anomaly of naturalizing foreigners while natives were unemployed, but did permit this realization to dampen his zeal for an immigration scheme. Others were less sanguine. Some economic writers took the paradox to heart and censured those who sought mere numbers of people. Sir Dalby Thomas wrote that although people were the wealth of a nation, "it is only meant, laborious and industrious people, and not such as are wholly unemployed; . . . the fewer such the better." An increase in the numbers of the idle was "so far from being national riches, that it is the surest and speediest way to inevitable poverty, famine, and nakedness." Labor, he agreed, was the basis of wealth, but only when workers were industrious, and "not by increase of people only."[54] The advancing theme of employment even cast doubt on the practically canonical proposition that an influx of wealthy foreigners would bring estates with them and enrich England. John Pollexfen, a member of the Board of Trade from 1696 to 1705, complained that persons of quality could pay for private acts of naturalization, but that the working people that were most wanted could not. Admitting the poor, he wrote,

> might probably tend more to the increase of riches than what can be expected by admitting the rich; for these may so far exceed the rich in number, that if kept to employments, might in time get more, than may probably be brought by the few rich that may come in.[55]

But it was crucial that poor immigrants be employed in some trade, for if the idle should come they would do England more harm than good, Pollexfen insisted. These seem obvious qualifications, yet they had scarcely appeared in the literature before the 1690s.

These early expressions of concern with employment marked the beginnings of a shift in the terms of economic discourse. As the rising star of employment began its steady climb towards the center of the constellation of economic policy goals, the ambitions to increase England's population by actively encouraging immigration began to be outshone. The change started in the 1690s, but its full impact was not felt until the 1720s and 1730s. Many observers after the Revolution, like Roger Coke, could still cavalierly dismiss such worries with the confident assurance that immigrants such as the silk-weavers of London could create more employment than they could fill themselves.[56] Charles Davenant, Inspector-General of Imports and Exports from 1703, and one of the most important new economic voices heard around the turn of the century, treated immigration proposals with more circumspection.

Davenant declared his allegiance to populousness as a prerequisite to national prosperity, while insisting that employment mattered more than mere numbers of people.[57] His importance, however, lies in his elaboration of the theme that employment and population were intimately related. A meager population depressed industriousness, he argued, for in thinly inhabited countries people always grew proud, poor, and lazy. But unlike the Restoration economic writers, he did not see a large population as an assurance of industriousness. A country could be populous and yet poor, he warned, "so that numbers, unless they are well employed, make the body politic big, but unwieldy; strong, but unactive; . . . theirs is a wrong opinion who think all mouths profit a country that consume its product."[58] National wealth depended upon the number of people well-employed, not upon numbers in themselves: a large and dense population was a condition but not a certain promise of national wealth. Conversely, employment could increase populousness. If the idle were made to earn their maintenance, they would not so often die from "diseases contracted under a slothful poverty."[59] In Davenant's view, population and employment acted upon each other as reciprocal and complementary forces in advancing England's wealth, and public policy should strive to stimulate both in a balanced fashion.

As economic observers and analysts after the Revolution came to place more stress on employment, they expressed a corollary concern with the problem of poverty. The multiplying ranks of the poor and the dramatically rising burden of the poor rates contributed to the insistence that immigrants be industrious and employed. William Petyt estimated the poor rates in 1680 at £400,000, and Sir Humphrey Mackworth put the figure at £700,000 in 1694, amounts that fall below one modern estimate of £665,000 in 1685 and £900,000 in 1701.[60] Whichever calculations are closer to the truth, there clearly occurred towards the end of the seventeenth century a rapid increase in the problem of poverty. The estimates of Gregory King that over half of England's people had annual expenses that exceeded their incomes only corroborated the fears that many observers had already expressed. To settle the question of whether the poor were seen in this period essentially as an economic or rather as a social problem would require a more searching inquiry than can be undertaken here. Charles Wilson has treated the element of social reform in mercantilist views of poverty and employment, and it will be necessary to return to this question later in this study.[61] It is important to an understanding of the debate over population and immigration, however, to recognize how prominent a place was occupied in the economic discourse by what Wilson has called the Great Debate of the Poor, especially from the 1690s onward.

The preoccupation with finding employment for the able poor assumed so prominent a place in the economic discourse after 1689 that it tended to cast a shadow over immigration proposals even in the writings of those who saw no conflict between the two ends. Edmund Halley, for example, argued that population growth was hindered by the unequal distribution of property that discouraged the poor from marrying.[62] Charles Povey lamented the increase of the poor, and suggested regulations to keep wages up to reduce their misery.[63] In the writings of John Bellers, a Quaker clothier and philanthropist, a sincere religious concern for the poor combined with a conviction that the nation's wealth lay in its laborers.[64] Bellers deplored the great loss England suffered by the neglect of its poor, their unemployment, and a general indifference to the number of laborers. He calculated that the nation lost nearly four million pounds a year by voluntary and involuntary unemployment. Despite his concern with poverty, Bellers supported populationist policies, declaring the "increase of regular laboring people" the key to national wealth. People could not be too numerous, so long as they were not idle, and a regular employment of the poor would encourage marriage and attract foreigners.[65]

The writer and projector James Puckle went further than most in deflecting the immigration debate into the issue of employment. He complained in his tract *England's Path to Wealth* (1700) that the lack of employment and the idleness of the poor obstructed aspirations to repopulate the nation. An active public policy of creating employment, Puckle argued, would cure England's population problems: "a full employment of the hands we have," he insisted, "is certainly the best way to get more; for such as our employment is for people, so many will our people be." The more that employment and trade expanded, he declared, the more would industrious people come from abroad, become tenants, enclose wastes, improve lands, increase manufactures, and enlarge the number of English products. Puckle then differed from most commentators in his day in viewing populousness as the result of full employment and prosperity, and not as one of its causes.[66] His was the voice of the future: it cried out not for an act of naturalization to encourage immigration, but for the employment and wealth that would attract foreigners and create a larger native population, a view that would triumph in the course of the eighteenth century. Nevertheless Puckle represented little more than a lone voice at the opening of the eighteenth century. The movement for a large-scale admission of foreign settlers was by no means moribund yet, despite the reservations that had begun to pepper the economic discourse. The pleas for a naturalization act continued, partisan sentiment on the issue had not yet reached its feverish zenith, and the test of the policy that had been discussed for so long came in the last years of the reign of Queen Anne. Although the intellectual initiative for an immigration scheme had begun to flag, political inertia pressed the proposals ineluctably forward.

Two other developments in the economic discourse after the Revolution require mention, both of them articulated forcefully by Charles Davenant. Davenant revealed in his writings a forward-looking conception of the economic role of the plantations that exemplified the increasingly imperial economic vision of the eighteenth century.[67] The colonies had not depopulated England, he protested, and there had been an influx of foreigners; but the nation nevertheless had to expand its population by encouraging immigration, for "countries that take no care to encourage an accession of strangers, in a course of time, will find plantations of pernicious consequence." It was necessary to balance the outflow with the inflow of people. To Davenant, England had committed itself by the expansion of its colonial domains and its emerging imperial stature, even if unwittingly, to the admission of immigrants. However reluctant the natives might be, they had to open a doorway to immigrants from Europe who would balance the numbers of those who left England for the New World. As an imperial commercial power, Davenant suggested, England had forfeited a comforting but stultifying social order of cultural homogeneity in favor of diversity and a dynamic mobility of people. He anticipated as well a plea that became common in the eighteenth century by urging that aliens be encouraged to settle directly in the plantations as well, where subjects were especially wanted.[68] In this way the English would be discouraged from leaving the mother country—but Davenant knew that these were merely fair words, for he had adumbrated a population system of imperial rather than insularly English dimensions.[69] The preeminence of the Board of Trade after its creation in 1696 in the formulation of a general imperial economic order that sought to integrate colonial with national policies symbolizes this shift in thinking. The consequence in the long term, however, was to tarnish the appeal of immigration schemes that took a narrowly English view of the dynamics of population movement.

The second development in economic discourse at the turn of the century revolved around another theme proclaimed by Davenant, that of political liberty as a factor in demographic change and economic growth. Davenant expressed great confidence in liberty and good government as engines of population growth: they could both attract immigrants from abroad and promote a rapid multiplication of the native population. Almost all countries in the world, he theorized, had been more or less populous depending upon how well they had secured liberty and property.[70] Roger Coke voiced similar sentiments, declaring that the strength of every nation rested not only on the number of its people, but on "the well ordering and governing of them."[71] The idea was not strictly new, as earlier economic writers had lavished praise upon religious freedoms, but the notion of liberty as a virtual ideology represented a development in economic thought that would bear rich fruit in the course of the eighteenth century. The importance of the doctrine that political liberty fostered prosperity increased with the gradual growth of political stability in England as the new century progressed.[72] By the middle of the eighteenth century, the proposition that liberty and good government promoted a large population and national wealth enjoyed the status of an article of faith. Indeed, the belief here anticipated by Davenant came to eclipse the movement for the admission of foreigners in ways that must be examined in due course. In the 1690s and 1700s it was an idea that, like the political settlement of the Revolution, remained precarious by its novelty. Confidence in the power of stable government to ensure an ample population by attracting immigrants and promoting procreation grew gradually with the conviction that the political and religious liberties that the English possessed were the blessings of a constitution unique amongst the nations of Europe, and with the growth of political stability itself.

At the same time that economic writers began to express doubts or reservations about admitting foreigners and finding employment for a large population, an eruption of publications appeared that reflected a surging hostility to foreign immigrants. Many Englishmen felt a jealous resentment of the Dutch and French Protestants who had come with William III to England

and had received lands and high offices from him. Some of this anger represented genuine cultural distaste, but much of it expressed partisan antagonism: denunciations of foreigners were understood as thinly veiled attacks on the government and the king himself. As Defoe wrote of these troubled years, "party spleen over-ran the whole nation," and "the word *Foreigner* was the shibboleth of a party, who made it popular, that they might the better affront that great foreigner, that had made them all denizens, I mean King William."[73] Resentment of the followers of William was codified in the Act of Succession (1700), which provided that no person born out of the dominions of the Crown, although naturalized or made a denizen, could be a member of the Privy Council or of Parliament, hold any office, or receive any grant of land from the Crown.[74] An almost identical clause in 1 Geo. I. c. 4 answered the same purpose for the German followers of the Hanoverians. The animosity expressed in the pamphlet literature, however, reveals a more profound distaste for alien immigrants than could have been provoked by the small number of Dutch and French who settled in England in the train of William, for by the 1690s the volume of Dutch migration was quite modest.

Some observers made no secret of their vexation with the Dutch presence and with the new regime. John Blanch complained bitterly in 1694 that the Dutch wanted a naturalization act in order to buy up English land and monopolize the nation's trade. The "real Whig" Samuel Johnson, Rector of Corringham, fumed in 1697 that no Englishman wanted a "stranger thrust in his nose," and that aliens, especially the Dutch, had "crept . . . into the great cities, or at Court or in the Church," where they lived upon the spoils of the nation. A general naturalization would spell disaster for English trade. The Dutch were friends and allies, Johnson admitted, but must England adopt them and give them the birthright of England, and the inheritance of Magna Carta?[75]

The Rights and Liberties of Englishmen Asserted (1701), a tract attributed to Thomas Wagstaffe, senior, a nonjuror, went further.[76] A veiled attack on William III, the tract condemned the admission of French immigrants. The open policy of admission had made England "swarm with outlandish faces"—a "mixed multitude" of all sorts of nations, religions, and trades, as another tract put it.[77] The English, freeborn subjects with their own rights, trades, and occupations, could not tolerate such unconscionable encroachments by the subjects of other kings or states.[78] Such attacks did not go unanswered: John Tutchin's poem *The Foreigners* (1700), for example, provoked Defoe's reply in *The True-Born Englishman* (1701), the definitive rebuttal to the carping of the xenophobes, and the only work in this exchange to escape oblivion. But the polemical offensive was powerful.

The most vehement of this wave of attacks on foreigners appeared as a printed version of a speech ostensibly delivered in the Commmons by Sir John Knight, Tory MP for Bristol. The speech was said to have been given in 1694 during the debates on a bill for a general naturalization. Its author, who had been knighted in 1682 for his exertions against the Dissenters, was at the time of the speech in correspondence with St. Germains, and he displayed his Jacobite zeal with a fierce virtuosity. Knight had the speech printed and distributed throughout the kingdom in hopes of raising a popular clamor. The tract failed to foment the sought-for disturbances, but Knight achieved his ultimate end. The House declared the tract a printed libel, ordered it burned by the common hangman, and censured its author; but the dangers of naturalization had been widely publicized, and the naturalization bill of that year was defeated.[79]

John Knight deftly enlisted all the principal objections to the admission of foreign settlers in an argument that culminated in a scarcely camouflaged denunciation of William III. As Knight declared in the climax to his speech, a general naturalization would

> bring as great afflictions on this nation as ever fell upon the Egyptians, and one of their plagues we have at this time very severe upon us; I mean, that of their land bringing forth frogs in abundance, even in the chambers of their kings: for there is no entering the courts of St. James's and Whitehall, the palaces of our hereditary kings, for the great noise and croaking of the frog-landers.[80]

Knight concluded with a motion to "first kick this bill out of the House, and then foreigners out of the kingdom."

The author of *An Answer to the Pretended Speech* (1694) denounced Knight's diatribe as a "Jesuitical and New Romish" work "crammed with lies or prevaracations." The means to profit by the settlement of foreigners, the tract argued, was to receive them not with bitter hatred but with open minds and hearts. The more liberally they were received, the more benefit they would be to the nation. Knight's Jacobite libels were an attempt to incite a popular uproar against foreigners, but the potential for a successful general naturalization lay in precisely the opposite spirit. What galled Knight, the tract claimed, was that immigrants would swear against popery. Would he prefer that they abjured Presbytery? As this defender of the government observed, the spite against foreign Protestants flowed from their firmness to William and the ministry. Knight could inspire genuine fears of foreigners only in those to whom he would lend his "Jacobite spectacles: the one of which I suppose to be a magnifying, and the other a multiplying glass."[81]

The denunciations hurled against immigrants by Knight and other pamphleteers reflected not only partisan but deeper ideological objections to the admission of foreigners. Although the diatribes of Tories, High Churchmen, and Country partisans applied most immediately to the Dutch, they were no less true of other groups of foreign Protestants, whose loyalties naturally lay with William and his Whig ministers. No lasting alliance could exist between immigrants and the High Church Tories, in whose eyes the religion of the foreign Protestants was as much anathema as that of the English

Dissenters. Nor was understanding likely between the landed gentry and those who, as aliens, could not own a square foot of land, and who were instrumental in establishing the new commercial order that threatened the traditional roots of power that lay in the country.[82] The monied interest of the City, dominated by Whigs and wealthy immigrant merchants and financiers, supported the government and the king's war policy. Foreigners worked in concert with the Whigs to effect the revolutionary changes in finance of the 1690s and thereafter. No more potent symbol of those changes existed than the Bank of England, founded in 1694, and modeled on the Bank of Amsterdam. Immigrant foreigners invested heavily in the variety of debt instruments created during these heady days of Revolution finance.[83] The alliance of immigrant Protestants and Whigs, forged in the political turmoil of James II's reign, was tempered in the difficult years of the 1690s to a resiliency that endured beyond the middle of the eighteenth century. The Tory hostility to foreign immigrants proved equally long-lasting.

Openly ideological arguments sometimes surfaced in the controversy, but much of the polemical cut and thrust continued to revolve around economic issues. Foreigners had come not for the sake of religion, argued the author of *The Rights and Liberties of Englishmen Asserted* (1701), but to exchange their poverty for the comforts of English prosperity. In view of the fawning treatment of foreigners, it was a wonder that "all the Roman Catholic beggars, banditties, and runnagadoes" in Europe had not arrived as pretended French Protestants.[84] The author of *A Brief History of Trade* (1702) groaned that unemployment so oppressed the nation that forty men stood ready to fill every small place that came open. Trade had declined precipitously, and there was not enough work for more than two-thirds of the people. Yet the folly of naturalization, an exotic idea imported from Holland, continued to be discussed. Compassion demanded the reception of genuine religious refugees, but most immigrants in the past had come hungry for the high wages that they could earn in England, and had undermined the labors of English tradesmen. The "inundation" of foreigners, most of them "of the meanest rank, and not much qualified above common beggars," had increased poverty and frustrated the poor laws. Foreigners undersold the natives, never served their seven years' apprenticeship, and usurped trade. John Blanch blamed the prevailing power of foreigners in the government of the corporation of London for frustrating the privileges of English merchants.[85] Naturalizations, a broadside from the City of London charged in 1699, betrayed the "rights of the younger brothers" whose opportunities in trade were increasingly seized by foreign interlopers. The quantity of employment was fixed, and every foreign tradesman had got his place by "knock[ing] one of our natives on the head."[86] No more people were wanted to work the land, Samuel Johnson argued, and there were already more hands in manufactures than could be employed—on the contrary, the nation suffered from a "glut of men." The commercial connections of foreigners were worthless, Johnson declared, since they traded only in "outlandish frippery and foreign knacks."[87]

Had not foreign merchants ruined their English counterparts, John Knight demanded in his inflammatory rhetoric? The Act of Navigation would be nullified by a free naturalization, the practice of sending the younger sons of gentlemen abroad as merchants' factors would be frustrated, and cunning foreigners would return to their own country laden with the plunder of their transitory stay in England.[88] Because of the dearness of provisions and the general lack of employment, native English artisans were already "half-starved" and grew more miserable with each passing day. More commodities were made in England, he claimed, than could be consumed at home or abroad. Should English artisans starve while Parliament let in strangers to live in garrets, pay no taxes, and undersell them? None of the 40,000 French in England had settled on the land to supply the lack of husbandmen, Knight claimed, nor would any other immigrants attracted by a general naturalization act.[89]

Satire as well as economic argument became a weapon in the war of words against foreigners after the Revolution. In doggerel verse *A Satyr against the French* (1691) declared that the Huguenots had demonstrated their gratitude for their kind reception by undermining the nation's trade and working cheaper than native tradesmen could. Englishmen could not live as ascetics, eating roots, and thanks to foreigners they faced beggary or starvation. *The Satyr* amplified the cry of the English laborers that foreigners would eat the bread out of their mouths. In *An Elegy on the Death of Trade* (1698), foreigners received similar abuse for usurping English trade. A satirist in 1694 suggested that "since foreigners have naturalized and adopted all our money, it is but reasonable that we should adopt and naturalize some of their men."[90]

Beyond economic considerations, the enemies of naturalization warned that foreign settlers would be enemies to the English state.[91] Naturalized immigrants would be politically disaffected, Samuel Johnson maintained: at worst a permanent Trojan horse of potential enemies, at best a political "dead-weight to the nation." Johnson, amongst others, urged that foreigners should be kept out of the kingdom, or expelled if they came in any numbers.[92] All were spies, charged another pamphleteer, ready to betray England's secrets.[93] A cranky tract of 1693 even accused the French and Dutch immigrants of a conspiracy to rise in rebellion with their 8,000 cases of small pistols, presumably of foreign manufacture.[94] The extravagant charity to the French refugees, another pamphlet charged, had allowed secret enemies to enter the kingdom, papists who would not qualm at taking a false oath and who were tools of the French king. Some 45,000 French Protestants had deluged London, but more than twice that number of French papists were employed as valets de chambre, cooks, and governesses, all biding their time till they could abet a French invasion by burning the city. The problem could only be redressed by seizing the effects of the French papists, expelling their owners, and sending the French Protestants to Ireland.[95]

Could anyone of sense and reason, demanded one xenophobic pamphlet-eer, "be so barbarous to his own bowels" as to undo his "natural-fellow-free-born subjects for any interloping canary-birds, or naturalized foreigners?" Would the clatter of wooden shoes resound on English streets?[96] No amount of persecution, *The Rights and Liberties* argued, could make the French Protestants enemies to their native country, and naturalizing them would not turn them to the English interest.[97] Wartime vulnerability to paranoia then excited polemicists to paint the most lurid picture of the threats posed by immigrants.

Eager to quash any hopes of assimilation, the opposition press presented a case of irreconcilably clashing cultures. Naturalized immigrants, the "new-made English (yet Dutchmen still)," as John Knight sneered, would never live up to their oaths of allegiance. Foreigners refused to mix with the En-glish, the author of *The Rights and Liberties of Englishmen* claimed, herding together and keeping a "general correspondency" in trade. Foreigners em-ployed only other foreigners, to the further loss of English workers. "All their charity centers in their own circle, . . . but their poor you are sure to have forever." These "scum," these "caterpillars," these "vermin," number-ing nearly 300,000, should, before there was "little or no English blood left amongst us," be sent to the wilderness of the colonies and out of England.[98] Thus an ugly xenophobia, inspired principally by partisanship, fear, and cultural distaste, though at times bordering on racism, had come by the turn of the century to inform at least the fringes of the debate over the admission of immigrants.

The proponents of naturalization, economists and others, were not deaf to the new wave of hostility against foreigners. Englishmen, complained Roger Coke, perversely presumed to "love Englishmen above all others," a prejudice that cost their nation dearly. Coke dismissed fears of popish immigrants, audaciously urging that Catholic artisans be welcomed: they would not be popish priests, but strangers to the English people and lan-guage, too busy earning their bread to threaten the Church of England. Their children could be made good Anglicans.[99] The anonymous author of *A Discourse of the Nature, Use, and Advantage of Trade* (1694) agreed that England's religious and political settlement would be safeguarded if naturalized foreigners were only required to take an oath and declaration of allegiance. Religious duties, he declared, should serve secular ends.[100] Foreigners who lived meanly and in garrets to avoid English antagonism, another pamphleteer argued, would live less poorly, marry and have fami-lies, and pay house-rent and taxes if they were sincerely encouraged.[101] Economic writers had begun to recognize the formidable obstacle to a suc-cessful naturalization posed by these fears and antagonisms, and began to plead for the renunciation of the spirit of hostility to strangers.

The immigrants themselves were not without a voice, and it is fitting to conclude our survey of the controversy on the eve of the General Naturalization Act of 1709 by attending to their response to the atmosphere of growing animosity. To the slanders heaped upon foreigners came an answer from Hilary Reneu in his preface to the second English edition of Jean Claude's *Les Plaintes des Protestants* (1707), one of the seminal texts of the Huguenot diaspora.[102] The French Protestants in England, Reneu told his readers, had been deeply disappointed that no concessions in favor of Protestants in France had been incorporated in the Peace of Ryswick in 1697. The refugees had then to abandon almost all hope of returning to their homeland, and the animosity of the English towards them therefore stung them all the more deeply. The refugees, Reneu defiantly argued, had increased all the revenues of the kingdom by their trade and correspondence with acquaintances settled in other lands. England had made an unequivocal gain, he claimed, by the wealth, amounting to at least £100 per person on average, that the refugees had brought with them from France. Landlords could attest to the benefit from the settlement of the French refugees, for the rents that they paid totaled perhaps £80,000 per year. The refugees paid both parish and national taxes, and increased the consumption of manufactures and the products of the land. The French Protestants in England paid the rent on their churches and the salaries of their ministers, in contrast to their brethren refugees in Holland. Those who had been naturalized had paid the proper charges to become legally English.[103]

The French Protestants offered this long list of their economic contributions to England, Reneu explained, by way of retort to those who accused them of taking the bread from Englishmen's mouths. Cunning political and religious partisans voiced such accusations only in order to render the refugees odious to the common people. He appealed to the Whig ministry, if only in the interests of its populationist economic policy, to stifle the truculent abuse the French suffered from the High Church party:

> if therefore all politicians agree, that multitudes of people make the glory of kings, and the riches of a country; why are then so many libels suffered here to be published, in opposition to those general maxims? The refugees think them under an obligation to declare it; and let the public know, that this evil proceeds from the enemies of their religion.[104]

The Whigs could not silence the opponents of naturalization, but the year after Reneu stated his plea on behalf of immigrants, a Parliament controlled by the Whig ministry at the height of its power finally passed the General Naturalization Act. The policy that parliamentarians, pamphleteers, and economic experts had so long debated would be put to the test, for in the wake of the act came the immigration of over ten thousand Germans from the Rhine Valley.

5

The Palatine Migration: The Great Experiment

In the space of a few months in the year 1709 thousands of Germans from the lands on both sides of the Rhine, most of them desperately poor, some near starvation, arrived in London. They had traveled from their homelands down the Rhine to Holland. From there they had taken ship to England, most of them at the expense of the English government. They believed that the English queen would transport them to a new life in the American plantations. By the end of the summer about 13,000 had arrived. The Whig ministry, though it at first encouraged the immigration, soon found itself burdened with the enormous expense of supporting hundreds of large German families. Thousands of people for whom no employment could be found in the fields or workshops of England, and whose hopes of being transported immediately to the American plantations were crushed, became not an asset to the nation and the ministry, but an acute embarrassment. Few could speak English, only a handful had any trade skills, and most were unable to work owing to age or ill-health. After months of futile attempts, it proved impossible to incorporate the immigrants into England. They were dispersed to Ireland, to America, and to other corners of the British dominions. Many, perhaps most, were eventually sent back to Germany. The immigration for which English economic writers had been pleading for decades proved, when it came at last, an unmitigated disaster.[1]

The immigration started only weeks after the passage of the General Naturalization Act of 1709, the culmination of all the proposals made since the Restoration. When the Germans began to land in large numbers in May of that year they arrived in a country that had not experienced a large-scale immigration for twenty-five years; a country in which the issue of the admission of foreign settlers, after decades of debate in economic tracts and in Parliament, had become polarized along party lines;[2] and a country whose natives had demonstrated towards earlier immigrants their hostility to foreign intruders who came to establish themselves in England, as they complained bitterly, to "eat the bread from the mouths" of Englishmen.

The "poor Palatines" the German immigrants were called in England, on account of both their poverty and their misfortune. They came in the greatest number from the Rhenish or Lower Palatinate, but also from many of the small principalities of western Germany. They came from both sides of the Rhine, from Hanau, Franconia, the archbishoprics of Mainz and Trier, from Hesse-Darmstadt, Nassau, Alsace, Baden, and other regions. From Switzerland north to the confluence of the Mosel and the Rhine, and eastwards far up the rivers Main and Neckar, people poured out of Germany and down the Rhine to Holland.[3] The causes of the sudden and vast emigration remain as obscure today as they were to the officials in both Germany and England who tried first to control and then stop the exodus. The devastations of war, religious oppression, economic hardship, and a campaign to encourage migration all played their part in provoking the "Palatines" to leave their own countries.[4] Unable even to earn their bread in their homeland, the Germans found the promise or even the chance of finding a livelihood in another country enough to draw them forth in their thousands on what they thought was a pilgrimage to a new world, but what became for most only a passage to years of misery.

The devastation from war that had wracked the Rhineland for decades was one of the most important causes of the migration. Marshal Turenne had ravaged the Palatinate in 1674, and in the winter of 1688–89 the French army had carried out a ruthless and systematic devastation of the region. Trier, Worms, and Speyer were laid waste. Marshal Villars ravaged the area once again in 1707. In April 1709, at the moment that the emigrants were leaving their homelands, the French again threatened the Rhineland principalities with invasion.[5] In their appeals for the assistance of the English queen and her subjects, the Palatines complained most bitterly of the ravages and exactions of the French, and English sympathy for the Germans depended largely upon their role as the victims of French aggression, an image that they diligently cultivated.[6] Moreover, the English felt a lingering connection with the Palatinate because of the dynastic tie established in the seventeenth century through Elizabeth, the daughter of James I.

English sympathy for the Palatines also arose from the belief, however ill-founded, that they were refugees from religious persecution. In 1709 the German lands still operated under the principle of *cuius regio, eius religio*: three confessions were officially recognized, Catholic, Lutheran, and Reformed (Calvinist), and a prince's subjects were to conform to his religion. But the doctrine represented a principle rather than a reality. In the Rhenish Palatinate all three confessions were actively and publicly practiced. Moreover, there had been an alternation of the faith of the recent Electors Palatine that had made a mockery of the ideal of religious uniformity.[7] Johann Wilhelm, the Elector at the time of the emigration of 1709, was a devout Catholic. Although he did not adopt a policy of overt persecution, his Protestant subjects for some years felt his disfavor as he connived at the harassments and persecutions perpetrated by his magistrates. These local officials, under

Jesuit influence, and acting with considerable independence from the Elector, made it their program to extirpate Calvinism.[8] The Elector himself, however, was no mere passive observer of the oppressions suffered by his Protestant subjects. In 1698 he expelled the French Protestants who had settled in the Palatinate a decade earlier; his motives, though cloaked in the pretense of avoiding hostility with France, were probably largely religious.[9] In 1702 the Protestant Estates of the Empire appealed to England, its most powerful and staunchly Protestant ally, to discourage the oppressions in the Palatinate. The Elector responded by issuing two edicts, in April and July of that year, to stop the persecutions committed by his magistrates. But the edicts proved ineffectual, and Queen Anne wrote to the Elector in February 1703 that as allies of the Emperor, all Protestant princes of the Reformed religion must present a united front against the common enemy of France and Spain, and that the local officials of the electorate must be ordered to stop harassing the Elector's Protestant subjects.[10] Finally, in November 1705 Johann Wilhelm issued a declaration in which he granted full liberty of conscience to all his subjects, Lutheran, Calvinist, and Catholic. From that time serious oppression of Protestants seems to have ceased.[11]

In June 1709, after the migration to England was well under way, the Protestant Consistory in the Palatinate issued a statement citing the 1705 declaration promising liberty of conscience, and dismissing as a "groundless pretence" the claims of religious persecution made by some of those who had gone down the Rhine in the hopes of settling in the New World.[12] The statement was issued, however, at the Elector's direction, so its reliability is less than certain. It is probably true that some of the Palatines were what Trevelyan called "genuine religious refugees of a good type";[13] but the vast majority had migrated to find a place where they could earn their bread, perhaps not itself an ignoble motive. Anton Wilhelm Boehme, pastor of the German Court Chapel of St. James, wrote that religious zeal was not the reason for the migration. Although he admitted that there was some harassment of Protesants in the Palatinate, he insisted that it was not important enough to justify emigration.[14] In England, however, the belief persisted that the Protestants of the Palatinate were persecuted by their prince, and Defoe wrote in the *Review* that "the Protestant religion seems to approach to an utter extirpation on that side." This belief was partly responsible for the charity that the Palatines enjoyed when they first arrived in England.[15]

The devastation of war led to the economic hardship from which the Germans thought they were escaping. Moreover, many of the German princes levied exorbitant taxes to support their ambitions to model their courts on Versailles, as well as to repair the devastation caused by the royal occupant of that palace. The severely cold winter of 1708–9 multiplied the suffering of their subjects. A bitterly cold frost seized all of Europe, and in England the ice fairs on the frozen surface of the Thames invited comparison to those held during the Great Frost of 1683–84.[16] But unlike the earlier frost, that of 1709 was followed by a poor spring and summer, so that food prices rose precipitously. The result was a dearth year, perhaps the worst in the late seventeenth and early eighteenth centuries. Bread sold at double its normal price. Economic conditions in Germany were similarly distressing; the severe winter had been especially disastrous for the many Palatines who were vinedressers, and who were left without the means to feed their families.[17]

Yet more than poverty and the hope of a better place to settle inspired the Palatines to leave Germany. The migration was not a dispersal, but a folk movement to one destination: England. Emigration to British North America via England was systematically promoted in southwestern Germany. English agents canvassed the Rhineland to encourage the Germans to leave their homeland, to travel to England, and from there to take ship to settle in the English colonies in North America, particularly in Pennsylvania and the Carolinas. Papers were dispersed and fixed on their church doors promising that if they came to England the queen would send them on to the plantations at her expense.[18] It is certain that the Lords Proprietors of the Carolinas encouraged the emigration by having broadsides distributed in Germany that promised very favorable land settlements in their colony, and other propagandists may have been active as well. Emigration to the North American colonies had fallen off decades earlier, and colonial promoters like William Penn sought settlers from the continent with pamphlets and other encouragements. As one of the original Proprietors under the charter of 1663, Shaftesbury, as we have seen, stressed the vital need of the colony for people, sponsoring the flattering descriptions of the Carolinas written by Locke. Pamphlets like *A Brief Description of the Province of Carolina* (1666) appeared in English to encourage emigration. John Lawson, the surveyor-general of the colony, published his *A New Voyage to Carolina* (1709), a fuller account than had up to then appeared, in the year of the Palatine migration. The value of the Proprietors' holdings depended upon the number of settlers they could obtain. Yet the report of the governor and council of the province to the Proprietors in September 1708 estimated the number of inhabitants at less than 10,000, and urged a policy to encourage "honest laborious people to come among us."[19]

Other interests may have been involved in promoting the migration. Two Swiss agents, François Louis Michel and George Ritter, were in negotation with the Proprietors in London, and may have been involved in the project. Later in 1709 they led a group of 650 Palatine settlers to the Carolinas. The Proprietors apparently hoped that when the Germans arrived in London their passage to America would be paid by the English government, thus gaining them settlers at almost no cost. The English Resident at Frankfurt-am-Main, Henry Davenant, interviewed Germans from various places and distributed a book that encouraged the people to migrate to the Carolinas.[20] The Proprietors may have brought about Davenant's promotion of the migration. But some evidence indicates that the English ministry itself at least connived at the advertisements and leaflets that appeared in Germany. The possible involvement of the English government in the affair led a German historian writing at the beginning of this century to accuse the English, not without some reason, of "double-dealing" and "cold-blooded falsehood" in their treatment of the migrants who had been enticed away from their homes by false promises.[21] Whether the government directly promoted the migration or not, it prolonged it by its generosity to the emigrants and by providing their passage from Rotterdam. The Palatines became the unwitting subjects of an experiment in immigration policy whose signal failure contributed to the fall of the government that had sponsored it.[22]

When a committee of the House of Commons investigated the Palatine immigration in 1711, its examination of several of the immigrants revealed that

> there were books and papers dispersed in the Palatinate, with the Queen's picture before the books, and the title pages in letters of gold (which from thence they called the Golden Book) to encourage them to come to England, in order to be sent to Carolina, or other her Majesty's plantations, to be settled there; the book is chiefly a commendation of that country.[23]

A book encouraging the migration circulated widely in the Rhine Valley, but whether it was a product of the Carolina Proprietors' project to entice settlers to America, or was of a different, and perhaps native German, origin, remains uncertain. It is most likely that the "Golden Book" of the committee report was that written by Joshua de Kocherthal, *Aussführlich und Umständlicher Bericht von der Berühmten Landschaft Carolina in dem Engelländischen America.*[24] Kocherthal's *Bericht* praised Carolina as a field for migration, and suggested that if German migrants petitioned the English queen for permission to make the crossing to England, they might be granted free passage on a royal ship from Holland. Kocherthal wrote from personal experience, for he had led a group of sixty-one Germans to England and from there to New York in the preceding year. He included in his book a letter from one of that party dated July 1708 that declared that the queen would support and naturalize all those who came out of Germany.[25] The small migration of 1708 played a crucial role therefore in provoking the mass movement of the following year. It presented the Germans of the Rhineland with an example, energetically publicized by Kocherthal, of the English queen's benevolence and nurtured dreams of a settlement in the New World.

In February 1708 Kocherthal, a Lutheran minister, after having failed to obtain the permission of the Elector Palatine to emigrate, applied to Davenant at Frankfurt for passes to enable his small group of German followers to enter England and from there to pass on to the American plantations. Davenant cautiously refused the passes on the ground that the Elector would be displeased, and wrote to London for instructions. Secretary of State

Henry Boyle responded ambiguously that the Germans could not be encouraged, either by money or passes, "in any public way," though their settlement in the colonies would be "very acceptable" and for the public good.[26] What Kocherthal was told unofficially cannot be known, but he set off at the head of his small party with apparent confidence that they would be assisted in reaching their destination. Those hopes were partially realized when the English Resident at Rotterdam issued the group passes for the crossing to Harwich at no charge.

As soon as he reached London with his followers, Kocherthal presented a petition representing that the group had come from the area of the Rhine and Neckar, had been rendered destitute by the devastations of the French army in the preceding year, and wished passage and assistance in establishing themselves in America.[27] On 20 April Boyle referred the petition to the Board of Trade, the body responsible not only for economic policy but for the administration of the American colonies. Two days later, after having heard Kocherthal, the Board informed Boyle that the group had no means of subsistence without Her Majesty's immediate relief. After a delay of two weeks the ministry resolved to grant the pleas of the Germans, and on 10 May warrants were issued for the payment of the group's support until they were transported to New York, and they were ordered to be made free denizens without charge. Fourteen more Germans joined the original group after Kocherthal's petition on their behalf in June. With Lord Lovelace, the governor of the province, the group set sail in October for New York.[28]

After orchestrating the small emigration of 1708, Kocherthal returned to London. He appeared before the Board of Trade at the end of 1709 to advocate a proposed project for establishing a wine industry in Carolina with German immigrants.[29] However, he took no direct part in encouraging the migration of 1709, rather, his influence on the mass exodus of that year came from his *Bericht*, which by 1709 had reached a fourth edition. The book was published in Frankfurt, the center from which news of the English colonies in America spread with the help of Davenant, and it was a splendid advertisement for the English plantations. Written in the flattering tone of modern promotional brochures for holiday or retirement communities, the tract praised the Carolinas for the healthfulness of their climate, their peace and security, the fruitfulness of the land and the vigor of the economy, the fishing and hunting—even the surprising enthusiasm of the English inhabitants for learning to speak German. Kocherthal claimed in the preface to the 1709 edition that the first edition had appeared in 1706 and sold out quickly, and that his account of the Carolinas was based on information that he had gathered in England in 1704. The book, however, cannot have been the only one of its kind to have circulated in Germany in 1709, since it contained none of the express promises from the queen that the immigrants insisted that they had received. Indeed, the *Bericht* even suggested that those who could not afford to pay for their own passage from England to America could become indentured servants; it made no explicit promises. Yet the kind treatment given the migrants of 1708 itself acted as a strong encouragement to the migration, and Bishop Burnet thought that the generosity shown to that small group, and the inflated accounts of their good fortune that circulated in Germany, provoked the mass migration of the following year.[30]

Nor was the immigration of 1708 the first example of such a project for colonial settlement. A scheme to settle 500 Swiss Protestants in Pennsylvania at English expense had been considered by the Board of Trade in 1706. Although the project was never carried out, the Board agreed that the Crown would pay the passage of the settlers from Rotterdam to America.[31] William Penn had for years been active in promoting the emigration of Germans to Pennsylvania, and he was identified by several contemporaries as the author of the Palatine migration, though there is no evidence that he was in any way involved in its encouragement.[32]

Finally, there was the newly-passed General Naturalization Act of 1709. Why did the bill of 1709 pass when its many predecessors had failed? Economic conditions had not changed greatly. The war on the continent dragged on with no foreseeable end. The Protestant interest stood on fairly firm ground. Complaints of depopulation had if anything become less strident. The answer lies in party politics. The 1708 general elections returned what Secretary Sunderland called the most Whig Parliament since 1688.[33] Whigs also dominated the Lords, and the coalition of the Whig Junto and the Marlborough–Godolphin ministry pressed through Parliament a number of Whig measures that had long languished. The General Naturalization Act was one of them. Edward Wortley Montagu, a staunch Whig and the husband of the celebrated letter-writer, moved for the introduction of a bill on 4 February 1709, citing the example of the King of Prussia's invitation to French refugees who had "fertilized an almost barren country." The bill was presented in the Commons on 14 February, and ten days later, after the counsel for the City of London had spoken against the measure on the ground that it would rob the City of its duties, it was read a second time and committed. In spite of the opposition of the Tory Earl of Nottingham, who sponsored a proposed amendment that would have required those naturalized to receive the sacrament in the Church of England rather than in any Protestant church, the bill passed on a decisive division of 203 to 77. In the Lords, Bishop Burnet spoke for the bill and it passed without amendment and with very little opposition. The bill received the royal assent on 23 March.[34]

After the fall of the Whig government in the summer of 1710, and the elections of that year, the Tory House of Commons blamed the disastrous Palatine migration on the naturalization act that the Whigs had passed. Certainly the issue split down party lines: the Whigs defended the act they had passed and took great efforts to make a success of the Palatine immigration, while the Tories uttered bitter complaints at the coming of the Palatines and refused to support attempts to find them employment in England. Professor Dickinson has explored in detail the partisan battle that made pawns of the poor Palatines.[35] But the Tory argument that the naturalization act was responsible for bringing the Palatines to England is untenable. Immigrants as poor as the Palatines could have gained little or nothing by becoming naturalized subjects, and almost none of them took advantage of the act. Of the 933 persons known to have been naturalized under the act in the year 1709 almost all bore French names.[36] More importantly, the Germans could not have learned of the act before they set out from their homelands, since it was passed only at the end of March, and the first group of immigrants arrived in May of that year, after several months' travel. Nor do the German sources mention the prospect of naturalization as a motive for the migrants. The Act of 1709 did not provoke the Palatine migration, although the disastrous results of the arrival of so many poor people in England at a time of economic dislocation certainly led its repeal, and discredited for decades to come any scheme that proposed to increase England's population and stimulate its trade by naturalizing foreigners.

The migration to New York in 1708 of Kocherthal and his small party can scarcely be called an overture to the sudden outpouring of people that came to England in the following year. The epic migration of 1709 was all the more remarkable for the short space of time in which it took place, for the first Palatines arrived in England in May and by the end of October the immigration had almost ceased. The first omen of the migration came in a "Memorial Relating to the Poor Protestants from the Palatinate," written in French and received through the German post in late December 1708 by James Dayrolle, British Resident at the Hague, who would soon become a principal figure in the promotion and management of the migration. The memorial stated that a number of families were traveling to England in order to pass over to the American colonies, and that 800 or 900 people had already arrived at Rotterdam after fleeing from persecution and oppression. It pleaded that the Duke of Marlborough obtain from the queen free passage for the poor people "as well as the great number soon to follow." The Palatines were embarrassed by their poverty, the memorial added, but most were peasants, robust, vigorous, and fit to work. If the group of Palatines described in the memorial crossed to England it did so unofficially, for no further reference to them exists. It is more likely that the memorial was sent in anticipation of the 900 Palatines that Dayrolle reported as having arrived at Rotterdam in the middle of April. If so, it was perhaps intended by those who were encouraging the migration and distributing advertisements in Germany— particularly the agents of the Proprietors of the Carolinas—as a means to prepare the English government for the waves of immigrants that arrived in Rotterdam several months later.[37]

The true beginning of the migration came when Dayrolle granted passes on 29 March to sixty families, who numbered about two hundred persons, and who wished to settle in Pennsylvania. The Dutch Admiralty in Rotterdam had already promised them assistance in paying for their crossing to England. Dayrolle on the same day wrote to Secretary Boyle in London that the Dutch had under consideration a general naturalization act similar to that just enacted in England. He implied that the German migrants might be lost to the Dutch if they were not snatched up by England. Marlborough had been informed of the Palatines' circumstances, and had promised to appeal to the queen on their behalf.[38] So the migration had begun, and its momentum did not slacken until the end of the summer.

In mid-April Dayrolle issued passes to two groups of several hundred Palatines, writing to Boyle that they were all "strong and laborious" people, and that they were "followed by a great many others."[39] The words were suspiciously similar to those used in the memorial of December, and give the first hint that Dayrolle's part in the transportation of the Germans was not without dissimulation; for when the Germans arrived in London it was found that very few were fit to work. A few days later Boyle informed Dayrolle that the transport ships used to carry troops and supplies to the Continent were to receive the poor people on board to carry them to England.[40] The ministry had determined not only to receive the Palatines but to provide their transportation from Holland, so desirable a set of immigrants did they seem from a distance. At the end of April, 852 of the Germans set sail for England on four government transports. Their subsistence had been paid for by private charity collected in Holland, for they were too poor to buy even their own provisions, much less to pay for their passage across the Channel.[41]

The magnitude of the migration had not yet become apparent to the English officials involved, but German princes fearful of a costly loss of population had already tried to stop the exodus of their subjects. Bans on propaganda and recruiting of migrants proved ineffectual. The borders of the patchwork of German principalities lay so close to one another that authorities could stop neither agents and promoters, nor emigrants.[42] On 28 April the desperate Elector Palatine published an order forbidding his subjects to emigrate on pain of death and confiscation of their goods.[43] The order had little effect. Ernst Ludwig, Landgraf of Hesse, whose principality bordered the Palatinate to the north, published an order at the end of April, less savage but no more successful, that required those who wished to emigrate to produce a memorial stating the reasons why they wished to leave and to obtain official permission before departing. The order also forbade them to sell their goods without official consent. Many emigrants must by that time already have departed, and these official measures failed to stem the flow of people northwards. The journey down the Rhine to Holland took perhaps eight weeks, and the large numbers of migrant poor excited curiosity in those who saw them making their slow way through the innumerable toll points and down the river. Some of their countrymen gave the migrants food, money, even clothing; others robbed them of the small savings they had managed to bring away with them.[44] Many had nothing left to lose, their only possession consisting of a letter of recommendation from their homes, signed and witnessed by local officials or clergy.[45] In a spirit of hope they set out in search of a new life in America, confident of the benevolent charity that they would receive from the English queen.

In the Hague, Dayrolle learned on 6 May of the Elector's proclamation forbidding emigration and of his order that two boatloads of people on their way down the Rhine be seized and imprisoned. Many had by that time sought to make their way to Rotterdam by land rather than risk apprehension on the river. More arrived in Rotterdam every day.[46] The ministry apparently had few scruples about offending its German ally, for although Davenant at Frankfurt was given leave to assure the Elector that the queen was not encouraging his subjects to leave, the queen herself did not write.[47] The English government had committed itself to receiving people whose emigration it knew had been proscribed by its ally. Only later did it learn of how little value they would be to England.

From the small principality of Nassau-Dillenburg a set of documents has survived relating to the 1709 migration.[48] The principality lay to the north of Frankfurt, and shared the Rhine as common border with the Rhenish Palatinate to the south. It comprised three towns and perhaps twenty villages, from whose small population more than a hundred people emigrated in 1709.[49] The documents are the result of an order issued to local officials on 23 May by the Elector Wilhelm that those who wished to undertake the expedition "to Pennsylvania" should be discouraged, and the sale of their goods forbidden. Accompanying the order was a decree that required from any person who wished to leave an official memorial with responses to a set of questions.[50]

The replies to the interrogatories provide a small but detailed sample of the emigrants. Of the nineteen heads of families whose responses survive, the oldest was sixty-three, the youngest twenty-five, and the mean age was thirty-six. All families were Lutheran, with the exception of three Reformed and one Catholic family. Most of the families included at least one child. All the emigrants stated that they wished to leave because of the bad times, the hardship caused by the war, or the high price of bread. The recurrent references to the afflictions of war summed up the migrants' complaints, although several respondents simply stated that they wished to leave in the hope of improving their fortune. None of the replies mentioned religion as a motive.[51]

The news of the English colonies in America had arrived in the small principality at the beginning of May, when some learned of the emigration from their Palatine neighbours.[52] One of the petitioners had seen the English Resident at Frankfurt and had returned with a sheaf of advertisements that he then distributed, and several others declared that they had heard of the Carolinas at Frankfurt. A carpenter from Eberhaussen, it was said, had come to encourage the migration, and had expounded the contents of the books about the Carolinas that circulated in the region.[53] The reports of the New World were disseminated primarily through the churches, and one of the officials in charge of collecting the memorials reported to the Elector that a preacher named Diess incited people to migrate by his stirring comparisons of the migration to America with the exodus of Israel from the bondage of Egypt—with Queen Anne presumably playing the part of Moses in parting the waters of both the Channel and the Atlantic.[54] Officials reported that some thought that the costs of their journey would be reimbursed when they reached London, others that the queen would give them bread until they could earn their own, and one that the queen would advance them the money necessary for the undertaking. None had the means to pay his own passage to America.[55] Of those who stated their occupations, all but one, a shepherd, were artisans. A shoemaker complained that because of the hard times he was forced to work for other masters, and that he could scarcely afford the very dear bread. Some petitioners were themselves immigrants to the German lands that they now sought to leave. Hardship was the common force that led them all to set out for a new life.[56]

In addition to the small number whose interrogatories survive, there were many who simply applied to Electoral officials for permission to leave.[57] After the report of the official concerned, the Elector issued, with few exceptions, a decree to allow the petitioner to leave on condition that he pay his debts. Perhaps it was thought futile to forbid the emigration of people whose disobedience would cost them so little—in any case the authorities in Nassau-Dillenburg imposed no draconian measures of the sort attempted elsewhere. The decrees became shorter and shorter as the summer wore on, until they consisted only of the word *dismissi* and the date. In the petitions, as in the longer depositions, the reason almost universally given for emigration was poverty and the hardship of the times. The Elector did not attempt to keep these destitute people in his principality against their will, but his complaints to his officials of their failure to pay their creditors, the loss of the number of his subjects, and the diminution of his revenues, became more strident as the migration continued.[58] As in the Palatinate, the exodus seems to have ended more on account of the coming of autumn than because of any measures taken by Wilhelm or by the English government.

At this early stage the Palatines held considerable appeal as potential subjects, and attempts were made to divert the migrants from their course towards England. An edict of the King of Prussia issued on 2 May offered asylum to "Protestant refugees" from France "or any other place," and promised them free naturalization and full trading rights.[59] Frederick I thus sought to follow the example set by his father Frederick William, the Great Elector, whose generous reception of the French refugees at the time of the revocation of the Edict of Nantes had earned him lasting renown.[60] The Prussian edict did not refer to the Palatines expressly, but the timing of its promulgation leaves little doubt that it was intended to attract them. Yet they had left their homelands with the intention of settling in America, and few were diverted by such offers.

The numbers arriving in Holland continued to increase. Dayrolle wrote from The Hague on 10 May that about a thousand more had arrived at Rotterdam, and that Marlborough intended to order them all shipped on transports as soon as possible.[61] Adam Cardonnel, Marlborough's secretary, wrote to Boyle that Marlborough suggested Dayrolle be appointed to manage the transportations,[62] and on Cardonnel's authority Dayrolle appointed two Dutch merchants as commissioners to supervise the matter. The two Dutch commissioners, Hendrick van Toren and John Suderman, requested approval from Cardonnel the next day to embark 1,283 Palatines. They wrote that the convoy then at Rotterdam was to sail for England before authorization from London could arrive, and warned that the private charity money they had received from the Dutch had been exhausted.[63] Cardonnel approved the embarkation, assured the commissioners that they would be reimbursed, and instructed them to prepare lists of those sent across the Channel.[64] The ministry now assumed the entire charge of providing for and transporting the Germans. The transports could not carry all of those arriving, and packetboats were instructed to receive any who possessed a pass or note from Dayrolle.[65] Cardonnel wrote to Secretary Tilson at the Treasury that "the convoy being ready to sail, his Grace has thought fit, not to lose any time, to give orders for shipping them off, so that you may soon expect to hear of them on your side, where," he concluded with unintended irony, "you will know best what is to be done with them."[66] At the same time, reports came that three more large vessels full of immigrants had arrived at Cologne and were coming down the Rhine.[67]

Dayrolle received authority from London on 17 May to make all arrangements for the Palatines at the government's expense, on the basis of Marlborough's recommendations that it was "the best method of taking care of them."[68] The English ministry apparently viewed the reception of the Germans as a long-term project rather than as a charitable expedient, for they instructed Dayrolle to send further accounts of his expenses on behalf of the migrants from time to time.[69] Nor is there any doubt that the ministry knew from the outset that the immigrants wished to be transported to the colonies, not to be settled in England, and that they were too poor to pay their own passage. But the ministry had not foreseen the number of Germans who now arrived at Rotterdam at the rate of about one thousand each week.[70]

Meanwhile in London Sunderland wrote on 3 May to the Board of Trade to enlist its assistance in settling the newly-arrived Germans in England. His letter was seized upon by the subsequent Tory ministry as the seed of what had by then become the scandal of the Palatine migration. Indeed, it embodied the ministry's crucial decision to adopt the theories of economic writers on the advantages of immigration and to make them a part of government policy. If Britain's wealth, as had long been argued, could be augmented by the accession of foreign settlers, the Whig government had in the Germans the ideal body of people to vindicate the policy of encouraging foreign settlements that they had just endorsed by the passage of the General Naturalization Act. Poor German Protestants were coming to England in hopes of settling in the American plantations, Sunderland informed the Board, but the queen believed that

> it would be much more for the advantage of her kingdoms, if a method could be found to settle them here in such manner as they might get a comfortable livelihood, instead of sending them to the West Indies, that it would be a great encouragement to others to follow their example, and that this addition to the number of Her Majesty's subjects would in all probability produce a proportionable increase of their trade and manufactures.[71]

At last the aspirations of the economic writers for a naturalization of foreigners to stimulate English trade and increase the nation's population seemed about to be realized. The Palatine migration was to be an experiment conducted by the Whig ministry to test their theories. Sunderland ordered the Board to consider how and in what part of England the Palatines might best be settled. They were mostly husbandmen and laborers, he added, "which renders it the easier to dispose of them to the advantage of the public."[72] But the fallacy of such reasoning was soon revealed, for on the very day that Sunderland enlisted the help of the Board the first group of Palatines arrived in England.

Soon after their arrival, the first set of migrants presented a petition in which they recounted their ruin by war and other hardships, and the necessity that had compelled them to leave their homes. The petition stated that they had been encouraged to come to England by the English Resident in Frankfurt and by the earlier charity to their "neighbours."[73] They appealed for immediate assistance, and on 5 May Sunderland instructed the Board of Trade to prepare a report on their condition so that they could be supported by the queen's charity according to their need.[74] From the moment the Germans arrived in England, then, the ministry found it necessary to support them with public funds, though that support was expected to end as soon as the migrants had found employment.

The Board of Trade appointed two German-speaking Lutheran ministers to perform the inquiry requested by Sunderland. John Tribbeko, chaplain to the queen's late consort, Prince George of Denmark, and George Andrew Ruperti, the minister of the German Lutheran Church in the Savoy, reported that the first group of immigrants consisted of 210 families comprising a total of 852 persons. Most of the men were husbandmen or vinedressers. Thirty-three of the families were Roman Catholic. Tribekko and Ruperti reported that all but a very few suffered from great physical want—many were almost naked. Twenty or even thirty people sometimes shared a single room, the ministers explained, and the sick outnumbered the well.[75]

The immediate response to the appalling poverty of the Palatines revealed a generosity that continued throughout the episode. On 16 May a warrant was issued for the payment of sixteen pounds per day to the initial group of 852 persons, and arrangements were made for their lodging.[76] As their numbers multiplied, the immigrants' charge on the civil list rose rapidly, eventually reaching £138 per day.[77] Throughout the migration the queen showed a keen personal interest in the poor people's fate, and her involvement contributed to the ministry's vigilance in caring for the migrants. The queen had been devoted to her husband, Prince George, who was German by birth, and her grief had been profound when he had died on 28 October 1708, only a few months earlier. That Anne wished to aid the coreligionists of her late consort must have been apparent to the Whig ministry, which never found it easy to endear itself to her—and Tribbeko, the late Prince's private chaplain, may have exercised considerable influence in eliciting the charity that the Palatines soon enjoyed.

The number of immigrants arriving in London increased rapidly, and although a few of the earliest group had enough money to hire their own lodging, most could only take shelter where kindness offered it.[78] The first group collected near the Tower, in St. Katherine's, Tower Ditch, Wapping, Nightingale Lane, and East-Smithfield. As more arrived it was found necessary to hire barns in Camberwell, Lambeth, Kennington, Walworth, Stockwell, and other places, and the Crown turned over capacious ropehouses in Deptford to their use. A physician was sent among them to treat the many who lay ill.[79]

As available accommodation filled up, the Board of Trade began to discuss schemes for housing the Palatines in tents set up in uninhabited areas outside the city.[80] But the Board applied itself especially to the problem posed to it by Sunderland of how to make the Germans able to support themselves. It repeatedly enquired whether any of them could spin, and offered them help in setting up in that craft, including a supply of flax or wool if necessary.[81] Almost none of the Palatines had worked in textiles, but the Board could not transcend such stereotyped solutions. On 17 May it reported ominously to Sunderland that it found "great difficulties in proposing a method to employ them in such manner as they may be able to support themselves here."[82] A few days later the Board learned that only 200 of the men then arrived were able and fit to support themselves by working, and that only 100 of the women could knit or spin; the rest were too young, too old, or too infirm to work.[83] On 23 May it decided to settle the Palatines outside the city in the hope that they could be employed in the harvest: most of them were peasant husbandmen, and although this would not answer as a permanent solution, at least they could be set to work. But Tribbeko and Ruperti reported the same day that 1,300 more Germans had just arrived from Holland, and the increasing exasperation felt by the Board members leaps from the pages of their journal. The Board already feared that hostility toward the migrants because of their distressing condition would make their settlement in England even more difficult. When they received a report, certainly exaggerated, of the good state of health of the first group to land, the Board eagerly resolved to "get the same advertised in the newspapers."[84] Yet twenty-five of the first group of 852 had already died, and rumors that the immigrants might spread a contagion may already have begun to circulate.[85]

Tribbeko and Ruperti continued to make surveys of the Palatines as they arrived and to report their findings to the Board. The information they compiled provides a fairly detailed picture of about half of the total number of Germans who arrived in 1709. It is impossible to state the precise number of the immigrants. Various lists were compiled, but none of them is complete. The four lists made by Tribbeko and Ruperti of those who arrived in London between 6 May and 15 June comprise a total of 6,520 persons.[86] The Dutch commissioners in Rotterdam made lists of all those embarked for England at the expense of the British government, lists that comprised over 10,000 names, excluding the 852 persons of the first group.[87] The total number of migrants documented then is 11,064, but two groups of about 1,000 each were transported in August and October by means of private charity collected in Holland,[88] and various smaller groups made their way to England without official approval or assistance, so that the total migration probably exceeded 13,000 persons.

The embarkation lists prepared in Holland stated only the names of the immigrants, but the lists prepared in London by the Lutheran ministers recorded the age, religion, and occupation of the male heads of families, as well as the ages and sex of children. The numbers of Germans represented in each of over twenty occupations appear in Table 4. The vast majority of the men were husbandmen or vinedressers. Of the 6,520 people listed as having arrived, only 1,560 were men able to state a trade in which they were fit to work; 1,848, or almost a third of the total, were Catholics; 2,676, or over 40 percent, were children under the age of fourteen years. The proportion of the Germans who could support themselves by their own labor was thus very low. Almost all of the men were married, and some of the families had ten or more members. The age of the heads of families ranged from fourteen to eighty-eight, with a mean of thirty-five.

Table 4

Occupations of Palatines	
husbandmen and vinedressers	1,033
carpenters	89
weavers	67
tailors	56

smiths	47
coopers and brewers	46
masons	46
shoemakers	37
bakers	34
millers	28
joiners	21
butchers	15
wheelwrights	14
schoolmasters	11
stocking weavers	6
tanners	6
herdsmen	4
	1,560

Source: [Defoe], *Brief History*

Many of the details of the migrants were rehearsed by Daniel Defoe in his *Brief History of the Poor Palatines*. At that time Defoe was in the service of Godolphin, as his long-standing patron Harley was out of office.[89] His writings on the Palatine affair, both in the *Review* and in the fifty-page *Brief History* were not only thinly veiled defenses of the Whig ministry's passage of the 1709 Act and reception of the Germans,[90] but a detailed presentation of his views on population and immigration.[91] Defoe wished to see the Palatines settled on wastelands, and thought that the settlement must be a planned one. It would be impossible to employ the Palatines by dispersing them, he declared: projectors who might wish to employ them would be unwilling to provide the necessary security to the parish where they were to be settled. Moreover, it would be barbarous to separate the Germans, who were in families, and who could help one another so long as they were kept together.[92] Defoe did not in principle oppose sending the migrants to the American plantations, but considered it a less profitable alternative than keeping them in England, or at least Britain.[93] The economic benefit should by preference accrue to the mother country. He prepared for Godolphin a scheme for a Palatine settlement in the New Forest, and described similar schemes in the *Review* and in the *Brief History*. The settlements were to comprise from fifty to 100 families each, large enough to form self-sufficient communities, but small enough to ensure that the immigrants would mingle with the natives and learn the language and customs of England. The settlers were to be of a mix of occupations so that "they may live by labouring one for another." These "little colonies" of immigrants, like forced plants raised in a hotbed, were to be based on the cultivation of formerly unexploited land, but as they grew their trade would expand to enrich the English natives who lived nearby.[94] The scheme would achieve the twin objectives of settling the Palatines and of improving land that lay waste, economically barren.

Under the auspices of the ministry, and likely at the urging of Defoe, the

Board of Trade took under consideration the plan of settling the Palatines on wastelands. In spite of its earlier warnings of how difficult it would be to settle the Palatines, the Board wrote confidently to Sunderland on 1 June that the immigrants promised to be valuable additions to England's population. The Board offered the minister a parade of the sanctified economic maxims of population and wealth. "A multitude of people," it wrote, "is the glory and strength of a government," and many hands would contribute to the nation's trade and wealth. The Dutch and Walloons admitted in Elizabeth's time had been a national advantage in Norwich, Canterbury, and Colchester. The Board admitted, however, that the earlier immigrants had brought stocks to set up new manufactures, whereas the poor Germans had neither stocks nor trade skills. Many were women and children, and some were "more fit for alms-houses than work-houses." The Board remarked upon the large scale of the migration, and warned that many more would follow unless they were discouraged "until those already arrived be disposed of." The Palatines could be settled on royal wastes, the Board suggested, or the queen could write to the *Custos Rotulorum* of each county to recommend that the Justices of the Peace consider how they might be employed outside the capital.[95] The Board had apparently seized on the promise of a settlement in the countryside for the uprooted German peasant farmers.

The day before the Board presented its report to Sunderland it had written to the Attorney General and Solicitor General for their immediate opinion on two questions: first, whether the Crown had the legal right to grant parcels of land in the forests and wastes to any subjects with license to build cottages, enclose land, and convert it to husbandry; and second, what security might be give to indemnify parishes from the settlement of poor families among them.[96] The prompt reply came that the Crown could grant wasteland for thirty-one years or three lives, with license to build, so long as one-third of the annual value of the land were reserved for rent upon the leases granted. In answer to the second question the law officers stated that no security was required by law for the settlement of foreigners who had never had any settlement in England before, since it was impossible for a JP to issue a warrant to remove the people to their last legal settlement. Foreigners were free to settle wherever they pleased when they arrived in England.[97] The law officers' report did not offer much encouragement to the Board's plan for a settlement on royal wastelands. Parishes would be loathe to receive foreigners who seemed almost certain to swell the poor rates, and who could not be removed. Moreover, it would be necessary to compensate anyone whose rights of commonage in the Crown's wastelands were infringed.

Yet a settlement on the wastes offered many advantages. Godolphin wrote to Newcastle that the queen had been very willing to agree to the proposal of a settlement in her forests, and the ministry seems to have given the proposal serious consideration.[98] Defoe elaborated an ambitious plan for a settlement on wastelands in his *Review,* later published it in his tract on the Palatine immigration, and many years later revived it in his *Tour.* But the scheme never became a reality.[99] Other plans for settling the Germans of course came under discussion. A project for a settlement at Rio de la Plata surfaced and was quickly dropped, as was one for sending the Palatines to the Canary Islands.[100] The Society of London for Mines Royal presented several memorials to the Board of Trade in which it offered to take a group of Palatines to its manor in Wales, where a model city could be established and some of the Germans employed in mining while others cultivated waste ground.[101] Nothing came of the proposal. Henry, Marquis of Kent, the Lord Chamberlain, and subsequently one of the commissioners appointed to supervise the settlement of the Germans, proposed that twenty or twenty-five families be settled on his lands in Herefordshire and Gloucestershire. He offered to allot twelve to twenty acres to each family for ninety-nine years or three lives at a nominal rent, to help to educate the German children, to employ as many of the men as possible on his estates, and to provide them with support for some time to supplement the royal bounty that they would continue to receive. The Board replied that the proposal was excessively generous, and that if he wished to grant the Germans charity, he could take some of them on as servants to improve his land. The Board's minutes reveal that it had begun to lose patience with such well-intentioned but uneconomical projects, for it calculated the cost of the proposed settlement at over £1,500, and resolved that "the intention was not to settle these people here upon a better foot than our own, but only to give them such employment as they may subsist thereby."[102] The difficulty of finding employment for the Palatines in England had already become painfully apparent.

The city of Canterbury offers an example of the resistance of local communities to the settlement of Germans among them. Sunderland wrote to the city's mayor praising the people of Canterbury for the charity they had traditionally shown to foreign immigrants. If the city could receive some of the "persecuted Protestants" from Germany, the queen would be greatly pleased. The Palatines were honest and industrious, Sunderland insisted, and would occupy empty houses and waste grounds to the benefit of the corporation.[103] The mayor responded that Canterbury could receive none of the Germans. Because of the decay of the trades of silk-weaving and wool-carding there was not work enough to employ the poor families already settled in the city.[104] Canterbury's refusal became a pattern for the government's futile attempts to settle the Palatines in England. The ministry might consider them an accession to the nation's wealth and encourage and finance their immigration, but the English people refused to have such poor foreigners settled amongst them, particularly in the very difficult economic times of 1709.

The desperate poverty of the Germans, however, cried out for immediate attention. The ministry could scarcely transport them at government expense from the miserable reed shacks that they had improvised on the dykes around the flooded fields of Rotterdam to the suburbs of London only to watch them starve and die of disease. It preferred the burden of supporting the poor people to the scandal of allowing them to die.[105] Public support was indispensable: their numbers were too great to be rapidly integrated into the English economy even in the best of times. By the middle of June over 7,000 had arrived. Private charity amounting to £800 had been distributed to them early in May, but by mid-June the government was spending eighty pounds per day from the civil list on their support. The purchase of German Bibles from Hamburg and plans to send 500 of the children to charity schools to learn English could not satisfy their pressing need for food and shelter.[106] Both the Archbishop of Canterbury and the Bishop of London replied curtly to the proposal sent to them by the Society for Propagating the Gospel in Foreign Parts that the "poor persecuted Palatines" be supplied with a German minister. They informed the Society that it ought not to meddle in the matter until the government had resolved how to dispose of the poor people.[107] The ministry even sent appeals for private charity to the Bank of England and to the East India Company.[108] The necessity of feeding the immigrants, both on humanitarian grounds and to avoid an acute political embarrassment to the ministry, took precedence for the time being over considerations of how to settle them.

Finally, on 7 June the Justices of the Peace for the county of Middlesex petitioned the queen that despite her generous bounty, the Germans were still in need of relief for their subsistence, and that a royal brief for the collection of charity would be a suitable means to raise the considerable sum of money still needed.[109] A Tory pamphlet claimed plausibly that the Whig ministry had procured the petition through some of its dependants in the commission of the peace of the county.[110] In any case, the queen granted the Middlesex petition and issued a letter patent and brief on 16 June. A week later the brief was extended from Middlesex to all of England. The letter patent described the oppressions and hardships suffered by the Palatines, and especially the Protestants, from the devastations of the French. It stated that of those that had been forced to leave their native country, 8,000 had arrived in England. The letter was worded to create the impression that the Germans were refugees rather than voluntary migrants, and sought to arouse a sense of solidarity with victims of French aggression. The clergy were directed to read the brief to their congregations and to exhort parishioners to contribute generously, and the letter promised that the proceeds of the collections would allow the Germans not only to support themselves, but to increase the nation's wealth. The ministry appointed over one hundred commissioners, many of them high officers of state, to administer the collection and distribution of the charity money and to do everything necessary to find employment for the immigrants.[111]

The bishops wrote to the clergy of their dioceses to encourage their collec-

tions on the brief, but not without hints of partisanship. The Whig Archbishop of Canterbury, Thomas Tilson, recounted the devastations the
Palatines had suffered at the hands of the French, and called them "refugees" attracted to England by the freedom and justice of its constitution and
government. "I am sensible," he warned, stressing populationist motives,

> that in these and like cases, divers prejudices do and will arise from the weakness
> of some, and the cunning craftiness of others. You will, therefore, do well, after
> mature consideration, to open this matter judiciously, and to show, as you have
> occasion, that the increase of people is a means, not of impoverishing or weaken-
> ing a nation, but of advancing the wealth and strength of it.[112]

It was feared that both partisan disgust and economic hostility to the foreigners would prevent a large collection. The Bishop of Worcester's pastoral
letter went much further, and denounced the Palatines' prince for having
denied them the free exercise of their religion and having "oppressed them
with unmerciful taxes." The Bishop of Norwich recalled the special place
of that city in receiving strangers. The Bishop of Ely boasted that England
had been famous in all times for showing kindness to strangers, and declared
it as "a reward from heaven" that as a consequence English trade had improved, manufactures had increased, and the strength of the nation had
risen.[113] The benefit to those who contributed generously might be more
than purely spiritual. By assisting the Palatines to gain a settlement in England the natives would promote the kingdom's wealth. Such was the import
of the pastoral letters. The response to the brief was to prove very generous,
but the money collected did not begin to come in for some time, and the
long-term problem of disposing of the Germans remained unresolved.

The Palatines now learned definitely that they would not be sent on to
America. A German source related that the queen had come out to inspect
some troops, was astonished at the numbers of the immigrants, and demanded why they had left their country. A leader amongst the Germans
responded boldly that they had come in reliance upon the promises contained in Her Majesty's gracious writings. The queen knew nothing of the
books or letters, nor did her Council. A proclamation was issued that no
one would be sent to Carolina or Pennsylvania, the account concluded,
"which frightened the poor people terribly, and they mourned their journey
at the discovery of the fraud."[114] The proclamation does not appear in any
other records, but it is reasonable that the government should have tried to
crush the Germans' hopes of reaching America, for those hopes could only
interfere with the resolution of the ministry to make England their new
home.

The Palatines continued to arrive in large numbers in June, and the problem of housing them became more acute as July drew near. On 21 June
Sunderland ordered enough tents to be erected on Blackheath and other
open areas around London to house the 7,000 Palatines already arrived, and

the additional 2,000 expected by the next favorable wind.[115] Two days later Tribbeko and Ruperti, exhausted by their task, presented a memorial requesting assistance in caring for the Palatines. It was impossible to find places to pitch the 1,000 tents allotted to them, they complained, and Treasury warrants only provided money for the support of only 4,000 people.[116] Godolphin wrote to Marlborough that the exchequer was very low, and that the Palatines were a great burden.[117] Over a month was to pass before the first returns on the royal brief began to filter in. The number of the immigrants had in only six weeks become so great that England could not maintain them—and still more came.

6

The Palatine Migration: Failure and Dispersal

By the beginning of June 1709 the Whig ministry's great experiment in immigration policy had turned into a juggernaut, and Dayrolle at Rotterdam was urgently requesting instructions in case the numbers of Germans should grow too fast. More of them arrived in Holland every day, he wrote, and "the whole Palatinate is ready to follow them poor and rich." A few days later he received a report that 3,000 more were coming down the Rhine, and that most of them were tradesmen. But those that arrived proved to be only more destitute peasants. Many Roman Catholics were among those camped in miserable conditions outside Rotterdam, Dayrolle advised the ministry, but Marlborough had decided that "there was no great inconveniency to let them go with the rest," and had ordered their transportation. This startling decision reflected the fact that many of the families contained both Protestants and Catholics—there seem to have existed few conflicts between those of different confessions amongst the migrants. Dayrolle reported that despite talk of religious persecution, the Germans were leaving their own countries not so much for the sake of religion as to escape the hardships they suffered from their own rulers and from the French. Whatever the motives of the migrants, Dayrolle warned Boyle that if the queen's bounty or any other encouragement continued "you may have half Germany if you please, for they are all flying away not only from the Palatinate, but from all other countries in the neighbourhood of the Rhine."[1] Yet the ministry stood fast, and the only reply that Dayrolle received to his plaintive requests for new instructions was Boyle's order that he continue to transport the indigent Germans as fast as they arrived. Dayrolle himself still vacillated between warnings that the migration could get out of control and recommendations of the Palatines as potential new subjects to increase England's population. He reported that although the charity money raised in Rotterdam had nearly been exhausted, the Dutch people had begun to grumble that the Dutch colonies as well as England should have the benefit of the German emigrants.[2]

Finally at the end of June the ministry resolved that the migration must be stopped. Boyle wrote to Dayrolle on 24 June that it would be impossible to support so many poor people if they continued to come over in such large numbers, and that the success of the whole migration might be frustrated by too large an influx of people. Dayrolle was instructed to make it known that no more Germans would be transported to England until those already arrived had been disposed of. Those already in Holland might be sent over, but he was to prevent the arrival of any more, and despite Marlborough's earlier order no more Catholics were to be transported.[3] Dayrolle ordered an advertisement placed in the *Gazette* of Cologne in hopes of stopping the migration, but warned Boyle at the same time that they came on account of the war, and that if England wanted these willing immigrants it should receive them now, since few would leave their countries once peace had been restored.[4] The appeal of such a large body of migrants made both Dayrolle and the ministers in London extremely reluctant to renounce an opportunity to receive them. Blinded by the mere numbers of the Palatines, the English authorities seem to have thought little of the poor state of the migrants and the small chance of a successful settlement, and as a result for a time in the middle of the summer they equivocated indecisively.

Adding to the ambivalence in London was the passage at this juncture by the States of Holland and West Friesland of a general naturalization act that applied expressly to religious refugees. The timing of the Dutch act may have been simply a coincidence or the result of miscommunication, since the citizens of Rotterdam were by now so anxious to be rid of the poor Germans that they considered granting them the money necessary for their passage to England.[5] Dayrolle forwarded to London a memorial from the Dutch commissioners in Rotterdam that praised in suspiciously exuberant terms the multiplication of a nation's people and the rare opportunity of receiving the Palatines.[6] The Dutch commissioners undoubtedly foresaw the disastrous consequences to Rotterdam should it become the receptacle of all the people traveling down the Rhine Valley intent on passing to England and then to America. As the go-betweens with the English Resident, they themselves must have been under considerable pressure from the citizens of Rotterdam, who by the first of June had already spent £1,200 on the Germans. Nor did they offer any excuses for the inconsistency of their attempts to rid themselves of the immigrants whose value they commended to the English government.

Dayrolle's dispatches reflect the pressure that the Dutch placed on him, and he began to urge schemes that seem to have been provided to him by the Dutch.[7] To such proposals Boyle responded firmly that they were "out of season" in view of the decision to receive no more of the Germans for the time being. Yet the ministry's resolve to stop the migration remained distinctly half-hearted, for Boyle often joined his warnings, through sympathy or hesitancy it is impossible to know, with concessions that Dayrolle might transport those Germans that had already arrived in Holland— concessions that not only nullified the decision to stop the migration but positively encouraged it. Dayrolle continued well into July to transport those that arrived, claiming to act on the advice of Lord Townshend, plenipotentiary in the negotiations for peace, and Robert Walpole, Secretary for War, and stressing that he must send all or none.[8]

At the same juncture—that is, by the middle of July—agents of the Lords Proprietors of the Carolinas began distributing a small leaflet, printed in German, that encouraged settlement in the Carolinas. The leaflets promised 100 acres of unsettled land in America to each man, woman, and child, free for the first ten years, and thereafter at an annual rent of a penny an acre. If they chose to settle in towns, the Palatines would have land on which to build for a term of ninety-nine years or three lives, for a pepper-corn rent.[9] The leaflets, a handful of which survive, were probably a later version of the advertisements distributed earlier in the Rhineland to induce the migration. They attest to the central role played by the Carolina Proprietors in encouraging the migration, even after the ministry had resolved that England would receive no more of the Germans. Nor did the Proprietors keep their overtures secret at this point, if they ever had. Indeed an English version of their advertisement appeared in the government publication the *London Gazette*. They also presented an alternative proposal to a committee of Council to take all the Palatines in England from fifteen to forty-five years of age for settlement in the Carolinas, though at the government's expense for their transportation there, at over ten pounds per person.[10] The ministry still held to its decision to settle the Germans in England, and took no action on the self-serving offer of the Proprietors.

Warnings filtered back to Germany of the fate of those who had migrated. A report of the beginning of August from Rotterdam written in a bastard mixture of Dutch and German, perhaps prepared by the Dutch authorities, warned those in the Rhineland that England could not pay the passage of people from Rotterdam to London, much less to America. The books about Carolina had been fabrications: if they had no money, the report urged, migrants should turn back. In London, the account concluded, many of the poor people were saved from starvation by the collections on the royal brief, though a "great part" had died.[11] An account from a German resident in London, perhaps written in the interests of the ministry, warned intending immigrants that because of the great cost the queen sent no one to America. Instead, they were settled in England as day laborers or servants. The account falsely stated that many ships full of people had been sent back to Holland, and charged that those who wished to entice rich families to Carolina at their own cost, not the queen, had distributed the books encouraging the migration.[12] These discouraging reports that exposed as false all of the promises that seem to have inspired the migration came too late, however, to prevent groups of Palatines from arriving even as late as October.

In Rotterdam, the city magistrates had forbidden ships to bring in more people and announced that no more alms could be given. The citizens, however, eager to be rid of the Germans, collected enough money to send 1,000 more Germans to England in the middle of August. Dayrolle suggested to Boyle that the ministry appeal directly to the Dutch government for assistance in stopping the migration.[13] He explained that the two Dutch commissioners had embarked yet another group of 1,000, thinking that they were doing England a great service in sending as many as they could. Boyle assured Dayrolle that Townshend would make an appeal to the Dutch government to put a stop to the transportations, and three days later instructed Dayrolle to do the same, "since it will be a very difficult matter to dispose of them in any manner of settlement before winter." The ministry foresaw the enormous cost of housing and supporting the Germans, and Boyle stressed that if despite admonitions to the contrary the people of Holland sent over any more Palatines, Dayrolle could assure them that they would be sent back.[14] In accordance with the ministry's decision, the Palatine Commissioners in London resolved early in September that if any more Germans were sent whose landing could not be prevented, they would receive no support in England.[15]

Dayrolle delivered a request to the States General that their Rotterdam Admiralty be ordered to stop further embarkations of the Palatines for England. The States replied shrewdly that they could not prevent those already in the United Provinces from passing to England, but promised that their representatives at Cologne and Frankfurt would warn the Germans against attempting to go to England and inform them that they would not be allowed to pass through Holland.[16] Dayrolle discovered at the same time that somebody in England was encouraging the migration despite the published warnings. An unidentified gentleman, he reported, had come on the packetboat from Harwich and boarded the transports at Brielle to distribute charity money and several thousand of the "little prints" encouraging the migration, and had urged the Palatines to send the writings to their friends in Germany. Four hundred more Germans had arrived at Rotterdam because of the encouragement of the "tickets," Dayrolle claimed, expressing his dismay that "these poor people are invited after that manner, to be miserable afterwards." He thought that the tickets came from the Proprietors of the Carolinas, "or some disaffected persons"—but the tickets must have been the same as those earlier printed by the Proprietors. It seems too absurd even for the High Church Tories of the reign of Queen Anne to have encouraged the migration in order to embarrass the Whig ministry with as many poor foreigners as possible.[17]

The advertisements to discourage the migration having failed conspicuously, in September the queen issued a royal proclamation, printed in German and distributed throughout the Rhineland, warning that no more people would be received or supported in England. Those who arrived after 1 October would be immediately returned home.[18] The proclamation sounded a note of finality, but the desperate people who had given up what little they had to journey to America could not believe that the benevolence of the queen, with which they had been enticed away from their homelands, could be so abruptly revoked. Late in September, 1,500 Palatines awaiting transportation in Holland petitioned for admission: "we have been enticed out of our native country," they proclaimed bitterly, "to serve Her Majesty in her [plantations], but coming here we find ourselves very much deceived, being well informed now that all the promises made in Her Majesty's name are nothing else but false reports." They had left in the hopes of having a peaceable settlement under the queen's protection, but they were now nearly dying of want. They could not return to their native lands, but they believed that they would be the last group to come to England, since the States General forbade any more Germans to pass into Dutch territory. Dayrolle wrote on behalf of the petitioners that they could not return, since "they doubt whether their prince will receive them, and if he does, they are sure to be barbarously used and exposed to all sort of injuries from the Roman Catholics."[19]

The appeal to religious sympathy, however, was of no avail. Sunderland, the minister most active in promoting the migration, replied that the petition had touched the queen with the misery of the poor people, but that the difficulty of settling those that had already come, "the great clamour that such numbers do raise in this time of scarcity," and the heavy expense to the government made it impossible to receive any more. Dayrolle was told "to be very plain with them" that they would not be admitted. If the government "should once vary from this resolution till these here are disposed of, there would be no end of their coming over." The ministry's resolution, however, still could not stop the migration. Dayrolle sheepishly reported on 11 October that 1,100 more Germans had embarked for England, "despite all my endeavours to prevent it."[20]

Intrigue surrounded the last transportations. A Mr. Wulsten had been instructed by the Palatine Commissioners to make inquiries amongst those just arrived in London regarding their transport across the Channel. On 14 October he reported to Sunderland that the people had been at Rotterdam for six weeks, and that many would have returned to their own country had not Mr. Trone [Toren], one of the Dutch commissioners in Rotterdam, told them that orders had come for sending them to England. Toren had even ordered the return of some of those who had already gone aboard boats to travel back up the Rhine.[21] Sunderland received a similar account from Sir Alexander Cairnes, one of the Commissioners in London. Cairnes had boarded every ship laden with Germans on the Thames to demand why they had persisted in coming after public notice had been given that no more of them would be received in England. They replied that Toren, acting under Mr. Dayrolle, had informed them of the order, but that after he had made a trip to The Hague, Toren had shipped them off, and received payment from them for their passage. The Germans and the ships' masters pressed Cairnes to let them go ashore. He replied that if they did so it would be at their own expense, and that they would receive no charity—but to Sunderland he confided that "if they be not soon taken care of, many of them will perish."[22]

In possession of these accounts of the duplicity of the Dutch commissioners, Sunderland wrote to Dayrolle on 18 October. He thought it "very extraordinary after all the endeavours that have been used to prevent it," that yet another 1,100 Palatines had come into the Rhine. He recounted the manner in which the last groups of Palatines had been "forced" to come to England, and concluded that

> this matter ought to be enquired into to the bottom, for it appears a very odd proceeding and Her Majesty does not doubt but you will have it cleared, because the commissary at Rotterdam who is mentioned . . . pretends to act under your name: and after having acted in this manner I hope they will not pretend to any reward or gratification from Her Majesty, for if this be true they do on the contrary deserve to be punished.[23]

Yet Sunderland's threats were in vain, for on 25 October Dayrolle reported that over a thousand more Palatines had been shipped by the magistrates of Rotterdam, "with what money I know not." He insisted that the Dutch commissioners had acted from wholly charitable motives, and that they deserved no blame for the continued transportations.[24] Yet Dayrolle's own involvement in the affair was at best dubious. He had proved completely ineffectual in preventing the Dutch from disposing of the Germans across the Channel, and he wrote to the Dutch commissioners on 5 November that his "intentions were good" in regard to the sending of the last group of Germans, implying that he had been involved in the decision to transport them despite his orders to the contrary from the ministry.[25]

The government carried out its threats to send the Germans back to Holland only in the case of two straggling groups that came in December, a gesture that came far too late to serve as a deterrent. One group of sixty-three, mostly women and children, landed at Sunderland on a collier that had brought them from Brielle. They were sent by pass warrant from the JPs of each county in a relay that ended in the parish of Bishopsgate, which refused to receive them. They were sent to join some others at Southwark to await deportation. The other group arrived first at Bow, and all ninety-three of them were ordered returned to Holland as the "most effectual way to prevent the coming over any more of those people," as Sunderland remarked.[26] By that time winter was at hand, and the season of the migration was in any case at an end.

By the time that winter put a stop to the migration, a concerted effort had been underway for months in England to settle the Germans. The newly constituted Palatine Commissioners met for the first time on 7 July, having given notice of their public meetings and invited proposals for settling the immigrants. A list of the Commissioners and of the occupations of the Palatines appeared in the *Gazette*, Ruperti began to translate the Anglican liturgy into German, and the Commissioners tackled the task of integrating the immigrants into the English economy. They gave notice on 20 July that any masters of ships were at liberty to employ as many of the Germans as wished to serve them. Applicants were referred to the stalls at the tent city at Blackheath, where officials awaited proposals for the employment of even the smallest number of people.[27]

The tent cities that blossomed around London attracted much comment, and visits to the Palatine camps became a popular excursion for curiosity seekers. Crowds of spectators from London thronged the camps, especially on Sundays when other entertainments were few. Defoe quoted a German who disapproved of the loose observance of the Sabbath in England, and who complained that thousands came out "to stare at us."[28] The camp became a kind of fair, with sports and drinking, and wagers placed upon feats that the Germans performed. The immigrants sold items of small value to the crowds, and they received much private charity from the visitors as well.[29] One Quaker tradesman brought wagonloads of cloth, and other benefactors donated thousands of shirts and pairs of shoes. The poor people could have subsisted on the charity of the queen alone, a German source claimed, but the daily contributions of merchants, gentlemen, and citizens lessened their hardship.[30] In contrast to the many reports of their poverty and illness, some visitors reported that the Palatines lived quite well, that their camps had become thriving tent cities, and that several marriages had been celebrated among them. But English observers had ample opportunity to witness the alien burial customs of the Germans,[31] and the reports of their well-being are belied by the continual accounts of illness and death that hung over the camps. Life in the camps was peaceful, although officers had to be appointed to distribute the lots of straw on which the migrants slept, the coal they burned, and to prevent what the Germans called *Weiberkriege* (women's wars) over the limited number of ovens available for cooking.[32]

Aside from Defoe's *Brief History* several publications appeared in connection with the attempt to settle the Palatines. *A Short and Easy Way for the Palatines to Learn English* (1709),[33] written in German and printed in gothic script, sought to instruct the immigrants in the English language and local customs. It claimed to contain "the most necessary words and common expressions," including the names of farm tools, and such indispensable phrases as "come, let us go to the ale-house." The tract included parallel texts of prayers translated into German from the Book of Common Prayer. The pamphlet exhorted its German readers to be thankful for the charity they received from the queen and their other benefactors, and to remember that they were strangers in the land. The greatest advantage of England, the tract advised, was that only the Protestant religion was established by law. Readers were advised to endear themselves to the English by speaking of the good news of victories against the French, and of the terrible devastastion of cities in the Rhineland that had caused them to flee. In a dialogue passage, two Palatines urged each other to be industrious and agreed that they would be glad to be able to get a living soon and relieve the nation of their expense. They praised the Palatine Commissioners and remarked upon the good wages paid in England, the liberty, and the freedom from heavy taxes that made the lot of the common people in England so much better than in their own country.[34] *A Short and Easy Way*, which may have been prepared by the German ministers retained by the ministry, sought not only to teach a few English phrases but to promote the settlement by providing the Germans with remarks that would fall gratefully upon English ears.

On the other hand, another pamphlet, *The Palatines' Catechism; or A True Description of their Camps at Blackheath and Camberwell, in a Dialogue between a High-Dutchman and an English Tradesman* (1709), provided its Tory author with an opportunity to reply to the Germans' apologists. "I think our charity ought to begin at home," his English tradesman growled; "the Palatines may be poor enough, but their coming hither can never make us rich (as has too often been learnedly worded) when we had so many before we could not tell what to do with them."[35] The tract's German character replied that England's poor would have more not less work if the immigrants could put under cultivation the vast wastelands of England. The Englishman scoffed at such misguided ideas, and warned that if they were too much indulged, the Palatines would become as much a plague upon England as the French refugees who had become the secret masters of the English by their dishonesty. After the "hot fit of foreign charity is over," the pamphlet declared, the Palatines might find it as hard to get employment as the English poor had since the Revolution.[36] The *Palatines' Catechism* articulated a lesson that any Tory catechumen might well learn by heart: the immigrants would subjugate the English if employed, and beggar them if not.

The conscience of the tradesmen of England seemed the prize fought for in the pamphlets on the Palatines, and in a Whig tract entitled *The State of the Palatines for 50 Years Past to this Present Time* (1710) there appeared a section entitled "The Palatines Case Humbly Offered to the Tradesmen of England." In this manifesto the Germans were made to express profuse thanks for the charity they had received and to entreat English tradesmen not to resent the charity of the queen, the aristocracy, and the gentry. Instead, those whose livelihoods might be under threat were invited to express a similar compassion and charity. Tradesmen should "lay aside all reflections and imprecations, and ill language against us," the tract pleaded.[37] The tract stressed that the immigrants sought the tolerance of the tradesmen and laborers whose employment they might usurp, or whose wages they might depress—for its author recognized that their hostility, not that of Tory agitators, represented the greatest obstacle to a successful settlement. Like other pamphleteers, the author of *The State of the Palatines* sought to evoke sympathy by vivid descriptions of the French destruction of the cities of the Palatinate, and of their cruelty to the inhabitants of the region.[38] An official publication in support of the settlement appeared as well, ordered by the Palatine Commissioners: *The Piety and Bounty of the Queen of Great Britain: with the Charitable Benevolence of her Loving Subjects, toward the Support and Settlement of the Distressed Protestant Palatines* (1709). The tract presented a collection of papers relating to the immigrants, and recommended them, in arguments similar to those of Defoe's *Brief History* (1709), as deserving subjects of charity and desirable settlers in England or in the plantations.

The pamphlets published in the defense of the Germans implicitly betrayed the growing animosity felt toward them. A German source confided that the English common people, already laboring under the burdens of the war, had become very sore (*geschwürig*) at the cost of supporting the immigrants.[39] But at least as important as the war were the depression of trade and the consequent lack of employment. The poor harvest meant even less demand than usual for agricultural laborers, and the exceptionally high prices of wheat led the government to put in force the old statutes against forestalling and engrossing, as the ministry feared the outbreak of riots. Many English natives felt real want, and it was said that in some places people looked more like skeletons than like human beings.[40] As Abel Boyer, a witness to the events, and himself a French refugee, later wrote,

> this falling out at such an unseasonable time, created great heartburnings among the common people, who did by no means like to see strangers come among them in that poor despicable manner, when [they] themselves lay under such discouragements, and being continually stirred up by bad instruments, could not be kept within the rules of common decency.[41]

Defoe wrote in July that English tradesmen "look upon the poor strangers as a cloud hovering over them, and which they think will every day break upon their particular [trade], and deluge all their labour."[42] The economic depression that coincided with the General Naturalization Act and the Palatine migration must take much of the blame for the disastrous events of 1709.

Occasionally the smoldering resentment of the English broke out into open flame. The Tory Thomas Hearne recorded an incident of late August that involved about forty Palatines. Several Englishmen in an alehouse made "some reflections upon the receiving of these people" as a group of the Germans passed by. To their misfortune, one of the Palatines understood English, and the group set upon the Englishmen and beat them "in a very rude and unhumane manner." They were, Hearne related indignantly, "dismissed with a soft reprimand" by the Justice of the Peace before whom they were brought.[43] The isolation of the Germans at their camps kept similar encounters between Germans and English laborers to a minimum. Yet a

German source recounted that an enormous English mob came to the camp at Blackheath in the dead of night with weapons to hew down all of the Catholics amongst them, and that violence was only averted when the papists took shelter amongst the Protestants.[44] The attempts to settle the people permanently in English parishes had little chance of success with the anger of the English natives at the point of an armed attack on their camp.

The futile attempt to settle a group of Palatines at Sundridge, a village three miles west of Sevenoaks, Kent, reflects the difficulties that faced the Commissioners in disposing of the Germans. At several vestry meetings in July Archdeacon Edward Tenison, the rector of Sundridge and a cousin of Archbishop Tenison, proposed that a small number of Palatines be received by the parish. The settlement would be made on the security of his promise to bear the expense of renting a house for them, and of paying the parish ten pounds for any of them regularly relieved by the parish in the following seven years. Like the Lord Chamberlain's proposal, Tenison's was excessively generous, but the parishioners resisted it fiercely. Some complained that the Germans were lazy and could not work, and vestry meetings ended in such noise and confusion that no other business could be transacted. Finally the parish agreed grudgingly to accept two families of not more than ten persons in all. News of the decision spread rapidly. Sundridge parishioners were told at the nearby town of Westerham that their rector was a "black-coat devil" who deserved to be knocked on the head. The country people in the area said there would be a rising if the Palatines came. In addition, one of the parishioners who had signed the agreement prepared by Tenison was boycotted for his cooperation in the scheme.[45]

The hapless families chosen for the settlement, whose members ranged in age from five to thirty-seven, arrived at the end of August, and Tenison employed them in his hop garden and provided a master to instruct them in weaving. Hatred of the settlers was almost unanimous, and only increased after their arrival. Tenison complained dejectedly that the most restrained of his neighbors talked "of pulling down my house and of firing my barns." Vile language and noisy clamors met the Germans when they ventured away from the house they had been given, and stones rained upon Tenison's gate.[46]

Discontent fermented for a month after the arrival of the immigrants. Then on 8 September a group of twenty-six men assembled at an alehouse, and, led by a bricklayer and a husbandman, marched "with shouting and hallowing" to the house the Germans had been given. The frightened Palatines took cover inside, where they were told through an interpreter that the mob had waylaid en route, that they must be gone in ten or twelve days "by foul means if not fair."[47] The rioters achieved their end, for although they were indicted, the Palatines had to leave the parish. Local Justices of the Peace did not punish the rioters, and Sunderland wrote to Sir John Philips, one of the Commissioners, for information on the failure to suppress such tumults. A jury impaneled for the trial took no notice of the charge they were given, Tenison complained, nor could anything that was said upon oath by the witnesses gain any verdict at Sundridge but in justification of the rioters.[48] Tenison remarked bitterly that if the government would let such violence go unpunished, private persons could do little. "The Palatines' fate in this parish," he lamented, "affords but an uncomfortable reflection upon the temper of the common sort of man."[49] His words, at least in the circumstances of 1709, proved all too prophetic.

Hostility to the Germans was by no means restricted to the laboring poor. Aside from the partisan antipathies of most Tories, the upper classes were more worried about the risk of infection from the Germans than the economic competition that they might present. Peter Wentworth wrote to Lord Raby on 22 July that many people resented the government's having brought over so many Palatines without knowing what to do with them, and that there were fears that "they would bring a plague among us, for they die in heaps at Blackheath, of malignant fevers and smallpox."[50] John Floyer wrote to wish Lady Dartmouth the recovery of her health, and "a better neighbourhood than the Palatines, which I fear have infected your pure air. Our country has whole loads of them and call them gipsies, not knowing the language and seeing their poor clothes."[51] A year later Lady Pye could still blame the Palatines for the deaths caused by an epidemic of smallpox, and in looking back at the migration two years later Swift fumed that "we lost in natives thrice the number of what we gained in foreigners" by the diseases the Palatines brought in.[52] In a more sympathetic vein Roger Kenyon wrote to his sister-in-law that he had visited the camp at Blackheath, and had found that all were very poor and many ill. "What freak brought these poor creatures hither," he wrote, "is not easy to guess; but it seems there had been some books sent among them . . . with flattering descriptions of Carolina and they are mad to go thither."[53]

By the beginning of August very few settlements for the Germans had been found in England. The Commissioners announced on 6 August that a fund would be established as security for any parishes that would receive the poor people. Those who could not earn their own subsistence would be supported from the fund.[54] Godolphin complained of the great expense of maintaining them, and the slowness of the steps towards settling them taken by the ponderously large Commission. He turned again to the Board of Trade that had dealt with—or rather failed to deal with—the migration in its early stages, and requested the Board to propose a way of speedily disposing of them.[55] The reply that he received could hardly have allayed Godolphin's financial worries, for the Board suggested that a premium of five pounds per head be offered to every parish or private person willing to receive or employ the Germans, that they be transported there at the queen's expense, and that the recipients execute as consideration for the money an acknowledgement that the Crown would no longer be responsible for them. Those not disposed of in that way, the Board concluded, could be sent to the plantations in America.[56] Thus the government had come at last to a choice between the undignified expedient of bribing its own people to take the Palatines off its hands, or of sending them at great expense to the destination for which they had originally left their homes in Germany.

The Board of Trade now began serious consideration of a settlement in the American colonies, a less desirable alternative in the eyes of the proponents of naturalization, but now a hopeful expedient. The Board made inquiries of the Treasury about Kocherthal's small group that had been sent to New York the preceding year.[57] It also approached the Carolina Proprietors, who responded on 11 August that they were willing to encourage the making of silk, the planting of rice, vineyards, and fruit, and the production of naval stores in their colony. They offered terms identical to those that had appeared in their earlier leaflets and advertisements—but the Board took no immediate action on the offer.[58] The ministry had not abandoned all hopes of a settlement in England, and on 17 August the Palatine Commissioners published the Board of Trade's five pound per head offer to persons and parishes that would accept a settlement of the foreigners.[59] News of the government offer excited much comment, and Ralph Palmer wrote to his nephew Ralph Verney that "the case of the Palatines is all our domestic talk." There were to be circular letters to all the parishes and vestries advertising the five pound settlement offer, Palmer declared, but "what to do with them is hard to imagine," he added, "and it is thought that Parliament will enquire into the invitation they had hither."[60] The pressure on the Whig ministry mounted as the embarrassment of the migration became more acute.

Fairly early in the summer the ministry had taken steps toward a settlement in Ireland. On 5 July Thomas Wharton, the Whig Lord Lieutenant of Ireland, wrote to Sunderland that he was promoting a settlement in Ireland and that he expected to be given a free hand in the matter by the Irish Parliament. The Germans would be welcome, he hoped, as immigrants far more desirable than the French Protestants in Ireland, who were mostly disbanded officers contributing nothing to the public good.[61] A few days later the Privy Council of Ireland joined Wharton in an address to the queen urging her to send as many of the Palatines as she thought fit.[62] At the end of the month the Commissioners in London resolved to send 500 of the largest families, all Protestant, to Ireland, where they were to be employed in husbandry and the manufacture of linen. The number soon grew to 821 families and a total of 3,073 persons.[63] On 8 August, the day before this large group set forth from London for Chester, where they were to embark for Dublin, the government issued orders to all mayors, Justices of the Peace, and other magistrates, to assist the Germans' journey to Chester, and to ensure that they were "kindly entertained and civilly used." The route had been carefully planned, and was published in the *Gazette*.[64] The government's precautions bear witness to the hostility that could be expected to erupt wherever the Germans appeared. Defoe thought it a "satire and oblique reproof" that a royal order was necessary to ensure that the foreigners were not mistreated on their journey—but some incidents did occur, and there might have been more of them without the order.[65]

The story of the Palatine settlement in Ireland need not be told in detail here. Its success was hardly greater than that of the attempted settlements in England. Some forty-three gentlemen drew the families from a pool, and received them on their estates, where the Germans paid much reduced rents and received a continuing allowance from the queen's bounty.[66] The authorities in London sent another 800 to Ireland in February 1710.[67] But the Palatines chafed in their Irish settlements, and before long some amongst them began to return to England. The Commissioners in England sent an agent, John Crockett, to Ireland to discover the cause of such returns and to prevent them. In Dublin, Crockett discovered that the Commissioners established for the Palatines in Ireland were issuing passes back to England under the authority of the Lord Lieutenant. Crockett protested, but was told by the chairman of the Commission that the Germans' return to England could not be stopped since they were "a free people." In fact, the Irish had become as anxious to get rid of the foreigners as were the English. The Irish Commissioners, Crockett reported, had offered the Germans free passage to Hamburg, but none had accepted. More scandalous, however, was the discovery that at least some of the Palatines had been paid ten shillings per head as passage money back to England. Those arriving back in England complained of hard usage in Ireland, and grumbled that they had received only a fraction of the subsistence money allotted to them.[68] Many who had set out for Ireland well-furnished with necessities, an opposition pamphleteer charged, had returned "naked and in the extremest misery."[69]

Some Palatines remained in Ireland, either living on the allowance provided for them and awaiting the opportunity of a peace to return to Germany, or gradually establishing themselves in the island.[70] Yet Archbishop King, one of the firmest supporters of the Irish settlement scheme, wrote in January 1711 that they "seem as far from a settlement as the first day they came into the kingdom."[71] The Commissioners in Ireland petitioned the queen from Dublin in April 1713 for additional money for the maintenance of the immigrants, stating that there were 263 of the original families still in Ireland, comprising a total of 979 persons, most of whom were settled on farms in the country.[72] The same Irish Commissioners, still trying six years after the first arrival of the Germans to fulfill their original brief, reported early in 1715 that the immigrants were "in a starving condition," and it was all that they could do to keep them from leaving Ireland.[73] It had proved necessary to appoint for them an agent who spoke German since they had not learned enough English to get on alone, and their Irish landlords and neighbors took every opportunity to cheat them.[74] The few who remained in Ireland formed small enclaves whose distinctive culture survived into this century.[75] But these tiny groups, cauterized against assimilation, scarcely represented a successful settlement.

The next group of Palatines to be disposed of met a happier fate. It had been a patent absurdity from the start for England to receive Roman Catholics, and Marlborough deserved the blame that the Tories were later so keen to heap upon him for having ordered the transportation of the papists along with the others, a decision that compromised the ministry and fatally discredited the attempted settlement. Early in August Luttrell reported that some of the Germans had renounced popery "and more of them, 'tis expected, will do the like."[76] In the event, of course, very few did. At the beginning of September a memorial from the Imperial envoy, Count Gallas, complained to the queen that many of the Germans held communion with the Church of Rome, attending mass at the Spanish chapel. Apparently the ragged Palatines were seen as less than pleasing additions to the divine office. Moreover, the imperial envoy indirectly represented the princes whose subjects the Germans had been, and the memorial requested that the Catholics be sent back to Germany. At the same juncture several thousand of the Palatines, most of them Catholics, petitioned the queen praying that she out of her goodness and justice pay their passage home. They had come, they explained, on the understanding that they could have the freedom to exercise their religion, and since that right was now denied them, they wished to return to Germany. Their request was readily granted. On 14 September the Commissioners announced that passes for the transportation of many of the Catholics had been ordered, and that all of that religion who wished it would be issued with passes and granted twenty shillings for the cost of their transportation and support to return to Germany.[77] The Treasury wrote chidingly to Dayrolle that 2,274 Roman Catholics had been found amongst the poor Palatines "supposed to have been all Protestants."[78] When the order was announced that the papists among them were to be shipped back, some of the Germans chose to change their religion and remain. An account written by one of them stated that 332 went to Lutheran churches, and 188 entered the German Reformed Church.[79] In the pamphlet published by the Commissioners, however, only forty names appeared as converts to the Lutheran Church in the Savoy.[80] Little less than a week after their petition the Catholics were on board ship and bound for Rotterdam, so eager was the ministry to dispose of such embarrassing and expensive charges. The total number returned was 2,257. Dayrolle reported from the Hague on 1 October that the Catholics had arrived and received their charity money of ten shillings for the journey back to Germany, "they praising and blessing Her Majesty and the whole English nation." They were soon to leave for the Rhineland, he added, "to the great satisfaction of the town of Rotterdam."[81]

Despite the settlement in Ireland and the return of the Catholics to Germany, thousands of the immigrants, the majority of those who had come, remained at the end of the summer in England and without a settlement. A measure of relief came in the collection on the royal brief, which was much larger than had been expected. In London and the area of the bills of mortality alone over £20,000 was collected.[82] A Tory pamphleteer complained peevishly that £300,000 had been collected for a "parcel of vagabonds who might have lived comfortably enough in their native country."[83] Receipts from the collection began to come in at the end of July, and continued until the end of the year. Disbursements began about the first of August, were greatest in August and September, and declined until they finally ceased in 1711, although December 1709 was the last month in which large payments were made. Many parishes donated very generously, as did Dissenters' congregations, and particularly Quaker meeting houses.[84] French refugees, Defoe declared, had set an example by their generosity: one Paul Girardot, an eminent French refugee merchant of London, gave £423. Other private persons with no political cause to promote gave very liberally.[85] The Whig magnates who had supported the General Naturalization Act, however, subscribed the largest amounts: the Duke of Newcastle, for example, gave £500.[86] The large collections from the City of London, whose opposition to naturalization and to the admission of foreigners had been unwavering, casts doubt upon how polarized was the sympathy for these poor aliens who had been enticed away from their homes—partisan fervor aside, a genuine sympathy for the Palatines seems to have been widespread. The Tory Lord Mayor, Sir Charles Duncombe, however, ostentatiously donated as little as was considered consistent with the dignity of his office, fifty pounds.[87] The sizes of contributions themselves represented powerful political statements, and in *The Tatler* Steele had his Isaac Bickerstaff vow to settle a pension on a Palatine family "and by that means give these unhappy strangers a taste of British property."[88]

Charity, however, generous it might be, would not solve the problem of the Palatines. Proposals for the employment of the immigrants continued to filter in to the government and to the Commissioners. William Reyner, under contract with the Navy to produce sailcloth, applied to employ 300 of the Germans for seven years in spinning and making the cloth.[89] But like most of the proposals, Reyner's was never carried through. Of those that were, almost all failed. The government itself sought to employ as many as it could: some worked on the construction of a canal at Windsor, and others in naval shipyards.[90] Some were employed by gentlemen in various parts of England as servants or laborers.[91] A German account stated that about 150 children were "bought" by the English, probably meaning that they were taken into English families to be raised as servants, in the manner of Moll Flanders.[92] Some communities offered to receive families and to build houses for them after the government's offer to parishes of five pounds per head to be rid of the people. A Commons committee reported in 1711 that many had been received in this way, "but in a very short time most of them returned, and were afterwards otherways disposed of."[93] The report of 1711 savored of Tory vengeance—but there is no reason to doubt its essential truth.

Small groups of Germans were settled here and there. Liverpool received 130; Chester received an unstated number, as did Edinburgh.[94] The City of Rochester agreed to take a handful of Palatine children and to sponsor their education. The county of Middlesex received several families at the urging of the Whig Lord Lieutenant, the Duke of Bedford. Merchants in Bideford and Barnstaple interested in the Newfoundland fishery proposed to employ several hundred; the two towns had received a large number of French refugees in the 1680s, mostly fishermen and mariners from the French maritime provinces, and the merchants may have hoped to derive a similar benefit from the Germans.[95] But it is uncertain whether their plans were carried out. The authorities sent sixteen families north to Sunderland with promises of land, but when they were made day-laborers they returned to London. Ten families went to Plymouth and found work, but complained that they earned too little to subsist, and slipped back to London in hopes of being returned to Germany. Two families received by Sir Matthew Dudley, one of the Palatine Commissioners, returned with the familiar complaints of hard usage.[96] Francis Drake took a few families in the West Country and Sir Ambrose Crowley, the iron-master, an equal number in the north. Drake wrote to Lord Cowper on 15 December that he was "sorry to say how very few are likely to answer. The men [are] lazy, very expecting, unthinking, and without the least tolerable concern for the good of those who are willing to employ them." Many of these complaints were undoubtedly justified. On the other hand, Defoe wrote that when the Palatines tried to work they were "kicked and abused and driven from their labour"; if they were hired to carry a burden, it was pulled off their backs in the streets and they were thrown into the gutter.[97] The fate of the families sent to Sundridge was undoubtedly repeated elsewhere. The Palatines were villains and victims in turn, but in neither role could they successfully become a part of the English nation.

A scheme to settle several hundred of the immigrants in the Scilly Islands proved abortive and added another episode to the farcical proceedings of the ministry and the Commissioners. One hundred families, comprising some 600 persons, were embarked on transport ships in October, with stores and provisions for settlement. When they learned of the plan, however, the inhabitants of the Islands protested that the Scillies were poor and could scarcely provide a livelihood for those already there. The transports never set sail for the Scillies, but the Germans were kept on board ship languishing until the end of December, when they were released to straggle back to Blackheath. The cost of the venture was £1,500.[98]

In answer to the Duke of Newcastle's inquiries, the Justices of the Peace for the East Riding expressed their readiness to assist the Palatines as they could. But the Justices of the Peace for Nottinghamshire answered a similar request with disingenuous regrets that since there were no manufactures in that county, they could do nothing.[99] Winter was approaching, and the Germans began to be moved in October to warehouses and barns, despite the protests of parish officers at the charge they might bring upon the poor rates, as well as the risk of infection. On 5 October Sunderland reproached the Board of Trade for its failure to have a quorum, and insisted that he wanted a speedy resolution of the Palatine problem. The Board defended itself with a report of what it had done to settle the immigrants, and denied its responsibility for the delay in disposing of them.[100] Secretary Boyle finally wrote to Walpole, Secretary for War, that commissioned officers should be sent among the Palatines to enlist any remaining papists who would enter the queen's service in Portugal. Unwanted in England, these least desirable of immigrants were considered acceptable as cannon-fodder overseas, and 150 of them so enlisted.[101]

The Germans' natural wish to be kept together as a community presented one of the greatest obstacles to a successful settlement in England. Because they knew no English, their apologists argued, separation would leave them without friends, without employment, and without God. White Kennet, one of the Commissioners, wrote to the Reverend Samuel Blackwell on 8 October that although groups of them had been sent to various parts of England, "they seem not inclined to stay when divided from one another." From such small settlements they always returned with complaints of hard usage. They wanted to go to the Carolinas, Kennet admitted, and there was no way to plant them in England without an act of Parliament to colonize them in one body and in one place.[102] The proposals of Defoe and others to settle the immigrants in large colonies had been scrutinized and abandoned by the ministry. Now as a desperate final solution the government considered what the Palatines themselves had always insisted they wanted, a settlement in the American plantations. Necessity demanded that the attempt to settle them in England, the government's central purpose in receiving the Palatines, be adandoned.

The Commissioners had announced as early as mid-July that they were resolved to settle as many Palatines as was convenient in "north Britain, Ireland, and the plantations."[103] The Board of Trade began to consider a settlement in Jamaica in August, and in mid-September the Commissioners delegated to the Board all responsibility for the consideration of colonial schemes. Jamaica received a great deal of consideration as the site of a settlement, but in the end very few Palatines were sent there.[104] Colonel Daniel Parke, governor of the Leeward Islands, offered to settle some on the islands of Nevis and St. Christopher, but he received no reply to his proposal.[105] A group of 500 was eventually settled in the Bahamas. Charles Carrington reported to the Board of Trade in 1722 that their settlement lay near Nassau, and that they were "an indolent, lazy tribe and good for little." The next year, however, Governor Phenney wrote to Lord Carteret that the

Palatines were "in a very flourishing condition," and that he "could wish for a great many more of them."[106] As in England, accounts of the immigrants in the plantations shed more light on the prejudices of the writer than on the character of the people.

The Carolina Proprietors, who had been instrumental in promoting the migration, continued to negotiate inconclusively with the Board of Trade until a company of Swiss promoters struck a bargain with the Proprietors to establish a settlement of Palatines in the colony. Two men, Christoph von Graffenreid and François Louis Michel, represented the consortium of Swiss entrepreneurs. In consultation with the Surveyor General of the Carolinas, John Lawson, who was then in London to see to the publication of his book on the province, Graffenreid decided to establish his settlement along the Neuse and Trent rivers. He purchased 5,000 acres from the Proprietors for the sum of fifty pounds early in August, and he was duly invested with the title of Landgrave and given a coat-of-arms. Baron von Graffenreid then assumed direction of the project and undertook negotiations with the Palatine Commissioners. Graffenreid agreed to establish a settlement in the Carolinas of 100 families, about 650 people, with the government paying the cost of transportation at £5 10s. each, and other incidental expenses to a total of £4,000. The Baron agreed to grant 250 acres to each Palatine family, and to provide a subsistence for the first year and other necessaries. Graffenreid subsequently purchased more land from the Proprietors so that he held a total of 17,500 acres when the enterprise began.[107] The Proprietors were very pleased with the arrangement, and wrote to the colonial governor that "nothing could more effectually contribute to the advancement of the province" than such projects to increase the number of its people.[108] Graffenreid selected only the young and fit from amongst the Germans, put them under the authority of John Lawson and Christopher Gale, Chief Justice of North Carolina, and arranged for a further 100 settlers to come directly from Switzerland.[109]

Lawson and the 650 Palatines set sail finally in January 1710, and, after a voyage of thirteen weeks in which about half the settlers died, they arrived in Virginia. Lawson remarked angrily that owing to the false economies taken by the government and the Swiss promoters, there were twice as many of the Germans on board "as ought to have been on a healthful ship." As the ships arrived one of them was plundered by a French privateer, leaving its passengers with nothing. The survivors of the voyage set off overland, selling to English settlers what few possessions remained to them, sometimes including their clothes, in order to buy enough food to subsist. They arrived at the site of the settlement, New Bern, named after Graffenreid's native city. Graffenreid himself arrived in the Carolinas in September 1710, leading the group of 100 Swiss. There he found the Palatines, as he admitted in his published account of the settlement, in "sickness, want, and desperation."[110]

The New Bern settlement struggled on, when in the summer of 1711 typhoid struck, killing many of the settlers. The Anglican missionary John Urmstone reported in July that only 300 Palatines were still alive, "and those ready to starve." However, their end came more swiftly. The native Tuscarora resented the white settlements, especially that of New Bern, as encroachments on their lands. When Lawson and Graffenreid set off on an exploratory journey in September 1711 they were captured by the Tuscarora who put Lawson to an excruciating death. Graffenreid was later released, but not in time to give warning of a large-scale attack by a confederation of tribes led by the Tuscarora.[111] On 22 September a massacre took place in which hundreds of people in and around New Bern, a witness reported, most of them Palatines, were "butchered after the most barbarous manner that can be expressed."[112] Some of those who survived the attacks scattered to other places. Baron Graffenreid himself resettled on the Potomac in the following year. The Carolina Palatine settlement had proved a debacle, and it was even rumored that the English settlers at New Bern had instigated the Tuscarora to destroy the hapless Germans. "Such encouragement," wrote Urmstone, "do the Proprietors give people to come into the colony."[113]

A report from the Board of Trade to the Lord Treasurer at the end of August foreshadowed the project by which England in the end disposed of the greatest part of the Germans. The Board concluded that if the Jamaica settlement proved not to be suitable, those foreigners not otherwise disposed of could be settled on wasteland in New York. Since that province was under royal government (that is, it was not proprietary) measures could be taken to prevent the settlers from creating manufactures that would compete with those of England, a possibility that always worried the authorities in London. The settlers would, the Board believed, provide a barrier against the Native Americans and French, intermarry with the Native Americans, and promote the fur trade. A manufacture of naval stores might be established, and vinedressers among the Germans could produce good wines in those parts of the American continent where wild vines grew.[114] The proposal for a settlement in New York remained in the background until the end of November, when the Board itself received from Colonel Hunter, the newly appointed governor of the province, a proposal to settle 3,000 Palatines on the Hudson River in places "abounding in pine trees" that could be used to establish a manufacture of pitch and tar for naval supplies. The Board gratefully embraced Hunter's scheme and recommended to the ministry on 5 December that 3,000 Palatines be sent to New York for the production of naval stores.[115]

The great appeal of the New York settlement lay in the certain employment that the naval stores manufacture would provide and the imperial purpose that it would serve. Virtually all of the pitch and tar used by the British navy came from the Baltic, although the Swedish monopoly there had been compromised by exports from Russia. English fears of reliance upon foreign sources for such vital commodities led to attempts to establish a manufacture of naval stores in the American plantations, and a bounty was paid for colonial naval stores from 1705.[116] As recently as March 1709 the Board of Trade had reminded the governor of New York of the importance to the British navy of American sources of pitch, tar, and masts.[117] The Board's report to the ministry on Colonel Hunter's proposal presented detailed calculations of how the manufacture could be established and operated. Mr. Bridger, Surveyor General of Woods on the Continent of America, was to instruct the Germans in the manufacture of naval stores from the pine trees that grew along the Hudson and Mohawk Rivers on tracts of land recently resumed by the Crown, and thus available for the settlement.[118] At last there seemed hope of turning the Palatines to gainful employment that would redound greatly to the benefit of Britain, though not through the channel of repopulation.

Yet the New York scheme fell under the same curse that frustrated the other attempts to settle the Palatines. The convoy did not finally leave England for America until April 1710, and 470 people died in the typically appalling conditions of the transatlantic voyage. Governor Hunter arrived in the first ship of the convoy in New York harbor on 16 June, too late in the year for the naval stores project to be started.[119] The migrants, who had been required to sign a covenant that bound them to work under the governor's direction on the naval stores manufacture, were settled along the Hudson River.[120] From the first planting of the settlement, the Palatines chafed under their servitude and sought the freedom to settle where they wished. The New World seemed to them a vast wilderness prison, and many still nurtured dreams of a destiny in the Carolinas. Internal disorders developed amongst the Germans, and the quarrels with Governor Hunter continued almost without interruption. A court was established to supervise the settlers, to see that their work on the manufacture of naval stores progressed, and to punish transgressors.[121] Refugees from the exactions of the French armies and the oppressions of their own German rulers, the Palatines now found themselves little better than slaves in the promised land to which they had looked for peace and liberty.

Finally, in May 1711, the frustrated Germans cast down their tools in mutiny and demanded the land originally promised them. Hunter, outraged by the ingratitude of the Palatines on whose behalf he had expended much of his personal fortune, summoned troops from Albany and intimidated the settlers into submission.[122] The project, however, was already doomed to failure, for reasons both political and natural. The pine trees that grew near the Hudson River were of a variety that produced little resin, and therefore it is doubtful that the extraction of pitch and tar for naval stores could ever have been profitable.[123] But political events in England led to the complete neglect of the project. Only two days before Hunter landed with the Palatines at New York, Sunderland, the member of the Whig ministry most active on behalf of the Palatines, was dismissed. Over the summer of 1710 the Whig ministers were by degrees removed, and the Tories who took their place were staunch opponents of naturalization and the avowed enemies of the Palatines. Governor Hunter's stream of letters to London pleading for financial support for the New York venture received no sympathy from the new government, and he vowed bitterly that the project would not fail on his account even if he were ruined.[124]

The historian of the Board of Trade in this period lays the blame for the starvation of the New York settlement not on the Board, whose membership shifted only very gradually from Whig to Tory after the ministerial revolution of 1710, but on the Treasury, whose refusal to support the project not only doomed it to gradual financial starvation, but ruined Governor Hunter, whose personal expenditures on the scheme were never reimbursed.[125] In 1712 Hunter had to inform the Germans that the naval stores project was a failure, that they were released from the obligation of their covenant, and that they must fend for themselves without further assistance from him or from the English government. Some remained in New York; others scattered to various parts of Pennsylvania and Carolina, where they settled on their own small farms; a few returned to Germany with tales of their odyssey that must have entranced the relatives and friends that they left behind years earlier when they set out for England and a new life.[126]

By the end of 1709 the Palatine problem had receded from the center stage of English affairs. Groups of several hundred at a time continued to be returned to Germany for the next three years. At the end of January 1710 almost 900 were shipped back to Holland at the government's expense. Their condition must have been very bad, for Dayrolle was told to deduct the charity money allowed for those that had died in the short passage across the Channel.[127] Another group of 741 was returned to Holland in early May 1710, after the Commissioners had resigned themselves to sending back "the remainder" of the Palatines.[128] But those who had gone to Ireland continued to trickle back to London, and the government could not prevent their return.[129] Late in February 1711 the government granted the petition of another group of 616 Catholics who requested the customary twenty shillings in order to return to Germany; as with all the groups, ten shillings was applied to the passage to Holland, and the other ten to the journey up the Rhine to Germany. In April, 380 more Germans, recently arrived from Ireland, received the standard stipend for the return journey.[130]

Early in 1711 the Palatines were still conspicuous enough in London for the Tories to make much press of them. A pamphleteer wrote that "the wretched spectacle these people made in crowds daily from the Poultry to the Royal Exchange" had provoked the Commons to enquire into their case. A Commons committee reported in April that "the Palatines have no subsistence, but what they get by their wives begging for them in the streets."[131] Still more came from Ireland, and an order in Council issued on 6 September

1711 stated that the Palatines returned from there grew "very burdensome to the parishes of Southwark and some other parts of the Town . . . and put people in fear of a contagious distemper from them." This group of 540 persons was ordered returned to Holland, and another 240 that had also returned from Ireland were shipped to Holland in June 1712.[132] The minister of the Prussian Church in the Savoy wrote indignantly that "the poor creatures have been perfectly deluded and tricked by ill people into this labyrinth," and were now scuttled off to an uncertain fate in Germany by an unsympathetic ministry.[133] Some Palatines did remain permanently in England, and references to them occur in parish registers till mid-century,[134] but there were no distinct settlements or communities. From the thousands who came in 1709 only a tiny remnant, the distillate of formidable hardship, survived as permanent additions to England's population. The rest bequeathed nothing to the nation but a bitter memory.

That memory was kept alive by the Tory malcontents who denounced the poor immigrants and the Whig ministry that had brought them to England, turning the popular resentment felt towards the Germans into a political weapon to discredit the government. The anger and discontent aroused by the reception of the Palatines contributed to the eruption of open violence during the Sacheverell trial early in 1710. Then, as during the Palatine migration, the Tory opposition used the cry of "the Church in danger" to exploit popular Anglican feeling and give an ideological color to cultural prejudice and economic anxieties. Most of the parochial clergy seem to have sympathized with the Tories, and "Church in danger" declamations resounded from the pulpits. The reception of the Palatines and the General Naturalization Act were denounced as threats to the Anglican establishment, and more generally the whole constitution in Church and state. Partisans capitalized on the widely-felt disgruntlement with the Whig immigration policy by publishing a list of the MPs who had voted for the act. The general election of 1710 returned a large Tory majority to the House of Commons, and the many country gentlemen, Tories sitting for the first time, longed to expose the abuses of the late ministry. They resented the high taxes necessary to continue the war that they accused the Whigs of having protracted, and saw their alliance with the monied interests, in which Jews, Dutchmen, Huguenots, and other foreigners were so conspicuous, as part of the hated war policy.[135] So a virulent xenophobia became a prominent feature of the new Tory government.

In January 1711 the Commons received a petition from the parish of St. Olave, Southwark, complaining that Palatines threatened the "utter ruin" of the parish. At the same time a bill was introduced to repeal the naturalization act. The new ministry seized the opportunity to expose the former Whig government and appointed a committee to inquire into the migration. The committee report presented to the House in April had an emphatic Tory bias. The October Club was then at the height of its power, with its members drinking toasts of "damnation to foreigners."[136] A pamphlet by Francis Hare, the Duke of Marlborough's chaplain, appeared in defence of the late ministry's management of the migration, reciting the maxim of the advantage of a large population, and vindicating both the Act of 1709 and the reception and support given the Germans. But at the same time Swift voiced the upwelling of Tory rage against naturalization schemes, fuming against the Whig ministry that had reduced "the birthright of an Englishman . . . to the value of twelve pence."[137] The bill to repeal the act failed to pass the House of Lords, not yet won over to the Tories, but a new repeal bill introduced in 1712 rapidly passed both Houses, and received the royal assent on 9 February of that year.[138] The official Tory verdict on the Palatine migration was embodied in the words of the Commons committee in 1711:

> The inviting and bringing over into this kingdom the poor Palatines, of all religions, at the public expense, was an extravagant and unreasonable charge to the kingdom, and a scandalous misapplication of the public money, tending to the increase and oppression of the poor of this kingdom, and of dangerous consequence to the constitution in church and state. Resolved, that whosoever advised the bringing over the poor Palatines into this kingdom was an enemy to the Queen, and this kingdom.[139]

The policy of admitting foreign settlers thus met with a resounding political defeat, in large part because of the disastrous Palatine migration. The migration had been far greater than England could accommodate, and the Germans' lack of skills made it nearly impossible for them to become integrated into the English society and economy. Moreover, the timing of the immigration had been dictated not by reasons of economic practicability, for a time of acute trade depression was hardly the auspicious moment for such a vast influx of poor foreigners, but by reasons of party political advantage. It is hardly surprising then that the Whig's great experiment in naturalization policy failed. The pleas of economic writers for sheer numbers of people had proved themselves to be very ill-conceived. The dreams of an England brimming with people vanished in the rude awakening of partisan tumult that reached a climax in Queen Anne's reign, nor could those dreams ever be fully recaptured thereafter.

Perhaps the greatest lesson of the Palatine migration was that the hostility of the natives could act as an insurmountable obstacle to a settlement of foreigners in England. Despite the efforts of the ministry, the Board of Trade, and the Palatine Commissioners, the antagonism of the English people, fomented by Tory activists, had doomed to failure the attempts to settle the Germans in England. At Sundridge and elsewhere, indeed wherever the unfortunate strangers went, they were reviled, assaulted, or driven away. Defoe declared that "the humour of the English working people is at this time so averse to foreigners, that some of them have declared that if they come to work among them, they will be occasion of their deaths."[140] His prophetic remarks at the beginning of July 1709 were amply confirmed. He had written then that the Palatines

> will meet with here all the discouragement and repulse that an ill-natured stranger-hating people can put upon them—till the government . . . shall be forced to disperse them again to such parts and places as they can.[141]

And so it happened. Within a few years of their arrival in 1709 only a handful of Palatines remained in England. The animosity of the English, the trade slump and resulting unemployment, and the Germans' lack of skills conspired to make settlement impossible. The consequent suffering of the misled Germans, and the expense of the many failed schemes to settle them, discredited for years to come the policy of encouraging immigration by offering the rights of British nationality to foreign settlers.

7

The Reception of Immigrants:
"The Bread from our Mouths"

This work began with the story of Jacques Fontaine, the French Protestant who encountered not only sympathy but very considerable animosity in his land of refuge.[1] Fontaine had in Taunton a taste of the True-Born Englishman's national pride and his vehement prejudices against foreigners. Many observers blamed the failure of the Palatine settlement on chauvinism, and denounced English xenophobia as the chief obstacle to a successful scheme for naturalization. Charges of English hostility have surfaced repeatedly in the course of this study. The fairness of such complaints, and the actual force of antagonism as an inhibition on immigration, have not yet been scrutinized. An attempt must be made to explore the reactions of English natives to foreigners, both favorable and unfavorable, and to chart the contours of public opinion towards immigrants. The subject is a very large one, and deserves a fuller treatment than can be accommodated here, but its important bearing on the immigration question demands at least a summary treatment.

English reactions to immigrants ranged from sympathetic assistance to physical assault. Expressions of hostility stand out in bold relief, but it would be misleading to suggest that antagonism dominated in English sentiment towards immigrants. If more confrontations than conciliations are portrayed here, if the scenes that have survived the passage of the centuries betray tension rather than harmony, the reason is that the gradual processes of accommodation, acculturation, and adaptation have left few records. Sympathy and kindness seldom left a paper trail, but the historian must be cautious not to forget them. Pitfalls also threaten any treatment of English reactions as separate from the process of adaptation by foreign immigrants, for this was a dialectical process that formed an essential unity. The contact between two peoples and cultures involves a process of give and take, a bilateral adaptation. The host culture accommodates and assimilates newcomers, who themselves undergo a process of acculturation. Both acculturation and assimilation progress by degrees, faster or slower, through frictions between the two cultural groups.[2] Tensions then, though they do not tell the whole story, play a dynamic role in the process of adjustment.

The acculturation of foreigners in early modern England, their loss of distinctive language, religion, marriage patterns, and cultural forms, deserves more attention than it has received.[3] Even less studied, however, have been the processes of assimilation of foreigners by the English and the ways in which English natives reacted to immigrants, the subjects of the present inquiry. A variety of factors bore on English reaction to immigrants. Religion shaped not only the debate over naturalization but the response of individuals and groups to foreign settlers as well. Economic considerations inspired the pleas for the admission of foreigners, and the economic self-interest of English tradesmen, artisans, manufacturers, and consumers, represented perhaps the most potent force in forging English attitudes towards foreigner settlers. Cultural configurations played a similarly important role in English reactions; indeed, an inquiry into English attitudes is essentially a history of mentalities, of enduring cultural patterns of thought and feeling. A rising barrier of cultural hostility and popular xenophobia confronted immigrants to England over the course of this period, as the formation and evolution of attitudes towards foreigners came increasingly to be molded by broader political and ideological changes in British society. By the middle of the eighteenth century, reactions to immigrants had become one facet of the cultural and ideological construction of English national identity.

Before the Revolution and the Toleration Act the question of religion dominated the immigration controversy in Parliament and in the press. The religion of immigrants contributed a great deal to the shaping of English reactions as well. The complexities of the religious side of English attitudes would themselves fill a thick volume, and the issues can only be summarized here. The brevity of treatment, however, must not be seen as calling into question their central importance to contemporaries. The secular tendencies of the period can easily be exaggerated, and if the edge of religious piety became blunted in the course of the eighteenth century, the ideological dimension of religion increased. The importance of religious considerations in shaping English attitudes towards foreigners ultimately derived from the centrality of religion to the English sense of self-identity: the English were a Protestant people, treading a middle way between the extremes of Catholicism and Reformed Protestantism. This sense of Englishness then naturally conditioned reactions to foreigners that focused directly upon religion.[4]

Religion, moreover, offers the most sensitive measure of the rapidity of assimilation and acculturation in the early modern period. The foreign churches such as those of the Dutch and French Protestants, not only in London but in provincial towns as well, protected and perpetuated the immigrants' culture, language, and sense of separate identity. The churches formed the focal point of every immigrant community, as well as providing a measure of insulation that slowed the process of anglicization. The decline in their membership is the best evidence available of the pace of assimilation, though it is by no means comprehensive, even for Protestant refugees whose distinct identities derived largely from their faith.[5] Moreover, the religious hostility that foreigners faced in England mediated the process of absorption, again in a dialectic process between majority and minority cultures.

Religious antagonism took as many forms as did the convictions, faiths, and prejudices of the time. But in fairness to their English hosts, it must be stressed that immigrants often received a compassionate welcome precisely on account of their religion. The English possessed a deep reservoir of sympathy for those who came as religious refugees, and particularly for the French Protestants who had suffered persecution at the hands of the popish and absolutist King of France. In their case political, religious, and ideological motives conspired to elicit a very favorable initial reaction. The generous reception given to Jacques Fontaine and his companions on their first arrival seems to have been the rule rather than the exception.

Sympathy for religious refugees of course depended upon widespread knowledge of their plight. The English government apparently sought to suppress news of the persecution of the Protestants of France, particularly under James II, though with only moderate diligence and an indifferent success. Most people probably learned of the French oppressions through the collections on the royal briefs sent out for the relief of the refugees. Descriptions of the persecution, as they gradually filtered into England, painted a lurid picture of the cruelest tortures, and Narcissus Luttrell in 1685 echoed the general English response when he called the persecution "more severe than any against the primitive Christians under the Roman Emperors." Tales of horror made good press, and details of the French *dragonnades* circulated widely after their victims began to arrive and recount their sufferings. The enthusiasm of the English to succour the refugees became itself an expression of national pride, a demonstration of England's leadership in promoting Protestant solidarity. The Palatines as well owed the sympathy and assistance that they received, at least in the early months of the migration, largely to their presentation to the English public as religious refugees.[6]

English generosity to newly-arrived refugees, or other immigrants, came relatively painlessly, for helpless victims and homeless strangers naturally excited compassion. But English opinion did not universally accept the members of the foreign churches established in England. Members of the foreign churches were Protestant, but not Anglican, and as such they stood as exceptions to the laws against Dissenters from the Established Church.[7] Anglicans, particularly those with High Church tendencies, felt ill at ease with this anomalous status, and with the lack of episcopacy in the Reformed churches. The French Protestants, after all, were Calvinists, and the French churches looked in the disturbing direction of Geneva for guidance on questions of practice and belief. As a consequence, considerable controversy in

England surrounded the question of whether the French churches established in London and elsewhere should preserve the Calvinist liturgy used in France or conform to the Anglican rite.[8] Soon after the establishment in 1661 of the most important of the conformist congregations, the French Church in the Savoy, John Durel, later Dean of Windsor, produced a French translation of the Book of Common Prayer for use in that and other conformist churches. From the time of the foundation of the Savoy church until the Revolution, the English authorities allowed French immigrants to found only conformist congregations in England. Robin Gwynn has argued plausibly that the government policy against the establishment of Nonconformist churches reduced the number of French Protestants who chose England as their land of refuge, though one can only speculate on how many potential immigrants were thereby lost.

The policy of imposing a Gallicized Anglican conformity upon the Huguenots reached its zenith in 1686, at the height of James II's persecution of Dissenters, when rumors of *quo warranto* proceedings against all Nonconformist French churches in England suggested the government's resolve to extirpate French Calvinism. The threat failed to materialize, and after the Revolution the policy of enforcing conformity to the Anglican liturgy lapsed. A strong shift thereafter towards nonconformity—that is, back to the Calvinist form of the litrugy—bore witness to the importance to French Protestant immigrants of liturgical freedom. Although in the 1680s conformist French Protestant congregations outnumbered Nonconformist congregations two to one, by the turn of the century the proportion had been reversed.[9]

Despite the ominous threats of James II's reign, nothing in the Restoration period compared with the attacks of Archbishop Laud on the foreign churches in the 1630s. Archbishop Tenison refused to give an opinion either for or against the foreign Reformed churches, but for the most part the Anglican establishment made no active opposition to the French, Dutch, or other foreign churches in England.[10] A conspicuous exception was Bishop Morley of Winchester, who demanded in 1668 that the minister of the French congregation at Southampton show by what authority he preached. The Bishop argued ingeniously that the exemption from the Act of Uniformity in favor of foreign churches applied only to those members of the congregations who were not natural-born subjects. Coetus, the committee of the French and Dutch churches of London, responded to Morley's attack by citing the example of the long-established congregations at Norwich, which had enjoyed protection for over a century. For the time the dispute blew over. In 1683, however, at the height of the Huguenot migration, the mayor of Southampton, acting, it is safe to assume, out of other than purely spiritual motives, complained to Bishop Morley that the French used their congregation as a shield from the laws against Dissenters. Morley, easily provoked on the issue, wrote to Bishop Compton of London in November of that year complaining that receiving such "Presbyterians" presented a danger to the Established Church, since they could too easily join with the English Dissenters, "the most inveterate and most irreconcilable of our enemies."[11] Throughout the period of the Restoration, English attitudes towards Protestant immigrants such as the Huguenots vacillated between the wish to buttress the Protestant interest and the contrary fear of encouraging Dissent; that ambivalence, in 1683 and at other times, prevented any concerted drive to alter the status quo arrangement of toleration.

Fearful of potential political repercussions, the French Church of London itself sought to minimize its dealings with the English Dissenters, and flatly refused to accept them as members. The foreign churches strove in this as in other respects not only to keep on good terms with the Established Church and the government but to provoke as little popular resentment amongst English natives as possible. Paradoxical proposals such as that of the corporation of Bristol in 1682 that fines levied upon English Dissenters be used to relieve French Protestants were perhaps intended to drive a wedge between English Dissenters and the foreign Protestants—certainly Bristol did not otherwise distinguish itself for friendliness towards immigrants. But such efforts were hardly necessary. The foreign churches flirted with English Dissent, but nothing more.

We possess very little evidence of the strictly religious feelings of English laymen towards foreigners. Differences in outward observance occasionally caused tension: the Calvinist practice of wearing hats during services so scandalized the English that some otherwise Nonconformist French churches resolved that the ministers at least should appear in church bareheaded.[12] Local English parishes showed little inclination to welcome the establishment of foreign churches in their midst, though their aversion was probably more cultural and economic than religious. The inhabitants of the parish of St. Martin Orgars in London, for example, petitioned the Lords in 1700 against a proposal to erect a French church there, complaining that it would "create a perpetual settlement of foreigners in the heart of the City" and have a detrimental religious as well as cultural effect on the inhabitants of the parish.[13] On the whole, however, no evidence suggests that any but High Church Anglicans harbored a large measure of purely religious hostility towards the foreign Protestants, though at times religious issues mingled with political, ideological, or economic antagonism.

One incident in Queen Anne's reign, however, provoked particularly strong popular religious resentment. In the spring of 1707 a small group of self-styled French *"inspirés"* reached England from the Cévennes, and the curious episode of the "French Prophets" began. The group's prophesying, speaking in tongues, and fervent preaching won them a certain number of followers but a far larger measure of contempt and hatred. Defoe condemned the "prevalency of this new delusion" in the *Review*, Lord Shaftesbury deplored such flagrant examples of enthusiasm in his *Characteristics*, and others charged that the French Prophets were disseminating Jacobite propoganda. By the end of 1708 they numbered 400, with twice as many English as Huguenot believers. Aroused by the growing popular resentment of the cult, the French Protestant population turned on the Prophets, excommunicated them, assaulted them, and successfully sued them for blasphemy and sedition. The French Church hurriedly published its disavowal of any connection with their absurdities in order to forestall the general odium that might fall upon all Huguenots in England. The climax of the episode came when the Prophets attempted to raise one Doctor Emms from the dead in a staged piece before a turbulent crowd. When the uncooperativeness of the deceased doctor became apparent, the Prophets barely escaped from the enraged mob that would have torn them apart. However, the power of faith allowed the cult to linger on for some time in a shadowy existence. The unfortunate episode of the Prophets did nothing to improve the reputation of the French Protestant churches in England or to assure Anglicans of the religious respectability of foreign settlers in general.[14]

Yet after the Revolution English suspicions attached increasingly not to the foreign Protestants in England but to the opposite pole of the religious spectrum. Most foreign immigrants came from religious traditions that were far more thoroughly Reformed than the Anglicanism of their English hosts, yet many, like Jacques Fontaine, found themselves accused of popery. By the mid-1670s the fear of popish immigrants surpassed anxieties over Protestant extremists.[15] No genuine threat existed that any number of Englishmen would convert to French Calvinism, or that the presence of the refugees would materially strengthen English Dissent—but might not some of the French be secret papists? The charges of surreptitious Catholicism reached their height in the early 1680s, when hysterical fears of popery in England and the mass influx of French refugees both reached a zenith. Rumors became so persistent that Charles II ordered an advertisement placed in the *Gazette* denying the "scandalous reports . . . daily spread abroad" that the French refugees were disguised papists. The foreign churches required immigrants to present authentic testimonials of their Protestantism, the announcement stated; anyone with proof that a refugee was a papist was to so inform the Bishop of London. The notice did not quell suspicions, and in 1683 fears of popery led to open rioting in Norwich in which the frenzied English inhabitants dragged French settlers through the streets, sacked their houses, and left one woman dead.[16]

Such violent outbursts betray far more than simply religious animosity, of course. By the 1680s, and certainly after the Revolution, anxieties over the risk that immigrants might be Catholic reflected broader ideological forces. In the eighteenth century disturbances or expressions of hostility motivated by fears of Catholic immigrants occurred sporadically, tending to ebb and flow with the perceived threat from Catholic continental powers, especially France. Generalized fears of Jacobitism could reinforce xenophobia. A memorial presented to the Commons in 1700 typifies the complaints that appeared in the eighteenth century, after the influx of French Protestants had largely ended. French papists, the petition charged, came to England as cooks, valets de chambre, butlers, and dancing-masters, all with "more access to persons of quality than the most honest French Protestant." In this way popery infiltrated England subtly in the highest places.[17] Denunciations of immigrants as secret Catholics reached their peaks at times of greatest threat, particularly during the Jacobite episodes of 1715 and 1745. In 1744, for example, a gathering of English footmen with a grievance against the French and Swiss immigrants who competed against them for jobs ended in a riot at the door of a Middlesex Justice who tried to prevent their meetings. The disturbance was provoked or excused in part by fears that the French in England were papists and "commissioned spies", preparing the way for invasion.[18] As the author of *French Snakes in British Clover* (1744) wrote, "the swarms of Frenchmen in the service of the families of Great Britain are inconsistent with the love of our religion and country." They presented the political risk of an internal enemy, the religious threat of Catholicism, and the cultural contagion of continental ways. The underlying grievances in disturbances such as that in 1744 clearly arose from economic and ideological resentment and the anxieties of war rather than concerns that could be called strictly religious.

Attitudes toward Jewish immigrants betray a complex mixture of motives, but religious difference dominated English reactions, no less after 1689 than before. The question of anti-Semitism lies beyond the scope of this study, but the contrast between the sentiments felt towards Jews and towards foreign Protestants demands notice. Religious practice may occasionally have excited repugnance, as when Samuel Pepys visited the newly-established synagogue in 1663 to witness a service, and left with his "mind strangely disturbed with them." Uninformed prejudice played a far more powerful role, however, and most anti-Semites simply hated the Jews on principle as crucifiers of Christ. Economic concerns played a minor role so long as the issue remained only admission rather than naturalization, with its accompanying privileges.

The right of the Jews to reside and exercise their religion in England fell under attack in 1664 when the Conventicle Act came into effect, in 1672 at the cancellation of Charles II's Declaration of Indulgence, and again in 1685 at the accession of James II. On each occasion the Jews petitioned the Crown for protection, and on each occasion the proceedings against them came to a halt.[19] The issue occupied a very minor place in public discourse, and the antagonism that existed was mostly passive.[20] The number of Jews settled in England was small, and the settlement was entirely limited to London. Although a handful of Jews pursued careers as merchants, the jealousy excited amongst their English competitors was apparently quite limited. On account of religion no Jew could become a freeman of the City of London, and Jews therefore could not trade at retail within the boundaries of the corporation. The City imposed a strict legal limit of twelve on the number of Jewish brokers to whom the Court of Aldermen issued licenses. Nor would the conflicting patterns of sabbaths and holy days permit the apprenticeship of Jews to Christian masters, so that the Jews presented no substantial threat of competition to English tradesmen. The strongest antipathy directed at immigrants, that of trade hostility, remained muted in the case of the small Jewish community, whose occupations presented little competition to native English artisans. Despite the occasional diatribes against them on religious grounds, the Jews on the whole received better treatment in England than in any other country in Europe in the period, except perhaps the United Provinces.[21]

Taking the period from the Restoration to the accession of George III as a whole, economic considerations weighed more heavily in English reactions to immigrants than questions of religion. If the policy of encouraging immigration arose from a desire to stimulate trade, resentment of the unfair competition presented by foreigners nurtured the most forceful opposition faced by immigrant settlers. Much of the enmity felt towards foreigners expressed itself through the corporations, jealous of their privileges, as Jacques Fontaine learned when he appeared before the city government of Taunton. As London's campaign against naturalizations demonstrates, the incorporated cities represented not only the interests of the merchants and tradesmen admitted as freemen, but their own corporate interest as well.[22] Yet despite the vigorous opposition to the admission of foreigners mounted by the City of London, and the rather more desultory resistance mounted by some of the other corporate cities, the most formidable source of animosity came from English tradesmen and artisans themselves.

Of course, not all immigrants confronted a hostile reception. Sociologists have identified two types of immigrant as archetypes that tend to provoke acute resentment in the host communities that they enter: the "sojourner laborer," willing to work for a lower wage rate than native workers; and the "middleman minority" engaged in trade or commerce. In seventeenth- and eighteenth-century England foreign laborers and artisans excited a far more angry reaction than higher-echelon tradesmen and merchants.[23] In this period, French, Jewish, and Dutch immigrants often took the role of middlemen and merchants. They occupied important commercial and financial positions out of all proportion to their absolute numbers and contributed to the financial revolution of the 1690s and thereafter. Many produced or traded in superior consumer goods, such as silk, silver, fine paper, and other articles aimed at an elite clientele.[24] Although they earned the political hatred of Tories by their commercial innovations and their alliance with the Whigs, they suffered very little hostility from the English merchants and financiers with whom they dealt every day. As members of a relatively privileged class, they were assimilated, or at least tolerated, very soon. Assimilation operated from the top of the social scale downward, and that difference reflects a more generalized class dimension apparent in English reactions to immigrants, for the elite generally gave a warm welcome to immigrants whom tradesmen and laborers resented as unscrupulous competitors.

English artisans, tradesmen, and laborers, and the chartered craft and trade guilds to which many of them belonged, presented the most powerful antagonism toward immigrants. They expressed their opposition to immigrants both directly, sometimes in open violence, and indirectly, through the exclusive powers of the corporate cities and the guilds. The attempts in the seventeenth and eighteenth centuries of the craft companies to exclude foreigners have their parallel in twentieth-century efforts of organized labor to exclude immigrant laborers,[25] and the early modern complaints have a distinctly familiar ring: foreigners took jobs from natives, undercut wage rates, and formed enclaves of alien culture in England. Immigrant craftsmen, tradesmen, and skilled laborers felt the anger of the English tradesmen who accused them of "eating the bread out of our mouths." Nor did English complaints represent simply xenophobia: foreign laborers accustomed to lower standards of diet and housing almost certainly were able to work for lower wages than those considered reasonable by English workmen.[26] The lesson was not lost on English workers. As Sir William Yonge remarked in 1753,

> though these people know nothing of the general interest of the kingdom, they very well understand their own interest, and know that the fewer labourers there are in their way, the higher wages they may insist on, or the fewer retailers there are of the commodity they deal in, the higher price they may exact.[27]

Economic self-interest formed the foundation stone of popular opposition to immigrant settlers.

Popular xenophobia of the sort that Tory opponents of immigration sought to excite betrayed a strong color of economic anxiety and was most intense in the corporate cities, whose artisans and petty tradesmen stood to lose the most by the arrival of foreign competitors. Indeed, the economic and popular political motives of antialien agitation can scarcely be disentangled.[28] The Tory, Country, and High Church opponents of immigration did not neglect to publicize their economic arguments, but they exploited as a fulcrum something much more powerful—popular prejudice against aliens. The entrenched distaste for foreigners amongst the common people can be seen as part of a popular political culture, as a reflection of economic self-interest, and as an expression of a growing sense of national identity and pride. Whatever the complexion of popular animus against foreigners, however, Tory and other opponents of naturalization sought to pose as paternalistic defenders of native Englishmen and their established birthright against Whiggish attempts to undermine those rights by admitting crafty Frenchmen, starving Germans, and parsimonious Dutchmen.

England's second and third largest cities, Bristol and Norwich, offer good examples of how popular urban politics influenced xenophobia. The city government of Norwich, staunchly paternalistic and Tory, fully supported the popular traditionalism of the city's artisans, including their hatred of foreigners. The corporation actively endorsed the freemen's restrictive trading privileges, and set itself firmly in opposition to the Whig and Dissenter elements associated with foreign immigrants.[29] Sir John Knight well represented his constituency of Bristol, another Tory and Jacobite stronghold, in his diatribes against foreigners. In 1751, upon receiving the news that a general naturalization bill had been defeated in Parliament, the people of Bristol demonstrated their sentiments towards immigration schemes by burning in effigy Josiah Tucker, Rector of St. Stephen's and one of the bills proponents.[30] Attention must focus on London, however, since most foreigners settled in and around the capital. G. S. DeKrey has documented the Tory loyalties of the popular elements in the metropolis, and it is in keeping with the known contours of popular politics that in London political partisanship conspired with economic anxieties to nurture in the trading and laboring classes an abiding resentment of foreign settlers.[31]

The first task of an immigrant such as Jacques Fontaine was to find a way to earn his living. This brought him into immediate conflict with English tradesmen, with the corporate cities, and with the chartered companies of craftsmen. Corporate and guild control over trades in London suffered a process of erosion in this period, as unfree trading and manufacturing expanded in the suburbs, but this only resulted in a heightened effort at strict enforcement of exclusive privileges.[32] Although most immigrants settled in London, many, such as the French silk-weavers of Spitalfields, chose to set up trades in the suburbs of the capital rather than attempt to become freemen. The corporation of London kept a very strict surveillance on those residing within its jurisdiction, and a long stay required a license. A committee sat regularly in the Guildhall in order to receive informations on foreigners trading in the City.[33] Neither London nor the other corporations wanted an accession of immigrant settlers. Certainly no English corporate city could rival the Dublin City Assembly's open admission of French to its liberty in the 1680s.[34] The governors of the corporation of Lincoln insisted emphatically in 1683 that French refugees would find no housing there, and that foreign settlers would be "no advantage to this city but a prejudice to [it] and all others." The mayor of Bristol wrote to the Privy Council in 1681 that the corporation was "utterly at a loss how to dispose of . . . these French already come, and those that may hereafter arrive."[35] The corporations expressed similar sentiments in connection with the Palatines, and attitudes changed little in the eighteenth century.

However unwanted, immigrants settled predominantly in the cities and especially in the capital. To exercise a trade without the freedom of the City, however, brought the authorities to one's door almost immediately. Natural-born Englishmen not free of the City were referred to as "foreigners," and had as little right to exercise a trade in London as any newly-arrived alien. But aliens suffered under greater disabilities. City statutes forbade even the son of an alien from becoming a freeman by apprenticeship to a trade. The only method available to immigrants was freedom by redemption. This meant the payment of a substantial fine, and aliens and the sons of aliens had to have the approval of the Court of Common Council in addition to the usual assent of the Court of Aldermen.[36] They were admitted only "for special reasons and after mature and serious deliberations," and denizens had no more rights in this regard than aliens. These requirements presented a formidable barrier, and the City admitted few immigrants to the freedom. A manuscript list compiled in 1700 named only twenty-six aliens or denizens who had been made free of the City in the preceding sixteen years.[37]

A few examples will illustrate the vigor with which London enforced its exclusive privileges. In 1676 the corporation admitted a Dutch cabinetmaker who had served his seven years' apprenticeship as a freeman by redemption in the Joiners' Company on the recommendation of the King and Council. A Dutch bricklayer who had worked on the royal fortifications and public works was similarly admitted in 1677. The Bishop of London in 1682 recommended to the Court of Aldermen one John Louis, an endenizened French Protestant. He was to be admitted to the freedom by redemption in the Goldsmiths' Company, but the Company balked, and the Court of Aldermen had to issue a second order several months later that Louis be admitted without delay.[38] The City government became less averse to the admission of aliens in the eighteenth century. In 1737 the City's governors altered the corporate ordinances to make freedom by apprenticeship available to the sons of aliens so long as their fathers had been naturalized before their birth. In 1751 the City admitted by apprenticeship to the Drapers' Company the son of an alien who had never been naturalized. Yet even admission to the freedom did not always secure an immigrant the right to exercise his trade in peace. A French button-seller who had lived in England for twenty years, had married an Englishwoman, had been endenizened, and had been made free of the City of London petitioned the Crown in 1677 that he had been "violently prosecuted" by several Englishmen of his trade.[39] Even surmounting the obstacles placed in the way by the corporations offered no absolute assurance of protection to immigrant tradesmen. The foreign churches, which sometimes acted as informal employment clearinghouses for their members, sought to protect immigrant tradesmen's right to work against the opposition of English tradesmen, the guilds, and the corporations. In 1663 the committee of the French and Dutch churches of London petitioned the king that he ensure that foreign artisans be able to exercise their trades without suits or molestation. The churches looked to the Crown for help when the harrassment of the native English threatened, as did individual foreign tradesmen.[40]

Beyond the freedom of the City, the requirement to serve a seven years' apprenticeship before practicing a trade presented another obstacle to foreign tradesmen. The issue of apprenticeship formed the central complaint in many of the petitions against foreigners from English tradesmen or from the craft guilds. Most of these were addressed to the Crown, for example the memorial of the silversmiths in 1668 complaining that Frenchmen were working outside their charter, and their similar petition of 1682 to preserve their privileges. A petition to the Crown in 1686 from the "handicraft and retail tradesmen" of London complained generally of aliens practicing trades in and around the City. The Company of Musicians petitioned the City's Common Council in 1693 against that most notorious brand of Frenchman, complaining that "many dancing-masters that are foreigners" keep "rude and disorderly schools," and demanding that only freemen, "such as are civilized persons" be allowed to exercise the trade.[41]

The petitions from Englishmen resentful of the foreign presence on their soil betray more than simply dull malice. Native artisans perceived themselves as possessing a sort of property right in their nationality, the "birthright of an Englishman," and their opposition to foreign settlers expressed their conviction that the encouragement and reception of immigrants infringed natal political and economic rights. Thus a conception of property rights grounded in proven skills and traditional and restrictive paternalist laws and customs conspired with an underlying cultural xenophobia to form an important feature of popular and artisanal culture.[42] English tradesmen saw foreigners in England as competing unfairly by subsisting on "roots," living in garrets, and employing outlandish manufacturing methods.[43] Such interlopers violated the accepted social norms within which all were expected to live and work. E. P. Thompson's notion of the moral economy of the crowd, the popular sense of certain traditional rights and customs within a paternalistic social order, sheds some light on popular attitudes towards immigrants.[44] Englishmen who petitioned against naturalization, attacked foreigners, or demonstrated against them derived a sense of legitimation from their belief that they acted in conformity with a consensus of opinion that the admission of foreigners violated traditional protective customs, as well as the very letter of the law. Historians have acknowledged the role of xenophobia amongst London's laborers, artisans, and petty tradesmen in provoking popular disturbances in this period.[45] Those who took action against foreigners—especially in the industrial suburbs of London—belonged to the same groups of tradesmen, craftsmen, and apprentices that most often participated in crowd action to express their disaffection and unrest.[46] Moreover, they could and did cite laws to back up their claims: antialien statutes from the reigns of Richard III, Henry VIII, and earlier, that had long since fallen into disuse but that had never been repealed. English tradesmen directed their complaints then not only at the foreigners themselves but at the authorities who connived at or actively encouraged their arrival. Those in authority, the Crown by protection, the Whigs by encouragement, brought immigrants to England and countenanced their unfair competition, circumvention of the apprenticeship laws, and flouting of customary trading practices. England's rulers, English tradesmen complained, had overturned the exclusive rights of natives, a form of property in their skills and legal status, by the admission of aliens.

In view of the bitterness felt against immigrants by many English workers it is hardly surprising that the government received a regular stream of petitions from foreign artisans complaining of harassment by the English. To such pleas the Crown responded promptly and effectually. The Privy Council Registers of the period are filled with cases of the harassment of immigrant tradesmen, mostly French or Dutch. The Council normally referred such petitions to the Attorney General; when the resolution of the grievance is recorded, it is almost without exception in favor of the prosecuted or otherwise molested immigrant. The Crown, then, acted very much as the protector of the immigrant tradesman.

The petitions represent a variety of trades. A French "fringe and twist" maker of Stepney complained in 1676 of harassment in spite of his having practiced his trade in England for ten years and trained two English apprentices. An endenizened French maker of watch chains complained in the same year that his money and goods, and even his clothes, had been seized, and he had been sued for their forfeiture, by some people pretending a statute of Richard III. The case was resolved in the victim's favor "especially since by his Majesty's grace and honour he is made a denizen." In 1677 and 1678 the Attorney General stayed prosecutions against a French goldsmith and against a group of Dutch buttonmakers. In 1685 four Englishmen broke into the house of Jeremy Parvet, a French clockmaker, assaulted his pregnant wife, and took all his goods and money, claiming that he had forfeited his property because he was an alien artificer, but the Council ordered the property restored. In 1699, the Council referred to the Attorney General a petition from a group of prosecuted French bakers with the remark that the king was concerned that such people be free to gain their livelihood. In 1701 French Protestant silk-throwsters and bakers in the suburbs of London complained that English masters had "totally hindered" their trades, and in 1702 three French silk-throwsters petitioned that their skills had aroused so much jealousy amongst native tradesmen that an action had been brought against them in Common Pleas. In 1703 French braziers petitioned for their release after being arrested for exercising their trade. They complained that the English braziers were not incorporated, and annexed certificates to their petition to prove that they had served their apprenticeships. Even two hapless Scots shoemakers suffered the indignity of a brief imprisonment in 1677 for not having served their seven years' apprenticeship in England. These examples, which could be multiplied, demonstrate not only the sympathetic response of the Crown to the fate of immigrant tradesmen, but how often the English intimidated or prosecuted foreign tradesmen.[47]

Such harassment was not confined to London and its environs, as the case of Jacques Fontaine at Taunton demonstrates. Similar troubles afflicted a French tailor who complained in 1687 of being molested in carrying on his trade in Norwich. In 1703 French Protestants at Bideford complained that the authorities had imprisoned them for following their callings. John Chardavoyne had sold drapery, hats, and stockings for twelve years at Plymouth, but became the target of harassment by the newly-elected mayor in 1701. In November 1702 Secretary Hedges wrote to the mayor of Southampton that two French linen drapers who had been settled in the town exercising their trade for many years had lately been troubled by the magistrates of the town. Hedges ordered that the immigrants be countenanced and encouraged. The French cutler Phillip Gariot petitioned in 1705 that he had practiced his trade in Southampton for twenty-five years, but that his wife, also a refugee, was now prosecuted for making mantuas. The mayor replied that "Garrett" and his father had been allowed to practice their trade unmolested, but that the poverty of the Company of Tailors was such that it could not allow its privileges to be invaded. A relative, James Gariot, had been similarly harassed in his trade only a few years earlier in Plymouth. The harassment in all these cases came from either the city corporations, the chartered craft guilds, or from individual English tradesmen.[48] To these miscellaneous examples, which could be multiplied, may be added three more detailed ones: the fishermen of Rye, the hatters of Wandsworth, and the weavers of London.

In October 1681 French Protestant mariners and fishermen settled in Rye presented a petition to the king. They had brought with them their boats, nets, and other implements, and sought royal protection to practice their trade as fishermen. This they soon received, on condition that they produce a certificate from the Archbishop of Canterbury or the Bishop of London affirming that they were genuine Protestant refugees. On 16 November the Council resolved to alter its earlier order, making the licenses granted to the fishermen valid for only one year.[49] Well before the year had passed, however, in March 1682, the Rye fishermen petitioned the king again. The mayor had disturbed them in their trade on the pretence that their nets were not of the same fashion as the English, and they had been assaulted by the townspeople as they were going to church. The Privy Council ordered that the harassment stop, but again in 1684 trouble erupted. The English fishermen threatened to burn the nets of the French, and Secretary Jenkins wrote to the mayor of Rye directing that the seizure of the nets be stopped until the Council had resolved the problem. The incensed English fishermen would not be stopped, and obtained an order for burning the nets of the French. Jenkins wrote again a few days later insisting that the foreigners must not be disturbed until the Council had heard the parties. The French fishermen failed to appear before the Council for a hearing on 17 April, but the stay on the order to burn their nets continued, and the controversy apparently died down.[50]

From at least the end of 1682 one Daniel Brulon supplied the Court and the City with the fish that the French at Rye caught—the xenophobia of the Aldermen apparently did not extend to culinary matters. But in December 1685 the mayor and inhabitants of Rye petitioned the king that Brulon's "ill usage" of the French might make them a burden and charge to the town, and the Council directed the Attorney General to proceed at law against Brulon. The governors of Rye found themselves caught in an embarrassing dilemma between their resentment of the French competitors to the native fishermen, and their fear that if the foreigners were too severely exploited by one of their own number they would fall onto the poor rates. The Brulon matter was sorted out, and the authorities in London thereafter regularly renewed the Frenchmen's licenses to fish. After years of silence the French complained in 1698 that the mayor forbad them to go to sea at night as they customarily had, and pleaded that they must do so to get a subsistence for their families, who then numbered 400 persons.[51] No further complaints appeared from Rye, and the foreign community seems thereafter to have been successfully assimilated. As elsewhere, the dying-out of complaints about harassment bears mute witness to the economic integration of immigrant tradesmen.

Perhaps the most persistent harassment of foreign tradesmen came from the Feltmakers' Company of London and focused on French Protestant hatters, most of whom settled in Wandsworth.[52] The corporation admitted the feltmakers as a City company only in 1650, and the guild's journeymen soon earned a reputation for tumultuousness: as early as 1666 the feltmakers petitioned the Court of Aldermen against the masters, wardens, and assistants of the company. In 1696 a delegation of journeymen negotiated with the masters of the company to prevent a reduction of wages, and two years later several journeymen were indicted for their combinations and collections of money against their own company. Indeed, the feltmakers were perhaps the first group of laborers in England to form an organized combination to raise wages.[53]

When French Protestant hatmakers arrived in England they soon had a taste of the feltmakers' militancy. In 1663 the journeymen petitioned the Court of Common Council that "we have oftimes met in debate and consideration" and remonstrated without success against the practice of the masters of the company employing foreigners. The masters and wardens of the company responded that the journeymen demanded unreasonable wages, and argued that if employing foreigners were forbidden, freemen would move to the suburbs outside the jurisdiction of the company. In 1675 a dispute arose between one James Caron, a hatmaker from Utrecht, and the feltmakers, who had attacked him and then brought suit against him for not having served his seven years' apprenticeship. Caron had settled in Lambeth with his family of ten and established a workshop there. The Privy Council ordered that the company admit Caron and drop its suits against him, provided that he take two English apprentices and employ no more than five foreign journeymen.[54] At the same time, rumors circulated that the English hatters would rise against their French competitors in order to drive away from London all workmen who were not natives.[55]

But the conflict did not reach any scale until the 1680s, when French hatmakers from around Rouen and Caudebec settled in Wandsworth and introduced hatmaking techniques unknown in England.[56] The arrival of these foreign interlopers with skills superior to their own outraged the English feltmakers, and only thanks to the protection of the Crown, which granted them licenses, could the French manage to practice their trade.[57] The Feltmakers' Company petitioned the king in 1685 complaining that French immigrants exercised the trade of hatmakers contrary to the company's charter and the statutes of Parliament. The Council referred the petition to the Attorney General, who recommended to the Committee for Trade that the French receive licenses *non obstante* the statute 1 Rich. III c. 9,[58] with certain restrictions.[59] The Council issued the licenses in April: the French were limited to two apprentices, English unless their own sons; they were to employ only such French as were already in England; and they must employ two Englishmen for each Frenchman. These negotiated terms did not satisfy the feltmakers. They complained to the Council in December of the same year that more French hatmakers had arrived since the first group had received their licenses, and that they sold hats "up and down the streets," leaving the English with very little trade.[60]

The feltmakers used more direct tactics as well and succeeded in intimidating some of the foreigners into leaving the country. In February 1686 the Privy Council was told that although he had obtained a license, one Gamaliel Martin "being threatened by the hatters to be ruined, he hath left all there, and is fled beyond sea."[61] Despite such intimidation, French hatmakers continued to arrive and to receive licenses to exercise their trade. Some had been naturalized, others had been settled in England for some years, but now nearly all scrambled for licenses in the hopes of escaping English harassment under the mantel of Crown protection. The government issued some of the licenses on condition that the recipient trade more than five miles from London and outside the jurisdiction of the Feltmakers' Company,[62] but molestations, arrests, and lawsuits persisted throughout the 1690s, with the Crown maintaining its policy of protection. In 1694 the Council ordered the Attorney General to mediate with the Feltmakers' Company and any others likely to prosecute the French, and to enter *noli prosequi* orders as necessary from time to time. The order was renewed in 1698 and 1701, but no more is heard of the dispute thereafter. As at Rye, by the early eighteenth century the French hatmakers had imparted their skills to the

English practitioners of the trade and achieved a modus vivendi with the natives.[63]

The Weavers' Company of London provides a final and quite different example of the friction between established English tradesmen and immigrants. A very large proportion of the French refugees who came to England in the late seventeenth century were weavers by trade. Over three-quarters of the immigrant tradesmen identified in the registers of the French Church of London between 1698 and 1706 worked in textile manufacture,[64] and recent research has borne out the truth of the conventional wisdom that French Protestant weavers made a crucial contribution to the establishment of the silk industry on a firm footing in England.[65] Alien weavers often exercised their trade outside the jurisdiction of the Company, or simply in defiance of its authority, for the Company could not strictly enforce its privileges against such large numbers of foreign workers.[66]

The Weavers' Company, however, unlike its sister craft guilds, admitted immigrants to membership so long as they presented proof of training and experience in the trade. Usually the Company required at least three years' residence in England before admission, and it remained very grudging in its admission of foreigners as masters. The Company accepted so many foreign journeymen, however, that it found it convenient to have its admission oath translated into French as early as 1672, a decade before the largest migrations from France. The Company diligently enforced one important qualification, however, regularly imposing fines for its violation: master weavers must employ at least as many English as foreign journeymen.[67]

Membership in either the Dutch or the French church of London facilitated admission to the Company, for the two churches had arrived at an understanding with the Company's governors. In 1666 the Company petitioned the king that it "groaned under great oppressions and discouragements . . . by aliens exercising their trade," and two years later the French and Dutch churches responded by seeking to placate the Company and to obtain assurances that those who came to England on account of religious persecution would be admitted as members. The Company and the foreign churches had struck a temporary bargain as early as 1653, and in 1670 they reached another settlement in negotiations before the Privy Council. The arrangement thereafter seems to have satisfied both parties. The churches obtained the right to represent their members before the Company, and the Company in turn benefited by the churches' help in distinguishing genuine Protestant refugees from other less-desirable foreigners. The foreign churches strove with much success to protect the rights of their members, particularly the large number who worked in the textile trade, but harassment still occurred: angry English tradesmen seized or cut from their looms the work of foreign artisans, and vexatious suits were occasionally brought. In view of the large number of immigrant tradesmen working as weavers, however, expressions of resentment and eruptions of hostility remained remarkably few.[68]

The generosity of the Weavers' Company towards immigrants, however, was more apparent than real. In contrast with the Feltmakers' Company, the masters held a firm control over the Weavers' Company. A deep fissure divided the trade between the larger masters who employed considerable numbers of weavers, and the journeymen weavers themselves, the skilled laborers.[69] The alliance of the Company with the foreign churches therefore represented at least in part the alliance of the master weavers, almost all English, with a clearinghouse of cheap foreign labor, vetted as safely Protestant. The English journeymen were well aware of this. As the "London Prentices" lamented in a doggerel verse broadside of 1685, "weavers all may curse their fates, because the French work under-rates."[70] The animosity of the English journeymen and apprentice weavers to the French immigrants who usurped their work broke out on several occasions into open violence that, although it never exacted a high cost in terms of property or human life, nevertheless attested to the simmering hostility that lay just beneath the surface. No riots in this period rivaled those against foreigners in London in the sixteenth century.[71] Immigrants suffered intimidation far more commonly than actual violence. The frequent incidents in which small groups of Englishmen broke into immigrants' houses and seized their possessions presented a more immediate threat than large-scale crowd assault. When violence did break out, however, the identity of the perpetrators was seldom in doubt—almost all the open physical attacks upon foreign tradesmen came from English tradesmen, journeymen and apprentices.

Incidents occurred over the course of the period, though naturally they tended to correspond with hard economic times. Complaints against foreign artisans brought demonstrators to the door of the Commons in 1664, and in 1670 the Lord Mayor held hearings to investigate an attempt by the apprentice tailors to incite an armed attack on French tradesmen.[72] In 1675 rioting erupted as weavers attacked the engine-looms (used to manufacture silk ribbon) that they called the "French invention," and that they claimed had left thousands of them without work. The weavers had complained repeatedly to the authorities about the looms, and had grounds for arguing that their use violated established trade laws. The rioting, which started early in August in the eastern manufacturing suburbs, involved a good deal of personal intimidation and the destruction of at least eighty-five engine-looms, although the attacks were not directed exclusively towards foreign artisans—the rioters were said to break into "their fellows' houses, French or English."[73] But the rioters' name for the looms betrays the association in the popular mind of foreigners and the dislocations caused by technological innovation. Some attackers did single out French weavers, destroying their materials and rifling their houses, and when rumors spread of an intended massacre of foreign tradesmen the government called in the King's Guards to restore order.[74]

Disturbances again threatened to erupt in London in August 1683. The riot against the French in Norwich that summer that led to one death has already been mentioned. By 9 August the authorities had ordered a troop of horse quartered in Islington, Hackney, and Mile End "to keep the weavers in order." The Earl of Sunderland wrote to the other Secretary of State, Leoline Jenkins that "if they have any just reason to complain of the French, the law is open," but they could not take justice into their own hands. Thomas Atterbury wrote to Jenkins on 27 August that the apprentice weavers "do cabal, and intend a petition to his Majesty . . . in opposition to the French weavers," and others said that "if they can get a sufficient number together they will rise and knock them [foreigners] on the head." The English weavers were meeting in public houses, the ministry was warned— some spoke of petitioning the Weavers' Company, but others warned of the presence of the trained bands stationed nearby. In the event, however, though the statutes against aliens of Richard III's reign became for a time the shibboleth of the discontented, no violence broke out.[75] A decade later, in 1693, Tory opponents of the general naturalization bill then pending in Parliament distributed "great bundles" of Sir John Knight's inflammatory speech amongst the silk weavers in Spitalfields, but the anticipated disturbance did not materialize, and troops quartered in Wandsworth in 1695 pacified the journeymen and apprentice dyers who had threatened to pull down the houses of French Protestant dyers there.[76] Again, in 1720 during the weavers' riots against printed calicoes, French calico-printers and weavers became targets of attack, though resentment against foreigners was incidental to the central grievances that led to the disturbances.[77]

By the early eighteenth century the wave of French immigrants of the 1680s and 1690s had settled into a peaceful coexistence with the native English. The few Palatines who remained in England merged with the general population. However, the growing number of Irish and Welsh laborers who journeyed to the Home Counties each summer to assist in the hay harvest, or to work in London, often faced an angry English populace.[78] At harvest-time, wrote a pamphleteer in 1748,

> the city is [so] pestered with thousands of Irish people . . . that it is troublesome walking the streets for fear their pitchforks should run in your eyes, and of a Sunday they swarm so thick . . . that the sight of them is shocking.[79]

Such temporary invasions of Irish could be tolerated. In July and August 1736, however, widespread rioting against Irish immigrant laborers erupted.[80] In that year the old church of St. Leonard's in Shoreditch was being demolished in preparation for the construction of the present church, designed by George Dance the Elder. The stonemason in charge of the project discharged a large number of English workmen and replaced them with Irish laborers who worked at one-half to one-third the wages of the English. This provocation, with the additional grievance that master weavers in nearby Spitalfields had begun to employ Irish at lower rates, brought violent mobs into the streets of Shoreditch, Spitalfields, and Whitechapel. The rioters attacked houses where the Irish were thought to lodge with cries of "down with the Irish." The crowds pulled down houses, rioters and victims alike were wounded, and one youth was killed. Similar tumults occurred in Dartford in Kent, and mobs arose in Southwark, Lambeth, and Tyburn Road to demand of intimidated passersby whether they were "for the English or the Irish." Observers numbered the mobs at as many as 4,000, and the ministry called up the Tower Guards and the militia; but the easily-dispersed crowds reappeared repeatedly for over a month. The Irish workmen at St. Leonard's were dismissed, and the disturbances finally burnt themselves out.[81]

English economic resentment of foreign settlers only very occasionally led to open hostilities, but the occasional outbreaks of violence bear witness to the rawness of the nerve touched by immigrant tradesmen. Yet the craft guilds and their members failed for the most part in their attempts to prevent immigrants from practicing trades in England. Two circumstances explain the success of the immigrants of the late seventeenth century, most of them French Protestants. One reason was the support of the Crown, which protected immigrants, especially those with novel trade skills, and regularly redressed the wrongs committed against them by their English competitors. The other and more important reason for the success of the French Protestants was the trade skills that they possessed. Those skills aroused the hostility of the natives, true, but they also gave immigrants a means to establish themselves in their adopted homeland, to carve out an economic niche for themselves in England. English artisans sought to preserve their traditional restrictive rights, what they saw as virtual property rights founded on traditional norms and integral to a popular political economy of artisanal culture. This claim of legitimacy in resisting foreign settlements native tradesmen was called simply "the birthright of an Englishman," as they used the formula "taking the bread from our mouths" to denote the transgression of this unwritten standard. Yet in the long term the resistance of English tradesmen was doomed to failure. In an increasingly commercial society, foreign immigrants who could augment the size of a stagnant population and who could contribute new craft techniques and a spirit of industriousness offered too much to England for the authorities to allow native tradesmen to harass them out of the country. For reasons of protecting social order, as well as economic and political motives, the English government could not wink at English tradesmen's resort to self-help persecutions.

Ironically, those immigrants which challenged the established English artisans most directly made the most successful settlement. The French refugees' possession of economically valuable skills allowed them to create a place for themselves in the English social and economic order. The importance of trade or craft skills can be demonstrated by contrasting the French with the other large immigrant group of the period, the Palatines. The ministry and the Crown went much further in supporting the Palatines than they had with the French Protestants, expending enormous sums on their subsistence and attempted settlement. But unlike the French, most of whom had some valuable skills, the Palatines were almost all unskilled peasants—the few vinedressers among them had little to offer England. Moreover, the pattern of English hostility toward the Palatines differed from that towards the French Protestants. The craft guilds and the corporate cities do not seem to have molested the Germans. The poorer class of English laborer on the other hand, precisely those with whom the newcomers would be competing for work, succeeded in frustrating every expedient adopted by the government to settle the Palatines in some sort of employment. The conspicuous poverty of the Germans convinced the English natives that they had come to eat the bread from their mouths.[82]

The very different fates of the French and the Germans then reflect the importance of trade skills to foreigners attempting to settle in England, even though such skills or innovative techniques aroused the antagonism of natives fearful of competitors and jealous of their birthright. Immigrants with useful trade skills encountered the greatest direct hostility from natives fearful of their competition; yet the failure of those defensive attacks in the long term betrays the underlying weakness of the guilds and corporate cities, and the inefficacy of artisans' attempts to exclude foreigners who infringed on the prescriptive rights that they viewed as part of their economic, cultural, and political inheritance. It was precisely the skilled artisans that successfully established themselves in England. They, unlike unskilled immigrants, managed to integrate themselves economically, to resist the hostility of the native English, and to gradually become an integral part of the English economy and society.

English attitudes towards immigrants cannot be fully explained on economic grounds, however, and even the addition of partisan political dynamics and religious considerations does not provide a full picture of the forces that conditioned the English reception of foreign settlers. Cultural and ideological dimensions of national difference impinged on English attitudes as well. A rich repertory of stereotypes of foreigners not only invited particular reactions to them when they set foot on English soil, but contributed to the coalescence of a strongly-felt sense of English—and at times British—national identity in the eighteenth century. Defining either public opinion or attitudes from historical sources of course presents formidable difficulties,[83] and in the case of foreigners one must distinguish between English views of domestic foreigners who had immigrated to England and foreigners abroad. In the most general terms, however, the pattern of English opinion conforms to the sociological model of ethnocentrism, that is the dichotomy between in-groups and out-groups. Foreigners, especially the visible ones who had come to England, stood outside the majority culture, and this otherness came to be particularly potent by the 1750s, in the very years when parliamentarians and publicists made the last concerted effort to make general naturalization a permanent national policy.

Sentiments toward foreigners did not necessarily grow out of direct personal experience, any more than they do today. Londoners had a continual exposure to immigrants and visitors, as had those who lived in a few of the larger towns, such as Norwich and Bristol, but most of the population probably never saw, or at least had dealings with, foreign immigrants. Popular prints provide the most helpful sources on English opinion, although literary sources, written either by English natives or by foreigners, also contributed to the creation of images of national character.[84] How far such prints and subliterary genres created as well as reflected opinion is a nice question. Perhaps the best answer lies in recognizing the dynamic interchange between representation in the prints or other media and a constantly evolving, often volatile, body of public opinion.[85] Graphic prints and popular literature offer a rich source on views of foreigners, but they must be used with caution. Some images of foreigners, for example those of the Spanish and the Russians, reflect little more than stale stereotypes of people with whom the English actually had relatively little contact in this period. Such representations tend to say more about international political circumstances than about deeper perceptions of national identity. The thrust of these materials in any case is perfectly clear: they expressed a robust chauvinism and perpetuated gross stereotypes, betraying, among other things, what Josiah Tucker called "the epidemical disorder of the country, an aversion to foreigners."[86]

Opinion about foreigners must be examined with reference to particular nationalities. Immigrants frequently voiced the complaint, however, that the English common people mistook Germans, Swiss, Danes, Swedes, Dutch, and Walloons for French. The natives seem to have had little difficulty in spotting foreigners by their speech, dress, or manner, but all were labeled as "foreigners," "strangers," or more colorfully as "French dogs." The term *French dog,* wrote the Swiss de Saussure, was "the greatest and most forcible insult that can be given to any man, and it is applied indifferently to all foreigners." Ironically, an observer in 1707 noted that the French refugees applied the odious epithet of "étrangers" to the English natives—cultural otherness could operate in both directions.[87]

Of the "mingled harvest of mankind" that came up the Thames,[88] perhaps the most detested at the beginning of the period were the Dutch. The Dutchman was associated with the hog or boar, a blunt and churlish creature given to drinking beer and eating butter. In the popular English conception he was lazy except where his own interests were concerned, a "slippery fellow" with a mean spirit of greed. The Dutch of all ranks, "from the boor to the burgomaster," as Swift wrote, possessed an "inferior sort of cunning" and a vulgar stolidity.[89] The Dutch came from a "quagmire isle," a "land of bogs to breed up hogs." They were "hogan mogans" whose coarse and oafish appearance belied their barrels of butter and money.[90] "High-Dutchmen," (that is, Germans) suffered little abuse in the prints and pamphlets, although the predominance of Germans among foreign mercenary troops contributed to their being seen as instruments of tyranny, symbols of a hated standing army, and impositions on the liberties of Englishmen.[91] Opposition to the first two Georges also cast a shadow over Germans more generally, but this was more a reflection of political and dynastic issues than of underlying national perceptions.

England images of Jews were particularly graphic, seizing upon the type of the Ashkenazim from eastern and central Europe rather than the Sephardim of Iberia, who were relatively much more assimilated to English culture. Stereotyped as peddlers of old clothes and other small items that could be carried on one's back, Jews were pictured as dressed in black caftans with long hair and beards, conspicuously foreign.[92] The virtual explosion of pamphlets, broadsides, and prints that accompanied passage of the short-lived Jewish Naturalization Act of 1753 betrayed the potential vehemence of anti-Semitic feeling in England, but it is notable that that hostility focused almost exclusively on trade and religion: race was scarcely a category by which otherness of Jews or other foreigners was judged.

England also received every year an accession of domestic foreigners from the Celtic fringe as visitors or permanent immigrants. Of these, the Scots provoked the most comment, and most contributed to the defining of the sense of English national identity in the middle years of the eighteenth century. It is for this reason, amongst others, that the national identity that developed in the middle years of the eighteenth century was principally of Englishness rather than Britishness, however much George III may have "gloried in the name of Briton."[93] Popular prints portrayed the Scots as backward and provincial, haughty and overbearing, scarcely better than dirty and penniless savages. At the opposite pole, many Scots, physicians for example, managed to make their entry into English society at a level high enough to arouse acute jealousy among the English. The odor of rebellion lingered round the Scots after the Fifteen and the Forty-Five, as did the stigma of the old alliance with absolutist and Catholic France.[94] Worst of all, the Scots were seen as predatory and cliquish fortune-seekers, as one print put it, as "a swarm of locusts from the north in search of profit and preferment" to batten on the greater wealth of the southern kingdom, aided by the arts of flattery, parsimony, and cunning. Charles Macklin satirized the type in the character of Sir Pertinax Macsycophant in his play *The True-Born Scotsman* (1764).[95] Feeling against the Scots reached its climax during the ministry of the Scots Earl of Bute.[96] One print of that time bore the title "The Caledonian Voyage to Money-Land"; another, depicting Scots descending on England in wagons and carriages, carried the title "We are all a Comeing." Another broadside, entitled "Scotch Amusements," portrayed Scots, including Bute, Mansfield, and other identifiable figures treading on English liberties, surrounded with all the paraphernalia of prejudice: a haggis kettle, basins of broth, ragged tartan clothes, barbaric Scots speech.[97]

The Irish stood no higher than the Scots in English opinion. Indeed, a German visitor at the end of the century remarked that the English were more averse to the Scots and Irish than to other foreigners.[98] The Irish came, often at first as seasonal laborers for the harvest, and settled in some of the poorest quarters of London and other cities. Many were unskilled laborers, often finding work in the building trade. Their Catholicism and poverty made the welcome they received from the English less than cordial. They were represented as either "Irish bog-trotters," that is, the poor and backward Catholic Irish peasantry, or "Irish fortune-hunters," the Anglo-Irish gentry in search of quick fortunes in England, usually, it was assumed, by an unscrupulous marriage to an English heiress. But large-scale migration of the Irish, and the coalescing of attitudes towards them, awaited the end of the eighteenth century.

The most powerful images and opinions referred to the French. By the time of the Restoration or soon thereafter, as a letter to Secretary Joseph Williamson in the 1660s put it "the humours of the people [were] very averse to anything of the French."[99] The English suffered from double vision in their image of the French. The French fop represented one stereotype. A popular ballad described the type as "a brisk young gallant newly arrived from France . . . garbed like any son of Croesus, perfumed, imbroidered, patched, and curled."[100] The French dandy was real enough, but he also personified the English resentment of French leadership in fashion, culture, and the arts, as well as the English taste for things foreign.[101] Evelyn denounced this French cultural hegemony in his *Tyrannus; or, The Mode* (1661) and a host of publications thereafter echoed his charge. *The English Lady's Complete Catechism*, a pamphlet of about 1695, complained that the fashionable in England must have everything about them either French or foreign, from their waiting-maids to their parrots. The French servants of the English upper classes suffered particular abuse, as did the *petit-maitres* with affected airs who were so often satirized on the stage. The "French manner" grated on English sensibilities, so much so that the French Church of London advised its members in 1697 to abandon their "proud and haughty airs" that antagonized the English.[102]

The English saw the French as over-dressed fawning rogues, given to philandering and intrigue, "accomplished Monsieurs" with "pert coxcomical looks,"[103] whose errors in English grammar and pronunciation, real or imagined, excited ridicule and parody ("it but three weeks since me came from France . . .").[104] Scarcely better were Gallicized Englishmen such as the

protagonist of Arthur Murphy's play *The Englishman from Paris* (1756) who
returns from the Continent a "ragout," vows that he wishes he "could obtain
an Act of Parliament to unnaturalize myself," and is attacked by a mob who
mistake him for a Frenchman, crying "no monsieurs, no wooden shoes, no
French spies."[105] In the eighteenth-century English mind, being French and
being English were two diametrically opposite states of existence.

These stereotypes represented more than literary or iconographic conven-
tions, for they expressed antipathies that played themselves out in the street
as well as in the press. Pierre Grosley found on his tour in 1765 that "the
most shocking abuse and ill language" met Frenchmen in England, especially
those of higher social station. To merely walk past the common people,
foreigners found, elicited litanies of "French dog, French bastard." While
passing through Chelsea, Grosley wrote, "a number of watermen drew themselves up in a line, and attacked [me] . . . with all the opprobrious terms
which the English language can supply, succeeding each other, like students
who defend a thesis." Grosley told as well of a group of Portuguese threatened by English laborers to "speak your damned French, if you dare."[106]
The Abbé le Blanc warned of the insults that attended anyone dressed in
the French manner, and de Saussure echoed him, advising that it was safest
to dress as simply as possible. Le Blanc thought that the stock character of
the Frenchman in the theatres played a powerful role in shaping the popular
prejudices of the English.[107] But English antipathy to the French had far
deeper cultural and ideological roots, however much le Blanc may have
been right that popular representations of foreigners contributed to English xenophobia.

English Gallophobia had another side, for the the opposite to the French
dandy was the penurious and oppressed French peasant. These two contrasting images of the French reflected Englishmen's conviction, by no
means wholly misplaced, that French society was polarized between the
magnificence of the great and the poverty of the mass of people. There were
two Frances and two kinds of Frenchman. This second sort of Frenchman
wore rags over his gaunt frame, clattered along in wooden shoes, munched
onions and garlic, and subsisted on *soupe maigre*. Fat popish priests and a
tyrannical monarch preyed upon his abjectness. In contrast to their dandified
compatriots, these French were notoriously parsimonious, living in lodg-
ings, eating vegetables, and making a joint of beef last a full two days.[108] As
one antinaturalization print put it:

> Wretched and tatter'd, full of Wants;
> Forlorn and friendless, hunger-bit,
> Hither he comes to ply his Wit,
> A Beggar first, and then a Thief
> If you deny the ask'd Relief;
> If you relieve his starving Need,
> Soon he'll requite the friendly deed;

Either he will your Pocket pick,
Or shew you some worse scurvy Trick[109]

Hogarth captured the contrasting French stereotypes in two prints: "The Gate of Calais; or, The Roast Beef of Old England" (1749) depicts the garlic-eating and sabot-shod French peasant, while "The Four Times of Day, Noon" (1738) satirizes the French fop, in this case just emerging from the French Protestant Eglise des Grecs, Hog Lane, London. The tendency of the English to bifurcate their images of foreigners, of the French, the Irish, the Jews, reinforced the comforting sense that England had achieved a middle way, that John Bull struck a happy medium of moderation between abject poverty and a corrupting luxury. Thus the stereotypes contributed in this as in other respects to the process of English national self-definition.

As Pepys wrote, "we do naturally all . . . hate the French."[110] Yet not everyone shared the common prejudices against the French and other foreigners. The Abbé le Blanc observed that, in contrast to the common people's insults, well-bred Englishmen displayed scrupulous courtesy to foreigners. Many continental visitors spoke of the effusive kindness of the English elite.[111] Of course, those foreigners themselves belonged to a broadly-defined elite, and most were sojourners rather than permanent settlers. Nevertheless, a real difference existed between elite and popular attitudes toward foreigners. Issues of party and ideology explain a good deal of this difference, for an open-minded reception of immigrants possessed strong overtones of Whiggish cosmopolitanism, while popular xenophobia allied itself with conservative Anglicanism, economic protectionism, and Toryism.[112] The political alignment of popular attitudes to foreigners, like partisan politics in Parliament, did not become clear till after the Revolution. Even then, both Whigs and Tories found occasions to exploit popular xenophobia, the Whigs warning of popery and Jacobite plots,[113] and the opposition proclaiming themselves the true patriots and defenders of traditional English liberty against foreign corruption and the betrayal of the Ancient Constitution.[114]

Yet by the middle of the eighteenth century a strong sentiment had developed that saw the Whigs as too culturally cosmopolitan, as the partisan embodiment of that aristocratic element in English society that embraced continental and other "exotic" tastes and ideas in defiance of the popular detestation of such things.[115] This cosmopolitanism offended the growing sense of national consciousness of the mass of Englishmen in the eighteenth century, and in the 1750s and 1760s xenophobia became what it had not perhaps been before, a buttress to a growing sense of national identity.[116]

There are many signs of the burgeoning of national feeling in the mid-eighteenth century as Englishness came to play a central part in the identity of the English people. The new personification Britannia, often symbolizing liberty, appeared at this time, as did John Bull, first in print and then in graphic representations. The ode "Rule, Britannia" was composed in 1740.[117] Histories of England and Britain, of which Hume's was only the most influential, enjoyed great popularity. Self-proclaimed patriots consciously attacked the cosmopolitan and Frenchified English tastes of the social elite. The belligerently English Hogarth, for example, carried on a campaign against foreign cultural influence in the arts.[118] In his print "Beer Street" he created an enduring visual emblem of robust Englishness. Handel turned by force of circumstances from cosmopolitan Italian opera, with its foreign *castrati* and *prime donne*, to oratorios imbued with indigenous Anglican feeling and whose Old Testament themes suggested that, like Israel, the English were a chosen people.[119] An increasingly national market and economy, a growing interest in tourism within Britain, as well as the tensions and trials of war all contributed to a more integrated and tightly woven social fabric and to a more conscious sense of Englishness. A developing sense of the otherness of those who did not enjoy the "birthright of an Englishman" contributed to this potent sense of national consciousness. The English image and perception of the foreigner betrays, by a sort of negative reflection, like the inverted image on the eye's retina, a growing sense of English identity.

Food and diet provide one example of the power of symbols in the definition of foreignness and Englishness,[120] for while gaunt foreigners ate roots and herbs (the French), frogs and butter (the Dutch), oats and haggis (the Scots), robust Englishmen feasted on roast beef and washed it down with beer—as the verse at the bottom of Hogarth's "Beer Street" proclaimed, water should be left to the French. From earthen dishes, a pamphleteer grumbled, foreign immigrants ate food that was fit only for dogs.[121] Partly a recognition that the English common people enjoyed a higher standard of living than their counterparts across the Channel, such elemental cultural facts as food, drink, and clothes provided another source of national pride and uniqueness. The English luxuriated in solid English-made woolens while foreigners shivered in ragged linen clothing. In the realm of manners and morals, again the English saw themselves as set apart from foreigners by their solid sincerity and unaffected, sometimes blunt, forthrightness, in contrast to foreign effeminacy, duplicity, and affectation.[122] The legal status of alien could be removed by the processes of denization or naturalization, but the cultural stigma of "foreigner" proved far harder to shed.

Attitudes toward foreigners then cannot be fully understood without exploring their relationship with the developing national consciousness in England. The images and stereotypes of foreigners briefly rehearsed here, nearly all pejorative, therefore constitute more than simply a catalog of English bigotry. These popular stereotypes and symbols convey in the language of metaphor a keen sense of the differences between foreigners and the English, and they thereby played an instrumental role in shaping the national self-image of the English themselves. The almost totemic images of foreigners go far towards defining the English view of the uniqueness of national character and reveal an increasingly intense sense of pride in being English, although prejudices against foreigners also reflected genuine cultural distaste.

Hatred of France in particular, the national embodiment of intolerance, popery, and absolutism, symbolized by the wooden shoes of the French peasant, acted as a foil to Englishmen's love of their "birthright" of liberty, the rule of law, and their balanced constitution. The antithesis of "wooden shoes" was the "liberty of the free-born Englishman." The English felt themselves unique for their liberty, their rule of law, and their balanced constitution.[123] That constitution was seen not simply in terms of politics, however, but as a constitution in Church and state, and English identity rested on a sense of the transcendent virtues of English Protestantism and the prophetic historical position of the English people. Anti-Catholicism strongly defined English national distinctiveness: wooden shoes represented popery as well as absolutism.

The vocabulary of national feeling often merged in the eighteenth century with that of popular xenophobia. In the 1730s protesting London crowds provoked by Walpole's excise bill chanted "no slavery, no excise, no wooden shoes!" Placards at the time of the Jewish Naturalization Act of 1753 juxtaposed distaste for Jewish and French immigrants with the slogan "no Jews, no wooden shoes!" In Bristol at the same time crowds chanted "no general naturalization, no Jews, no French bottle-makers, no lowering wages of labouring men to four-pence a day and garlic!"[124] These popular cries betray the many dimensions involved in the English response to immigrants. Cultural xenophobia and stereotypes of foreigners, the economic self-interest of tradesmen and the corporate cities, political conflict between Whig and Tory, City and Country, and finally a growing sense of national identity in England, all contributed to the complex reaction of English natives to immigrant settlers. The antagonism was not overwhelming: foreigners came to England in large numbers, and many eventually became integral members of English society. The resentments and popular prejudices of the natives, however, presented a formidable obstacle to the schemes for large-scale naturalizations that continuted to be promoted both in the economic discourse and in Parliament until after the middle of the eighteenth century.

8

The Debate to 1760: The Waning of Populationism

The notorious failure of the Palatine migration and the short-lived Act of 1709 deflected but did not extinguish the debate over naturalization. The economic discourse on population and immigration continued to evolve. Those on all sides, however, long shunned any political action that would have revived the lingering rancor left by the episode of 1709. From the repeal of the naturalization act in 1712 until almost the middle of the century not even the brashest Whig attempted to introduce a general naturalization bill in Parliament. When immigration figured in political discourse it did so primarily as a Tory instrument to denigrate Whig economic policy. Only in 1746, during a period of revived interest in the policy of encouraging immigration, did the Commons again consider such a bill. Thereafter, for a handful of years, the issue again became as combustible as it had been in the reign of Queen Anne. From the repeal of the 1709 Act to the 1740s, however, adversaries in the controversy over immigration confronted one another not in the political arena but in economic and political publications and in the growing segment of the national and regional press devoted to economic issues.

Towards the end of Queen Anne's reign the reverberations of the disastrous General Naturalization Act and the Palatine migration still echoed in the pamphlet literature and mingled with the discordant crescendo of polemics over the Hanoverian succession. The enemies of naturalization continued to denounce, even after its repeal in 1712, those who had sponsored the 1709 Act. Swift reviled those "who love a Dutchman, a Palatine, or even a Frenchman, better than a Briton," and who imagined that "trade can never flourish unless the country becomes a common receptacle for all nations, religions, and languages." In his *History of the Four Last Years* (1714), he declared that all the foreigners acquired by the act only increased the number of Dissenters, and grumbled with some justice that "the public was a loser by every individual among" the Palatines, who had come like "infants dropped at the door."[1]

Swift's partisan bile expressed the resentment that he and other Tories felt at the accession of George I. The issue of naturalization became one facet of the controversy over the Hanoverian succession, and for a few years it assumed more a political than an economic cast. Just as they had in the 1690s in the case of William III, diatribes against foreigners after 1714 implied partisan resentment of the new monarch. Indeed, the bitterness of the discourse on immigration deepened in the years immediately after the Hanoverian accession, despite the earlier repeal of the Act of 1709. In his notorious tract *English Advice to the Freeholders of England* (1714), Francis Atterbury, Bishop of Rochester, attempting to save the Tory cause, denounced the Whigs for their schemes of naturalization "whereby they would graft so many new exotic scions, of quite different and of base species, as entirely to alter the property of the old honest English stock." The Whigs, Atterbury complained, had betrayed the ethnic integrity of England in order to martial foreigners as additional forces in their political camp—an unconscionable opportunism that sold out the rights of Englishmen to the "outlandish craving cormorants" who had the new king's affection.[2] Such complaints about foreigners pulled only the thinnest of veils across the animosity felt towards the new royal family. As Bernard Mandeville, himself a Dutch immigrant and a staunch Whig, wrote in the ironically titled *The Mischiefs that ought Justly to be Apprehended from a Whig-Government* (1714), "the High-flyers in speaking of the King so often repeat the word stranger . . . only because they know that among ignorant and ill bred people, it is an invidious name" that assured an emotional response.[3] Nor did George I take any pains to make himself agreeable to English opinion, refusing to learn even a smattering of the language of his new kingdom, and thus reinforcing the xenophobic arguments of his adversaries.[4]

Debate continued for many years after the accession of George I over the naturalization of the small number of Germans who followed the Elector of Hanover to his new realms. The most notorious exchange occurred in 1717 between John Toland and an anonymous Tory pamphleteer. Toland, an outspoken Whig deist and a perhaps slightly embarrassing champion of the Hanoverian succession, had published in 1714 an impassioned and eccentric tract in favor of the naturalization of the Jews. That tract, though enlightened in its arguments, represented little more than a gesture of provocation in view of the events of a few years earlier, but Toland was soon embroiled in a more immediate controversy.[5] In 1717 he published *The State-Anatomy of Great Britain*, a blatantly pro-Hanoverian tract that suggested, amongst other things, that some of King George's German followers ought to be raised to the peerage—despite the prohibition on such ennoblements in the Act of Settlement of 1701.[6] Toland recognized that the naturalization issue was essentially partisan and ideological—"when they abuse the Germans, it is to wound the Royal family through their sides," he remarked—and he condemned the repeal of the General Naturalization Act as the work of religious bigots and political saboteurs who craved revenge for the establish-ment of the Hanoverian succession.[7]

Toland's tract provoked a reply, *An Argument Proving that the Design of Employing and Ennobling Foreigners is a Treasonable Conspiracy against the Constitution* (1717), sometimes improbably attributed to Defoe.[8] The author of *An Argument* denounced "the design of prostituting the illustrious blood of our nobility to foreigners" as a way to subject "a free and glorious nation, to the breath of a covetous Dutchman, a mercenary Frenchman, a haughty, insolent Spaniard, or a lewd, assassinating Italian." In addition to such ethnic and cultural pollution, the tract argued, the admission and ennoblement of foreigners would open the flood gates to religious heresy and schism.[9]

Toland responded with *The Second Part of the State-Anatomy* (1717), reciting the threadbare praises of the United Provinces' open-door policy toward immigrants, the virtues of religious toleration, and the necessity of a law for liberal naturalization. The French refugees had become useful and loyal subjects, Toland observed, and Hanoverian Germans, more akin to the English in language and manners, would bring a similar benefit to the nation (he scrupulously avoided mentioning the recent Palatine fiasco).[10] Toland denounced the machinations of the enemies of the Hanoverian succession, whom he charged had distributed broadsheets[11] warning of the arrival in London of large numbers of foreigners who formed an advance guard of a conquering German army.[12] The discontent aroused by such rumors had, he suggested, contributed to the Jacobite rising of 1715.

The final tract in this exchange, *A Farther Argument against Ennobling Foreigners* (1717), repeated the condemnation of naturalizations or ennoble-ments of foreigners, but retreated a bit from its author's earlier racial dia-tribes by remarking that "our business is not now so much about mixing of blood, though that is not insignificant, but about mixing our politics".[13] The admission rang true, for the exchange over the naturalization of the followers of George I concerned high politics rather than social or economic policy. Certainly the number of immigrants from Hanover in the early eighteenth century could have had no effect on the English population. In any case, the debate of 1717 over the naturalization of Germans and their admission to the English nobility soon died out, though high-ranking Germans contin-ued to receive private grants of naturalization from Parliament over the several succeeding decades.

The broader political contours of the population and immigration question crystallized at the time of the accession of George I in a way that lasted until nearly the middle of the century. The Whig policy of encouraging immi-gration suffered a severe embarrassment by the disastrous Palatine migra-tion, and that debacle had a lasting effect on Whig economic and social policy. The cosmopolitan Lord Stanhope, who served in effect as first minis-ter in the years immediately following the accession of George I, betrayed some sympathy towards a policy of liberal admissions of immigrants to England. In 1714, with Queen Anne in extremis, he had relied on his connections with the immigrant community in obtaining promises from the French Protestants in England, as well as from City merchants, of financial and armed support to secure the Hanoverian succession.[14] The eclipse of a liberal immigration policy may have been in part owing to the contest for power among the Whigs after 1714 between the Walpole–Townshend and the Sunderland–Stanhope factions—Sunderland, after all, had orchestrated the attempted settlement of the Palatines. But even had Walpole not emerged as the leader of the Whigs, probably nothing could have been done in the immediate wake of the failed Act of 1709, for the new regime would have betrayed a remarkable lack of political tact if it had embarked on so unpopular a policy as the encouragement of large-scale immigration.

Nevertheless, the now-traditional alliance between City financial interests, immigrants, and the Whigs, all intent on preserving the Revolution Settlement, persisted and gained strength under the House of Hanover. The Whig committment to a liberal admission policy held firm in principle. As Walpole came into the ascendant, however, the chances of any sort of active political concessions for foreigners in England dimmed. Walpole demonstrated no intolerance towards immigrants, nor did he neglect economic matters during his years in power,[15] but his personal involvement in the Palatine episode had provided a lesson that so astute a politician was unlikely to forget, and he scrupulously avoided such an explosive issue as naturalization. Moreover, by the time of the 1722 election that marks his firm establishment of control, the Whig party had divided into Court and Country factions. Country interests, whether Tory or Whig, never looked kindly upon the reception, much less the encouragement, of foreign immigrants, whether from motives of demographic engineering or party principle. Indeed, Walpole ingeniously appropriated from the Tories one of the most powerful forces in popular politics, xenophobia, and turned his new weapon on those who had used it in the preceding reign. The Whig government could now denounce Tories as potential Jacobites who would bring in a hated, foreign, and papist royal house. By making Jacobite dangers the object of popular hatred and fears their avowed hatred of foreigners was deftly turned against the Tories.[16] In consequence of this new political and ideological configuration, the Whigs in the 1720s and 1730s allowed the policy of naturalization to slip silently from the political platform of the party and of the government. Only in the 1740s, after the fall of Walpole, did Parliament again address the question of altering immigration and nationality law.

The opposition to Walpole, whether that of the Country Whigs or Country Tories, revealed far less inclination to promote immigration schemes than the ministry. Immigrants settled almost wholly in towns, and their reception only accelerated the process of commercialization that landed interests witnessed with considerable misgivings. Indeed, Country writers often cited foreign influence and aristocratic cosmopolitanism as the chief corroding agents acting upon English morals and the British constitution through Walpole's system of power. Bolingbroke's attacks on the ministry in *The Craftsman* decried the new commercial and financial social order and expressed the resentment of the gentry towards, as one of their number wrote, a government that had ruined "those that have only land to depend on to enrich Dutch, Jews, French, and other foreigners, scoundrel stock jobbers and tally jobbers who have been sucking our vitals for many years."[17] If Bolingbroke represented the civic humanist tradition,[18] it will be clear that he and his partisans had no wish to see an influx of foreign settlers who would threaten the integrity and homogeneity of English civic culture. So long as xenophobia supplied so powerful a weapon to political polemicists—and it grew more powerful with the blossoming of national feeling in the first half of the eighteenth century—the promotion of laws to encourage immigration posed formidable risks to any party. The quiescence of the issue after 1715 bears witness to the tendency towards political stability that stamped these decades, and that followed the political frenzy of Queen Anne's reign.[19] Few issues were more divisive than naturalization schemes. During the age of Walpole a change in immigration policy simply ceased to be an immediate political possibility.[20]

Despite its banishment from parliamentary politics, immigration did not cease to be an economic issue. The proponents of naturalization in the first half of the eighteenth century, however, often qualified their proposals in a way that the earlier economic writers seldom had. The reservations expressed in the 1690s proved prophetic of eighteenth-century views of immigration. Many tracts still advocated schemes for naturalization. Perhaps the most articulate and cogent arguments for the admission of foreign settlers appeared towards the middle of the century. But a long-term view of the economic literature reveals the 1690s and the 1700s as a watershed after which the movement for encouraging immigration gradually lost its momentum. The decline of populationism coincided with fundamental changes in England's economy and demographic circumstances, as well as in the early economic writers' ideas about population, employment, and the problem of the poor. Full employment came to be seen as the necessary condition for a successful reception of foreign settlers; worries grew that immigration could worsen the problem of poverty; and the belief gradually emerged that populousness represented not a means to prosperity but purely the result of a thriving trade and a benevolent and free government. By mid-century many observers doubted that population could be increased by deliberate government policy, and some even questioned the desirability of having more people. Despite these mounting doubts, however, a sizable, though declining, body of writers in the first half of the century still saw a naturalization of foreign Protestants as the fastest, easiest, and best way to expand England's population.

The character of the economic discourse changed in the eighteenth century as the media for its expression evolved. Economic publications became less numerous after the turn of the century, as the remarkable blossoming of economic discourse after the Restoration began to fade.[21] Bolingbroke's proposed trade treaty with France elicited a surge of tracts and polemical pamphlets,[22] as did the South Sea Bubble affair, but the first half of the eighteenth century as a whole witnessed a volume of works on trade that fell well below that of the latter part of the seventeenth century. The new essay literature of the eighteenth century filled some of the gap. As Addison's famous paeon to the Royal Exchange in number sixty-nine of the *Spectator* testifies, commerce became more and more respectable amongst those who wished to consider themselves as members of the polite classes. If it would be too much to say that trade became gentrified, at least an understanding of trade became gentrified, and by the middle of the century the most eminent philosophers, following the example of John Locke, did not disdain to write on economic subjects. The new periodicals that appeared from the 1730s onward such as the *Gentleman's Magazine* and the *London Magazine* gave trade matters an important place in their pages, and contributed to making commercial literacy a necessary attainment for the middle class and gentry who formed the bulk of their readership. Indeed, the periodical form, once well established, offered polemicists a way to reach more people than they could with a pamphlet.[23] So too did the rising number of newspapers, as provincial newspapers appeared after the turn of the century to augment those published in London.

Despite occasional setbacks to the press, such as the stamp duty on pamphlets and newpapers imposed in 1712, additional forums for the expression of opinion on trade issues continued to develop.[24] Although the volume of print devoted to economic discourse may have declined, the diversity of sources in which that discourse unfolded increased, and the breadth of its audience very likely expanded. Nevertheless, the drive towards new ways of thinking about economic matters subsided. The economy suffered few dramatic setbacks in the first half of the eighteenth century, and the pressure to voice economic proposals was consequently less urgent than in the dark days of the 1660s or in the turbulent 1690s. With no acute depression of any length, English trade, though it did not quite thrive, at least enjoyed stability and considerable commercial growth.[25] Walpole's policy of peace lessened both the strains on the state's finances and the need for manpower. Population did not decline, though neither did it grow at a significant rate.[26] In these economic conditions, the fears of depopulation that had fueled the immigration controversy, though not forgotten, no longer offered compelling motives for a reform of immigration policy.

The most important economic publicists of the first several decades of the eighteenth century was Daniel Defoe, and his writings offer perhaps the best point of departure for a description of how thought about population and immigration evolved in this period.[27] Defoe tirelessly campaigned, as has been shown, on behalf of the Act of 1709 and the Palatine migration, and his ideas in many respects represent a summing up of the arguments for immigration that had matured over the preceding fifty years. From the appearance of his earliest works, Defoe energetically promoted naturalization schemes as part of a general populationist economic policy. In an early work, *Lex Talionis* (1698), he proclaimed that "no number of foreigners can be prejudicial to England"; a million immigrants, "of whatever nation," would employ land and people by their consumption of the nation's provisions.[28] He elaborated the same views in the notable pamphlet *Giving Alms no Charity* (1704), and maintained that even two million foreign settlers could bring only good, since "multitudes of people make trade, [and] trade makes wealth." Colchester, Canterbury, and Norwich flourished in manufactures, he declared, because of the reception of Flemish migrants in the sixteenth century. He contrasted the generous encouragement given to foreigners in Elizabeth's reign with the complaints and ill treatment that met the recent Protestant refugees from France. Over 50,000 thousand of them had come to England, but 500,000 more "would be both useful and profitable to this nation."[29] Defoe never doubted that immigrants would quickly be assimilated by English society; he insisted that the "True-Born Englishman" had been a foreigner only a few generations ago.

Defoe's ardent populationism, then, lay at the heart of his vision of the English economy, and like the Restoration economic theorists before him, he conceived no limits to population growth. It was, he insisted in the *Brief History*, "the constant and experimented principle of all the rational part of mankind, that people are the riches, honour, and strength of a nation, and that wealth increases in an equal proportion to the additional numbers of inhabitants."[30] In this view Defoe betrayed a rather old-fashioned notion of the economic order, but in other respects his views looked forward to the future. In particular, his eagerness to portray the interests of land and commerce as entirely reconcilable in terms of immigration policy differs from the more strictly mercantile economic vision of many of the Restoration thinkers, and suggests his and other observers' hope of forging a less-divided community of economic and political interests in the years after the reign of Queen Anne.

"People are indeed the essential of commerce, and the more people, the more trade," Defoe proclaimed in the *Review*.[31] The potential benefits for trade of a larger population constituted almost an economic dogma. But Defoe stressed as well the rewards for landed wealth and agricultural productivity of an accession of foreign settlers. A reciprocal relation existed between land and population in his view, and this premise led him to urge the settlement of foreign immigrants on England's wastelands, as his proposals to the Marlborough–Godolphin ministry testify. He agreed with some of the more vehement opponents of immigration schemes that too many people worked in trades while laborers were sadly lacking on the land, but he optimistically believed that an accession of immigrants could be used as an instrument to correct this imbalance. In his ambition to settle immigrants on the land, Defoe stood apart from earlier economic writers, who seldom expressed opinions on where newcomers should be settled.[32] Other observers in these years shared his interest in settling immigrants on the land. Erasmus Philips, a tract-writer and essayist, warned in *An Appeal to Common Sense* (1720) against the excesses of the South Sea scheme, and proposed turning the frenzy of speculation in the Company's stock to public account. The Crown, he suggested, should grant wastelands to the South Sea Company, which could then sell the land to foreign immigrants enticed to England by an offer of naturalization. Like Defoe, Philips expressed an abiding confidence in the powers of an act like that passed in 1709 to entice new settlers to England; and also like Defoe, Philips counted the benefit of populousness as the expansion in the measure of aggregate demand, particularly for agricultural products, and the consequent improvements in the cultivation of land.[33]

Although the preoccupation with settling immigrants on the land may at first glance seem backward-looking in the rapidly commercializing economy of eighteenth-century England, in fact Defoe and Philips sought to articulate a new basis for an active immigration policy that recognized, if tacitly, the importance of land in the Whig dispensation of the Hanoverian age. Defoe's grand scheme for settling the Palatines on wastelands came to nothing in the end, and he expressed his disappointment in its failure.[34] Yet he continued to promote projects to encourage immigrant settlements to the end of his career. He set forth proposals similar to the one that he had advocated for the Palatines in his *Tour*, and in such works from the very end of his life as *Atlas Maritimus* (1728), *A Plan of the English Commerce* (1730), and *A Brief State of the Inland or Home Trade, of England* (1730).

Most economic writers of the early eighteenth century, however, took a more cautious approach to pleading for the encouragement of immigration, and laid increasing stress on the necessity of employment. The writings of Bernard Mandeville, not usually considered a writer on trade, but important to an understanding of the immigration controversy, must be seen in the light of this change in the discourse.[35] Mandeville acknowledged the desirability of a large population, but his ideas on this as on other social questions bore the stamp of his eccentricity. The notorious paradox expressed in his *Fable of the Bees* held that private vices brought public benefits, that is, that the "vice" of luxury amongst the elite promoted the economic growth and prosperity of society as a whole.[36] His views on the poor and on employment, and thus on immigration, grew directly from this central principle, for it assumed that society consisted of two classes of persons: consumers and producers. Mandeville saw national wealth and power as depending upon a large population of laborious poor who "have nothing to stir them up to labour, but their wants, which it is prudence to relieve, but folly to cure." He embraced with a ruthless logic the traditional view that wages must be kept low to force the poor to work, for the whole fabric of society depended upon a constant supply of "willing hands for all the drudgery of hard and dirty labour."[37] Mandeville followed the venerable moralist's distinction between those denied the opportunity of employment and the slothful who refused to work, but he did so in very sophisticated terms of the human psychology of diligence, industriousness, and sloth.[38]

In Mandeville's view populousness provided one stimulus to the industriousness of the laboring classes. In the sort of "frugal and honest society" that he disdained, economic stagnation would admit of no increase in population; but in a prosperous commercial society, complete with avarice and luxury, population must grow.[39] The admission of immigrants would provide a measure of this expanded population. The English mob, he admitted, might grumble because foreigners forced them to be more industrious, but popular resentment should not be permitted to frustrate the broader public interest. At worst, Mandeville wrote in a pleasing simile, receiving immigrants resembled the planting of trees: "they are chargeable at first, take up that ground which might be otherwise employed, and perhaps yield little or no profit to him that plants them; but then his posterity often make ten pounds for every six pence he laid out."[40]

Yet Mandeville did not advocate an active government policy to encourage immigration, since, he held, a country that possessed a sufficient reservoir of employment "must always be thronged and can never want people." To provide the opportunity of employment to everyone was enough, and to that end a government must promote manufactures and agriculture, the first to draw vast numbers of people into a nation, the second to maintain them there.[41] Mandeville, then, subscribed to the traditional views that prosperity demanded a large and growing population and that laborers must be compelled to productivity—views that were then under attack. His preference for government measures to provide the poor with employment rather than to actively encourage immigration, however, typified progressive economic discourse of his day, for the concern with employment that had emerged in the 1690s became the central theme in economic discourse in the course of the first half of the eighteenth century.

The growing insistence on providing employment compromised traditional pleas for populousness and the principle of a liberal immigration policy. The language of economic publications shifted from "people" and "numbers" to "labor" and "employment." The paradox of receiving foreigners while natives suffered from poverty and lack of work became more disturbing and undermined the pleas for a larger population. As David Clayton wrote in *A Short System of Trade* (1719), "a multitude of people are the real . . . riches of [a nation] if fully and profitably employed. But if those multitudes are idle, it is quite the reverse." In the same year John Cary echoed those sentiments, declaring that "people are the wealth of a nation, yet it can only be so, where we find employment for them, otherwise they must be a burden to it." Cary, a Bristol merchant, contributed to the refinement of the balance of trade doctrine to include the criterion that the better trade was that which created the most employment at home.[42] The partisans of particular trades began to boast that they provided a large measure of employment for the poor, and consequently deserved special privileges.[43] Other observers argued on the contrary that the diversity of employments that arose in a commercial society like that of England represented one of its great advantages.[44] Some daring souls even argued that the poor had a claim of right to employment: George Blewett wrote in 1725 that those without employment had "a right to a maintenance some way or other, and . . . society is under an obligation to employ them, or . . . maintain them unemployed."[45] The question of employment increasingly supplanted demographic issues in the economic discourse.

Defoe insisted that immigrants would not usurp employment, and that ample work existed in England for foreigners and natives alike. English laborers earned much more than their counterparts in other countries, he observed, and their high wages offered convincing proof that England lacked people, not employment.[46] Many remained unconvinced. The author of *Some Thoughts Concerning Government* (1731) asserted that the state had the twin duties of increasing population and providing employment. Marriage and procreation should be encouraged and rewarded, for the power of a nation depended upon the number of its inhabitants. Yet, the author of *Some Thoughts* warned, proper laws must be passed and implemented to keep all the inhabitants constantly employed according to their different orders and occupations; otherwise, populousness would avail nothing. A nation must therefore take measures to employ its people and to oblige them to be industrious, by "a due coercive power exercised over them."[47] The enhanced importance attributed to stimulating employment arose then from the conviction that a larger population alone, whether expanded by immigration or otherwise, would not necessarily ensure full employment.

Other observers saw the provision of employment as the only active economic policy that a nation could adopt, and insisted that population would take care of itself. "Does not every one know," declared the author of *A Letter from a Merchant who has left off Trade* (1738),

> that the people of a country always increase both by generation, and by the accession of foreigners, in proportion as the trade and manufactures of that country increase? When multitudes of poor are starving for want of employment, it frightens most of them from marrying, and instead of inviting foreigners to come and settle among you, it forces many of your poor to go seek for employment in foreign countries.[48]

According to this view, the only means to populousness lay in the creation of employment. Matthew Dekker, Dutch immigrant merchant, director of the East India Company for thirty years, and Tory MP, subscribed to this principle, expressing it as a maxim of state economic policy that "such as your employment is for people, so many will your people be."[49] Whatever stimulated trade employed the poor, Dekker declared, employment increased the number of people, and increasing the number of employed people increased trade and wealth. Freedom of trade and the sense of security created by political liberty would attract immigrant sailors, fishermen, and manufacturers as needed. But immigration, and populousness in general, Dekker insisted, were consequences of a thriving trade, and therefore not the proximate concern of government.[50] Thomas Baston expressed similar sentiments in 1716: "where trade is, there will be employment; where employment is, thither will people resort . . . would we once make trade to flourish, we need not doubt but people from all parts of the universe would resort hither." Both John Bellers and Joseph Harris also saw full employment of the poor as the best inducement to draw foreigners into England.[51] Prosperity and employment would act as regulators on the volume of immigrants and on the size and density of population.

The problems of poverty and employment represented two sides of the same coin, for poverty invariably followed closely upon unemployment in the preindustrial economy. The choice by publicists to speak in terms of poverty, however, often signaled a deeper disillusionment with populationist policies than that expressed by the proemployment school. Lawrence Braddon's sensationally entitled tract *The Miseries of the Poor are a National Sin, Shame, and Charge* (1717) offers a good example of the heightened concern with poverty and unemployment. Braddon claimed that England had nearly two million able but unemployed poor and that the poor rates exceeded £1,200,000 a year. He insisted that the poor must be provided with employment enough for them to earn the necessaries of life. The dream of multitudes of people had a strong seductive power, since no nation could be rich or powerful without being populous, but neither procreation nor immigration ought to be encouraged until all the native poor were employed or relieved of want. Otherwise, Braddon insisted, a large population would prove a burden and a curse, bringing national poverty rather than prosperity.[52] Moreover, only the prospect of ample employment, not hollow promises of legal rights by naturalization, would effectively attract foreign settlers. But invitations to foreigners must await a new economic dispensation for the English poor at home.

Of course complaints about the incongruity of widespread poverty and the admission of large numbers of immigrants had long been voiced, but they now found a deeper resonance and a more general assent. Defoe himself had earlier complained that England was "burdened with a crowd of clamouring, unemployed, unprovided-for poor people". He insisted that when he referred to "people as the great subject of trade," he meant "such as ought to be numbered among the people, not the passive, [and] good for nothing." The idle poor chose to beg rather than work, and beggars could be banished from England by putting the laws in execution against them. Three beggars in four, he exclaimed angrily, could work and support themselves by their labor if they chose.[53] Economic policy must therefore, he insisted, apply the canon of industriousness to judge the value of any laborers, native or foreign:

> Numbers of people are without question the strength and wealth of a nation; we most readily grant the general. But then it must be numbers of legally settled inhabitants, not numbers of vagrant and wandering people. Settled inhabitants are industrious, labourious, and lend their helping hands to all the exigencies of the whole body, whether publick or private. . . . These are the inhabitants whose numbers are of import in a government; and if we had two millions or three millions of such more than we have the kingdom would be still so much the richer and stronger.[54]

Immigrants willing and able to work would always be a beneficial addition to the nation, "though they brought nothing with them but their hands."[55] The fears of worsening the problem of unemployment, and of admitting masses of poor foreigners, Defoe insisted, had no foundation in fact. For a growing body of economic writers in the first half of the eighteenth century, however, Defoe's arguments had lost their cogency.

Workhouses offered one option for forcing the unemployed to work. The establishment of workhouses began in Bristol in 1696, but only in the 1720s, with Parliament's passage of an act enabling any parish to found such a workhouse, did this method of imposing discipline on the unemployed poor become general. Some 150 parishes built such institutions, and they enjoyed a considerable body of supporters amongst economic writers, churchmen, and civil servants. But from the outset other observers, such as Lawrence Braddon, denounced them as so many acknowledgments of failure. Even the defenders of the workhouse principle for dealing with poverty, such as Bishop Berkeley, Joshua Gee, and John Cary, saw little to praise in the realities as opposed to the potentialities of workhouses. Their penal quality made them mute witnesses to the misery of the poor rather than solutions to the problem of poverty. And none, not even the model foundation at Bristol, was ever financially self-supporting. The workhouses failed to reduce the problem of poverty, and the appalling conditions of many of them offended the increasingly sympathetic attitude towards the poor.[56]

The reservations voiced about immigration schemes betray the erosion of the optimistic faith that poverty could be abated and population dramatically increased at the same time. Moreover, the eighteenth century witnessed a growing concern for the plight of the poor that reflected more than economic anxieties or concern for social order. Complaints at the burden of poor relief betrayed more than simply self-interested grumbling on the part of those who paid the rates; many observers accused the existing poor laws of actually contributing to depopulation through parish officers' discouraging marriage amongst the poor in order to lower the potential burden on the parish.[57] But beyond the purely economic side of poverty, a more sympathetic attitude towards the sufferings of the poor arose in the eighteenth century as a humanitarian sentiment took root. The Third Earl of Shaftesbury's *Characteristics* (1711) gave the first intellectual expression to the idea of benevolence, and the charity schools that appeared around the turn of the century testify in concrete terms to the same impulse, though their creation also betrayed a desire to discipline the poor.[58] Mandeville scandalized opinion in part because the English had come to see philanthropic endeavours as not only morally but materially proper. Richard Steele spoke for many when he praised the charity schools as "the greatest instances of public spirit the age has produced."[59] Religious influences played a role in the emerging humanitarianism, but philosophical works such as Francis Hutcheson's *Inquiry into the Original of our Ideas of Beauty and Virtue* (1725) that relied on the sentiments of natural religion rather than the injunctions to charity of the Established Church played a larger part in nurturing notions of sympathy and compassion. A concern for the fate of the poor formed an element of Enlightenment humanism and faith in the essential benevolence of the natural order, as well as in the meliorative powers of the state.[60]

Compassion alone however cannot explain the alterations in economic thinking about poverty. James Bonar has suggested that the question of population was in the seventeenth century one of room (thus the concern with wastelands), and in the eighteenth century one of food. If so, the change reflected the growing sense that subsistence consisted of more than simply enough to prevent starvation. A sympathetic attitude to the poor suggested that incentives to labor could be as important as deterrents to idleness. A growing body of economic opinion applauded high real wages, as the view developed that productivity could be increased by a real wage that kept the laborer happier and healthier. Poverty and underemployment came to be seen as undermining the relative productivity of the English laborer, which was generally recognized as one of England's greatest economic assets. The gradual acceptance of the belief in the potential of raising the productivity of labor discredited the assumption that immigrants must be encouraged to flood the labor market with people in order to keep wages low and enforce industriousness. These developments in economic thought naturally cast a shadow over the proposals to encourage immigration.[61] Indeed, a paradox arose as it became difficult to reconcile the notion of individual welfare and happiness with calls for a densely-packed population. J. Bennet's maxim in *The National Merchant* (1736) that "the true and ultimate end of every government is the . . . happiness and increase of the people"[62] mingled incongruously the old and the new views of the laboring population.

As Jacob Vanderlint, a merchant of London, wrote in his tract *Money Answers All Things* (1734), the strength and interest of every state lay in its having as many subjects as could be supported "in a happy condition"—thus making happiness, or the standard of living, part of the formula for an optimal population. Vanderlint thus expressed the growing sentiment that the welfare of the poor represented an important social goal in itself. Laborers had sufficient employment, Vanderlint declared, only when their wages rose to "the just value of labour," which provided them with "the decent and comfortable support of a middling family . . . in that station of life," a standard that would embarrass many governments today. The revolutionary nature of Vanderlint's ideas, so far from the convenient theory of keeping the poor miserable, will be immediately apparent. The increase or decrease in the population of a nation depended upon the nation's trade, and a flourishing trade caused people to gravitate toward the new employment that it created. Despite such inherent economic mechanisms for migration, however, Vanderlint warned that a state could have a greater population "than the land it contains can well support." The land under cultivation must increase in proportion to any growth of population in order to feed the additional people, and if it could not be increased then the excess population must leave.[63] Vanderlint's view that public policy should promote a minimal standard of life anticipated the fears of overpopulation that had virtually disappeared for almost a century from the writings of English economic writers, but that resurfaced in the 1750s and thereafter.

The increasing importance attributed to the colonial trade marked another development in economic thought in the eighteenth century that influenced the controversy over population and immigration. As we have seen, the plantations were in the seventeenth century as often considered a detriment as an advantage to the mother country's commerce and population. In the eighteenth century, however, fewer and fewer observers considered the colonies a disadvantage to England, and many would have agreed with the panegyric of Bennet in *The National Merchant* that "the advantages we receive from our colonies are of a nature more certain, more durable, and . . . more profitable to Great Britain than any other commerce whatever."[64] So far from resenting the colonies as drains through which England lost people, economic commentators came to praise overseas possessions as means by which home employment and thus population could be expanded. The merchant Joshua Gee, for example, in his *The Trade and Navigation of Great Britain* (1729) lavished praise on the colonial trade as supplying England with raw materials that stimulated the manufactures that would in turn ensure a full employment of the poor. Over a million poor people, Gee proclaimed, could be employed if the colonial trade were managed correctly. One controversialist even declared that every laborer occupied in America created employment for three people in England. By creating employment, the colonial trade would correct any lack of people in England—so far had economic thought moved from the Restoration disparagements of costly plantations.[65]

Yet one result of the more positive view of the colonies was the realization that their need for people far outstripped that of England. If England had uncultivated wastelands, how meagre they were in comparison with the seemingly limitless wilderness of America! Bennet argued that the poor who burdened the English economy could be employed in the colonies where their labor would be worth twice its value in England. It was, he conceded, axiomatic that "the wealth of a nation consists in numbers of people well employed," but religion and natural sentiments suggested the multiplication of fellow countrymen rather than the naturalization of foreigners. In America Englishmen would breed faster than at home, and the limitless extent of land there could accommodate foreigners as well.[66] Thus the American colonies came to be seen as excellent breeding grounds, indeed virtual demographic hothouses, to increase the total transAtlantic population of English-speaking peoples. In short, thinking about population policy began to embrace not simply England but the entirety of the imperial dominions of the Crown.

The growth of British North America provided an example of how quickly population could increase in favorable circumstances, which tended to dispel the fears of depopulation of England. Between 1675 and 1740 the population of British North America increased some fourfold, and it was often said (by Franklin, Adam Smith, and Hume, for example) that the American population could double every twenty-five years.[67] American economic writers themselves clamored for immigration and the increase of the population generally.[68] Immigration to America encountered little of the native hostility and presented few of the political problems that plagued it in England. As a result, English economic writers, as they became convinced that a larger colonial population benefited England, embraced proposals to encourage the migration of foreigners to America even at England's expense—a French Protestant might do more good for England in Georgia than in Norfolk.

Consonant with this line of thought was Parliament's passage in 1740 of an act to provide for the naturalization of foreign Protestants who had resided for seven years or more in any of the American colonies.[69] The relative liberality of the act, which contained alternative procedures for Jews and Quakers, contrasted with the lack of any legal concessions to immigrants in England in these years. The Act of 1740 bears witness to the pressing need of settlers in the New World, as well as to how much less controversial—certainly from the perspective of Westminster—was the reception of foreigners in America than in England. Of course the departure of people from the British Isles to North America represented something rather different. Emigration from Britain, and especially from England, could still arouse vociferous opposition, as it did during the large-scale emigration of the early 1770s, but such expressions of resistance were only sporadic; observers had very little to say, for example, about the transportation of roughly 50,000 convicts to America in the period 1718–75.[70]

In sum then, the growth in political stability, a policy of peace, the new stress on employment, the growing concern with the plight of the poor of England, and the favorable view of trade with the colonies and their powers of population growth, all conspired to erode fears that England had too few people, and contributed to the retreat from economic and political discourse of proposals for the encouragement of immigration. Yet in the 1740s and 1750s the issue thrust itself into the public arena again as several bills for a general naturalization were introduced in Parliament and the naturalization question exploded into public controversy despite the enfeeblement over the several preceding decades of its theoretical and demographic foundations.

"That the strength and riches of a society consists in the number of the people," wrote Henry Fielding in 1751, "is an assertion which hath attained the force of a maxim in politics."[71] But political maxims deserve the greatest distrust; they too often embody nothing more than the ossified memory of a truth whose day has passed. By the middle of the eighteenth century the force behind the pleas for populousness would seem to have been spent. Yet in November 1746, after a gap of almost forty years, a bill was introduced in the Commons for an act of general naturalization of foreign Protestants.[72] As in 1709 the initiative was partisan, led by the Whig Robert Nugent, an ally of the ministry and one of the Members for Bristol. Nugent, an Irishman born appropriately enough in the year 1709, friend to Pope and Goldsmith, husband in succession to two wealthy heiresses, had attached himself to the Pelhams at an opportune moment, and in 1754 he was rewarded with appointment as a Lord of the Treasury.[73] As befitted his party allegiances and the preoccupations of his constituency, he was an energetic and consistent supporter of measures to improve trade.[74] But why, after decades, did Nugent—with the approval of the ministry—revive the divisive issue of an immigration scheme?

With the fall of Walpole in 1742 the complexion of politics changed, as factions within the Whig camp struggled for predominance. The so-called Broadbottom Administration of the Pelhams that consolidated its power at the beginning of 1746 provided a much freer atmosphere for the introduction of a variety of Whig measures than had prevailed during the Walpole years. Moreover, a revived populationism appeared in the 1740s. The rate of demographic growth remained modest at mid-century—more rapid growth awaited the 1770s. More importantly, England, and Britain generally, experienced a far more pressing need of manpower from the 1740s onward. War with Spain began in 1739 and this merged with the general European and colonial conflict of the War of the Austrian Succession. Mobilizing troops for action on the continent, defeating the Jacobite forces of the Forty-Five, and manning the Royal Navy on which rode Britain's blue-water policy made the need of population acutely apparent. These challenges were redoubled by the dawning vision, focused by war, of an actively imperial British world role, as the costs of defending hegemony in the West Indies, in North America, and increasingly in India as well, wrought formidable transformations in the power of the state and its financial operations. John Brewer has explored the relations between state financial powers and the period of active war that began in the 1740s.[75] Another consequence of the new belligerence and the emerging imperial vision of Britain was a reborn populationism.

Patriotism and population went hand in hand, as did, seemingly, sympathy and self-interest. The celebrated opening of Captain Coram's Foundling Hospital in 1742, for example, symbolized not only the sentiment of compassion for the poor and the growing spirit of philanthropy but a revived eagerness to preserve and increase England's population. Hospitals multiplied in these years—hospitals to reform prostitutes to more procreative ways of life, lying-in hospitals to provide maternal care, hospitals for a variety of diseases that inflated the death rate—reforms that all reflected the revived populationist preoccupations of the period after about 1740.[76] Robert Nugent's resuscitation of schemes for general naturalization betrayed a more general concern with population.

Yet opposition to the measure remained as resilient as in earlier years, indeed more so. The opponents of naturalization quickly rallied at the introduction of Nugent's bill. In February the Commons received a petition against the bill from the City of London, which argued that the measure "would be greatly prejudicial to the revenues, trade, and liberties" of the City. The proceeds of the City's alien duties would be lost, and natives would be deprived of many valuable branches of their trade and their religious and civil rights greatly endangered. In March the Commons received a similar petition from the City of Westminster protesting patriotically that the bill "must divide and weaken the purest Established Church, and endanger the best system of government that human judgement is capable of forming." The Pelham ministry, fearing popular discontent with the measure, gave it little support, and in April the Commons on a division of 78 to 50 postponed consideration of the committee report on the bill.[77]

Events repeated themselves in the following session, when Nugent presented a bill on 4 December 1747.[78] The City immediately petitioned against it, and Tory MPs wrote circular letters urging that petitions be presented against the proposal when Parliament met again after the holidays. Pamphlets, newspaper articles, and periodical pieces appeared both for and against a general naturalization, and those opposed to it eagerly rekindled memories of the controversial act of Queen Anne's reign. On 3 February the Commons received a petition against the bill from the inhabitants of the City of Westminster, and the next day a well-attended and long debate ended when a motion for the commitment of the bill failed on a division of 167 to 103.[79]

Despite these defeats the perseverant Nugent introduced yet another bill in February 1751. The sheriffs of the City of London wasted no time in presenting their petition against the proposal, but the bill received a second reading and was committed before the Commons was deluged with petitions against it, the harvest of the Tory party's diligence in mobilizing opposition. Petitions poured in from the corporate towns, from Bristol, Salisbury, Thetford, Rochester, Southampton, Oxford, Reading, and Gloucester, all denouncing the proposed general naturalization scheme. The petitions voiced time-worn complaints: such an act would induce only the poorest foreign Protestants to come; foreign mariners would take naturalization and never reside in England, thereby frustrating the navigation acts (Rochester); the dearness of labor was caused by the high prices of the necessaries of life, so that foreign laborers would work cheaper than natives, who could not live so frugally (Southampton); the bill would deprive natives of employment, increase the poor rates, endanger England's "happy establishment of civil and religious rights," and would "pour in upon us none but the poor and outcast of other nations" (Salisbury); "it might be made use of by evil persons to instil uneasiness into the minds of" subjects and bring in people of "different persuasions," thus increasing schism (Reading); not one trade in England suffered from a want of hands, and the poor laws would be overburdened with foreigners (Gloucester). The barrage of petitions from the corporations, as well as another surge of publications against the proposal, would certainly have been enough to ensure the defeat of the bill, but the coup de grace was applied when opponents of the proposal presented the House with the old petition of 1711 from St. Olave's parish, the report of the Tory Commons Committee of 1711 on the petition, and the resulting representation to the queen, all condemning the 1709 Act and the reception of the Palatines. The 1751 bill, the last one for a general naturalization in the eighteenth century, was lost.[80] Britain's law of nationality and naturalization would remain unchanged until well into the nineteenth century.

One short-lived change in nationality law did occur in these years, in fact a postscript, but in another sense a climax, to the mid-century agitation for a general naturalization law. In 1753 Parliament passed the Jewish Naturalization Act, the so-called Jew Bill, amidst a furious controversy that forced the ministry to ignominiously repeal the measure at the beginning of the next parliamentary session.[81] The furor over the Jewish Naturalization Act, which allowed Jews to obtain private acts of naturalization in Parliament by the procedure already available to Protestants,[82] unfolded along very different lines from the debate over populationist immigration schemes. Many of the sixty or so tracts provoked by the act claimed that the question was a wholly religious one having little to do with trade.[83] Certainly those who attacked the act used largely religious arguments—but that does not prove that their motivation had any element of the spiritual about it. The City of London proved itself the act's most virulent enemy, and not because of the piety of the Court of Aldermen. The popular clamor against the act, replete with ugly scenes of anti-Semitism encouraged by Tory agitators, led to its hasty repeal. Although the Act of 1753 was not intended to encourage large-scale immigration,[84] and did not directly concern the population question, the events surrounding its short life reveal the same conflicting interests of trade and religion, the same narrow-minded fear of foreigners, and the same political partisanship, that figured so prominently in the controversies surrounding the bills for the general naturalization of foreign Protestants, the century-long history of which came to an end with the failure of the bill of 1751.[85]

Josiah Tucker, rector of St. Stephen's, Bristol, and later Dean of Gloucester, served as the most prominent spokesman for the revived populationism of the mid-eighteenth century. His pleas for the encouragement of immigration and for the passage of Nugent's parliamentary bills marked the last substantial contribution to economic discourse in the controvery that had begun a century earlier. Tucker enjoyed a reputation as an expert on economic matters, and R. H. Tawney called him "the greatest English exponent [of political arithmetic] before the days of Adam Smith." Although Tucker wrote voluminously, and his views were highly respected, he was unable to break free from the old mercantilist prejudices, for example against the colonies, that Adam Smith finally laid to rest a few years later. He began his career as a publicist with the advocacy of immigration schemes (another example of his conservatism), for the populationism of the 1740s and 1750s enjoyed more support in political circles than amongst economic theorists. Nor did his championing of naturalization increase Tucker's popularity. He complained of the "fury and resentment" occasioned by his tracts on naturalization, and when the news reached Bristol in April 1751 of the defeat of the general naturalization bill then pending in Parliament the bells were rung and several effigies of Tucker, an ally and friend of Nugent, were paraded about the town and then cast into bonfires "with all the marks of detestation and contempt" of which the Bristol populace were capable.[86]

Tucker was a staunch populationist who echoed the truism that "numbers of inhabitants are the strength, riches, and security" of a nation. In sparsely populated countries, he believed, people lived beyond the pale of civilization, existing like "the brute savages of the woods and mountains." He subscribed to the traditional view that England had been depopulated by the plantations, and that "the gallows and electioneering, spirituous liquors and debauchery, have destroyed their millions." He consequently condemned as absurd the notion that England had too many people. Populousness tended to promote industry and good morals, Tucker argued, which in turn promoted populousness. There were too many bachelors, and marriages produced too few children, he declared, offering lengthy proposals for increasing English fertility in his unpublished treatise *The Elements of Commerce and Theory of Taxes* (1755).[87]

Like most of his contemporaries, Tucker viewed employment as the cornerstone of economic prosperity. The test for all "points of commerce," he wrote, was "which scheme tends to find a constant employ for most hands at home, and to export most labour abroad?" He christened his theory of wealth—hardly novel but articulated with perspicuity—the "balance of industry": this formula would be the talisman of national prosperity. No effect of diminishing returns would follow upon an increase in population, Tucker insisted, since one man's labor created a proportional amount of employment for another, and immigrants would banish laziness and debauchery by their example. A naturalization bill could never pass, he warned, on the condition that employment must be found for foreigners before they arrived—should more children be prevented from being born until all were provided with prospective employment?[88] Adult immigrants would immediately enrich the nation with their industry. They would come as a gentle stream, not as a torrent, and they would be the industrious rather than beggars, for the poor would not be encouraged to migrate by an offer of naturalization. He scoffed at the inconsistency in the two principal arguments against naturalization that charged on the one hand that England would be deluged by foreign beggars and on the other that immigrants would undercut the natives and take the bread from their mouths.[89]

Despite his efforts, Tucker saw one naturalization bill after another introduced by his friend Nugent and then defeated in the space of a few years. In a chapter of one of his tracts entitled "Historical Remarks on the Disposition and Behaviour of the Natives of this Island towards Foreigners" he denounced the "narrow spirit and perverseness" of the English, and "the epidemical disorder of the country, an aversion to foreigners," echoing Defoe's frustrated complaints of a half-century earlier. How different from this, he lamented, was the policy with regard to the colonies, where the value of numbers of people was justly regarded. By 1755 he declared in exasperation that "this harmless word [naturalization] has by art and industry been made such a bugbear, that the very sound of it carries dread and terror." He proposed instead a set of reforms that would have amounted to de facto naturalization without the name, and suggested that the proposed privileges be considered as a national advertisement and be announced in foreign gazettes several times a year. But the cause was already lost. The last flurry of attempts to promulgate a general naturalization act had failed, enthusiasm soon evaporated, and the movement to encourage immigration, by the 1750s largely shorn of its theoretical and empirical underpinnings, would soon become a thing of the past.[90]

Other tracts written at the time of the mid-century controversy more truly represent the evolution of thought about population in the first half of the century than Tucker's. Even those who wrote in favor of the bills did so with a pronounced reserve. Many of the old arguments saw the light again, but some new reasoning entered the debate. The rise of the unincorporated towns in which the industrial revolution was about to be born offered an

example of the advantages of free trade and free entry: Birmingham flourished because of its free admission of migrants from within England, why
could the nation not do likewise with respect to migrants from abroad? The
very high mortality rate of London led one pamphleteer to suggest that
naturalized foreigners could take the place of Englishmen in the urban
breach, and natives could then be preserved on the farms and in manufacturing towns. Other observers posed the new argument that the increase in
the number of laborers by a naturalization would help to prevent, as the
Gentleman's Magazine put it in 1751, "the combinations of journeymen so
loudly complained of and severely felt throughout the kingdom." Another
argument held that since foreigners owned a large proportion of the public
debt, according to Tucker as much as fifteen or twenty million pounds, they
should be naturalized and required to reside in the kingdom so that they
would spend their income and dividends at home rather than abroad.[91]

But those who argued against the policy of naturalization in the 1740s and
1750s prevailed. Jonas Hanway, merchant, philanthropist, and a prolific
writer on a variety of public questions,[92] vowed in his tract against the Jew
Bill that England already had more people than could be fully employed.
The nation wanted not new people but new trades in which to employ those
already here. The "number of the working poor . . . constitute the chief
riches of a nation," Hanway urged, but the cost of maintaining the unemployed poor weighed heavily on the whole nation. The solution lay in the
reform of the idle and profligate English poor rather than in immigration, he
declared.[93] Other observers, such as Thomas Alcock and Thomas Salmon,
agreed that however valuable migrants might be for the colonies, they could
do little but multiply poverty in England.[94]

An episode involving the Prince of Wales, the future George III, casts
considerable light on the discrediting of the policy of encouraging immigration.[95] In the late 1750s the Prince's tutor and future minister the Earl of
Bute had his royal charge write several essays on trade. One essay of 1757
entitled "On Industry in Great Britain" addressed the "problem" of the
high cost of labor in England and the "idleness and debauchery" of English
laborers. There were too few people in England, the Prince wrote, and the
best way to stimulate industry, keep the poor rates down, and improve
manufactures, was by a general naturalization of foreign Protestants. The
ideas expressed in the Prince's essay reflect his familiarity with Dean
Tucker's writings; indeed, the Bishop of Norwich, the Prince's preceptor,
had asked Tucker to write a treatise on trade for the instruction of the royal
pupil. Tucker temporized and then declined the request, explaining that the
Prince's popularity might be compromised by an association with someone
whose economic ideas had earned him the distinction of being burnt in effigy
in England's second largest city.[96] The point was well made, and apparently
well taken, for the Prince in his later essays on trade made no mention of
immigration schemes. The desire to create the image of a popular monarch

who could symbolize the patriotic unity of the nation made such unpopular proposals untenable.[97] The episode reveals the importance of the continuing animosity toward foreigners, heightened by growing nationalist sentiment, in scotching naturalization schemes.

At the same time that the last gusts of controversy swirled around general naturalization schemes, interest revived in the project of the political arithmeticians to determine the exact population of England. With growing concern in the 1740s and 1750s about manpower and demographic stagnation, a numbering of the people suggested itself as a useful tool of governance, and a bill for a national census was introduced and debated in Parliament in 1753.[98] As Joseph Massie remarked, the widely differing estimates of population bruited about in the 1750s rested on a very slender foundation of evidence. An anonymous pamphleteer asserted that the primary reason for a census was to decide the question whether a naturalization of foreigners were necessary; but in fact the whole populationist drive of mid-century might be discredited or reinforced by the results of an enumeration.[99] It was argued in the Commons, however, and widely felt, that a numbering of the people would apprise foreign enemies of the nation's strength and pose a threat to English liberty by allowing "place-men and tax-masters" to extort private information from freeborn subjects. The principle of liberty and the specter of wooden shoes, either foreign or domestic, prevailed with the Commons and the bill was dropped.[100]

Curiosity over the nation's actual population was nevertheless not so easily dispelled, for the dynamics of population became ever more tied to the nature of the British imperial polity. Indeed, the remainder of the century witnessed a protracted controversy, brought to a climax with the census of 1801, over whether England's population had increased or declined since the Revolution. This new exchange over the question of population, which has been recounted and analyzed by D. V. Glass,[101] must be distinguished from the debate over population and immigration that went before it. In fact, the two controversies, though obviously related to one another, only overlapped chronologically for a few years in the middle of the eighteenth century. The difference can be summed-up in a simple semantic distinction: the earlier debate concerned populousness and the later, population. Whereas up to the 1750s writers generally began with the normative proposition that England needed more people and proposed positive policy measures to promote populousness, in the second half of the century controversy revolved around the state of the actual population, as investigators groped towards a science of demography and vital statistics. The participants in the discourse over population in the latter half of the century concerned themselves far less than their predecessors had with prescriptive measures—in short, they were less actuated by immediate and direct policy motives. It is nevertheless worth glancing at the beginnings of the later

debate in order to note the transition from issues of immigration and populousness to those of demography proper.

The first phase in the controversy began with the publication in the *Philosophical Transactions* of an essay by William Brackenridge in 1755, and
developed into an exchange between him and Richard Forster. Their debate
principally concerned the method by which population could reliably be
measured in default of a census, but Brackenridge also argued that England's population growth had stagnated and that the country was "but
thinly peopled," for the normative side of the issue was far from a dead letter.
Immigration, he thought, had helped to compensate for natural decrease: "if
it was not for the accession of foreigners, and those who come from Scotland
and Ireland, the increase would be very inconsiderable, if any at all; which
by the way shows the reasonableness and good policy of encouraging foreigners to settle among us."[102] This argument, however, was by the 1760s
becoming somewhat out-of-date, since the terms of reference in connection
with population were being redefined to make the criterion for population
policy the good of the British Isles, or the whole of the British dominions,
not just that of England. Indeed, the opposition to emigration to America
that flared up in the sixties and seventies suggests the change, since nearly
all of those emigrants came from Scotland and Ireland rather than from
England.[103]

Forster countered that the measure of employment would naturally lead
to the correct size of population, and insisted that if foreigners were invited
in they must be immediately "re-exported."[104] The exchange between Forster and Brackenridge proved inconclusive, but the controversy was reani-
mated in a much more public debate begun by Richard Price's laments
over depopulation beginning about 1770 and embodied in his *Essay on the
Population of England and Wales* (1780). The furor raised by Price's assertions extends beyond the chronological limits of this study, but as a footnote
to the immigration controversy it reveals the enduring interest in the question of Britain's population in a period when very little reliable population
information was available.[105]

While the study of population departed from the issue of immigration, the
middle years of the eighteenth century witnessed a burgeoning of interest
in economic analysis that was international in scope. Economic thinkers
benefited from the cosmopolitan intellectual networks of the Enlightenment
and translations (especially between English and French) of works on commercial and demographic subjects became common.[106] Montesquieu's *De
l'Esprit des Lois* (1748) in particular acted as a catalyst to political and
economic thought throughout Europe.[107] The Scottish Enlightenment thinkers, above all Adam Smith, contributed to the creation of a recognized
science of political economy.[108] Some years earlier, and in the very different

economic and political conditions of France, the first true school of economists, the physiocrats, arrived at a view of population similar to that emerging in Britain.

In the eighteenth century, many observers in France worried about depopulation,[109] but the physiocrats concluded that the attempt to increase
wealth by increasing population would prove futile. The Irish merchant and
writer Richard Cantillon, a precursor of the physiocratic school, argued in
his treatise, *Essai sur la Nature du Commerce en Général*,[110] that the number of laboring people in a nation corresponded with the amount of employment available by which they could earn their subsistence. The means of
subsistence, the measure of which depended upon the state of agriculture
and the standard of living acceptable to people, Cantillon held, placed a limit
on population. Only by increasing employment and the productivity of land
could the number of people be increased.[111] These premises suggested the
obvious conclusion that schemes which sought to artificially expand population beyond the level that the structure of the economy could accommodate,
such as attempts to encourage immigration, could achieve nothing.

The Marquis of Mirabeau, father of the great orator of the Revolution,
was inspired by his admiration for Cantillon to publish a work in 1757 entitled *L'Ami des Hommes*. Mirabeau argued, in accordance with the tract's
subtitle, *Traité de la Population*, that a nation's wealth could be augmented
by increasing the number of its people.[112] From this traditional populationist
attitude Mirabeau was promptly weaned by François Quesnay, the founder
of the physiocratic school, and the author of the celebrated *Tableau Economique* (1759). Mirabeau, describing his first meeting with Quesnay,
wrote that

> I had reasoned in this way: wealth is the fruit which comes from the land for the
> use of men; the labour of man alone possesses the capacity to increase wealth.
> Thus the more men there are, the more labour will there be; the more labour there
> is, the more wealth there will be. The way to achieve prosperity is therefore: (1)
> to increase men; (2) through these men, to increase productive labour; (3) through
> this labour, to increase wealth. In this position I felt myself invulnerable, . . . but
> my critic [Quesnay] did not beat about the bush with me, and told me quite plainly
> that I had put the cart before the horse. . . . My man asked me to do the same
> honour to men as is done to sheep, since anyone who wants to increase his flock
> begins by increasing his grazing land.[113]

Quesnay and his followers arrived at what a biologist might call the habitat
theory of population: land and food determined the number of people in a
state, and influencing population size by direct means was impossible. Quesnay declared in his *Tableau Economique* that wealth determined the extent
of population. By wealth he meant the revenue of the state, and that was
determined by the "produit net," the product of agriculture. He even warned

that the population could grow too large for the well-being of the state by placing an excessive pressure on the means of subsistence.[114] In concert with the growing stress on productivity in English economic thought, Quesnay insisted that the quality and not the quantity of population determined the wealth of a nation. Economic thinkers at the middle of the century increasingly saw populousness then not as an absolute but as a relative quality. Whether the physiocratic view of populousness as a consequence rather than as a cause foreshadowed the Malthusianism to come, it did contribute to the divorce of demographic policy from the immediate concerns of economists.

An exchange between Montesquieu and David Hume, an example of the international flow of economic ideas in the period, betrayed another new facet of thought about population. Montesquieu had written in his *Persian Letters* that Europe had gradually been depopulated, and made similar arguments in *De l'Esprit des Lois*, saying that the ancient world had enjoyed a far larger population than did modern Europe.[115] Hume attacked this theory in his discourse "Of the Populousness of Ancient Nations" (1752), an essay that has usually been treated as one of the products of the quarrel over the superiority of the Ancients or the Moderns, or the Battle of the Books, but which expressed with Hume's inimitable clarity a new vision of population dynamics.

Montesquieu had named a severe or despotic government as one of the causes of depopulation, but Hume made much more of this idea, arguing that even the most absolute of modern governments allowed more liberty than any ancient polity had, in particular because of the institution of slavery. Since liberty created the great and fundamental condition for a large population, Hume argued, modern Europe must be more populous than was the ancient world. Although earlier writers, most notably Charles Davenant, had cited liberty as one of England's attractions to immigrants, Hume was amongst the first to declare that liberty was the mediating cause of populousness.[116] The relation between commerce and liberty became a popular subject of controversy, as some argued that only by commerce could liberty be achieved, and by others that liberty was the precondition of commerce.[117] On all sides the close relation between commerce and political liberty was acknowledged, for in mid-eighteenth century England the ideology of liberty reached an apotheosis. "The cause of Liberty," wrote Peter Williamson without embarrassment in his *Occasional Reflections* (1758), "is the cause of God himself"—and as England was the home of liberty the English nation enjoyed a special divine grace. As Blackstone proclaimed, "The idea and practice of . . . political or civil liberty flourish in their highest vigour in these kingdoms, where it falls little short of perfection."[118]

Economic writers joined the chorus in singing the praises of liberty.[119] Josiah Tucker eagerly informed his readers that foreigners loved English liberty and would crowd to enjoy the blessings of a free state and to engage in the commerce that itself rendered men free.[120] It would be naive to suggest that economic ideas succeeded each other like dynasties by the death without issue of the last male heir,[121] but by the middle of the eighteenth century liberty had been proclaimed as the criterion for the greatness of the British constitution, the envy of Europe, and enthroned as the supreme economic virtue for ensuring that a nation's population was sufficient and its trade secure.[122] The greatness and power of a state, an anonymous tract of 1753 argued, "consist in the number of its inhabitants, their industry, and their freedom." Freedom had become an end in itself. Benjamin Franklin, in his *Observations Concerning the Increase of Mankind* (1751), blamed "bad government and insecure property" as a principal reason for the decline of a nation's population. Hume declared in 1752 that "every wise, just, and mild government, by rendering the condition of its subjects easy and secure, will always abound most in people." Even Rousseau, by temperament hardly an economic thinker, completed in *The Social Contract* (1762) the apotheosis in the international republic of letters of liberty and good government as the engines of population growth. To the question "What is the best government?" he replied that the surest mark of the preservation and prosperity of the members of any state was their numbers: "the government under which, without external aids, without naturalization or colonies, the citizens increase and multiply most is beyond question the best."[123]

Liberty formed the foundation of human happiness, for a benign government that secured liberty ensured the well-being of its people.[124] Happiness, that elusive quality so dear to the eighteenth-century mind, became a factor in the demographic equation as well as in economic views of productivity. As Hume insisted, good government, liberty, and happiness determined population: "wherever there are most happiness and virtue, and wisest institutions, there will also be most people." Malachy Postlethwayt took the notion to its logical conclusion by articulating a "balance of happiness" principle of population: "if the inhabitants of one country enjoy more happiness than those of others, the latter will resort to the former of their own accord."[125] The eighteenth century created a veritable cult of happiness that ideally excluded no man or woman, however humble, but the stress on individual happiness, as we have seen, undermined the idea that a larger population was ipso facto better.[126] William Paley tried to resolve the contradiction with the utilitarian argument that a large population was desirable in order to achieve "the greatest quantity of happiness in a given tract of land."[127] But the incongruity of such a mixture of bastard mercantilist and utilitarian standards bears out the inconsistency of attempts to justify striving to increase population by active laws when the main principle of government policy was identified as the liberty and happiness of the people.[128]

Moreover, the spread of the notion that a cognizable natural law operated upon human affairs further undermined confidence in positive measures to increase population. The view that the state only needed to provide certain conditions, such as liberty, for commerce and society to thrive, supplanted the mercantilist conviction that the state must intervene in order to promote national wealth and power. Adam Smith's invisible hand could extend to guide the size of the population as well as to direct the price of turnips. The idea of an equilibrium in population size, postulated two centuries earlier by Botero but forgotten during the reign of the mercantilists, now gained adherents.[129] Indeed, the intellectual foundations for this change had been laid half a century earlier, for the fundamentally interventionist assumptions of the political arithmeticians who promoted immigration schemes and other populationist policies had been irretrievably compromised by the triumph of Newtonianism. William Petty died in 1687, the same year that saw the publication of Newton's *Principia*, and although the Newtonian vision of an ordered universe operating according to observable laws took a long time to penetrate economic thought, the conclusion must sooner or later be reached—and had been reached by the middle of the century—that population too followed the rules of a natural balanced order that political intervention could not alter. The scientists and philosophers saw this first. William Derham in his Boyle Lecture of 1713, *Physico-Theology*, interpreted patterns of births, marriages, and deaths, as evidence that a divinely established equilibrium created "a certain rate or proportion of the propagation of mankind."[130]

Beyond the idea of equilibrium, of course, lurked the fear of surfeit. The principle of natural limits gained ground in the eighteenth century and imbued thinking about population. Even Arthur Young, a conventional thinker in economic matters, questioned the value of what he called "indiscriminate population" and declared that a nation might even decrease in the number of its people and yet make great advances "in every point of real consequence." No fear could be more vain than that of a prosperous nation wanting subjects, proclaimed the cautiously orthodox *Politician's Dictionary* (1775), since "population will take care of itself."[131] After the middle of the century English writers on trade seldom expressed concern that a larger population was needed, the warnings of Richard Price notwithstanding. On the contrary, some observers began to voice complaints about the risk of overpopulation. A tract of 1748 warned in words reminiscent of those of a century and more earlier that

> our people being once esteemed the riches of our country . . . it may be thought they cannot swell to a number that may oppress it; but the judgement is relative, for . . . the swelling number, and its increase, will over-burden our country, if it remains in its present condition.

Franklin insisted that the admission of foreign immigrants into a country that already had as many inhabitants as its employments and provisions for subsistence allowed would not increase the number of people; any underpopulation would soon be filled by natural generation. The determinant of population growth, he wrote, was "the ease and convenience of supporting a family," and this would strictly limit growth in fully settled regions such as Britain or Europe. Population regulated itself, for nations resembled "a polypus: take away a limb, [and] its place is soon supplied."[132]

A preoccupation with the means of subsistence and a fear of overpopulation went hand in hand, and those observers who adhered to the pessimistic view anticipated many of the ideas popularized by Malthus at the end of the century. It is no coincidence that many of them were, like Malthus, clergymen. Clergymen perhaps naturally preferred a settled agrarian society to a dynamic society based on commerce, which was associated even by its defenders with sophistication, luxury, and a less than traditional moral ambience. William Bell, a divine and fellow of Magdalene College, Cambridge, provides an example. Bell earned one of Lord Townshend's prizes for essays on trade subjects by an essay published in 1756 under the title *A Dissertation on the Following Subject: What Causes Principally Contribute to Render a Nation Populous? And What Effect Has the Populousness of a Nation on its Trade?*[133] Bell argued in a remarkable anticipation of Malthus that the ability to obtain the means of subsistence limits procreation, and that agriculture places definite limits on the ability of laborers to earn enough for the necessaries of life. William Temple of Trowbridge, a writer on trade of the old stamp, was incensed by Bell's attack upon any active attempts to increase population, and upon Britain's commercial economic and social order generally, and published a countertract. But even his retort, which praised liberty and trade as means to increase population, made only a token apology for the policy of encouraging immigration.[134]

Robert Wallace, a friendly adversary of Hume's, expressed views similar to those of Bell. Wallace agreed with Hume that "that government policy is best, where most people are happy and easy," and that such beneficent and secure states were likely to have ample populations. But the causes of low population, Wallace held, were moral, and the vices encouraged by a commercial economy would eventually undermine agriculture, and limit the food supply. Even in the best-governed state land was ultimately limited, and thus a constraint on population always imposed itself, accelerated by the exhaustion of the fertility of the soil, so that the ulitimate fate of overpopulation would befall all human societies in accordance with "the order of nature itself."[135]

The flavor of Enlightenment pessimism, as well as the resemblance to Malthus's ideas, will be apparent, but it must not be thought that a new fear of overpopulation was confined to a clique of clergymen.[136] The belief that food supply imposed a limit on the size of population assumed increasing importance in Britain and on the continent in the second half of the eighteenth century.[137] Britain stood on the threshold of a dynamic demographic expansion that in less than forty years' time awoke new and more dire predictions of overpopulation. While no economic writers prophesied a demographic explosion, the previous fears of depopulation had largely evaporated by the accession of George III to the British throne in 1760. The intellectual and demographic motives for encouraging immigration to increase the native population had disappeared.

Conclusion

The controversy over immigration in the seventeenth and eighteenth centuries revolved around the central question of population. One of the objects of this study has been to relate the evolving thought on population and immigration as closely as possible to the economic, political, and social circumstances in which it developed. The attempt to make the economic writings more comprehensible, to deepen the meaning of economic discourse, has necessitated framing that discourse more firmly within its historical context. This in turn has meant the use of narrower chronological units than most historians have chosen, with a resulting stress on the evolution of ideas, a portrait in which change assumes at least as prominent a position as continuity.

The pleas for the naturalization of foreign Protestants cannot be divorced from, indeed were largely inspired by, the economic dislocations and the fears of depopulation that characterized the unsettled age of the Restoration. The controversy over immigration, however, falls naturally into three periods. The first stage began with the Restoration and continued through the 1680s, when the naturalization movement began and developed, fueled by the fears of population loss caused by the plague of 1665 and the economic crisis of the late 1660s. The 1670s witnessed the refinement of the arguments for the admission of foreigners as a remedy for the continuing stagnation of the economy. In the 1680s, a time of better trade, the controversy became imbued with the political and religious issues that dominated that decade. At this time also the organized opposition of the City of London, motivated by the desire to preserve its alien duties, first became an important force. The arrival of large numbers of French Protestant refugees around the time of the revocation of the Edict of Nantes in 1685 added a new dimension to the debate, though it deflected the lines of the discourse surprisingly little.

With the Revolution of 1688 the contours of the controversy changed dramatically, and its second phase began. From the Restoration to the Revolution the issue of religious toleration for Protestant Dissenters had been inseparably interwoven with that of the encouragement of immigration. After the Revolution the policy of toleration thrust the religious question to the periphery of the controversy, but at the same time the immigration issue split permanently along the ideological lines of Whig–latitudinarian and Tory–High Church parties. The party division over the issue reached the zenith of its divisiveness at the time of the General Naturalization Act of 1709, the culmination of the many abortive bills introduced in Parliament from the time of the Restoration. Indeed only because of the politicization of the issue did the Act of 1709 pass, since as an economic issue it had never gathered enough support in Paliament to become law.

Yet the Whig Act of 1709 came on the eve of the Palatine migration that would spell its doom. The Whig ministry's decision to embrace the German migration as an opportunity to put the policy into effect proved a costly mistake. The failure of the many attempts to settle the Palatines in England arose in part from the Germans' lack of any useful trade skills, in part from the assiduous opposition of the Tories, and in part from the Palatines' reluctance to settle in England after having been enticed to migrate on the basis of promises that they would be sent to America. The animosity that met the Palatines was symptomatic of the reactions of English natives, who feared that immigrants would "underwork and undersell" them. Yet English xenophobia also reflected cultural chauvinism and a sincere national pride in the "birthright of an Englishman." Antagonism towards foreign settlers and the opposition to immigration schemes were counterbalanced by the protection afforded by the Crown and its officers, protection that proved particularly important for the many immigrants, especially the French Prot-estants that arrived in the 1680s and 1690s, who possessed trade skills that made them a genuine threat to native tradesmen.

Despite the disastrous Palatine migration, the immigration movement was not completely discredited and the first half of the eighteenth century marks the third phase of the debate. In the eighteenth century concern grew over unemployment and poverty, and the well-being of the mass of laboring peo-ple came to figure in economic thinking. These developments dampened the concern for a larger population. The several attempts to pass a general naturalization act around the middle of the eighteenth century represented a revived populationism, but this new concern for the numbers of people followed different channels of expression from the earlier focus on immigra-tion. By mid-century the theoretical foundations of the pleas for the admis-sion of foreign settlers had suffered a great deal of erosion, and most observers saw population no longer as a cause of wealth but as one of the consequences of prosperity. Moreover, heightened sympathy for the poor and a growing school of thought that high wages encouraged high productiv-ity meant that a large population was no longer sought simply to keep wages low in order to discipline workers to industrious labor. The new stress on happiness and on liberty as policy goals signalled the end of the mercantilist era, and the demise of populationism as a matter of state economic policy, as incipient fears of overpopulation even began to be expressed.

The naturalization movement lasted almost precisely one hundred years, corresponding remarkably well with the findings of demographic historians that the size of England's population stagnated and sometimes actually declined during this period.[1] Although contemporaries could not have known very precisely the real state of the nation's population in the seventeenth and eighteenth centuries, economic changes that were conditioned by the number and density of England's people inspired their concern with under-population. The story of the immigration controversy therefore provides a necessary supplement to the conclusions of demographic historians on the actual quantitative state of England's population in the early modern period.

Yet an offer of general naturalization did not prove a feasible way to achieve the ends, most importantly the expansion of England's trade, sought by its advocates. The low numbers of naturalizations and denizations, even when the procedures were made cheap and simple from 1681 to 1688 and from 1709 to 1712, bear out the truth of William Petty's observation that offers of naturalization would attract few foreigners. The two largest groups of immigrants during the period were the French Protestants, who came to escape from religious persecution, and the Palatines, who came in reliance on promises of cheap land and favorable settlements in America. Some of these migrants sought naturalization once they had arrived in England, but the number who settled in England because of the chance of acquiring the legal privileges of English or British subjects must have been very small.

An offer of cheap naturalization was the wrong way to encourage immigration. Was the encouragement of immigration the right way to increase England's population? Again the economic writers' enthusiasm seems to have been misplaced. While in the economic and demographic circumstances of the period an increase in population ought to have had a stimulating effect, the desire to encourage large-scale immigration, rather than a gradual influx of people, risked the sort of disastrous outcome that followed the Palatine migration. Despite the groans of observers like Daniel Defoe at the vast extent of wastelands, in fact England had relatively little unoccupied land suitable for settlement and cultivation. Moreover, as the work of historical demographers has demonstrated, the preindustrial demographic regime possessed its own equilibrating mechanisms, particularly that of age at first marriage, by which the size of population directed itself, if crudely, towards an optimum level. Large-scale migrations therefore challenged the ability of the preindustrial economy to absorb newcomers, although England was able to integrate the regular flow of individual immigrants, particularly those who came to work as servants, that arrived without causing any substantial disruption. While active policies to encourage immigration by recruitment proved problematic, a liberal policy of reception seems to have contributed to English economic growth.

The distinction between recruitment and reception suggests other criteria that determined the potential success of an immigration scheme. Many of the advocates of immigration made no qualification that foreigners should possess trade skills, yet the Palatine migration illustrates the results of such indiscriminate zeal for mere numbers. The economy was most able to accommodate those with novel skills, but even those trained in trades that were already practiced in England enjoyed far more success than unskilled immigrants. In an increasingly commercial society in which both inland and foreign trade were growing at substantial rates, at least in the longer term, proficiencies that could contribute to the expansion of manufacture or exchange found a fairly ready acceptance. Agricultural laborers on the other hand were not wanted in a period when wages in the countryside were already low and the agrarian sector was undergoing difficult adjustments in the process of commercialization. Since immigrants tended to settle in urban areas, and especially in and around London, those in possession of urban skills proved to be the most assimilable.

The timing of large-scale migrations placed another condition on the possible benefit to be had from the arrival of foreign settlers. Large numbers of people tended to be on the move in this period because of the disruptions of war: the Palatines are a prime example. Yet these opportunities for England to recruit large numbers of migrants came at the times when, also owing to the disruptions of war, the English economy proved least able to absorb and provide employment for more people. This paradoxical situation formed part of a larger complication with immigration schemes: the craving for immigrants arose from economic hardships, yet those economic problems made the assimilation of settlers more difficult. Immigrants were sought when the economy was depressed, and therefore when the demand for labor was at its feeblest. In terms of the timing of migration, a more flexible and opportunistic policy sensitive to changes in international circumstances, such as that pursued in Holland in the 1680s, might have allowed England to exploit the shifting course of events abroad that made desirable immigrants available. A general naturalization law was far too blunt an instrument to serve this end. Yet party politics and an underlying current of xenophobia made a more nuanced approach virtually impossible.

Were the anti-immigrationists right in opposing naturalization schemes then? Few of their motives—High Church intolerance, economic self-interest, Tory partisanship, the preservation of corporate privileges, resistance to change—inspire admiration. Yet the opponents of naturalization saw clearly that the arrival of large numbers of foreign settlers in a short time would provoke a hostility on the part of the native English that would make a successful settlement exceedingly difficult. The anti-immigrationists, unlike their adversaries, recognized, and often exploited to their own ends, the cultural obstacles to the reception of immigrants. Cultural animosity to immigrants was indeed formidable, although strictly racial considerations, despite occasional references to the dangers of mixing blood, occupied only a peripheral place in the English reaction to foreign settlers. In view of the power of popular xenophobia, the success of an immigration policy depended not only upon its selectivity in terms of the economic role to be filled by newcomers, but upon its capacity to select those who shared considerable similarities of culture and religion with their English hosts. Only if the need for population had been more acute than it was could these cultural obstacles have been ignored without endangering the success of an immigration policy.

Despite the important place it held in the economic discourse, the immigration movement perhaps never could have borne fruit, at least as it was conceived by its promoters. In any case, by the 1760s England stood on the threshold of a dramatic expansion of its population, and the lingering appetite for more people soon would be finally assuaged. The epitaph of the immigration controversy had been written by Addison in the *Spectator* as early as 1711:

> When I was got into this way of thinking I presently grew conceited of the argument [for naturalization] and was just preparing to write a letter of advice to a Member of Parliament for the opening the freedom of our towns and trades, for taking away all manner of distinctions between the natives and foreigners, and removing every other obstacle to the increase of the people. But as soon as I had recollected with what inimitable eloquence my fellow-labourers had exaggerated the mischiefs of selling the birthright of Britons for a shilling, of spoiling the pure British blood with foreign mixtures, of introducing a confusion of languages and religions, and of letting in strangers to eat the bread out of the mouths of our own people, I became so humble as to let my project fall to the ground, and leave my country to increase by the ordinary way of generation.[2]

The recasting of Britain's immigration policy would await the nineteenth century, and the continuing debate over population after the middle of the eighteenth century evolved as a very different discourse from what had gone before, a discourse in which immigration played a very minor role.

Notes

CHAPTER 1. INTRODUCTION

1. Jacques Fontaine, *Memoirs of a Huguenot Family*, 122, 146–50, 155.

2. By the General Naturalization Act of 1844, 7 & 8 Vict. c. 66.

3. This book addresses the immigration issue in regard to England rather than Britain. Scots and other non–English Britons were usually thought of as foreigners during this period, and their arrival must be treated under the head of immigration. Nevertheless, the question of immigration policy was increasingly assimilated into a broader British, and indeed imperial, political configuration in the course of the eighteenth century. Moreover, the economic discourse of which the immigration controversy formed a part reflected a commercialization of society that embraced in one degree or another the entire English-speaking world.

4. James Bonar, *Theories of Population from Raleigh to Arthur Young* is an elegant but impressionistic set of studies of particular writer's ideas, and concentrates on the debate over the relative populations of town and country. See also, Charles Emil Strangeland, *Pre-Malthusian Doctrines*. More helpful is E. P. Hutchinson, *The Population Debate: the Development of Conflicting Theories up to 1900* (Boston: 1967).

5. See E. A. Wrigley and R. S. Schofield, *The Population History of England, 1541–1871*.

6. D. V. Glass, *Numbering the People*.

7. See, e.g., the collection of essays in D. C. Coleman, ed., *Revisions in Mercantilism*, and Walter E. Minchinton, *Mercantilism: System or Expediency?* (Boston: 1967).

8. This reductionist view has at times been wrongly associated with remarks in B. E. Supple, *Commercial Crisis and Change in England, 1600–1642*, 197–98, but Professor Supple's treatment is very far from such a simplistic interpretation.

9. An early example of this tendency is Maurice P. Ashley, *Financial and Commercial Policy under the Cromwellian Protectorate* (Oxford: 1934). Nor has this bias been absent from the recent literature. The work of J. C. D. Clark, in its eagerness to overturn a perceived economic reductionism, turns to a similarly flawed political and ideological treatment of causation. Clark, *English Society 1688–1832*.

10. A. W. Coats, "Economic Thought and Poor Law Policy," 39–51, 39–40. and Mark Blaug, "Economic Theory and Economic History," 111–16, 115 make pleas for this sort of integration.

11. An extremely important exception in the area of Anglo-American migration is Bernard Bailyn's monumental reconstruction of the movement of people to British North America in the 1770s, *Voyagers to the West: A Passage in the Peopling of America on the Eve of the Revolution* (New York, N.Y.: 1986). Most studies, however, have focused on the nineteenth and twentieth centuries, for example, Colin Holmes, *John Bull's Island: Immigration and British Society, 1871–1971* (London, 1988);

James Walvin, *Passage to Britain: Immigration in British History and Politics* (Harmondsworth: 1984).

12. Samuel Smiles, *Huguenots: Their Settlements, Churches, and Industries;* R. L. Poole, *A History of the Huguenots of the Dispersion;* William Cunningham, *Alien Immigrants to England.*

13. One reason for this is the nature of the surviving documents, the bulk of which are ecclesiastical. The celebration of the tercentenary of the revocation of the Edict of Nantes in 1685 produced a number of works on the seventeenth-century Huguenot migration, the most important of which is Robin D. Gwynn, *Huguenot Heritage.* Very useful on trades is *The Quiet Conquest: The Huguenots 1685 to 1985,* Tessa Murdock, ed. (London, 1985). An important work on the earlier migration of the sixteenth century, also ecclesiastical in focus, is Andrew Pettegree, *Foreign Protestant Communities.*

14. Bernard Cottrett, *The Huguenots in England.*

15. Denys Hay, ed., *New Cambridge Modern History,* 1:335–38.

16. Leslie Page Moch, *Moving Europeans,* 26–31; John Edwards, *The Jews;* Mack Walker, *The Salzburg Transaction.*

17. J. S. Bromley, ed., *New Cambridge Modern History,* 6: 30–31.

18. Pettegree, *Foreign Protestant Communities.*

19. Warren C. Scoville, *The Persecution of Huguenots.*

20. French refugees were often stopped when they landed in England to ensure that they were not spies. Those without passes were usually promptly released. *CSPD* (1693), 177; *CSPD* (1695), 9; *CSPD* (1692), 310, 403; I. Abrahams, "Passes Issued to Jews," 24–33, 24. The passes were simple one-page printed forms with blanks to be filled in and were not difficult to obtain. PRO, SP 34/11/167 (passes issued January 1709). The packetboats that transported foreign mails served as well to convey travelers to and from the continent. The cost of the journey was about ten shillings around 1700, including the fees of the customs officers who were charged with the duty of ensuring that those disembarking possessed passes and were not carrying contraband goods. H. D. Traill and J. S. Mann, eds., *Social England,* 4 (1903):822.

21. Wrigley and Schofield, *Population,* 159, 185–7, 195, 219–28; see Charles Wilson, *England's Apprenticeship,* 374.

22. I. Scouloudi, *Returns of Strangers in the Metropolis.*

23. The information that can be gleaned from them has mostly been published in the *Proceedings of the Huguenot Society of London.* On the problems of reconstitution, see R. D. Gwynn, "The Ecclesiastical Organization of French Protestants in England in the Later Seventeenth Century" (unpublished Ph.D. thesis), 390–91.

24. G. C. Gibbs, "The Reception of the Huguenots in England and the Dutch Republic," 275–306, 295–97.

25. R. D. Gwynn, "The Arrival of Huguenot Refugees," 366–73; Gwynn, "Distribution," 404–36. Gwynn, "Distribution: London," 509–68; *Les Huguenots,* 109.

26. Josiah Child, *Brief Observations Concerning Trade* (1668), xi.

27. This can be seen vividly in the registers of foreign churches published in the various *Publications* of the Huguenot Society. The only systematic study of the acculturation and assimilation of a particular immigrant community in this period examines the French community at Bristol: R. Mayo, "Les Huguenots a Bristol" (unpublished dissertation).

28. Cottrett, *Huguenots in England,* 177–79.

29. James Walvin, *The Black Presence,* 62; M. Dorothy George, *London Life,* 139–146.

30. Robert Sommerville, *The Savoy Manor,* 80; *The Case of the High German*

Reformed Protestant Congregation in London, 4–5, 13–14; J. G. Burckhardt, *Kirchen-Geschichte der Deutschen Gemeinden in London*; Guildhall MS 8356, fols. 3–52 (baptismal register, Hamburg Lutheran Church).

31. Ole Peter Grell, "From Persecution to Integration," 97–128.

32. J. H. Hessels, ed., *Register of the Attestations or Certificates of Membership,* &c., 72–176.

33. L. Hagberg, *Djacob Serenius,* 421–23; J. E. Pinnington, "Anglican Openness," 133–48, 146; PRO, PC 2/64/138 (petition and order for Greek Church).

34. Cecil Roth, *History of the Jews,* 158–172; David S. Katz, *Philo-Semitism.*

35. H. Pollins, *Economic History,* 43, 47–48; Roth, *History of the Jews,* passim; H. S. Q. Henriques, *Return of the Jews,* 97–98; Todd M. Endelman, *Jews of Georgian England,* 124, 168, 171–72, 175.

36. George, *London Life,* 120–21.

37. Gwynn, "Distribution: London"; M. Dorothy George, "London," 1:160–96, 179; W. H. Quarrell and Margaret Mare, eds., *London in 1710,* 12, 27–28; M. Corbyn, *Observations on the Past Growth . . . of London,* 22.

38. See Joan Thirsk, *Economic Policy and Projects,* 43–44.

39. Vincent B. Redstone, "Settlements of Ipswich," 183–204; PRO, SP 29/423/123 (memorandum, April 1683); P. Pett, *Happy Future State,* 257; A. F. W. Papillon, *Memoirs,* 118–19.

40. Gwynn, *Huguenot Heritage,* chaps. 4 and 5; E. Lipson, *Economic History,* 3:56; Wilson, *Apprenticeship;* C. G. A. Clay, *Economic Expansion,* 2:81–83.

41. For a more complete treatment of the issues addressed here see Daniel Statt, "The Birthright of an Englishman: The Practice of Naturalization and Denization of Immigrants under the Later Stuarts and Early Hanoverians," *PHSL* 25 (1989): 61–74.

42. 7 *Coke's Reports* 1a; M. J. Jones, *British Nationality Law,* 52–57; Clive Parry, *Nationality and Citizenship Laws,* 40–43, 52–56.

43. The Navigation Act of 1669, 12 Car. II c. 18, and that of 1663, 15 Car. II c. 7, required that the master and three-quarters of the crew of ships trading with the English dominions be English, and forbade aliens to exercise the trades of merchant or factor in the plantations.

44. A. K. Cockburn, *Nationality or, The Law Relating to Subjects,* 149; *Collingwood v. Pace,* Vaughan 274, 86 Engl. Rep. 262 (1664), 265; 12 Car. II c. 18, ii; 15 Car. II c. 15.

45. Parry, *Nationality and Citizenship,* 38, 49–52; Shaw, *1603–1700,* vi–viii; *Calvin's Case,* 7 *Coke's Rep.,* 25b; Sir Edward Coke, *First Part of the Institutes,* sec. 1, p. 8; G. L. Beer, *The Old Colonial System,* 1:70.

46. Sheila Lambert, *Bills and Acts,* 62, 32, 86, 38; C. Strateman, ed., *The Liverpool Tractate,* xxii; BM, OPL 356.m.3 (108); *CSPD* (Feb.–Dec. 1685), 238 (petition of June 1685); George Clark, *The Later Stuarts,* 56; *The Report of the Select Committee of the House of Commons on Fees and Salaries of the Servants of the House, 22 February 1732,* reprinted in O. C. Williams, *Clerical Organization,* 305–12.

47. Shaw, *1603–1700,* xxxiii, 124, 176, 180, 232; Parry, *Nationality and Citizenship,* 49–53; J. G. Burckhardt, *Kirchen Geschichte,* 11.

48. In contrast to the nationality law of most modern states, English law did not require residence for a space of time for either naturalization or denization.

49. Order in Council of 28 July 1681, reprinted in Shaw, *1603–1700,* 124–25; General Naturalization Act, 7 Anne c. 5.

50. The grants under the Order are recorded in the Secretary of State's Entry Book, and run as a parallel series to those grants made under the usual procedure and enrolled on the Patent Rolls. Naturalizations under the Act of 1709 were to be enrolled in the records of the courts in which petitioners took the oaths, including

Chancery, Queen's Bench, Exchequer, Common Pleas, in Quarter Sessions where the petitioner was resident, or in open court in Scotland. Lists survive only for Queen's Bench, Exchequer, and the Middlesex Quarter Sessions. An unknown number of naturalizations were enrolled in Common Pleas, but no one took the oaths in Chancery. Since most immigrants settled in and around London, the complete total would probably not be substantially greater than that given here. The surviving lists have been published in Shaw, *1701–1800*, and in W. & S. Minet, *Supplement to Dr. Shaw's Letters of Denization*, sec 2, 11–34.

51. I. Scouloudi, and A. P. Hands, *French Refugees Relieved.*

CHAPTER 2. THE FOUNDATIONS OF THE DEBATE

1. J. C. D. Clark, *English Society 1688–1832.*
2. Joyce Oldham Appleby, *Economic Thought,* 103.
3. Ralph Davis, *A Commercial Revolution.*
4. F. J. Levy, "How Information Spread," 11–34, 23.
5. Peter Burke, "Popular Culture," 143–62, 154.
6. Keith Wrightson, *English Society,* 193–94; Keith Thomas, "The Meaning of Literacy in Early Modern England", in *The Written Word: Literacy in Transition,* ed. Gerd Baumann (Oxford, 1986), 97–131.
7. *Craftsman,* 4 October 1729. See Edward Robinson, *Coffee House,* 106–7, 183; *The Character of a Coffee House* (1673); Bryant Lillywhite, *London Coffee Houses;* Ellis Aytoun, *The Penny Universities.*
8. Addison reckoned that at "a modest computation" twenty readers saw each copy of the *Spectator,* and the *Review* was as well known in its day; *Spectator,* no. 10 (12 March 1711).
9. John Brewer, *Sinews of Power,* 241–42.
10. Ibid.; Jeremy Black, "Print-Run," 345.
11. Tim Harris, *London Crowds,* 107.
12. J. R. Moore, "Defoe's *Some Seasonable Queries,*" 179–86, 183–85. Two typical examples are Roger Coke's *A Treatise wherein is Demonstrated* (1670) and Nicholas Barbon's widely-read *A Discourse of Trade* (1690).
13. Wrightson, *Society,* 194.
14. Margaret Spufford, *Small Books,* 45, 116–23; John Houghton, *A Collection for Improvement.*
15. David Ogg, *England,* 510–12.
16. It is this inconsistency and the lack of a set of accepted assumptions that has led some to question the usefulness of the term *mercantilism.* See E. A. J. Johnson, *Predecessors of Adam Smith,* 3–4; D. C. Coleman, "Labour in the English Economy," 280–95; D. C. Coleman, "Mercantilism Revisited," 773–91.
17. W. A. Speck, "Political Propaganda," 17–32, 27.
18. Keith Tribe, *Economic Discourse,* 35, 51, 81, 91, 145.
19. B. E. Supple, *Commercial Crisis,* 201–11; Eric Roll, *Economic Thought,* 68–76; B. Suviranta, *Balance of Trade.*
20. Richard Haines, *Prevention of Poverty,* 93; E. Lipson, *Economic History,* 3:84–86.
21. See Furniss, *Laborer,* passim; Jacob Viner, "Power versus Plenty", 61–91, 69–70.
22. Roger Coke, *Discourse of Trade* (1670), preface; Defoe, *Review,* 6:138 (1709).
23. Petty, *Treatise of Taxes and Contributions* (1662), in Hull, *Writings,* 1:68; Petty, *Verbum Sapienti,* in Hull, *Writings,* 1:110; on the male-female symbolism of land and labor, see W. A. Weisskopf, *Psychology of Economics,* 144–46. Charles

Davenant wrote in 1698 that "the wealth of all nations arises from the labour and industry of the people": Davenant, *Discourses on the Public Revenues, Part I* (1698), in Whitworth, *Works*, 1:138.

24. Hay, *Remarks on the Laws Relating to the Poor* (1735), 19.

25. Tucker, *Reflections on the Expediency of a Law for the Naturalization of Foreign Protestants, Part II* (1752), 19.

26. Viner, "Power versus Plenty," 69–74, points out that the belief in a fixed sum of global wealth contributed to a conception of economic rivalry that was analogous to the rivalry of military power; the preoccupation with labor, however, primarily concerned economic rather than military motives. See chap. 4.

27. Petyt, in McCulloch, *Tracts*, 458, 299. In the seventeenth- and eighteenth-century, economic writers' stress on labor can be detected an adumbration of Marx's labor theory of value. Like Marx, some early-modern observers recognized the paradoxically low share of national income enjoyed by labor compared to the value created by it.

28. Joan Thirsk, *Economic Policy and Projects;* Neil McKendrick, John Brewer, and J. H. Plumb, *The Birth of a Consumer Society.*

29. Locke, *Second Treatise of Government* (1690), sec. 40 (see also sec. 27); Sheridan, *A Discourse of the Rise and Power of Parliaments* (1677), 188; Marquis of Lansdowne, *Petty Papers*, 1:182.

30. Hutchison, *Political Economy*, 18.

31. Ibid., 20.

32. William Harrison, *Description of England*, 218; William Hunt, *The Puritan Moment*, 65–66, 69–70; Christopher Hill, *The World Turned Upside Down*, chapter 3.

33. E. A. Wrigley and R. S. Schofield, *Population History*, 258.

34. In Thirsk and Cooper, *Documents*, 757–58.

35. Charles Emil Strangeland, *Pre-Malthusian Doctrines*, 111–115.

36. David Cressy, *Coming Over*, 130–43; Mildred Campbell, "Of People either too Few or too Many," 169–201.

37. Bland, *Trade Revived* (1659), 6.

38. Petty, *Treatise of Taxes* (1662), 16; Child, *New Discourse*, 192, xi, 12; Sheridan, *Rise and Power* (1677), 186; Nicholas Barbon, *Discourse of Trade* (1690), 55; Roger Coke, *A Treatise Wherein is Demonstrated . .* (1671), 2.

39. Defoe, *Review*, 6:135 (2 July 1709).

40. Hutchison, *Political Economy*, 94–95.

41. W. C. Scoville, *Persecution of Huguenots.*

42. They accomplished this by sending to England the royal agent Usson de Bonrepaus. Robin D. Gwynn, *Huguenot Heritage*, 60, 131–32.

43. Joseph John Spengler, *French Predecessors*, 23–36; Charles W. Cole, *Colbert and a Century of French Mercantilism*, 2:463–72; René Gonnard, *Histoire des Doctrines*, 131–32; Sébastien le Prestre de Vauban, *An Essay for a General Tax* (1710); Pierre Goubert, *The Ancien Régime*, 45 (reprinted census); Boisguillebert, *Le détail de la France* (1695), 36; Bossuet, *Politique tirée*, bk. 10, art. 1, propos. 9 and 10; Henry Higgs, *The Physiocrats.*

44. K. Schuenemann, *Österreich Bevölkerungspolitik*, 3, et seq.; Hutchison, *Political Economy*, 90–92; Karl Pribram, *A History of Economic Reasoning* (Baltimore, 1983), 89–93; John A. Garraty, *Unemployment in History*, 37; Theodor Ludwig Lau, *Aufrichtiger Verschlag*, vol. 1, sec. i–ix; George Rudé, *Europe in the Eighteenth Century*, 26; Ingomar Bog, "Mercantilism in Germany," 162–89.

45. As Joseph Schumpeter remarked of the early economic writers, "until the middle of the eighteenth century they were as nearly unanimous in this 'popula-

tionist' attitude as they have ever been in anything": *History of Economic Analysis,* 251.

46. Hutchison, *Political Economy,* 18.

47. Furniss, *Laborer,* 28–29; J. Goring, "Social Change," 185–97, 185–86; *HMC Report,* House of Lords MSS, vol. 6, new ser., Addenda (1514–1714), 43–44 (engrossed Commons bill of December 1597).

48. Maurice P. Ashley, *Financial and Commercial Policy,* 151–52.

49. Charles Wilson, "The Immigrant in English History," 1–16, 10–11.

50. Thomas Violet, *The Advancement of Merchandize,* 17–18; Robinson, *Certain Proposals in order to the Peoples Freedom* (1652), 6, 12–13.

51. *To His Highness the Lord Protector . . . the Humble Addresses of M. B. I.* [1656], introduction, 1–3.

52. *CSPD* (1661–2), 80 (2 September).

53. Quoted in William Letwin, *Origins of Scientific Economics,* 112.

54. A point made clear by Thomas Sprat in his *The History of the Institution, Design, and Progress of the Royal Society of London* (1667).

55. Hutchison, *Political Economy,* 6, 43.

56. Maurice Ashley, *England in the Seventeenth Century,* 157; Robert K. Merton, *Science, Technology, and Society.* The Baconian influence here is obvious, for Bacon had called for the compilation of a general history of trade. See Charles Webster, *The Great Instauration.*

57. Philip Kreager, "New Light on Graunt," 129–40.

58. Hull, *Writings,* 1:xxxiv–xxxviii; *DNB,* sub Petty; Johnson, *Predecessors,* 91.

59. *Treatise,* 67, 49.

60. Fortrey, *England's Interest,* 217–19, 226, 244.

61. Ibid., 219.

62. Ibid., 219–24. See chapter 3.

63. See chap. 3; Coleman, "Labour"; Furniss, *Laborer,* chaps. 4 and 5.

64. Fortrey, *England's Interest,* 224–26.

65. Ibid., "to the reader."

66. *Reasons Humbly Offered to the Parliament by the Free-Born Merchants of England* [1660].

67. *To the Right Honourable the Commons in Parliament Assembled: The Humble Petition of the Native Merchants of England* [1660]. *Coloring* and *covering* were terms used interchangeably to describe the illegal practice of entering imported goods in the name of a native or naturalized subject in order to evade higher alien customs and duties.

68. *The Great Evil of Naturalizing Aliens Discovered by the City's Reply to the Aliens' Petition* [1660].

69. 12 Car. II c. 4.

70. Hale's tract is to be found in BM Stowe MS 163, fols. 146–69. It was first published in c. 1695, and is summarized, though somewhat misleadingly, in E. Heward, *Matthew Hale,* 145–46.

71. *DNB,* sub Hale; Gilbert Burnet, *Life of Hale,* 42–43.

72. Charles Emil Strangeland, *Pre-Malthusian Doctrines,* 148–49.

73. Peter Buck, "Seventeenth-Century Political Arithmetic," 67–84, 73–74.

74. Hale, *Primitive Origination,* 205; Hale, *A Discourse touching Provision for the Poor* (1673), chap. 3.

75. *Biographia Britannia,* 6:2475–81; E. P. Hutchinson, *The Population Debate,* 56–57; Burnet, *Life of Hale,* 47.

76. Appleby, *Economic Thought,* 276.

77. The French Protestants offer only one example of the importance of such

trade connections, created in their case because the diaspora from France extended to many of the countries of Europe and indeed beyond. D. W. Jones, "London Merchants and the Crisis of the 1690s," in *Crisis and Order in English Towns, 1500–1700*, P. Clark and P. Slack, eds. (London, 1972), 311–55, 328–30.

78. It was by no means only naturalized aliens who were guilty of such frauds. A 1705 report of the Commissioners of the Customs to the Lord Treasurer concluded that both native and naturalized subjects colored aliens' goods for import duties and for the "drawback" on goods exported "out of time" (English importers had twelve months and alien importers only nine months to drawback the duties paid on goods re-exported). The Commissioners condemned the practice as detrimental to the City and the queen's customs revenues, and as a discouragement to English merchants who traded fairly. CLRO, Alchin Box Q/XCVVII, no. 5.

79. In this argument Hale came close to expressing a racial motive for opposing the reception of immigrants. The conventional wisdom that the idea of race emerged only at the end of the eighteenth century, in conjunction with the spirit of nationalism, is perhaps too simple a formula. Yet it is true that arguments based on race seldom surfaced in the seventeenth-and eighteenth-century debate over the admission of foreigners, and the omission is important, since few political issues provide a more fertile medium for the growth of odious arguments of race than those of immigration and nationality. Chapter 7 provides a fuller treatment of this question.

80. See chap. 7.

81. To judge by the number of references to the tract, it must, like many such works, have circulated in manuscript before its publication.

CHAPTER 3. POPULATIONISM, RELIGION, AND IMMIGRATION

1. "To the King's Most Excellent Majesty, the Humble Petition of Divers Shopkeepers, Tradesmen, and Artificers" (1660), and "Opinion of the Council of Trade upon Shopkeepers' Petition," (14 March 1660/61), both in Thirsk and Cooper, *Documents*, 735–38.

2. Caroline Robbins, "A Note on General Naturalization," 168–77, 173—she acknowledges, the traditional view has been that the Crown indeed favored immigration more than did Parliament.

3. This traditional argument was repeated, for example, by Sir John Holland in his speech on a general naturalization bill on 4 May 1664, printed in Robbins, "A Note on General Naturalization," 176.

4. 15 Car. II c. 15.

5. The general naturalization act in Ireland, 14 & 15 Car. II c. 13 (Ireland), was continued by 4 Wm. & Mary c. 2 and 2 Ann. c. 14, and was made perpetual in 1718 by 4 Geo. I c. 9.

6. *CJ* VIII, 555 (2 May 1664), 557 (4 May 1664); Robbins, "A Note on General Naturalization," 175–77.

7. An unpublished thesis offers the most thorough attempt to determine the partisan alignment on the issue through an analysis of tellers' lists: M. R. Thorp, "The English Government and the Huguenot Settlement, 1680–1702" (Ph.D. thesis, University of Wisconsin, 1972), 223–24. The conclusion is indecisive.

8. David Ogg, *England in the Reign of Charles II*, 311–17, 321; Maurice Lee, Jr., *The Cabal*, 172–73; Roger Thomas, "Comprehension and Indulgence," 191–253, 195–97.

9. *CJ* IX, 22, 29, 30, 33; Grey's *Debates*, 1:56; *Diary of John Milward*, ed. Robbins, 152–53; B. D. Henning, ed., *History of Parliament*, 1:653–56; Grey's *Debates*, 1:56.

10. Thomas, "Comprehension and Indulgence," 196–204; Lee, *Cabal*, 173–78; Gilbert Burnet, *Life of Hale,* 189–90.

11. *LJ* XII, 274, 365–6, 375, 378; *CSPV*, (1669–70), 310–11 (London, Venetian Resident to Doge, 12 December 1670); *HMC 8th Report*, App., pt. i, p. 149 (amended draft of the bill); *CJ* IX, 175, 186.

12. Lee, *Cabal*, 197; Thomas, "Comprehension and Indulgence", 206–9; J. R. Jones, *Country and Court,* 175.

13. Thomas, "Comprehension and Indulgence," 209–15; Lee, *Cabal*, 194–201; Ogg, *Reign of Charles II*, 365–69; John Miller, *Popery and Politics.*

14. Robbins, "A Note on General Naturalization," 171, 173.

15. "His Majesty's Declaration against the French," 9 February 1666, PRO, SP 29/147/65; "His Majesty's Declaration against the States General," 17 March 1672, PRO, SP 29/304/22.

16. PRO, SP 29/311/87–89.

17. PRO, PC 2/65/172 (28 March 1676, petition of French artisan who had come in reliance on declaration of 1666); *HMC 9th Report*, App., pt. ii, pp. 79–80 (20 February 1677, petition of members of French Church in the Savoy who had immigrated in reliance on the 1666 declaration); PRO, PC 2/65/426 (22 December 1676, petition of Dutch bricklayer who had relied on the 1672 declaration).

18. "His Majesty's Declaration to all his Loving Subjects" (15 March 1672), in J. P. Kenyon, *The Stuart Constitution,* 407–8.

19. *LJ* XII, 521–22, 527, 575–76; *CJ* IX, 250, 267, 275; *Parl. Hist.*, 4:577–79; *DNB*, sub Coventry; Basil Duke Henning, ed., *The History of Parliament*, 2:243–45, 653–55; Grey's *Debates*, 2:154–57; *Diary of Sir Edward Dering, 1670–1673*, ed B. D. Henning, 159; *HMC 9th Report*, App., pt. ii, p. 19 (amended draft of bill); Thirsk and Cooper, *Documents*, 744–45 (Lords' bill).

20. D. R. Lacey, *Dissent and Parliamentary Politics*, 71–72.

21. *DNB*, sub Bethel; Bethel, *Present Interest*, 2, 13–17.

22. *DNB*, sub Sheridan; Sheridan, *Discourse*, 180, 189–90.

23. Sheridan, *Discourse*, 191–92.

24. Scott, *Companies*, 1:265, 278–79.

25. Joan Thirsk, ed., *The Agrarian History,* 5(ii):75–76; C. Clay, "Price of Freehold Land," 173–89, 174–77; *Diary of Samuel Pepys*, eds. R. Latham and W. Matthews, 8:84–5, 158 (27 February and 9 April 1667); Josiah Child, *New Discourse of Trade*, xxxviii; William Petyt, *Britannia Languens*, in McCulloch, *Tracts*, 285.

26. Charles Wilson, *England's Apprenticeship*, 215; Scott, *Companies*, 1:288–99; *CSPD* (1671–72), 87–88; C. D. Chandaman, *English Public Revenues*, 307–09; *CSPD* (1675–76), 499 (Thomas Overbury to [?], 8 January 1676); Haines, *The Prevention of Poverty: or, A Discourse of the Causes of the Decay of Trade, Fall of Lands, and Want of Money* (1674), 1, 4.

27. F. L. Carsten, ed., *New Cambridge Modern History,* 20; F. A. Wrigley and R. S. Schofield, *Population History of England*, 208–9, 230.

28. The plague in Marseilles occasioned Defoe's *Journal of the Plague Year* (1722). Paul Slack, *Impact of Plague*, 245, 69; Ogg, *Reign of Charles II*, 292.

29. B. E. Supple, *Commercial Crisis and Change*, 197–98.

30. Joyce Oldham Appleby, *Economic Thought and Ideology.* Lawrence Stone and Jeanne C. Fawtier Stone, *An Open Elite? England 1540–1880* (Oxford, 1984); one need not accept the Stones's argument in its entirety to acknowledge the persistence of the English elite.

31. Child has received the highest accolade of some historians of economic doctrine: that of being a precursor of Adam Smith. But Child was no theorist. He was a substantial merchant immersed in the practice of trade, the largest stockholder of

the East India Company by 1673, and his economic ideas were more a reflection of current opinion than of a profoundly original mind or an intention to establish a consistent set of doctrines. William Letwin, *Sir Josiah Child: Merchant Economist* (Boston, 1959); *DNB*, sub Child. Child's first tract, *Brief Observations Concerning Trade and Interest of Money*, appeared in 1668 under the initials J. C. His *New Discourse of Trade* (1693) incorporated the *Brief Observations*, and was probably written between 1668 and 1670. The two tracts will be treated together here, since Child's essential arguments changed little, but it must be remembered that the forceful influence of the *New Discourse* awaited the 1690s. See Letwin, *Child*, appendix 2, p. 32.

32. *New Discourse* (references are to the 4th edition, n.d.), preface, 194–95.

33. *Grand Concern*, 23–25.

34. Reynell, *English Interest*, 17–18.

35. Coventry, *An Essay Concerning the Decay of Rents* [c. 1670], BM Sloane MS 3828, fols. 205–10, reprinted in Thirsk and Cooper, *Documents*, 79–84.

36. Reynell, *English Interest*, 65–67, 59, 8.

37. *Grand Concern*, 23–25; Child, *New Discourse*, 14, 104, et seq.; *An Humble Address with Some Proposals for the Future Preventing of the Decrease of the Inhabitants of this Realm* (1677), 2, 3–5; *The Royal Fishing Revived* (1670), in *Harl. Misc.*, 7:403–8.

38. *An Humble Address with Some Proposals for the Future Preventing of the Decrease of the Inhabitants of this Realm* (1677), 2, 3–5; *The Royal Fishing Revived* (1670), in *Harl. Misc.*, 7:403–8. The fisheries struck contemporaries as perhaps the best example of the power of labor to create a surplus, since the value of the industry's product seemed to come almost wholly from labor.

39. Coke, *A Discourse of Trade. In Two Parts* (1670), 7, 9–12, 13, 54–55; Coke, *A Treatise Wherein is Demonstrated* (1671), 7.

40. Reynell, *English Interest*, 65–67, 59, 8. Reynell has been praised for his advanced views by Joan Thirsk, *Economic Policy and Projects*, 141–42.

41. Mildred Campbell, "Of People either too Few or too Many," 169–201, 189–92.

42. Robbins, "A Note on Good Naturalization," 172.

43. Ralph Davis, *A Commercial Revolution*, 18–19.

44. Child, *New Discourse*, 192, 196, 201–3.

45. Although many were published only years later, Petty's tracts circulated widely in manuscript copies: Alessandro Roncaglia, *Petty: The Origins of Political Economy* (Cardiff, 1985), 15. The chronology of Petty's writings is outlined in Hutchison, *Political Economy*, 29.

46. See, e.g., the remarks of Charles Davenant in *Discourses on the Public Revenue, Part I* (1698), in Whitworth, *Works*, 1:129.

47. *Petty Papers*, vol. 2, passim; *A Treatise of Ireland* (1687), postscript; "Ten Tools for Making the Crown and State of England more Powerful than any other now in Europe," in *Petty Papers*, 1:255–56.

48. *Trade Revived* (1681), pp. 61–2.

49. *An Essay Concerning the Multiplication of Mankind* (1686), 30–31; *Trade Revived*, 61–2. On the relative populations of town and country, see James Bonar, *Theories of Population from Raleigh to Arthur Young* (1931; New York, 1966).

50. The pattern is admirably described in E. A. Wrigley, "A Simple Model of London's Importance in Changing English Society and Economy 1650–1750," *Past & Present* 37 (1967), 44–70.

51. John Houghton, *A Collection of Letters for the Improvement of Husbandry and Trade*, 2 vols. (1681–83), 1 (1682): 49; *Proposals Moderately Offered for the Full Peopling and Inhabiting the City of London* (1672), 3, 5–6.

52. BM Sloane MS 3828, fols. 52.205–10, reprinted in Thirsk and Cooper, *Documents*, 79–84.

53. *CJ* IX, 15; Letwin, *Child*, 13, et seq.; *LJ* XII, 254 (25 October 1669).

54. The proceedings of the Committee are reprinted in Thirsk and Cooper, *Documents*, 68–79, and calendared in *HMC 8th Report*, App., pp. 133–36.

55. Thirsk and Cooper, *Documents*, 69–70.

56. Papillon was born in England, but was the son of an immigrant, and was a deacon of the French Church of London: *Memoirs*, ed. A. F. W. Papillon, 71–72; Thirsk and Cooper, *Documents*, 71, 73.

57. Thirsk and Cooper, *Documents*, 76–77, 79; *LJ* XII, 273–4, 284.

58. Coke, the grandson of the great common lawyer, was a Tory publicist perhaps better known for his political than for his economic works. Coke published three economic tracts in the 1670s, however: *A Discourse of Trade: In Two Parts* (1670); *A Treatise wherein is Demonstrated that the Church and State of England are in Equal Danger with the Trade of it* (1671); Coke, *England's Improvement: In Two Parts* (1675); *DNB*, sub Coke.

59. Coke, *England's Improvement*, 11–12; Coke, *Treatise*, 11.

60. Coke, *England's Improvement*, 2–3, 19–20; Coke, *Treatise*, 8.

61. Child, *New Discourse*, 150–51, 181–82; "For the Right Honourable the Lords of the Committee of Trade" [1668–69?], in Thirsk and Cooper, *Documents*, 740–41. On the hostility of English tradesmen, see chapter 7.

62. Reynell, *English Interest*, 63–4, 59–61.

63. Moreover, natural increase was threatened by the "spirit of madness" that led men to keep mistresses rather than marry and have children: *Grand Concern*, 23.

64. *Grand Concern*, 23–5.

65. Philip W. Buck, *Mercantilism*, 92–93; Thomas Manley, *Usury at Six Per Cent* (1669). 17–20.

66. Petty, *Verbum Sapienti* (1663), 114; *Treatise of Taxes* (1663), 67, 49; *Petty-Southwell Correspondence*, 219; William D. Grampp, "The Liberal Elements" 465–501; Petty, *The Political Anatomy of Ireland* (1691), 98–9.

67. A typical expression of this view is given in Petty, *A Treatise of Taxes* (1662), 67. A significant minority, including Defoe, advocated high wages. The difference arose from a largely unconscious, or unexpressed, disagreement over the elasticity of demand for English goods in foreign markets. Assuming that the balance of trade determined national wealth, if demand were elastic, then low wages would be preferable, lest English products be priced out of foreign markets as uncompetitive. If demand were inelastic, then high wages for English workers would be preferable, since they represented a greater increment of value added to raw materials in the process of manufacture, and a greater return to the nation when sold abroad. See Furniss, *Laborer*, 167–69.

68. Petty wrote *Political Arithmetic* in part as a rejoinder to Coke's economic theories. Petty and Coke present a suggestive contrast in methodologies, for Petty was very strongly imbued with an empirical Baconian approach to economic questions, while Coke adopted a rationalist deductive method inspired by Cartesianism. Coke's Euclidian expression of economic questions in the form of geometric axioms and propositions, valiant attempt though it was, hardly suited the purpose, but it at least imposed a logical order almost wholly lacking in Petty's works. This divergence in approach betrays the search of the early economic writers for a methodology and a language suitable to the new economic discourse whose boundaries they were marking out. On the Baconian underpinnings of early economic thought, see Karl Pribram, *A History of Economic Reasoning* (Baltimore, 1983), 65–68; Buck, *Politics*

of Mercantilism, 64–5; Hutchison, *Political Economy*, 28–41; William Letwin, *The Origins of Scientific Economics* (London, 1963), 135.

69. *Discourse*, 7, 9–12, 13, 54–55; *Treatise*, 7.

70. Child, *New Discourse*, 14, 104, et seq.

71. Coleman, "Labour in Seventeenth Century," 280–95; Furniss, *Laborer*.

72. Coleman, "Labour in Seventeenth Century"; E. P. Thompson, "Time, Work-Discipline, and Industrial Capitalism," 38–72; Mark Blaug, "Economic Theory," 111–116, 115.

73. R. H. Tawney, *Religion and Capitalism*.

74. Hale, quoted in Hutchison, *Political Economy*, 395.

75. *Grand Concern*, 25.

76. *Political Arithmetic* (1690), 88, 11–12, 25; *Petty Papers*, 1:261.

77. *Political Arithmetic* (1690), 30–31.

78. Nehemiah Grew was also notable for proposing a very different scheme for the encouragement of immigration from the usual one of a general naturalization act. He recognized that different inducements would be necessary in order to attract different classes of foreigners. To farmers the state could offer wasteland for settlement; to artisans the free exercise of their trades and high wages; to merchants the promise of naturalization. So to each occupational group that England wished to attract an inducement could be offered that would be genuinely attractive. Grew, *The Means of a Most Ample Increase of the Wealth and Strength of England* (1707), in E. A. J. Johnson, *Predecessors of Adam Smith* (New York, 1937), 136–37.

79. "Character of Holland" (1653).

80. A. T. Van Deursen, *Plain Lives*, chap. 2.

81. G. C. Gibbs, "Reception of the Huguenots", 275–306, 295–304; H. P. N. Nusteling, "The Netherlands and the Huguenot Emigrés," 17–34, 22–27.

82. Jean Tirel, *Lettres Fraternelles d'un prisonnier publiées par Eva Avigdor en collaboration avec Elizabeth Labrousse* (Paris, 1986), 55–62, 108–10.

83. See, e.g., *England's Interest Asserted* (1669), 33.

84. Appleby, *Economic Thought*, chap. 4, treats the influence of the Dutch experience upon the developing economic discourse in England.

85. *DNB*, sub Temple: T. B. Macaulay, "Sir William Temple," 1:195–272, 274.

86. Temple, *Observations upon the United Provinces of the Netherlands*, 215–18.

87. *Essay on Trade in Ireland* (1673), in *Miscellanea* (1680), 100.

88. *Observations*, 211–12.

89. Sheridan, *Rise and Power of Parliaments*, 185; Bethel, *An Account of the French Usurpation upon the Trade of England* (1679), 15; Davenant, *An Essay upon the Probable Method of Making a People Gainers in the Balance of Trade* (1699), in Whitworth, *Works*, 1:73; Davenant, quoted in William Wood, *Survey of Trade* (1718), 314; Coke, *Reflections upon the East India and Royal African Companies* (1695), 15.

90. René Gonnard, *Histoire des Doctrines*, 215. Modern sociologists have theorized that density stimulates technological improvements through increased social interaction and a greater necessity for invention: Robert K. Merton, *Science, Technology, and Society*, 209–16.

91. *Grand Concern*, in *Harl. Misc.*, 8:13–61, 23.

92. Child courageously argued that the Jews ought to be included in a general naturalization. The opponents of the Jews' admission were, he claimed, mostly merchants, who complained of unfair competition. Child retorted that the more trades the Jews entered and improved, the better; if the Jews were thriftier than the English, they would provide a good example. Though English merchants might suffer, they were only a small fraction of the nation. Many Jews had brought over large estates,

and if only they had the freedom and protection that they enjoyed in Holland, many more would settle permanently in England. All men were by nature alike, he counseled, and "fear is the cause of hatred." A grudging acquiescence in the Jews' presence would never achieve as much as a full legal toleration. Child's arguments went unheeded, but they illustrate the degree to which those who envisioned England as destined for greatness as a trading nation were willing to jettison traditional social, religious, and cultural controls. *New Discourse*, chap. 7.

93. Arthur O. Lovejoy, *The Great Chain of Being*.

94. Mark Goldie, "The Theory of Religious Intolerance" 331–68.

95. *England's Improvement*, 2–3, 11–12, 19–20, 5; *Treatise*, 8, 11.

96. *Brief Observations*, 6; *Observations Examined*, 18.

97. Appleby, *Economic Ideology*, chaps. 7, 8, and 9.

98. Jones, *Country and Court*, 218–19; Scott, *Companies*, 1:311–12; Chandaman, *Public Revenue*, 307–9; Wilson, *Apprenticeship*, 182–83, 215–16.

99. Pett, *Future State*, 122; *England's Wants* (1685), in *Somer's Tracts*, 9:222.

100. Robin Gwynn, *Huguenot Heritage*, chaps. 4 and 5; Warren C. Scoville, "Diffusion of Technology," 294–311, 392–411.

101. See e.g., George Hickes, *The True Notion of Persecution Stated* (1681), and Samuel Bolde, *A Sermon* (1682).

102. James II did issue two briefs for charitable collections, and cited, though probably with little sincerity, the encouragement of immigration in his Declaration of Indulgence of 1687. R. D. Gwynn, "Treatment of Huguenot Refugees," Much work has been done on the charitable collections: W. A. Shaw, "The English Government and the Relief of Protestant Refugees," 662–83; C. Pascal, "Secours Distribués," 264–67; R. A. Sundstrom, "French Huguenots and the Civil List," 219–35; R. Smith, "Financial Aid," 248–56.

103. *A Letter of Several French Ministers Fled into Germany* [1687?], 1–2; *An Answer to a Paper Importing a Petition of the Archbishop of Canterbury* (1688), 3.

104. Gwynn, "Treatment of Huguenot Refugees"; see also G. C. Gibbs, "Reception of the Huguenots," 275–306.

105. *Evelyn's Diary*, 4:485 (3 November 1685).

106. *LJ* XIII, 47, 87, 90, 103, 105; *HMC 9th Report*, App., pt. ii, p. 88 (amended draft of bill, 26 March 1677); Guildhall MS 7412, 1:102–3 (Coetus minute book, 4 March 1677, recording order from Lords committee to Savoy Church to "present such a bill as they desired"); *CJ* IX, 416–17, 462; *HMC 9th Report*, App., pt. ii, pp. 79–80 (petition from French Church in Savoy); *LJ* XIII, 47 (20 February 1677).

107. *LJ* XIII, 258, 267, 285, 287 (passed 13 July 1678); the Dutch Church and French Church, whose joint committee was called *Coetus,* urged a clause that would have required foreign artisans who wished to work under the act to obtain a certificate from one of the foreign churches: Guildhall MS 7412, 1:106–8 (Coetus minute book, 24 March, 26 May, 29 May 1678); *HMC 9th Report*, App., pt. ii, p. 120 (petition of Weavers' Company, arguments of counsel, amended draft of bill).

108. *CJ* IX, 730 (6 June 1685); *Reasons Humbly Offered by the Inhabitants of the City and Liberty of Westminster* (1685).

109. *LJ* XIII, 719, 722, 728; *HMC House of Lords MSS, 1678–88*, pp. 259–60 (draft bill, 17 December 1680); *The Correspondence of Henry Savile*, ed. W. D. Cooper (London, 1858), 176 (20 January 1681).

110. *CJ* IX, 696 (32 December 1680); Grey's *Debates*, 8:225–26; *History of Parliament*, 1:686–89; *DNB*, sub Knight.

111. *CJ* IX, 738, 752, (29 June 1685), 755 (1 July 1685); BM Lansdowne MS 256, fols 117–22 (manuscript draft of bill, n.d.); *Memoirs of Sir John Reresby*, ed.

A. Browning, 382; Roger North, *Autobiography,* in *Lives of the Norths,* ed. A. Jessop, 3:180–85; *CJ* IX, 761 (19 November 1685).

112. *Present State,* 61–2.

113. *Factum of the French and other Protestants in the Savoy,* PRO, SP 30/G.

114. *An Apology,* prologue.

115. The largest collection of the broadsides is held by the Corporation of London Record Office, Alchin Box Q/XCVII, no. 5.

116. Daniel Statt, "Controversy over Immigration," 45–61.

117. C. Carlton, *The Court of Orphans,* 93, 97–101; 5 & 6 Wm. & Mary c. 10; J. R. Kellett, "Financial Crisis," 220–47; I. G. Doolittle, "City of London's Debt," 46–59.

118. *The History of Naturalization* [c.1685] insisted that naturalization positively diminished the nation's population rather than increasing it, and that the accession of foreigners would not counteract the loss of natural-born Englishmen.

119. Virtually all the broadsides also concluded with pleas that if acts of naturalization must be passed, they should contain provisos that the persons naturalized not be exempt from the payment to the City of London of any duties owing to them.

CHAPTER 4. REVOLUTION AND ECONOMIC FERMENT

1. In Goldsmith/Kress Collection: Steele, *Proclamations,* 1:479.

2. See chapter 7.

3. E. Neville Williams, *Eighteenth-Century Constitution,* 64 (Godolphin to William III, 1693).

4. *CJ* X, 86 (13 April 1689), 373 (10 April 1690), XI, 21 (6 December 1693), 28 (12 December 1693); Henry Horwitz, *Parliament,* 190; *Parl. Hist.,* 5:849; *CJ* XI, 47, 107, 113, 129; *CJ* XI, 408 (22 January 1696).

5. *CJ* XI, 697 (8 February 1697), 714–16, 724 (19 February–2 March); *CJ* XII, 61 (25 January 1698).

6. *Several Letters Written by some French Protestants now Refuged in Germany* (1690), 34.

7. *DNB,* sub Tindal; Tindal, *The Power of the Magistrate* (1697), 171–3.

8. Hugh Trevor-Roper, "Toleration and Religion," 389–408.

9. For example, *A Letter to a Country Gentleman: Setting forth the Causes of the Decay and Ruin of Trade* (1698).

10. Scott, *Companies,* 1:326, 334; David Ogg, *James II and William III,* 435.

11. P. G. M. Dickson, *The Financial Revolution in England.*

12. Scott, *Companies,* 1:375, 385–86; T. S. Ashton, *Economic Fluctuations in England,* 16–17, 115–17; K. F. Helleiner, "The Vital Revolution,"

13. Hutchison, *Political Economy,* 56–57.

14. The act, however, had been in abeyance from 1679 to 1684: Ogg, *James II and William III,* 510–12; L. Hanson, *Government and the Press,* 7, 14; see chap. 2.

15. Joyce Oldham Appleby, *Economic Thought and Ideology,* chap. 9; J. G. A. Pocock, *Macchiavellian Moment,* 424–25.

16. The struggle of France and England over some of the French Protestant artisans amply illustrates this point: R. H. George, "A Mercantilist Episode," *Journal of Business and Economic History* 3 (1930–31): 264–71.

17. In *A Discourse Concerning Coining* (1696), 52; Barbon was active in the building industry as a real estate developer.

18. W. H. [William Harris], *Remarks on the Affairs and Trade of England and Ireland* (1691), 54, 71.

19. Locke, *Some Considerations of the Consequences of the Lowering of Interest* (1692), 100; Barbon, *A Discourse of Trade* (1690), 60–61.

20. On the question of the Protestants' departure having weakened France, see Warren C. Scoville, *Persecution of Huguenots.*

21. Coke, *Reflections upon the East-Indy and Royal African Companies* (1695), 21–22.

22. For example, Sir Francis Brewster, *Essays on Trade and Navigation* (1695), 7–10; and Matthew Tindal, *The Power of the Magistrate* (1697), 171–73.

23. John Brewer, *The Sinews of Power,* 11, 24, 37–45.

24. Geoffrey Parker, *The Military Revolution,* 43.

25. D. S. Chandler, *Art of War,* 304.

26. Peter Laslett, "John Locke," 137–64.

27. Hutchison, *Political Economy,* 61, 71–72; Karen Iverson Vaughn, *John Locke.*

28. Appleby, *Economic Thought,* 254.

29. *For a General Naturalization* (1693), in David Resnick, "Locke," 368–88, which briefly analyzes Locke's views on the issue and reprints his manuscript tract.

30. Appleby makes much of this division in the economic literature, attributing free-trade ideas to the merchants and mercantilist protectionist views to the manufacturers: *Economic Thought,* chap. 9.

31. For a good summary of Pocock's arguments, see Larry Dickey, "The Pocockian Moment," *Journal of British Studies* 26 (1987): 96–107.

32. Linda Colley, *In Defiance of Oligarchy.*

33. Resnick, "Locke," 374.

34. Lois G. Schwoerer, *No Standing Armies! The Antiarmy Ideology in Seventeenth-Century England* (Baltimore, 1974).

35. Macchiavelli, *Discourses,* bk. 2, chaps. 3, 4; James Bonar, *Theories of Population,* 53; E. P. Hutchinson, *Population Debate,* 41–2; Resnick, "Locke," 370–74.

36. Mildred Campbell, "Of People," 169–201.

37. Giovanni Botero, *Ragion di Stato* (Venice, 1598), in *Giovanni Botero,* eds. P. J. Waley and D. P. Waley, 143–47; Hutchinson, *Population Debate,* 18–19.

38. Or less often to France.

39. Helleiner, "Revolution," 80; Colin Brooks, "Projecting," 31–36; Wrigley and Schofield, *Population,* 208–9.

40. Published in *Philosophical Transactions of the Royal Society* 17, no. 196 (1693): 596–610.

41. Geoffrey Holmes, "Gregory King," 41–68.

42. *Two Tracts,* ed. George E. Barnett, 13, 16–19, 21–23, 27, 31, 51, 56.

43. After the turn of the century fewer attempts to measure the nation's population were undertaken, perhaps because improved financial policy made the issue less pressing. Brooks, "Projecting," 35.

44. Dugard, *A Discourse,* 2–3.

45. Grew, a member of the Royal Society, wrote a memorandum addressed to the Queen in 1707 entitled *The Means of a Most Ample Increase of the Wealth and Strength of England.* The manuscript is described in E. A. J. Johnson, *Predecessors of Adam Smith,* chap. 7.

46. Johnson, *Predecessors of Adam Smith,* 133–35.

47. The Births, Marriages, and Burials Act, 6 & 7 Wm. & Mary c. 6, imposed a one shilling per annum duty on bachelors over twenty-five and childless widowers: see Brooks, "Projecting," 31–33.

48. Mackworth, *England's Glory by a Royal Bank* (1694), 19–21.

49. Grew, *The Means,* in Johnson, *Predecessors of Adam Smith,* 133–35.

50. Brewster, the Lord Mayor of Dublin in 1674, wrote on both English and Irish trade: *DNB,* sub Brewster; Brewster, *Essays on Trade and Navigation* (1695), 7–10.

51. Heckscher called the paradox "a contradiction never resolved": Eli F. Heckscher, *Mercantilism*, 2:162.

52. This is one explanation offered by D. C. Coleman, "Labour in the English Economy," 280–95, 288–91, and espoused with enthusiasm by Joyce Appleby, *Economic Thought*, 136–44; see also, A. W. Coats, "The Relief of Poverty, Attitudes to Labour, and Economic Change in England, 1660–1782," *International Review of Social History* 21 (1976): 98–115, 104.

53. These are the words used by Appleby, *Economic Thought*, 155.

54. Thomas, *An Historical Account of the Rise and Growth of the West-India Colonies* (1690), 2–4.

55. Pollexfen, *A Discourse of Trade, Coin, and of Ways and Means to Gain and Retain Riches* (1697), 51–53.

56. Coke, *Reflections*, 14.

57. *An Essay upon the Probable Method of Making a People Gainers in the Balance of Trade* (1699), in Whitworth, *Works*, 2:202, 184, 187, 192, 195, 173; *An Essay upon Ways and Means of Supplying the War* (1695), in Whitworth, *Works*, 1:74–75.

58. Davenant, *Ways and Means*, 74.

59. Davenant, *Probable Methods*, 185–86.

60. William Petyt, *Britannia Languens* (1680), in McCulloch, *Tracts*, 378; Mackworth, *England's Glory*, 24; Max Beloff, *Public Order and Popular Disturbances: 1660–1714* (Oxford, 1938), 11.

61. Charles Wilson, "The Other Face of Mercantilism," in *Revisions in Mercantilism*, ed. D. C. Coleman (London, 1969), 118–39.

62. An opinion shared with respect to France by the most eminent French economic writer of the time, Boisguillebert; Joseph John Spengler, *French Predecessors of Malthus*, 34–35.

63. Halley, *Degrees of Mortality*, 46; Povey, *The Unhappiness of England*, 47–54.

64. Bellers was later praised by Robert Owen and Marx for the advanced view of labor that he expounded in his many economic tracts: *DNB*, sub Bellers; Anna Ruth Fry, *John Bellers, 1654–1725; John Bellers: His Life, Times, and Writings*, George Clarke, ed. (London, 1987).

65. Bellers, *Essays about the Poor* (1699), 56, 63–64; *A Supplement to the Proposal for a Colledge of Industry* (1696), in *Bellers*, Clarke, ed., 74–76. Bellers was best known for his schemes for a college of industry, a sort of workhouse, though deserving, as he said, "a name more grateful." The colleges would provide the poor with education, "all conveniences of living," and employment. Bellers's workhouse scheme, like that of Lawrence Braddon, aimed at the establishment of what were essentially utopian communities—thus Robert Owens's fascination with Bellers's ideas when his writings were rediscovered in the nineteenth century. Other observers saw workhouses as deterrents or punishments for the willfully idle, though the ostensible object was reform rather than punishment. Bellers, *Proposals for Raising a Colledge* (1696), in *Bellers*, Clarke, ed., 63; ibid., 19–21; John A. Garraty, *Unemployment in History* 44–49; Lawrence Braddon, *An Abstract of the Draught of a Bill for Relieving, Reforming, and Employing the Poor* (1717); A. W. Coats, "Economic Thought," 39–51.

66. Puckle, *England's Path to Wealth and Honour* (1700), preface, 35.

67. D. Waddell, "A Biographical Sketch," 279–88.

68. *Discourses on the Public Revenues, Part II* (1698), in Whitworth, *Works*, 2:3–7, 113–14, *Probable Method*, 186–87; *Ways and Means*, 74–75.

69. Other observers thought in purely economic terms. Nehemiah Grew, for example, argued that keeping home wages comparable to those in the plantations would

discourage emigration. Johnson, *Predecessors*, 133–35. But Davenant's broader vision proved in the event the more prescient.

70. *Probable Method*, 185–86. Davenant elaborated upon the necessity of religious toleration in his *Essays upon Peace at Home and War Abroad* (1704).

71. Coke, *Reflections*, 14.

72. J. H. Plumb, *Political Stability*.

73. Defoe, *Review*, 5:602 (15 March 1709).

74. 12 & 13 Wm. III c. 2, sec. 2.

75. Blanch, *The Interest of England Considered in an Essay upon Wool* (1694), 53–54; Johnson, *Confutation of a Letter* (1697), 323–38; *DNB*, sub Johnson; Caroline Robbins, *The Eighteenth-Century Commonwealthmen*, 113–14, 5–6. Yet Johnson's fellow "real whig" Robert Molesworth, an Irish and English MP, supported naturalization: Robbins, ibid. On Johnson, see Melinda Zook, "Early Whig Ideology, Ancient Constitutionalism, and the Reverend Samuel Johnson," *Journal of British Studies* 32 (1993): 139–65.

76. *British Library General Catalogue*.

77. *A Brief History of Trade*, 24, 31.

78. *Rights and Liberties*, 18–20, 22.

79. *DNB*, sub Knight; *Parl. Hist.*, 5:849–57.

80. *Parl. Hist.*, 5:856–57. At that date, the epithet "frog" referred only to the Dutch.

81. *An Answer to the Pretended Speech* (1694), 2, 8–9, 14–17, 22–23, 28.

82. W. A. Speck, "Conflict in Society," 135–54, 137.

83. See Dickson, *Financial Revolution*, passim; Isaac Kramnick, *Bolingbroke and his Circle: The Politics of Nostalgia in the Age of Walpole* (Cambridge, Mass.: 1968), 42.

84. *Rights and Liberties*, 3–11, 14–16, 21–24.

85. Blanch, *The Interest of England Considered in an Essay upon Wool* (1694), 53–4.

86. *Brief History*, 24, 31, 33–39, 127, 132–34; *An Humble Address to the Honourable House of Commons* (1699), in Thirsk and Cooper, *Documents*, 747–49.

87. *Confutation*, 335–36, 333.

88. *Parl. Hist.*, 5:851–54.

89. *Parl. Hist.*, 5:854–56.

90. *A Satyr*, pp. 11–12; *An Elegy*, in *Harl. Misc.*, 10: 357–58; *A Catalogue of Books of the Newest Fashion* [1694], in *Harl. Misc.*, 12:259.

91. *Brief History*, passim.

92. *Confutation*, 335–36, 333.

93. *Rights and Liberties*, 3–11, 14–16, 21–24.

94. *A Supplement to His Majesty's Speech* (1693), in John Rylands Library, 18–20.

95. *An Humble Address to the Honourable House of Commons on the Behalf of the Traders of England against Naturalizing Aliens* (1699), in Thirsk and Cooper, *Documents*, 747–49.

96. *Canary-Birds Naturalized in Utopia* [1708?], 2. This is the earliest use of the symbol of wooden shoes in reference to foreign immigrants that I have seen in the economic literature, though its potent use as an emblem of absolutism certainly occurred earlier, for example in the Whigs' antipopery processions in London in the 1680s.

97. *Rights and Liberties*, 18–20, 22.

98. *Rights and Liberties*, 135–36, 140, 119, 163. The Jews were not exempt from the rising hostility to foreigners. *The Jews Charter* (1702) and *A Historical and Law*

Treatise against the Jews (1703) were both vehement diatribes againt "the enemies of the cross of Christ" on religious and economic grounds. Sir Richard Baker, *The Jews Charter*, preface. *The Jews' Case* (1697) quoted William Prynne's attack against the Jews, and urged that they be required to pay alien customs rates. With the exception of these publications, and an occasional crank pamphlet, the literature on foreign Jews remained scant.

99. Coke, *Reflections*, 17, 19–21.

100. *A Discourse*, 26, 29.

101. *An Answer to the Pretended Speech* (1694), 2, 8–9, 14–17.

102. *Plaintes* was one of the most important works denouncing the persecution of Protestants in France; it is reproduced in E. Arbor, ed., *Torments of the Protestant Slaves*, 413–31.

103. *Plaintes*, 423–24.

104. *Plaintes*, 425.

CHAPTER 5. THE PALATINE MIGRATION: THE GREAT EXPERIMENT

1. The only lengthy treatment of the migration is nearly sixty years old: W. A. Knittle, *The Early Eighteenth Century Palatine Emigration*. Knittle was principally concerned with the German migration to New York. The only recent treatment is H. T. Dickinson, "Poor Palatines," which is concerned with the partisan aspect of the migration.

2. Dickinson, "Poor Palatines."

3. [Daniel Defoe], *A Brief History* (1709), 20–21; *Canaan*.

4. The term *Palatine* will be used here, as it was by contemporaries, to describe all of the peoples who migrated from the Rhineland to England in 1709.

5. J. S. Bromley, ed., *New Cambridge Modern History*, 6:233; Luttrell, *Relation*, 6:426.

6. *The Piety and Bounty of the Queen of Great Britain* (1709), 2; Defoe, *Brief History*, 24–25.

7. B. G. Stuvens, *Ausführlicher Bericht, passim*.

8. L. Häusser, *Geschichte*, 2:821.

9. Ibid., 2:811; Stuvens, *Ausführlicher Bericht*, 983–84.

10. Häusser, *Geschichte*, 824, 821; *Letters of Queen Anne*, B. C. Brown, ed., 114–15 (Saint James, Queen Anne to Elector Palatine, 20 Feb. 1703).

11. *Declaration Lately Published* (1707).

12. Defoe, *Brief History*, 47–8.

13. G. M. Trevelyan, *England under Queen Anne*, 3:37.

14. *Canaan*, 15, 24.

15. Defoe, *Review*, 6:103 (2 June 1709); *Declaration*, 6.

16. Trevelyan, *Queen Anne*, 2:394–95; Luttrell, *Relation*, 6:394–95.

17. E. LeRoy Ladurie, "Histoire et Climat," 3–34, 21; A. B. Faust, "Deutschen in Amerika," 59; Gilbert Burnet, *History*, 6:38.

18. Defoe, *Review*, 6:179–80 (16 July 1709); *CJ* XVI, 597. On the highly-developed network of agents operating around the printing center of Frankfurt, see A. G. Roeber, *Palatines, Liberty, and Property* (Baltimore, 1993), 116–21.

19. Richard S. Dunn, "William Penn," 322–329; Mildred Campbell, "Of People either too Few or too Many," 193–95; Council Report, 1708, reprinted in *South Carolina,*, eds. E. D. Johnson and K. L. Johnson, 63–64.

20. J. Goebel, "Briefe," *passim;* J. Goebel, "Neue Dokumente," 181–82.

21. Goebel, "Neue Dokumente," 182–83.

22. On the promotion of emigration, see Hans Fenske, "Die Deutsche Auswanderung," *Mitteilungen des Historischen Vereins der Pfalz* 76 (1978): 183–220; Hans Fenske, "International Migration: Germany in the Eighteenth Century," *Central European History* 3 (1980): 332–47.

23. *CJ* XVI, 597.

24. *Detailed and Circumstantial Account (1709)*.

25. Kocherthal, *Bericht*, 28, 79–80.

26. *CJ* XVI, 597.

27. PRO, CO 323/6/55 (Boyle to Board of Trade, 20 April 1708).

28. *CSPA* (1706–8), 720–21 (Board of Trade to Boyle, 22 April 1708), 744–75; Kocherthal, *Bericht*, 78; *BTJ* (1704–8), 482–84; *CJ* XVI, 597; *Colonial History of the State of New York*, E. B. O'Callaghan, ed., 5: 44, 53 (Board of Trade to Boyle, 29 June 1708).

29. PRO, CO 5/1049/155 (Board of Trade Journal, 27 December 1709).

30. Kocherthal, *Bericht, passim;* Burnet, *History*, 6; 37–38.

31. PRO, CO 5/3/28 (Board of Trade to Sec. Hedges, 13 March 1705–6).

32. John Oldmixon, *The History of England, 435*.

33. J. R. Jones, *Country and Court, 333*.

34. *CJ* XVI, 93, 108, 123, 143; *LJ* XVIII, 667–68, 680; *Parl. Hist.*, 6: 780–83; Abel Boyer, *Reign of Queen Anne, 7*:290; Burnet, *History*, 5: 411; Luttrell, *Relation,* 6: 418 (15 March 1708/09).

35. Dickinson, "Palatines."

36. Shaw, *1701–1800*, from which the above figure was derived; see Daniel Statt, "The Birthright of an Englishman: The Practice of Naturalization and Denization of Immigrants under the Later Stuarts and Early Hanoverians," *PHSL* 25 (1989): 61–74.

37. PRO, SP 84/232/8 ("Memorial Touchant les Pauvres Protestants venant du Palatinas," 24 December 1708); *CSPA* (1710–11), 287–90 (New York, Governor Hunter to Board of Trade, 28 November 1710).

38. PRO, SP 84/232/91–92, 109 (The Hague, Dayrolle to Boyle, 29 March and 19 April).

39. PRO, SP 84/232/108–109 (19 April).

40. BM Add. MS 15866, fol. 166 (Boyle to Dayrolle, 20 April); PRO, SP 44/108/ 59 (Sunderland to Commissioners for Transports, 23 April).

41. PRO, CO 388/76/56ii (Report to Board of Trade, 9 May); SP 87/4/280 (The Hague, Suderman and Toren to Cardonnel, 11 May, copy).

42. Fenske, "Migration," 339–40; Robert A. Selig, "Emigration," 4–5.

43. Luttrell, *Relation,* 6: 434.

44. Goebel, "Neue Dokumente," 195–96; Kocherthal, *Bericht*, 77.

45. *BTJ* (1704–8), 518.

46. PRO, SP 84/232/124 (The Hague, Dayrolle to Boyle, 6 May).

47. BM Add. MS 4743, fol. 109 (Boyle to Mr. Davenant, 10 May 1709).

48. The documents were printed in the articles cited above, Goebel, "Neue Dokumente" and "Briefe".

49. Goebel, "Briefe," 126.

50. Goebel, "Neue Dokumente," 183–84.

51. Ibid., *passim*

52. Ibid., 189–90.

53. Ibid., 185, 191, 185–86.

54. Goebel, "Briefe," 141, 136.

55. Goebel, "Neue Dokumente," 185, 189.

56. Goebel, "Briefe," 151, 143.

57. Their petitions appear in ibid., 139–79.

58. Ibid., 181–83 (Dillenburg, order of 30 August 1709 to all officials).

59. *Piety and Bounty*, 65–66.

60. Defoe, *Brief History*, 5; *Reception of the Palatines Vindicated* (1711), 4.

61. PRO, SP 84/232/125 (to Boyle, 10 May).

62. PRO, SP 84/232/125 (10 May).

63. PRO, SP, 84/232/280–281 (Rotterdam, Suderman and Toren to Cardonnel, 11 May 1709).

64. PRO, SP 87/4/282 (The Hague, Cardonnel to Suderman and Toren, 11 May, copy).

65. PRO, SP 87/4/278 (The Hague, Cardonnel to Mr. Vanderpool, 17 May).

66. PRO, SP 87/4/284 (The Hague, 13 May).

67. Luttrell, *Relation*, 6: 440.

68. BM Add. MS 15866, fol. 170.

69. BM Add. MS 15866, fol. 172.

70. PRO, SP 84/232/140 (The Hague, Dayrolle to Boyle, 7 June 1709); BTJ, 1709–15, pp. 33–4 (18 May 1709).

71. PRO, CO 388/76/54.

72. PRO, CO 388/76/54.

73. BM Add. MS 61649, fol. 66 (n.d., n.p.).

74. PRO, CO 388/76/55; SP 44/108/67.

75. PRO, CO 388/76/56; *CSPA* (1708–9), 296 (9 May 1709).

76. *BTJ* (1709–15), 33; *Cal. Tr. Bks.*, 23 (ii): 172 (warrant for payments to Ruperti and Tribbeko, 16 May 1709); Defoe, *Brief History*, 34.

77. BM Add. MS 17677 DDD, fol. 205 (L'Hermitage to States General, 21 June 1709).

78. *Canaan*, 106.

79. Defoe, *Brief History*, 32.

80. PRO, CO 388/76/60 (23 May 1709).

81. *BTJ* (1709–15), 35–38 (21 and 23 May 1709).

82. PRO, CO 389/36/404–5 (Stamford, Meadows, and Monckton to Sunderland.

83. *BTJ* (1709–15), 35 (21 May).

84. Ibid.; PRO, CO, 388/76/60.

85. *BTJ* (1709–15), 38 (25 May).

86. The lists in PRO, CO 388/76/56ii, 64, and 68–70 have been printed: "Lists of Germans from the Palatinate who Came to England in 1709," *New York Genealogical and Biographical Record*, vols. 40 and 41 (1909–10; reprinted, Baltimore, 1965).

87. The embarkation lists appear in PRO T.1 119/6–10, 19–26, 68–72, and 79–82, and were printed in part in Appendix C of Knittle, *The Palatine Emigration*.

88. BM Add. MS 15866, fol. 192 (9 October 1709).

89. Peter Earle, *World of Defoe*, 14; J. A. Downie, *Robert Harley*, 78–79.

90. J. R. Moore, introduction to Defoe, *Brief History*, vii.

91. For a more complete account of Defoe's views on the immigration question, see Daniel Statt, "Daniel Defoe and Immigration," *Eighteenth-Century Studies* 24 (1991): 293–313.

92. *Review*, 6: 199–200, 203–4.

93. *Review*, 6: 181–87; Defoe, *Brief History*, 39–42.

94. G. D. H. Cole, ed., *A Tour*, 1: 200–6; B.M. Add. MS 61649, fols. 76–78, 80–81 (manuscript proposals of c. 20 June 1709); Defoe, *Brief History*, 42–44. The optimum size of rural settlements of immigrants for rapid assimilation is modernly thought to be from fifteen to twenty-five families: R. A. Grauman, "Methods of Studying the

Cultural Assimilation of Immigrants" (unpublished M.Sc. [Econ.] thesis, London School of Economics, 1951).

95. PRO, CO 389/36/414–20.

96. PRO, CO 388/76/63.

97. PRO, CO 388/76/63.

98. *HMC Report*, Portland MSS, 2: 207 (3 June 1709); BM Add. MS 61649, fols. 80–81.

99. *Review*, 6: *passim;* Defoe, *A Tour*, 1: 200–6.

100. Defoe, *Brief History*, 37–38.

101. PRO, CO 388/76/58, 65i, 76 (23 May, 1 June, 23 June).

102. PRO, CO 388/76/66i, 67 (11 June 1709); *BTJ* (1709–15), 46–47.

103. PRO, SP 44/108/87 (4 June).

104. BM Add. MS 61649, fol. 75 (17 June 1709).

105. PRO, SP 87/4/184 (1 June).

106. Defoe, *Brief History*, 33.

107. *Journal of the Society for Propagating the Gospel*, 1: 164, 170, in *Ecclesiastical Records*, H. Hastings, ed., 2: 1738–39 (20 May and 3 June).

108. PRO, SP 44/108/92 (Sunderland to Bank of England and to East India Company, 14 June 1709).

109. *Piety and Bounty*, 3.

110. *A View of the Queen's Enemies in the Poor Palatines* (1710), 4.

111. *Piety and Bounty*, 4–10.

112. Abel Boyer, *Annals* 8, Appendix 3, 42–43.

113. Ibid., 44, 56, 51–52.

114. *Canaan*, 95–96.

115. PRO, SP 44/108/96 (Sunderland to Board of Ordnance).

116. *Cal. Tr. Bks.*, 23 (ii): 226 (24 June 1709).

117. *Marlborough-Godolphin Correspondence*, ed. H. L. Snyder, 3: 1293 (24 June).

Chapter 6. The Palatine Migration: Failure and Dispersal

1. PRO, SP 84/232/138, 144 (The Hague, Dayrolle to Boyle, 1 June and 14 June).

2. PRO, SP 84/232/138.

3. BM Add. MS 15866, fol. 176.

4. PRO, SP 84/232/168 (1 July).

5. *Piety and Bounty,* 66–67; PRO, SP 84/232/182 (Placaet of 7 July 1709).

6. PRO, SP 84/232/169 (1 July).

7. PRO, SP 84/232/138 (The Hague, Dayrolle to Boyle, 1 June); BM Add. MS 15866, fols. 178–180 (Boyle to Dayrolle, 5 and 12 July).

8. PRO, SP 84/232/185, 188 (The Hague, Dayrolle to Boyle, 15 and 19 July); SP 104/74/91 (Boyle to Dayrolle, 15 and 19 July).

9. PRO, SP 84/232/229 (15 July).

10. *London Gazette*, 14–16 July 1709; Luttrell, *Relation,* 6: 465 (16 July 1709).

11. Goebel, "Briefe," 171–73 (Rotterdam, Albertus Dooren, 1 August 1709).

12. Ibid., 180 (Ezechiel de Hailenberg to the Chancellor, 18 August 1709).

13. PRO, SP 84/232/212 (The Hague, Dayrolle to Boyle, 12 August).

14. BM Add. MS 61534, fol. 171 (The Hague, Dayrolle to Tilson, 23 August); BM Add. MS 15866, fols. 185, 187 (Boyle to Dayrolle, 23 and 26 August).

15. BM Add. MS 15866, fol. 190 (Boyle to Dayrolle, 9 September).

16. PRO, SP 84/232/225 (The Hague, Dayrolle to Boyle, 2 September); SP 84/232/232 ("L'Estrait des Resolutions de L. H. P. les États Généraux des Provinces Unies," 26 September 1709, N.S.).

17. PRO, SP 84/232/230 (The Hague, Dayrolle to Boyle, 5 September); SP 84/232/225 (The Hague, Dayrolle to Boyle, 2 September).

18. *Canaan* 10, 92–93.

19. PRO, SP 84/232/242–243 (received 28 September 1709).

20. BM Add. MS 15866, fol. 192 (9 October 1709); PRO, SP 84/232/268.

21. PRO, SP 104/74/98 (G. D. Wulsten to Mr. Dupre, Clerk of Palatine Commissioners, 14 October 1709).

22. BM Add. MS 15866, fol. 195 (Cairnes to Sunderland, 15 October).

23. PRO, SP 104/74/97.

24. PRO, SP 84/232/289, 297 (to Sunderland, 25 October, to Boyle, 28 October).

25. PRO, SP 84/232/301.

26. BM Add. MS 61649, fols. 102, 106 (Sunderland to Commissioners, 22 and 26 December 1709); BM Add. MS 61652, fol. 194 (Sunderland to Commissioners, 26 December, copy).

27. *London Gazette*, 6 July 1709; Luttrell, *Relation,* 6: 461, 463; *Piety and Bounty,* 62.

28. Defoe, *Review*, 6: 242 (23 August 1709).

29. Luttrell, *Relation,* 6: 488; *State of the Palatines* (1710), 16.

30. *Wentworth Papers,* ed. J. J. Cartwright, 97 (French newsletter, 24 July to 4 August); *Canaan*, 107–8.

31. *Wentworth Papers*, ed. Cartwright, 97; *The Palatines Catechism* (1709), in *Ecclesiastical Records*, H. Hastings, ed., 1817–20, 1820.

32. *Canaan*, 105–6.

33. Subtitled, *Oder eine Kurze Unleitung zur Englischen Sprach, zum Nutz der Armen Pfaeltzer; nebst Angehaengten Englischen und Teutschen A B C* (1710).

34. *Short and Easy Way*, 38, 40.

35. *Palatines Catechism*, 1818.

36. Ibid.

37. *State of the Palatines*, 6.

38. Ibid., 4–5.

39. *Canaan*, 7–8.

40. T. S. Ashton, *Economic Fluctuations*, 17.

41. Abel Boyer, *Memoirs of Queen Anne* (1729).

42. Defoe, *Review*, 6: 179 (16 July 1709).

43. *Remarks of Thomas Hearne*, ed. C. E. Doble, 2: 239–40.

44. *Canaan*, 108.

45. BM Add. MS 61611, fols. 111–12 (information of Nicholas Roberts, October 1709).

46. BM Add. MS 61611, fols. 85–86 (agreement of 31 July 1709, copy; Sundridge, Tenison to Sunderland(?), 31 August 1709).

47. BM Add. MS 61611, fols. 87–88 (Sundridge, Tenison to Sunderland(?), 9 September 1709; information of Melchior Springley, 9 October 1709, copy).

48. BM Add. MS 61611, fol. 89 (James Montague to the Attorney General, 16 September 1709); PRO, SP 44/108/151 (22 September 1709); SP 34/11/49–50 (Sundridge, Tenison to Sunderland(?), 13 October 1709).

49. BM Add. MS 61611, fols. 87–88 (to Sunderland, 9 September 1709).

50. *Wentworth Papers*, ed. Cartwright, 96.

51. *HMC Report*, Dartmouth MSS, 3: 147 (Lichfield, 23 August 1709).

52. *HMC Report,* Portland MSS, 4: 549 (Lady Pye to Abigail Hartley, 15 July 1710); Swift, *The Examiner,* no. 45 (7 June 1711).

53. *HMC 14th Report* App. 5, Kenyon MSS, pp. 442–43 (2 August 1709).

54. *London Gazette,* 4–6 August 1709.

55. PRO, CO 388/76/84 (J. Taylor at Treasury to Mr. Popple, 6 August 1709).

56. PRO, CO 389/36/441–43 (Board of Trade to Lord Treasurer, 9 August 1709).

57. *BTJ,* (1708–15), 61–62.

58. PRO, CO 5/289/223 (Proprietors to Commissioners, 11 August 1709); *CSPA* (1708–9), 445–46 (Proprietors to Board of Trade, 11 August 1709).

59. *London Gazette,* 18–20 August 1709.

60. *HMC 7th Report,* App., p. 507 (17 August 1709).

61. PRO, SP Ireland 63/366/144–45 (Dublin).

62. *Notes and Queries,* 1st ser., 11 (1855): 88; *HMC 8th Report,* App., p. 47 (7 July).

63. *London Gazette,* 30 July-2 August 1709; *Cal. Tr. Papers,* 119, (1680–1720), 153–54; PRO, SP 67/3/416 (Boyle to Lord Lieutenant, 9 August 1709).

64. *London Gazette,* 6–9 August 1709, 25–29 August; Luttrell, *Relation,* 6: 474 (9 August).

65. Defoe, *Review,* 6: 241–42 (23 August).

66. BM Add. MS 35933, fol. 12 (Dublin, Irish Palatine Commissioners to Lord Justices of Ireland, c. 10 August 1710).

67. *CJ* XVI, 598.

68. BM Add. MS 35933, fols. 12–13.

69. *View of the Queen's Enemies in the Palatines,* 8.

70. *Canaan,* 8; BM Add. MS 35933, fols. 18–19 (Dublin, Irish Commissioners to Lord Justices of Ireland, 15 February 1711).

71. Quoted in H. T. Dickinson, "Poor Palatines," 479 (to Secretary Dawson, c. 30 January 1711).

72. *Cal. Tr. Papers,* (1680–1720), 160: 475 (Dublin, 4 April 1713).

73. *Cal. Tr. Papers,* 1680–1720), 188: 79 (Dublin, to Lord Lieutenant, 8 February 1715).

74. BM Add. MS 35933, fols. 27, 29 (6 January 1718); *Cal.Tr. Papers* (1680–1720), 160: 475 (4 April).

75. W. A. Knittle, *The Early Eighteenth Century Palatine Emigration,* 92–95.

76. Luttrell, *Relation,* 6: 473 (6 August 1709).

77. *Piety and Bounty,* 63; *Collections of Thomas Hearne,* 2: 446 (petition to Queen, 8 September 1709).

78. *Cal. Tr. Bks.,* vol. 23, ii, p. 361 (J. Taylor to Dayrolle, 15 September 1709).

79. *Canaan,* 105.

80. *Piety and Bounty,* 64–65.

81. PRO, T.1/119/93/98, 136–53 (Treasury Money Book, 22 October 1709); SP 84/232/260 (The Hague, Dayrolle to Boyle, 1 October 1709).

82. CLRO, 36B, ex-Guildhall MS 282; BM Add. MS 17677 DDD, fol. 254 (L'Hermitage to States General, 19 August 1709).

83. *View of the Queen's Enemies,* 6–7. There is no record of the actual total.

84. CLRO 36B, ex-Guildhall MS 282 (Chamber of London, "An Account of Moneys Received upon Her Majesty's Brief for the . . . poor Palatines"). The fund was liquidated in March 1712.

85. Defoe, *Review,* 6: 230 (16 August 1709); Luttrell, *Relation,* 6: 472 (4 August 1709).

86. Dickinson, "Palatines," 471; *View of Queen's Enemies,* 6; *HMC Reports,* Portland MSS, 2: 207 (Newcastle to Lord Somers, 15 August 1709).

87. *View of the Queen's Enemies*, 6; *DNB*, sub Duncombe; Gary Stuart DeKrey, *Fractured Society*, 194–95.

88. *The Tatler*, no. 124 (24 January 1710).

89. *Cal. Tr. Bks.*, vol. 23, ii, p. 394 (petition to Treasury, 20 October 1709).

90. BM Add. MS 17677 DDD, fol. 254 (L'Hermitage to States General, 19 August 1709); *Cal. Tr. Bks.*, vols. 23, ii, pp. 351–52 (William Lowndes to Navy Commissioners, 8 September 1709).

91. Defoe, *Brief History*, 46.

92. *Canaan*, 112.

93. BM Add. MS 17677 DDD, fol. 254; *CJ* XVI, 598.

94. PRO, SP 44/108/155 (Sunderland to Mayor of Liverpool, 6 October 1709); *HMC 8th Report*, App., p. 395 (Lords of Council to Mayor of Chester, 29 June 1709); *Ecclesiastical Records*, ed. Hastings, 3: 1829–30; *Canaan*, 113.

95. Dickinson, "Palatines," 476; Luttrell, *Relation*, 6: 496; C. E. Lart, "Huguenot Settlements," 286–98.

96. *Canaan*, 110–11; BM Lansdowne MS 1013, fol. 126 verso (White Kennet to the Reverend Samuel Blackwell, 8 October 1709).

97. *Canaan*, 8; *State of the Palatines*, 10; Drake quoted in Dickinson, "Palatines," 477; Defoe, *Review*, 6: 175 (14 July).

98. *CJ* XVI, 598; PRO, SP 34/11/47 (draft commission, Queen to Thomas Ekines, 20 October 1709); SP 44/108/161, 188 (Sunderland to Commissioners, 26 October and 30 December 1709).

99. *HMC Reports*, Portland MSS, 2: 207 (Beverley, 20 July 1709).

100. *CJ* XVI, 596; *Canaan*, 103; PRO, CO 388/76/84 (5 October 1709).

101. PRO, SP 44/107/267 (Boyle to Walpole, 17 August 1709); *Ecclesiastical Records*, ed. Hastings, 3: 1831.

102. Burnet, *History*, 6: 38–39; BM Lansdowne MS 1013, fols. 126–27.

103. *Piety and Bounty*, 62 (20 July 1709).

104. *BTJ*, (1709–15), 65 (24 August 1709); *CSPA*, (1708–9), 465 (Bendysh to Popple, 16 September 1709); I. K. Steele, *Politics of Colonial Policy;* 118–20; Luttrell, *Relation*, 6: 613–14 (3 August 1710)

105. *CSPA*, (1710–11), 95–6 (Antigua, 11 May 1710, to Sunderland).

106. *CSPA*, (1717–18), 29, 60, 403; PRO, CO 23/2/75 (New Providence, 4 May 1722); CO 23/13/147 (New Providence, 24 December 1723).

107. Hugh T. Lefler and William S. Powell, *North Carolina*, 60–62; *CSPA*, (1708–9), 445–46, 471 (Proprietors to Board of Trade, 11 August 1709, and Proprietors to Receiver General of North Carolina, 22 September 1709); PRO, CO 5/289/229 (warrant from Proprietors to Deputy Governor, 8 September 1709); SP 44/108/163 (Sunderland to Commissioners, 3 October 1709).

108. PRO, CO 5/289/232.

109. *Graffenreid's Account*, ed. Vincent H. Todd, 47–48; Hugh T. Lefler and Albert Ray Newsome, 56–58.

110. *Graffenreid's Account*, ed. Todd, 51; John Lawson, introduction, xxiv–xxx; Lefler and Newsome, *Southern State*, 51.

111. *Graffenreid's Account*, ed. Todd, 73–75; Lawson, *Voyage*, introduction, xxx–xxxvii; Lefler and Newsome, *Southern State*, 62–64.

112. Letter of Christopher Gale to colonial governor, quoted in Lefler and Newsome, *Southern State*, 64.

113. *Graffenreid's Account*, ed. Todd, 74–75, 89.

114. PRO, CO 5/1121/387–91 (30 August 1709).

115. PRO, CO 5/1121/465–69 (30 November 1709).; *Cal. Tr. Bks.*, vol. 24, ii, pp. 147–48.

116. J. S. Bromley, ed., *New Cambridge Modern History*, 6: 841–42; *Several Grievances* (1700); 3 & 4 Anne c. 9.

117. *Documents Relative to New York,* ed. E. B. O'Callaghan, 5: 72 (to Lord Lovelace, 28 March 1709).

118. *Cal. Tr. Bks.* vol. 24, ii, pp. 147–48.

119. S. H. Cobb, *Story of the Palatines,* 125.

120. *BTJ,* (1709–15), 106 (Sunderland to Board, 20 December 1709).

121. *Documents Relative to New York,* ed. O'Callaghan, 3: 609–70; this summary is based largely on the accounts of the New York settlement contained in both Cobb and Knittle.

122. *BTJ,* (1709–15), 290 (New York, George Clark, Secretary of New York, to Board, 30 May 1711).

123. Cobb, *Palatines,* 173–74.

124. *Cal. Tr. Papers,* (1680–1720), 137: 311 (New York, Robert Hunter to Lowndes, 12 September 1711).

125. Steele, *Colonial Policy,* 131–32.

126. Cobb, *Palatines, passim; Canaan, passim*; A. G. Roeber, *Palatines, Liberty, and Property.*

127. *Cal. Tr. Bks.,* vol. 24, ii, pp. 153–54 (J. Taylor to Dayrolle, 31 January 1710); BM Add. MS 15866, fols. 197, 200 (Boyle to Dayrolle, 20 January 1710).

128. *Cal. Tr. Bks.,* vol. 24, ii, p. 269 (Lowndes to Dayrolle, 2 May 1710), 283 (Lowndes to Spencer Compton, 10 May 1710).

129. BM Add. MS 35933, fol. 16 (Dublin, Ormonde to Lords Justices of Ireland, 12 December 1710); *Cal. Tr. Bks.,* vol. 25, ii, p. 24 (Treasury Lords to Irish Revenue Commissioners, 9 March 1711).

130. *Cal. Tr. Bks.,* vol. 25, ii, pp. 183–84 (Treasury warrant to Chamberlain of City of London, 23 February 1711), 199–200 (Lowndes to Bendysh, 3 March 1711), 244 (memorial of Bendysh, 10 April 1711).

131. *View of Queen's Enemies,* 8; *CJ* XVI, 596.

132. PRO, PC 2/83/307 (Order in Council, 6 September 1711); *Cal. Tr. Bks.,* vol. 25, ii, pp. 446–47 (warrant, 13 September 1711).

133. *HMC Reports,* Portland MSS, 5: 183–84 (J. J. Caesar to John Chamberlayne(?), 16 June 1712); *Cal. Tr. Bks.,* vol. 26, ii, pp. 317–18 (J. Taylor to Mr. Southwell, 14 June 1712).

134. *Notes and Queries,* 3d ser., 1 (1862), 252.

135. Henry Horwitz, *Revolution Politicks,* 223–25; Geoffrey Holmes, "The Sacheverell Riots," 59–62; [John Toland], *The State Anatomy of Great Britain* (1717), 55–56; Geoffrey Holmes, *The Trial of Doctor Sacheverell,* 45–47.

136. *CJ* XVI, 456–57 (15 January 1711); J. R. Jones, *Country and Court* 344–45.

137. Hare, *The Reception of the Palatines Vindicated* (1711), 37, 40; Swift, *The Examiner,* no. 26 (25 January 1711).

138. *CJ* XVII, 24 (22 December 1711); *CJ* XIX, 209, 374.

139. *CJ* XVI, 598.

140. *Review,* 6: 211 (28 July 1709).

141. *Review,* 6: 153–54.

Chapter 7. The Reception of Immigrants: "The Bread from our Mouths"

1. Jacques Fontaine, *Memoirs,* 122, 146–50, 155.

2. R. A. Grauman, "Methods of Studying the Cultural Assimilation of Immi-

grants" (unpublished M.Sc. [Econ.] thesis, London School of Economics, 1951), 335, et seq.

3. The most important works are Bernard Cottret, *The Huguenots in England* and R. Mayo, "Les Huguenots a Bristol, 1681–1791," 2 parts (unpublished thesis, University of Lille, 1966).

4. Linda Colley, *Britons*, chap. 1.

5. The most exhaustive treatment of the French churches in England is R. D. Gwynn, "The Ecclesiastical Organization of French Protestants in England in the Later Seventeenth Century, with Specific Reference to London" (unpublished Ph.D. thesis, University of London, 1976).

6. E. S. DeBeer, "The Revocation of the Edict of Nantes," 303, 306.

7. The Act of Uniformity of 1662 provided that the penalties it imposed would "not extend to the foreigners or aliens of the foreign reformed churches": 14 Car. II c. 4.

8. J. E. Pinnington, "Anglican Openness," 137–38.

9. Lambeth Palace Library, MSS 1122, i, no. 13; *Diary of John Evelyn*, ed. E. S. DeBeer, 3: 545; Gwynn, "Ecclesiastical Organization," 161, 405; R. D. Gwynn, "Distribution of Huguenot Refugees," 435–36; *CSPD* (Jan. 1686-May 1687), 149–50.

10. C. W. Chitty, "Aliens in England to 1600," 194–97; Pinnington, "Openness," 138.

11. Guildhall MS 7412, I, p. 97 (Coetus minute book, 14 October 1668); M. R. Thorp, "The Anti-Huguenot Undercurrent," 578–79; Bodleian Library, Rawlinson MS C984, fols. 48, 50.

12. Samuel Smiles, *Huguenots*, 284; Gwynn, "Ecclesiastical Organization," 92; Henri Misson de Valbourg, *Memoirs*, 83–84.

13. *Reasons against Erecting a French Church* (1700), 9–10.

14. Defoe, *Review*, 5: 131 (12 June 1708); Shaftesbury, *Characteristics of Men*, 1: 20–21 ("A Letter Concerning Enthusiasm"); Max Beloff, *Public Order*, 48; *Harl. Misc.*, 11: 64–65; Hillel Schwartz, *Knaves, Fools, Madmen*, 17–18, 21, 14–15; Hillel Schwartz, *The French Prophets*.

15. Of course, denunciations of foreigners as Catholics occurred from the beginning of the period. The fire of London was blamed on French papists, as the inscription on the Monument attests, and many French and Dutch in London were arrested, imprisoned, and interrogated after the fire. Confessions were elicited, including one that 300 Frenchmen had plotted to burn the city. The victims of the fire sought a scapegoat, and foreigners were convenient candidates. A contemporary account describes a foreigner, himself a victim of the fire, whose mumbled Latin prayer as he tried to remove his belongings from the path of the flames was not understood by the crowd, and who nearly met his end when the cry arose "he is a Frenchman, kill him. . . ." J. E. Hearsey, *London and the Great Fire*, 137; *A True and Faithful Account of the . . . Late Dreadful Burning of the City of London* (1667), in *Somer's Tracts*, 7: 615–28; PRO, SP 29/443/47 (crank verse warning that "the nation it is almost quite undone by French men", 1666); *CSPD*, Addenda (1660–85), 205 (pamphlet accusation of July 1667); *Observations Both Historical and Moral upon the Burning of London* (n.d.), in *Harl. Misc.*, 7: 324, 326.

16. *London Gazette*, no. 1661 (17–20 October 1681); PRO, PC 2/69/374–375 (Order in Council); R. L. Poole, *History of the Huguenots*, 77; PRO, SP 29/43/188 (Norwich, Pierre Chauvin to John Chardin, 4 September 1683).

17. *HMC Reports*, Portland MSS, 8: 67–68 (Memorial to House of Commons, 24 February 1700).

18. The footmen even published a tract, by "True Blue," to argue their case and

defend themselves against charges of riot. *The Justice and the Footmen* (1744), 12–15, 18–20.

19. *The Diary of Samuel Pepys*, eds. R. Latham and W. Mathews, 4: 335; H. S. Q. Henriques, *Return of the Jews,* 99–103, 105–10.

20. On English anti-Semitism after the Revolution, see David S. Katz, "The Jews of England and 1688," in *From Persecution to Toleration*, eds. Ole Peter Grell, et al. (Oxford, 1991), 217–50.

21. H. S. Q. Henriques, *Jews and the English Law,* 199–200; Cecil Roth, *History of the Jews,* 203.

22. See chap. 3.

23. E. Bonacich, "Ethnic Antagonism." 547–59; E. Bonacich, "Middleman Minorities," 583–94.

24. P. G. M. Dickson, *Financial Revolution in England;* Charles Wilson, introduction to William Cunningham, *Alien Immigrants:* xvii; Charles Wilson, *England's Apprenticeship,* 195.

25. See, e.g., Kenneth Lunn, "Immigrants and British Labour's Response," 48.

26. M. D. George, *England in Transition,* 25; Edward Chamberlayne, *Angliae Notitia* (1669), 445; Joan Thirsk, *Economic Policy,* 118; C. Nicholson, *Strangers to England,* 52, 55.

27. *Parl. Hist.,* 14: 1303 (speaking on bill to permit exportation of wool from Ireland to Britain, 26 March 1753).

28. Nicholas Rogers, "Popular Politics," 77–78.

29. Michael Mullett, "Popular Culture," 131–35.

30. *Gentleman's Magazine,* 21 (1751): 186; Nicholas Rogers, "Popular Jacobitism," 123–41.

31. Gary Stuart DeKrey, *Fractured Society.*

32. J. R. Kellett, "The Breakdown of Gild and Corporation Control," 381–83; Michael John Walker, "The Extent of Guild Control of Trades in England"; E. Lipson, *Economic History,* 3: 343–51; D. W. Jones, "London Merchants," 311–12.

33. A. Pulling, *A Practical Treatise,* 60–64; V. Pearl, "Change and Stability," 3–34, 17–18; CLRO, Rep. 96/16 (order re foreigners, 10 November 1691).

34. See, e.g., Dublin City Assembly Roll, XV, membrane no. 109.

35. *HMC 14th Report,* App., pt. viii, MSS of Corporation of Lincoln, 109 (Sir Thomas Meres, MP for Lincoln, to Mayor, 14 December 1681); PRO, SP 29/417/142 (Mayor of Bristol to Privy Council, 10 December 1681).

36. The fine was about 46 shillings.

37. Pulling, *Treatise,* 64; CLRO, Jor. 48/235 (45s. 8d. paid in 1676); CLRO, Rep. 88/70 (46s. 7d. paid in 1682); CLRO, Rep. 94/60 (resolution of 4 November 1688); CLRO, Misc. MSS 42.2 ("An Account of Naturalizations from Anno Domini 1684," n.d.).

38. CLRO, Jor. 48/235 (Dutch cabinetmaker, 9 May 1676); PRO, PC 2/65/426 (petition of Dutch bricklayer, 22 December 1676); CLRO, Jor. 299b (Dutch bricklayer, 2 April 1677); CLRO, Rep., 87/215–16, 88/70 (John Louis, 26 July 1682 and 5 February 1683).

39. CLRO, Jor. 58/41/44, 56 (repeal of act of Court of October, 16th. Eliz.); CLRO, Jor. 59/349–50 (admission of Henri Fournier, 24 September 1751); PRO, PC 2/65/433 (petition of buttonseller, 10 January 1677).

40. Guildhall MS 7412, 1: 85 (Coetus minute book, June 1663); CLRO, *Remembrancia,* 9, fols. 34–35; *CSPD* (1660–61), 363 (petition of shopkeepers, 24 November 1660, and Committee report, 14 March 1661).

41. *Calendar of State Papers Venetian* (1666–68), 317–18 (Venetian Ambassador to Doge, 16 November 1668); *The Loyal Protestant and True Domestick Intelligence,*

no. 194 (15 August 1682); Public Record Office (PRO), PC 2/71/280 (petition of handicraftmen, 28 May 1686); CLRO, Jor. 51/300–301 (petition of Musicians, 9 March 1693).

42. For an elaboration of this interpretation of artisans' conceptions of property rights, see Michael Sonenscher, *The Hatters of Eighteenth Century France* (Berkeley, 1987).

43. *The Rights and Liberties of Englishmen Asserted* (1701).

44. Thompson, "The Moral Economy of the English Crowd in the Eighteenth Century," *P & P* 50 (1971): 76–136, 78–79, 83.

45. Atherton, *Political Prints*, 85; Mullett, "Popular Culture," 132–35.

46. Rogers, "Popular Politics," 84–86.

47. PRO, PC 2/65/172 (fringe and twist, 28 March 1676); PC 2/65/370 (watch chains, 8 November 1676); PC 2/66/51 (goldsmith, 20 June 1677); PC 2/66/341, 352 (buttonmakers, May 1678); PC 2/71/44 (clockmakers, 29 April 1685); *CSPD* (1699–1700 [bakers, 22 May 1699]); PRO, PC 2/78/203 (silk throwsters and bakers, 15 May 1701); *CSPD* (1702–3), 443–44 (silk-throwsters' petition, 14 November 1702); *CSPD* (1703–4), 376 (braziers' petition, 23 December 1703); PRO, PC 2/65/105 (Scots).

48. PRO, PC 2/79/99 (Norwich, 2 March 1687); PC 2/79/463 (Bideford, 25 November 1703); PC 2/78/228 (Plymouth, 28 June 1701); *CSPD* (1702–3), 304 (linen-drapers in Southampton, 20 November 1702); *HMC Report*, Portland MSS, 8: 375–76 (petition of Phillip Gariot, 25 August 1705; letter from Mayor, 13 August); *CSPD* (1700–2), 352 (Sir C. Hedges to Mayor of Portsmouth, 5 June 1701, to stop harassment of cutler).

49. PRO, PC 2/69/373 (petition, 19 October 1681); PC 2/69/379 (licences granted, 26 October 1681); PC 2/69/404 (term reduced, 16 November 1681).

50. PRO, PC 2/69/482–483 (petition, 22 March 1682); *CSPD* (Oct. 1683-April 1684), 334 (Sec. Jenkins to Mayor of Rye, 22 March 1684); PRO, PC 2/70/134 (petition of fishermen, 26 March 1684); 143 (17 April, failure to appear for hearing).

51. PRO, PC 2/69/610 (relating to Brulon's contract to supply the Court with fish, 12 January 1683); PC 2/71/87, 90 (petition of Mayor, 4 December 1685, reference to Attorney General, 11 December 1685); PC 2/71/105 (Samuel Pepys's motion to renew licences, 5 February 1685); PC 2/77/222 (petition of fishermen, 25 August 1698).

52. R. A. Shaw, R. D. Gwynn, and P. Thomas, *Huguenots in Wandsworth.*

53. CLRO, Rep. 60/204 (admission of Company, 23 July 1650); CLRO, Rep. 72/73 (petition of journeymen, 6 December 1666); H. Pelling, *British Trade Unionism*, 21.

54. CLRO, Jor. 45/311 (petition, 3 May 1663); PRO, PC 2/65/55, 171 (petition of Caron, 10 December, and Order in Council); Tim Harris, *London Crowds*, 202.

55. Harris, *London Crowds*, 202 (August 1675).

56. See W. C. Scoville, "Diffusion of Technology, I," 303–04.

57. The Privy Council Registers for James's reign are full of references to the dispute.

58. One of the most commonly cited of the old statutes forbidding aliens to work in England.

59. PRO, PC 2/71/11, 39 (Committee for Trade report to Council, 8 April 1685; petition of feltmakers, 13 February 1685); *CSPD* (1685), 94 (Attorney General's report, 14 March 1685).

60. PRO, PC 2/71/91 (petition, 18 December 1685).

61. PRO, PC 2/71/202 (report re. Martin, 11 February 1686).

62. PRO, PC 2/71/143 (licences granted 28 May 1686); PC 2/71/164 (naturalized hatmaker licenced, 8 October 1686); PC 2/71/212 (licences, 18 March 1687); PC 2/71/212 (licences, 7 December 1688); PC 2/73/188 (licences, 11 July 1689); PC 2/71/155 (licences for trade "above five miles from London," 17 July 1686).

63. PRO, PC 2/73/415 (molestations, 27 March 1690); PC 2/75/408, 442 (order to Attorney General, 3 May 1694); *CSPD* (1698), 236 (proceedings on petition from French hatters, 9 May 1698); PRO, PC 2/78/242 (order renewed, 31 July 1701).

64. Minet, *Threadneedle Street Registers,* xx.

65. P. Thornton and N. Rothstein, "Importance of the Huguenots," 60–88.

66. Minet, *Threadneedle Street Registers,* xx; F. Warner, *Silk Industry,* 51.

67. Alfred Plummer, *Weavers' Company,* 151, 160, 154–57; W. C. Waller, ed., *Extracts from the Court Books,* 54.

68. Plummer, *Weavers' Company,* 154; PRO, PC 2/59/61 (petition of Company against French, 3 August 1666); Waller, ed. *Extracts,* 9 (proposals of 1653); Guildhall MS 7412, 1: 125 (Coetus minute book, report of molestations, February 1690); PRO, SP 32/13/142 ("The Case of the French Protestant Weavers" [c. 1690]); *CSPD* (1702–3), 723.

69. Plummer, *Company, passim*; R. M. Dunn, "London Weavers' Riot," 13–23, 13.

70. Quoted in Lipson, *Economic History,* 3: 61.

71. Risings occurred against foreigners in 1517, 1519, 1586, and 1593: Tim Harris, *London Crowds,* 31; C. W. Chitty, "Aliens in England in the Sixteenth Century," 142–43.

72. Caroline Robbins, "A Note on General Naturalization," 173; PRO, SP 29/274/205–206 (handwritten broadside and depositions of those involved, April 1670).

73. John Stevenson, *Popular Disturbances,* 120–21; Harris, *London Crowds,* 191–202; Plummer, *Weavers' Company,* 165; *HMC 7th Report,* App., 465–66 (11 August, William Fall to Sir Ralph Verney), 492 (12 August, William Denton to same).

74. On 16 August Sir John Holland wrote to Lord Yarmouth that fear was spreading at the "dangerous discontent that the silk weavers and others have taken up against the French inhabitants in the City and suburbs, robbing them, as they conceive, of their trade and livelihood." *CSPD* (1675–76), 253 (R. M. to Sir Francis Radcliffe, August 1675); *HMC 6th Report,* App., pt. i, p. 372 (Holland to Lord Yarmouth, 16 August 1675); *CSPV* (1673–75), 449 (30 August 1675, Venetian Resident to Doge); Harris, *London Crowds,* 191–202.

75. *CSPD* (July–September 1683), 267 (Sunderland to Jenkins, 9 August 1683); *CSPD* (1683), 325, 330 (Atterbury to Jenkins, 25, 27 August; information of a weaver); PRO, SP 29/431/21 (same).

76. *Answer to a Pretended Speech* (1694), 11, 25; PRO, SP 44/100/169 (Shrewsbury to Mr. Blathwayt, 18 November 1695).

77. George Rudé, *Hanoverian London,* 185–87; Guildhall Library, A.1.3 no. 64 (affidavit of attacked weaver and resolution of Court of Weavers' Company, 10 May 1720).

78. *Parl. Hist.,* 14: 146 (4 February 1748, debate over bill for naturalizing foreign Protestants); *Parl. Hist.,* 14: 1302–3 (speech of Sir William Yonge, 26 March 1753).

79. *Seasonable Observations . . . on a General Naturalization* (1748), 9.

80. George Rudé is the historian of the riots of 1736, and the following is largely based on his accounts.

81. H. J. Bradley, *Shoreditch Church,* 27–30; PRO, SP 78/212/229 (State Papers, France, Holles Newcastle to Earl Waldegrave and Mr. Keene, 5 August 1736); George Rudé, *Paris and London in the Eighteenth Century* (London, 1970), 204–12; George Rudé, "London Riots of 1736," 53–63; J. P. Malcolm, 275; *Gentleman's Magazine,* 6: (1736): 422 (26 July), 485 (1 August).

82. Defoe, *Review,* 6: 211 (28 July 1709), 6: 175 (14 July 1709); A. Boyer, *Memoirs of Queen Anne,* 123.

83. See F. H. Allport, "Science of Public Opinion," 7–23.

256 FOREIGNERS AND ENGLISHMEN

84. It is dangerous, however, to use the remarks of visitors to gauge the opinions of immigrants. The difference is that between the stalls and the stage, between the audience and the players. The immigrant must become a part of the culture that a visitor merely observes.

85. Roy Porter, "Seeing the Past," 198–99; Michael Duffy, *Englishman and Foreigner* 14; Atherton, *Political Prints*.

86. *A Winter Evening's Conversation*, a dialogue tract of 1748, was typical in its characterizations: Tartuffe, a French Protestant, Vanderghelt, a Dutch factor and remitter, Achitophel, a Portuguese Jewish remitter all symbolized well-defined English stereotypes. Josiah Tucker, *Reflections on Naturalization,* Part 1, (1752), 62.

87. William Herbert, *Considerations in Favour of Strangers Residing in England* (1662), 13; *A Foreign View of England,* Madame Van Muyden, ed., 112; J. P. Denis, *A Plot Discovered* (1722), 11–12.

88. The phrase is James Thomson's, in *Liberty,* part v (1736).

89. Swift, *The History of the Last Four Years,* in *Works of Jonathan Swift,* ed. Walter Scott, 5: 47.

90. *The Danger of the Church and Kingdom from Foreigners Considered* (1721), 6; Atherton, *Political Prints*, 88; *The Dutch Boare Dissected; or, A Description of Hogg-Land* (1665), in Duffy, *Englishman*, 82–83.

91. Duffy, *Englishman*, 15.

92. Roth, *History of Jews,* 199; Todd M. Endelman, *Jews of Georgian England,* 182; *Gentleman's Magazine* (1753), 385; T. W. Perry, *Public Opinion,* 8–9.

93. For a different interpretation, see Linda Colley, *Britons,* and Linda Colley, "The Apotheosis of George III," 94–129.

94. Atherton, *Political Prints*, 209–16; Duffy, *Englishman*, 13, 19–22.

95. The play received its first performance in Dublin in 1764, but did not appear on the stage in London until 1781, when its title became *The Man of the World*.

96. Lewis Namier, *Structure of Politics,* 101–2.

97. Duffy, *Englishman*, 18–19, 196–97; Colley, *Britons*, chap 3.

98. Friedrich August Wendeborn, *A View of England,* 1: 266–67.

99. PRO, SP 29/337/no. 177, quoted in Gwynn, "Ecclesiastical Organization," 237; Before about the mid-seventeenth century, hostility had been directed more often towards the Spanish: Duffy, *Englishman*, 25.

100. *The Monsieur's Misfortunes; or, The Shammer Shammed* [c. 1690]. In this as in most of the broadsides, the Frenchman is made by his English opponents to cut a very sad figure.

101. Gerald Newman, *English Nationalism,* chap. 2.

102. Quoted in Gwynn, "Ecclesiastical Organization," 261.

103. Atherton, *Political Prints*, 85.

104. *French Snakes in British Clover* (1744), 9–10; "The French Dancing-Master's Misfortune at the English Masquerade" [c. 1690], in *Selden's Collection of Ballads*, vol. 5, no. 434, The Pepys Library, Magdalene College, Cambridge.

105. Arthur Murphy, *The Englishman from Paris* (1756). The play was never performed.

106. P. J. Grosley, *A Tour to London; or, New Observations on England, and its Inhabitants*, translated by Thomas Nugent, 2 vols. (1772), 1 84–85.

107. J. B. Le Blanc, *Letters on the English and French Nations,* 2 vols., (London, 1747), quoted in E. Smith, *Foreign Visitors,* 35–39; *Foreign View of England,* ed. Van Muyden, 111.

108. *The Town Spy* (1729), 9. The London commissioners of sewers complained in 1686 that the foreigners living in Spitalfields had made the area noisome with the

refuse of the cabbages and roots that they lived on. *HMC 11th Report*, App., pt. v, Dartmouth MSS, p. 129 D (29 January 1686, William Smythe to Lord Dartmouth).

109. *The Dreadful Consequences of a General Naturalization* (1751), broadside reprinted in Duffy, *Englishman*, 162–63.

110. *Diary* of Samuel Pepys, 2: 188.

111. Le Blanc, *Letters on the English and French Nations,* 1:93; Rosamond Bayne-Powell, *Travellers,* 138–39; [Andrew Henderson], *The Case of the Jews Considered* (1753), 21.

112. Mullett, "Popular Culture," 133–34. See also Jeremy Black, "Ideology," 184–216.

113. Whig exploitation of xenophobia dates from the reign of Charles II: Harris, *London Crowds*, 214–16.

114. Hugh Cunningham, "Language," 10.

115. For a detailed exploration of these themes, see Newman, *English Nationalism.*

116. See Newman, *English Nationalism*; John Pocock, "England," in *National Consciousness, History, and Political Culture in Early-Modern Europe*, ed. Orest Ranum (Baltimore, 1975), 98–117; Atherton, *Political Prints*, 105; Colley, "Apotheosis of George III," and *Britons.*

117. Atherton, *Political Prints*, 94; "Rule, Britannia!" first appeared in the last scene of *Alfred: A Masque,* by David Mallet and James Thomson, a circumstance that recalls the role of the myth of the Ancient Constitution and the Norman Yoke in the development of English national identity, as well as the self-conscious patriotism of the opposition that surrounded the Prince of Wales.

118. Black, "Ideology"; Derek Jarrett, *Age of Hogarth;* Newman, *English Nationalism*, 63–65.

119. See, for example, the print derived from Hogarth, *The Opera House, or the Italian Eunuch's Glory: Humbly Inscribed to those Generous Encouragers of Foreigners and Ruiners of England* [1735?], in Duffy, *Englishman*, 132–33; Colley, *Britons*, 31–33.

120. Mullett, "Popular Culture," 135.

121. *A Brief History of Trade* (1702), 24, 31, 33–39, 127, 132–34.

122. Newman, *English Nationalism*, chap. 6.

123. H. T. Dickinson, *Liberty and Property,* 159–62; Atherton, *Political Prints*, 85; Newman, *English Nationalism*, 67–77.

124. George, *England in Transition*, 26; Rudé, *Paris and London*, 322; Hilary Reneu, *Les Plaintes des Protestantes* (1707), preface, 429; G. B. Hertz, *British Imperialism*, 67; Linda Colley, *Oligarchy*, 155.

CHAPTER 8. THE DEBATE TO 1760: THE WANING OF POPULATIONISM

1. *The Examiner*, no. 22 (28 December 1710); *A History*, in *Prose Works of Swift*, H. Davis, ed., 6: 94–95.

2. In *Somer's Tracts*, 13: 537–38.

3. [B. Mandeville], *The Mischiefs*, ed. H. T. Dickinson (Los Angeles, 1975), 9.

4. The City of London in 1714 attempted to exploit the popular distaste for the Hanoverians by introducing in the Commons a bill "for the better preventing the covering of alien goods imported." Broadsides appeared both in favor and against the bill, denunciations echoed of foreigners defrauding the customs, but the bill failed.

5. *Reasons for Naturalizing the Jews in Great Britain and Ireland* (1714); see

John Toland, *Gründe für die Einbürgerung der Juden in Grossbritannien und Irland*, ed. H. Mainsuch (Stuttgart, 1965).

6. *State-Anatomy* (1717), 5th ed., 57.

7. Ibid., 56.

8. The attribution rests on slender evidence—certainly the tract contradicts the bulk of Defoe's writings. See P. N. Furbank and W. R. Owen, *The Canonisation of Daniel Defoe* (New Haven, 1988) 156–60.

9. *An Argument*, 5, 21, 75.

10. *The Second Part of the State-Anatomy*, 2d ed. (1717), 78–79, preface; *The State-Anatomy of Great Britain*, 5th ed. (1717), 56–57.

11. A broadsheet entitled *Advice from the Custom-House about the Importation of Foreigners to Starve our own Poor* (1715).

12. Toland, *Second Part*, preface.

13. *A Farther Argument against Ennobling Foreigners* (1717), 35.

14. Basil Williams, *Stanhope*, 142–44.

15. Michael Jubb, "Economic Policy," 121–44.

16. J. H. Plumb, *Political Stability*, 170–71; W. A. Speck, *Stability and Strife*, chaps. 8 and 9.

17. *HMC Rep.*, Portland MSS, 7: 96 (10 March 1702), quoted in Issac Kramnick, *Bolingbroke and his Circle: The Politics of Nostalgia in the Age of Walpole* (Cambridge, Mass., 1968), 61; see 63, 70, chap. 7.

18. J. G. A. Pocock, *Macchiavellian Moment*, 447–48; J. G. A. Pocock, *Virtue, Commerce, and History*. See chap. 4.

19. Plumb, *Political Stability*.

20. A good summary of the party divisions of the eighteenth century appears in E. Neville Williams, *Eighteenth-Century Constitution*, 173–76.

21. Hutchison, *Political Economy*, 54.

22. See D. C. Coleman, "Politics and Economics," 187–211.

23. John Brewer, *Party Ideology*, 16, 142–48.

24. On the effect of the 1712 stamp duty, see Michael Harris, "The Structure, Ownership, and Control of the Press, 1620–1780," in *Newspaper History: from the Seventeenth Century to the Present Day*, eds. George Boyce, et al. (London, 1987), 79–105; 84–87, 92.

25. T. S. Ashton, *Economic Fluctuations in England*, 142–50.

26. E. A. Wrigley and R. S. Schofield, *Population History*, 208–9.

27. Recent scholarship has generally recognized the importance of Defoe's output of economic and political pamphlets, although there is no definitive analytical study of his economic ideas. Peter Earle, *The World of Defoe* (London, 1976) is less a study of his economic ideas than an examination of his age through Defoe's eyes. Literary historians have used his economic writings and ideas to interpret his fictional narratives, and in turn used the imaginative writings as illustrations of his views on trade. See M. E. Novak, *Economics and the Fiction of Daniel Defoe* (Berkeley, 1962), Bram Dijkstra, *Defoe and Economics: The Fortunes of Roxana in the History of Interpretation* (New York, 1987), and T. K. Meier, *Defoe and the Defense of Commerce* (Victoria, British Columbia, 1987). For a more detailed examination of Defoe's views on immigration, see Daniel Statt, "Defoe and Immigration," *Eighteenth-Century Studies* 24 (1991): 293–313.

28. Defoe, *Lex Talionis*.

29. *Giving Alms no Charity* (London, 1704), 23, 5–8. The Edict of Nantes had been revoked in 1685, and Defoe's estimate of the number of French immigrants to settle in England corresponds closely with modern ones: R. D. Gwynn, "Arrival of Huguenot Refugees," 366–73.

30. Defoe, *Brief History*, 18.

31. "The more populous, the more trade, and the more trade, the more populous, and the more of both, must needs produce riches" (*Review*, 6: 135).

32. Defoe, *Lex Talionis*, 25; Defoe *Review*, 2: 69; 5: 603; 6: 165, 143, 168–70.

33. Philips, *An Appeal*, 18, 20–24; *The State of the Nation* (1725), 46–48.

34. *Review*, 6: 154, 158, 243.

35. M. M. Goldsmith, *Private Vices, Public Virtues: Bernard Mandeville's Social and Political Thought* (Cambridge, 1985), 124, argues that Mandeville was not "an economic theorist at all"; but his not having published a discourse of trade does not make his influential ideas any less relevant to the question at hand. Mandeville is an extremely refractory subject for analysis, it is true, precisely because his *Fable* is written as a long chain of intentional paradoxes. He was irrepressibly mischievous and impious, as when he suggested in his *Modest Defence of Publick Stews* (1724) that Parliament pass an act "for encouraging the importation of foreign women" to satisfy the demand of England's brothels. *Modest Defence*, 65–66. It is dangerous to take too seriously any of his more outrageous remarks—one can almost hear the laughter of his shadow. His importance to the development of economic and social thought, however, can scarcely be denied.

36. The standard edition of *The Fable* cited here is that of the 2d ed. of 1729, edited by F. B. Kaye, 2 vols. (Oxford, 1924).

37. *Fable*, 1: 194; 2: 259, 351.

38. *Fable*, 1: 242–45, 2: 113–19. See Malcolm Jack, "Progress and Corruption in the Eighteenth Century: Mandeville's 'Private Vices, Public Benefits'," *Journal of the History of Ideas* 37 (1976): 369–76.

39. *Fable*, 1: 200–1 (original pagination). Mandeville's ideas were important in the gradual redefinition of "virtue" in the eighteenth century and in the debate over luxury. See T. A Horne, *The Social Thought of Bernard Mandeville: Virtue and Commerce in Early Eighteenth Century England* (New York, 1978).

40. *The Mischiefs* (1714), 12–13.

41. *Fable*, 1: 184, 197.

42. Clayton, *A Short System*, 7; Cary, *An Essay towards Regulating the Trade*, 48.

43. For example John Haynes's pleas on behalf of the woollen trade in *Great Britain's Glory* (1715).

44. Arthur Dobbs, *An Essay on the Trade and Improvement of Ireland* (Dublin, 1729), 13–14, 17.

45. [George Blewett (Bluet)], *An Enquiry whether a general Practice of Virtue tends to the Wealth or Poverty . . . of a People* (1725), 4. As the title indicates, the book was written as a refutation of Mandeville's *Fable*.

46. Defoe, *Brief History*, 1; *Review*, 2: 53; 4: 31–36; on the question of high wages, see Richard C. Wiles, "The Theory of Wages," 123–24.

47. A. D., *Some Thoughts* (Dublin, 1731), 27, 30.

48. *A Letter*, 52.

49. *DNB*, sub Decker; *An Essay on the Causes of the Decline of the Foreign Trade* (1744), 62; the tract was perhaps the last great defence of the balance of trade doctrine.

50. Dekker, *Essay*, 65, 62–63, 93, 25.

51. [Thomas Baston], *Thoughts on Trade, and a Public Spirit* (1716), 22; Bellers, *An Essay for Employing the Able Poor* (1714), 38; Harris, *An Essay upon Money and Coins* (1757), in J. R. McCulloch, *Old and Scarce Tracts on Money* (1856; London, 1933), 368.

52. *Miseries of Poor*, ii–iii, vii, 123–25.

53. Defoe, *Review*, 6: 137, 135, 138; *Giving Alms No Charity*, 9.

54. Defoe, *A Brief State of the Inland*, 227.

55. Defoe, *An Essay at Removing National Prejudices*, 6.

56. John A. Garraty, *Unemployment in History*, 45–48; [George Berkeley], *Essay towards Preventing the Ruin of Great Britain* (1721), 6–7, 12–14; Samuel Johnston, *The Advantages of Employing the Poor*, 10–11; A. D., *Some Thoughts*, p. 32; *An Enquiry into the Causes of the Encrease and Miseries of the Poor of England* (1738), 3, 5–7; Braddon, *Miseries*, introduction, iv, xix–xx, 7, 9, 18, 20.

57. Furniss, *Laborer*, 36–37.

58. A. W. Coats, "Economic Thought," 39–51.

59. Quoted in Bernard Mandeville, *The Fable of the Bees*, ed. Phillip Harth (London, 1970), introduction, 36.

60. Daniel A. Baugh, "Poverty," 75; Norman S. Fiering, "Compassion," 195–218; John B. Radner, "Art of Sympathy," 189–210.

61. James Bonar, *Theories of Population*, 36; A. W. Coats, "Changing Attitudes to Labour," 36–37; Coats, "Economic Thought," 40–41, 45, 49; cf.: Dorothy Marshall, *English Poor*, 14, 23, 54; Wiles, "Theory of Wages," 113–26; Furniss, *Laborer*, chap. 6.

62. Bennet, *National Merchant*, 6.

63. Vanderlint, *Money*, 99–100, 8, 133–34, 8.

64. Bennet, *National Merchant*, 8–9.

65. Gee, *The Trade*, ii, vii–viii, x, 36–40, 70, 75–76, 87–88, 108–9, conclusion, 15; Richard Forster, "A Letter," 464.

66. Bennet, *The National Merchant*, 42, 128.

67. Smith, *Wealth of Nations*, bk. 3, chap. 4; E. P. Hutchinson, *Population Debate*, 112–13.

68. E. A. J. Johnson, *American Economic Thought*, 108–9.

69. 13 Geo. II. c. 7.

70. Bernard Bailyn, *Voyagers to the West*, 26–30, 36, 43, 57, 294.

71. Fielding, *An Enquiry into the Late Increase of Robbers* (1751), quoted in Furniss, *Laborer*, 23.

72. *CJ* XXV, 195.

73. At this time he represented the borough of Saint Mawes, Cornwall.

74. George Shelton, *Dean Tucker*, 138–40; R. Sedgwick, ed., *History of Parliament*, 2: 302–3.

75. John Brewer, *Sinews of Power*.

76. Paul Langford, *Commercial People*, 145–49.

77. *CJ* XXV, 269–70, 319–20, 334.

78. Ibid., 449.

79. Ibid., 469 (16 Dec. petition), XXVI, 29; *Seasonable Observations on the Naturalization Bill* (1748), p. 3; *London Magazine*, 15 (1748): 91 (petition of 3 February); *Gentleman's Magazine*, 18 (1748): 90; *The London Evening-Post*, no. 3140 (17–19 December 1747).

80. *CJ* XXVI, 29, 53, 72, 80, 84, 123, 133, 137, 139–40, 170–71; *Parl. Hist.*, 14: 971–72.

81. 26 Geo. II c. 26.

82. The act was therefore in no sense a "general" act but an exemption for Jews from the requirement of receiving the sacrament before obtaining a private naturalization act.

83. *A Modest Apology for the Citizens and Merchants of London* (1753), 1; *Remarks on the Reverend Mr. Tucker's Letter on Naturalization* (1753), 4; *An Apology for the Naturalization of the Jews* (1753), 23; Perry, *Jew Bill*, 90.

84. The act was sponsored by Jews already in England, and could not have inspired any substantial migration. See Philo-Patriae, *Considerations on the Bill* (1753), 23–24, 55–59.

85. It is noteworthy, however, that charges circulated in 1753 that the earlier failed bills for a general naturalization had been introduced to smooth the passage of the Jew Bill. One may well doubt the properties of political lubrication of so controversial a measure as general naturalization, but if the allegations were true they would provide a partial explanation for the introduction of the three successive bills of 1746, 1747, and 1751. See T. W. Perry, *Jew Bill*.

86. *DNB*, sub Tucker; R. H. Tawney, *Religion*, 24, 195; Tucker, *Reflections on the Expediencey of a Law for the Naturalization of Foreign Protestants* (1752), preface; Tucker, *A Brief Essay on the Advantages and Disadvantages which Respectively Attend France and Great Britain, with Regard to Trade* (1753), 91; *Gentleman's Magazine*, 21 (1751): 186. The best work on Tucker is Shelton, *Dean Tucker*. On the Tory and Jacobite tradition in Bristol, see Nicholas Rogers, "Popular Jacobitism in Provincial Context: Eighteenth-Century Bristol and Norwich," in *The Jacobite Challenge*, eds. Eveline Cruickshanks and Jeremy Black (Edinburgh, 1988), 123–41.

87. Tucker, *The Elements of Commerce and Theory of Taxes* (1755), 83, 63, 67, 89–90, 67–80; Tucker, *Reflections on Naturalization* (1752), 18.

88. Tucker, *Reflections*, part II, "Important Queries," 12; *Elements of Commerce*, 103; "Queries," 14, 9–10; *Elements of Commerce*, 63; "Queries," 11, 15.

89. Tucker, *Elements of Commerce*, 82, 89–89; "Queries," 38–39; *Reflections*, 63–64, v; "Queries," 31, 44–47, *Elements of Commerce*, 80, 64.

90. Tucker, *Reflections*, 11, 62; "Queries," 16, 27; *Elements of Commerce*, 83–87.

91. Tucker, *A Brief Essay*, 88; *Gentleman's Magazine*, 14 (December 1749): 559; *An Essay on the Naturalization of Foreigners*, 2d ed. (1762), 11; Tucker, *A Brief Essay*, 90; *Reflections on Various Subjects* (1752), 94; Tucker, "Queries," 27; *An Apology for the Naturalization of the Jews* (1753), 26; *The Expediency of a General Naturalization of Foreign Protestants* (1747), 11; [Philip Carteret Webb], *The Bill Permitting the Jews to be Naturalized by Parliament* (1753), 2.

92. See James Stephen Taylor, *Jonas Hanway, Founder of the Marine Society: Charity and Policy in Eighteenth-Century Britain* (Berkeley, 1985).

93. *DNB*, sub Hanway; Jonas Hanway, *A Review of the Proposed Naturalization of the Jews* (1753), 25–26, 28–29.

94. *Considerations Concerning the Expediency of a General Naturalization of Foreign Protestants* (1747), 6; Thomas Alcock, vicar of Runcorn in Cheshire, in *Observations on the Defects of the Poor Laws* (1752), 19–20; Thomas Salmon, *Considerations on the Bill for a General Naturalization* (1748), 4. Some opponents of immigration schemes preferred the language of the True-born Englishman: "Anglo-Nativus" declared sullenly in 1747 that the attempt to admit foreigners would "corrupt and impoverish the few [English] that remain untainted by French ragouts and Italian effeminacy": *A Letter to Sir John Phillips, Bart.* (1747), 5.

95. The following account is based on John L. Bullion, "From 'the French and Dutch are more sober, frugal, and industrious' to the 'nobler' position: Attitudes of the Prince of Wales toward a General Naturalization and a Popular Monarchy, 1757–1760," in *Studies in Eighteenth-Century Culture* 17 (1987): 159–72.

96. Tucker was not quite this explicit about the "many jealousies" raised against him, but his intent is clear. Tucker's account appears in the preface to his *Four Tracts* (1774).

97. Ibid., 159–67.

98. "An act for taking and registering an annual account of the total number of

people and the total number of marriages, births, and deaths . . . in Great Britain," *Parl. Hist.* 14: 1318–22.

99. Massie, *Calculations of Taxes for a Family* (1756), 6–12; *A Letter to a Member of Parliament, on the Registering and Numbering the People of Great Britain* (London, 1753), in *The Development of Population Statistics*, ed. D. V. Glass (Farnborough, 1973), 8–9.

100. *Parl. Hist.* 14: 1318–22.

101. D. V. Glass, *Numbering the People;* see also E. C. K. Gonner, "The Population of England in the Eighteenth Century," *Journal of the Royal Statistical Society* 76 (1913): 261–303.

102. *Philosophical Transactions* 49, i (1755): 275–76, 280.

103. See ibid.; Bailyn, *Voyagers.*

104. *Philosophical Transactions* 50, i (1757): 463.

105. See Gonner, "Population," 265–80; Glass, *Numbering*, chapter 2.

106. For example, Turgot's translation of Tucker's *Reflections on the Expediency of a Law for Naturalization* under the title *Questions importantes sur le commerce* (1756).

107. Hutchison, *Political Economy*, 188–89, 221; Joseph John Spengler, *Predecessors*, 382.

108. *Wealth and Virtue;* eds. Istvan Hont and Michael Ignatieff.

109. Spengler, *Predecessors*, 77–86.

110. Probably written between 1728 and 1730, and first published in 1755, in French. See Antoin E. Murphy, *Richard Cantillon: Entrepreneur and Economist* (Oxford, 1986), 246, and Elizabeth Fox-Genovese, *The Origins of Physiocracy* (Ithaca, N.Y., 1976).

111. Cantillon, *Essai*, ed. Henry Higgs (London, 1931), 25, 27, 67, 85. For a survey of physiocracy see Henry Higgs, *The Physiocrats: Six Lectures on the French Economistes of the Eighteenth Century* (London, 1897), and Elizabeth Fox-Genovese, *The Origins of Physiocracy: Economic Revolution and Social Order in Eighteenth-Century France* (Ithaca, 1976).

112. Spengler, *Predecessors*, 128–30.

113. Ronald L. Meek, *Economics of Physiocracy,* 16–18.

114. *Quesnay's Tableau Economique*, Marguerite Kuczynski and Ronald Meek, eds., 19–20; Gianni Vaggi, *Economics of François Quesnay.*

115. *Lettres Persanes* (1721), no. 113, 117; *De l'Esprit* (1748), book 23, sections 10–26.

116. See *David Hume: Writings on Economics*, Eugene Rotwein, ed. (London, 1955), lxxxix; Hume, *Essay of the Populousness of Ancient Nations,* 1: 384 et seq.

117. See Albert O. Hirschman, *The Passions and the Interests: Political Arguments for Capitalism before its Triumph* (Princeton, 1977), 70–96; Adam Smith, *Wealth of Nations*, bk 3, iv, 4; Donald Winch, *Adam Smith's Politics: An Essay in Historiographic Revision* (Cambridge, 1978), chapter 4.

118. [Williamson], *Reflections*, 8, 87; William Blackstone, *Commentaries on the Laws of England*, 1: 123.

119. Defoe too had laid particular stress on liberty as the great magnet to attract immigrants, "the great star of Britain's constellation, which shines as a beacon to oppressed peoples." Liberty would "make all the world fly to you if they can" to escape tyranny. *Brief History*, 23. Erasmus Philips expressed similar faith in the "charms of liberty" in attracting foreign settlers. Philips, *An Appeal*, 18, 20–24.

120. Tucker, *Elements of Commerce*, 82, 89–89; "Queries," 31, 38–39; 44–47; *Reflections*, 63–64, v; *Elements of Commerce*, 80, 64.

121. Nor was the idea new that freedom led to a large population: Machiavelli had asserted this in *The Discourses* (1531; Harmondsworth, 1983), bk. 2, 2: 280.

122. H. T. Dickinson, *Liberty and Property.*

123. *Reflections upon Naturalization, Corporations, and Companies* (1753), 3; Franklin, *Observations*, in J. R. McCulloch, *Select Tracts*, 168, 171; Hume, *Essay of the Populousness of Ancient Nations* 1: 384; Rousseau, *Social Contract*, bk. 2, chap. 9, 231.

124. The argument is, of course, tautological.

125. Hume, *Of Populousness*, in *Writings*, Rotwein, ed., 112; Postlethwayt, *Commercial Interest*, 2: 367–532.

126. A. R. Humphreys, *Augustan World*, 164.

127. Paley, *Principles of Political Philosophy*, 2: bk. 6, chap. 2, 368–69.

128. Another important attempt to reconcile happiness, liberty, and populousness is [Jean François, Marquis de Chastellux], *An Essay on Public Happiness*, 2 vols. (1774), 2: 180 et seq.

129. Botero, *Della Ragione di Stato* (1598; English translation, 1606); see Alessandro Roncaglia, *Petty: The Origins of Political Economy* (Cardiff, 1985), 59–60, 108; in the eighteenth century as well, Italians such as Genovesi were in the vanguard with the idea of equilibrium, or a *populazione giusta*: Karl Pribram, *Economic Reasoning*, 87–88.

130. Derham, *Physico-Theology*, 174–177. This treatment is based on Peter Buck, "Seventeenth-Century Political Arithmetic," 83.

131. Hume described natural limits in "Of the Jealousy of Trade" (1758), quoted in Hutchison, *Political Economy*, 209; Arthur Young, *Proposals to the Legislature for Numbering the People* (London, 1771), 21, 25–26; *The Politician's Dictionary* (London, 1775), 158.

132. T. W., *The Natural Interest of Great Britain*, 2d ed. (1748), 31; Franklin, *Observations*, in J. R. McCulloch, *Tracts*, 165–72, 165–69, 171–72.

133. See J. R. Raven, "Viscount Townshend and the Cambridge Prize for Trade Theory, 1754–1756," *Historical Journal* 28 (1985): 535–55, esp. 549.

134. Bell, *A Dissertation*, 9–10, 17; Temple, *A Vindication of Commerce and the Arts* (1758), 5–6, 44, 64.

135. Wallace, *Characteristics of the Present Political State of Great Britain* (1758), 38; *Various Prospects of Mankind* (1761), 114, 116, 121; Wallace, *A Dissertation on the Numbers of Mankind in Ancient and Modern Times* (1753), 148–51; Robert B. Luehrs, "Population and Utopia," 313–35.

136. Indeed, the agrarian bent of the proto-Malthusians fit very well with both the economic circumstances of France and with physiocratic doctrine.

137. Hutchinson, *The Population Debate*, 117–22; Schumpeter attributed the "anti-populationism" in England after the mid-eighteenth century to the economic displacements and resulting unemployment caused by the early stages of the industrial revolution: *History of Economic Analysis* (London, 1954), 252. This may be a partial answer, although those economic changes had only just begun, and the explanation also ignores the correlation between changes in demography and changes in economic ideas.

CONCLUSION

1. E. A. Wrigley and R. S. Schofield, *Population History*, 208–9.

2. Addison, *Spectator*, no. 200 (19 October 1711).

Bibliography

Manuscript Sources

Oxford, Bodleian Library:

Rawlinson MS, C984, fols. 48, 50   Bishop Morley letters

London, British Library:

OPL 356.m.3	Papers of Robert Harper
OPL 357.B.1	Clerks of Parliament Papers
Lansdowne MS 256, fols. 117–122	Draft of bill
Lansdowne MS 691	N. Grew MS tract
Lansdowne MS 1013, fols. 126–27	W. Kennet letters
Stowe MS 163, fols. 146–69	M. Hale MS tract

Additional MSS:

4743	Papers of Henry Davenant
15866	Diplomatic Correspondence of James Dayrolle
17677	Copies of Correspondence and State Papers from The Hague
35933	Hardwicke Papers Blenheim Papers
61534	Letters re United Provinces
61611	Letters from E. Tilson re Palatines
61649	Correspondence re Palatines
61652	Letter book copies of Sunderland's correspondence as Secretary of State

London, Corporation of London Record Office:

36-B, ex-Guildhall MS 282	Chamber of London Accounts
Rep	Repertories of the Court of Aldermen
Jor	Journals of the Court of Common Council
Alchin Box MSS	Miscellaneous MSS
Misc. MSS 42.2	Collection of tracts

Cases and Counsel Opinions
Remembrancia, 9

London, Guildhall Library:

MS 7412   Coetus Minute Book
MS 8356   Register of Baptisms, Hamburg Lutheran Church

London, House of Lords Record Office:
House of Lords Papers, 1707

London, Lambeth Palace Library:

MS 1122i, no. 13   Collection of Papers re French Protestants

London, Public Record Office:

PC 2	Privy Council Registers
T.1	Treasury Board Papers
SP 29 & 30	State Papers Domestic, Charles II
SP 30/G	"Factum of the French"
SP 32	State Papers Domestic, William and Mary
SP 34	State Papers Domestic, Anne
SP 44	Entry Books, 1661–1828, Secretary's Letter Books
SP 67	Entry Books, 1681–1783, Secretary's Letter Books
SP 84	State Papers Foreign, Holland
SP 87	Military Expeditions
SP 104	Entry Books, 1571–1783
SP Ireland 63	Elizabeth to George III
CO 5	Colonial Papers, America and West Indies, Original Correspondence
CO 23	Colonial Papers, Bahamas
CO 323	Colonial Papers, General Original Correspondence
CO 388	Board of Trade Papers, Original Correspondence
CO 389	Board of Trade Entry Books

PRINTED SOURCES

An Account of Moneys Received upon Her Majesty's Brief for the Relief, Subsistence, and Settlement of the Poor distressed Palatines. 1712.

Alcock, Thomas. *Observations on the Defects of the Poor Laws, and on the Causes and Consequences of the Great Increase and Burden of the Poor.* Oxford: 1752.

"Anglo-Nativus," *A Letter to Sir John Phillips, Bart., Occasioned by a Bill Brought into Parliament to Naturalize Foreign Protestants.* 1747.

An Answer to the Pretended Speech Said to be Spoken Off-hand in the House of Commons, by one of the Members for Bristol. 1694.

An Apology for the Naturalization of the Jews. By a True Believer. 1753.

An Apology for the Protestants of France, in Reference to the Persecutions they are under at this Day; in Six Letters. 1683.

An Argument Proving that the Design of Employing and Enobling Foreigners, is a Treasonable Conspiracy against the Constitution, Dangerous to the Kingdom, an Affront to the Nobility of Scotland in Particular and Dishonourable to the Peerage of Britain in General. 1717.

Barbon, Nicholas. *A Discourse Concerning . . . the New Money.* 1696.

―――. *A Discourse of Trade.* 1690.

[Baston, Thomas.] *Thoughts on Trade, and a Publick Spirit.* 1716.

Bell, William. *A Dissertation on the Following Subject: What Causes Principally Contribute to Render a Nation Populous? And what Effect has the Populousness of a Nation on its Trade?.* 1756.

Bellers, John. *A Supplement to the Proposal for a Colledge of Industry,* 1696. In *John Bellers,* edited by George Clarke.

―――. *Essays about the Poor, Manufactures, Trade, Plantations, and Immorality.* 1699.

―――. *To the Lords and other Commissioners, Appointed by the Queen to Take Care of the Poor Palatines.* 1709.

―――. *An Essay for Employing the Able Poor.* 1714.

Bennet, John. The National Merchant; or, Discourses on Commerce. 1736.

[Berkeley, George.] *The Querist, Containing Several Queries, Proposed to the Consideration of the Public.* Dublin, 1725 [1735.]

[Bethel, Slingsby.] *The Present Interest of England Stated. By a Lover of his King and Country.* 1671.

―――. *An Account of the French Usurpation upon the Trade of England, and what Great Damage the English do Yearly Sustain by their Commerce, and how the Same may be Retrenched, and England Improved in Riches, Land, Interest.* 1679.

―――. *The Interest of Princes and States.* 1680.

[Blanch, John.] *The Interest of England Considered in an Essay upon Wool.* 1694.

―――. *An Abstract of the Grievances of Trade which Oppress our Poor.* 1694.

[Bland, John.] *Trade Revived; or, A Way Proposed to Restore, Increase, Enrich, Strengthen and Preserve the Decayed and even Dying Trade of this our English Nation.* 1659.

Boisguillebert, Pierre Le Pesant de. *Le détail de la France.* 1695.

Bolde, Samuel. *A Sermon against Persecution.* 1682.

Bossuet, Jacques-Bénigne. *Politique tirée des propres paroles de l'écriture sainte.* 1709.

Botero, Giovanni, *Ragion di Stato.* Venice, 1598. In *Giovanni Botero: The Reason of State,* edited by P. J. Waley and D. P. Waley. London: 1956, book 7, chapter 11.

Boyer, Abel. *The History of King William the Third.* 1703.

―――. *The History of the Reign of Queen Anne, Digested into Annals.* 10 vols. 1712.

―――. *Memoirs of Queen Anne: Being a Compleat Supplement to the History of her Reign, wherein the Transactions of the Four Last Years are Fully Related.* 1729.

————. *The History of Queen Anne.* 1735.

Braddon, Lawrence. *The Miseries of the Poor are a National Sin, Shame, and Charge.* 1717.

Brewster, Francis. *Essays on Trade and Navigation. In Five Parts.* 1693/94.

————. *New Essays on Trade.* 1702.

A Brief and Summary Narrative of the Many Mischiefs and Inconveniences in Former Times as Well as of Late Years, Occasioned by Naturalizing of Aliens. [c. 1690.]

A Brief History of Trade in England. 1702.

The Brief Observations Examined. 1668.

The British Merchant; or, A Review of the Trade of Great Britain. 12 numbers. 1719.

Burckhardt, Johann Gottlieb. *Kirchen-Geschichte der Deutschen Gemeinden in London: Nebst Historischen Beilagen und Predigten.* Tübingen, 1798.

Burn, Richard. *The Justice of the Peace, and Parish Officer.* 2d ed. 2 vols. 1756.

By the King and Queen, A Declaration for Encouraging of French Protestants to Transport themselves into this Kingdom. 1689.

Canary-Birds Naturalized in Utopia. [1709.]

[Cantillon, Richard.] *Essai sur la Nature du Commerce en Général.* Edited by Henry Higgs. 1931.

[Care, Henry.] *Animadversions on a Late Paper, Entitled a Letter to a Dissenter.* 1687.

[Carter, William.] *England's Interest Asserted, in the Improvement of its Native Commodities; and more Especially the Manufacture of Wool.* 1699.

Cary, John. *An Essay on the State of England in Relation to its Trade, its Poor, and its Taxes, for Carrying on the Present War against France.* Bristol: 1695.

————. *A Discourse Concerning the East-India Trade, shewing how it is Unprofitable to the Kingdom of England.* 1699.

————. *An Essay towards Regulating the Trade, and Employing the Poor of this Kingdom.* 2d ed. Appended: "An Essay towards Paying off the Publick Debts." 1719.

In Case any Proviso Should be Offered to the Bill of Naturalization. [c. 1697.]

The Case of Richard Pierce, Citizen and Grocer of London, Farmer and Collector of the Duties of Package, Scavage, Balliage, and Portage. [c. 1690.]

The Case of the City of London, in Relation to the Bill for a General Naturalization of all Foreign Protestants. [c. 1709.]

The Case of the High German Reformed Protestant Congregation in London. 1758.

The Case of the Jews Stated. 1690.

The Case of the Merchants of Great Britain, Residing at Home, or in the British Factories in Foreign Countries, with respect to Persons Obtaining Acts of Naturalization, without any purpose of continuing in these Kingdoms. [1752.]

The Case of the Poor French Refugees. [c. 1697.]

A Catalogue of Books of the Newest Fashion to be Sold by Auction, at the Whig's Coffee-House. [1694.] In *Harl. Misc.,* 12:257.

Chalmers, George. *Political Annals of the Present United Colonies.* 1780.

[Chamberlayne, Edward.] *England's Wants; or, Several Proposals Probably Beneficial for England, Humbly Offered to the Consideration of all Good Patriots in both Houses of Parliament.* 1667; 1685 edition.

The Character of a Coffee House. 1673.

[Child, Josiah.] *Brief Observations Concerning Trade, and Interest of Money.* 1668.

Child, Josiah. *A New Discourse of Trade.* 4th ed. n.d. (1st ed., 1693).

[Claude, Jean.] *An Account of the Persecutions in France.* 1686.

Clayton, David. *A Short System of Trade; or, An Account of what in Trade must Necessarily be Advantageous to the Nation, and what must of Consequence be Detrimental.* 1719.

Coke, Sir Edward. *The First Part of the Institutes,* 1670.

Coke, Roger. *A Discourse of Trade. In Two Parts.* 1670.

————. *A Treatise wherein is Demonstrated, that the Church and State of England are in Equal Danger with the Trade of it.* 1671.

————. *England's Improvements. In Two Parts.* 1675.

————. *Reflections upon the East-Indy and Royal African Companies. With Animadversions Concerning the Naturalization of Foreigners.* 1695.

Colonel Pierce his Candour and Fairness with the City. [c. 1705.]

Colsoni, F. *Le Guide de Londres pour les Estrangers.* 1693.

A Confutation of the Reasons for Naturalizing the Jews. 1715.

Considerations Concerning the Expediency of a General Naturalization of Foreign Protestants, and Others. 1747.

Considerations upon the Mischief that May Arise from Granting too much Indulgence to Foreigners. 1735.

[Corbyn, Morris.] *Observations on the Past Growth and Present State of the City of London.* 1751.

[Coventry, William.] *An Essay Concerning the Decay of Rents and their Remedies.* [c. 1670.] In Thirsk and Cooper, *Documents,* 79–84.

The Craftsman.

The Crisis; or, An Alarm to Britannia's True Protestant Sons. 1754.

The Danger of the Church and Kingdom from Foreigners Considered. 1721.

Das Verlangte, nicht Erlangte Canaan. Frankfurt and Leipzig: 1711.

Davenant, Charles. *An Essay upon Ways and Means of Supplying the War.* 1695. In Whitworth, *Works,* 1:1–81.

————. *Discourses on the Public Revenues, and on the Trade of England. Part I.* 1698. In Whitworth, *Works,* 1:125–342.

————. *Discourses on the Public Revenues, and on Trade. Part II.* 1698. In Whitworth, *Works,* 1:343–459, and 2:1–162.

————. *An Essay upon the Probable Methods of Making a People Gainers in the Balance of Trade.* 1699. In Whitworth, *Works,* 2:161–382.

The Declaration Lately Published, in favour of his Protestant Subjects, by the Elector Palatine. 1707.

[Defoe, Daniel ?.] *Some Seasonable Queries on the Third Head, viz. A General Naturalization.* [1694.]

[Defoe, Daniel.] *Lex Talionis; or, An Enquiry into the most Proper Ways to Prevent the Persecution of the Protestants in France.* 1698.

Defoe, Daniel. *The True-Born Englishman: A Satyr.* 1703. In *Later Stuart Tracts,* ed. George A. Aitken. London: 1903.

[Defoe, Daniel.] *Giving Alms no Charity, and Employing the Poor a Grievance to the Nation.* 1704.

————. *An Essay at Removing National Prejudices against a Union with Scotland. Part I.* 1706.

————. *A Brief History of the Poor Palatine Refugees lately Arrived in England.* 1709.

————. *The Review.* 1708–12. Facsimile ed. Edited by A. W. Secord. 12 vols. New York: 1938.

————. *The Manufacturer; or, The British Trade Truly Stated.* 86 numbers. 1719–20.

————. *The Great Law of Subordination Considered; or, The Insolence and Unsufferable Behaviour of Servants in England Duly Enquired Into.* 1724.

————. *Atlas Maritimus & Commercialis; or, A General View of the World, so far as Relates to Trade and Navigation.* 1728.

Defoe, Daniel. *A Brief State of the Island or Home Trade.* London: 1730. In *The Versatile Defoe: An Anthology of Uncollected Writings of Daniel Defoe.* Edited by L. A. Curtis. London: 1979.

[Defoe, Daniel.] *A Plan of the English Commerce.* 2d ed. 1730.

Defoe, Daniel. *The Complete English Tradesman.* 1840 ed.

————. *A Tour through the Whole Island of Great Britain.* Edited by G. D. H. Cole. 2 vols. 1928.

————. *Robinson Crusoe.* Everyman ed. 1977.

————. *Roxana.* Oxford University Press ed. 1981.

[Dekker, Matthew.] *An Essay on the Causes of the Decline of the Foreign Trade, Consequently of the Value of the Lands of Britain, and on the Means to Restore Both.* 1744.

Denis, Jean Baptist. *A Plot Discovered: Carried on Boldly these many Years by False Brethren . . . in a Book Entitled The Spirit of the French Refugees Manifested.* 1722.

Derham, William. *Physico-Theology: or, A Demonstration of the Being and Attributes of God, from his Works of Creation.* London: 1714.

Detailed and Circumstantial Account of the Celebrated Land of Carolina. Situated in English America. 4th ed. Frankfurt: 1709.

A Dialogue betwixt Whig And Tory, alias Williamite and Jacobite. 1693.

A Discourse Concerning Trade, and that in Particular of the East-Indies, wherein Several Weighty Propositions are Fully Discussed, and the State of the East-India Company is Faithfully Stated. 1689.

A Discourse of the Nature, Use and Advantages of Trade. Proposing Some Considerations for the Promotion and Advancement thereof. 1694.

Dobbs, Arthur. *An Essay on the Trade and Improvement of Ireland.* Dublin: 1729.

Downes, Theophilus. *A Discourse Concerning the Signification of Allegiance.* 1689.

Dubourdieu, Jean-Armand. *An Appeal to the English Nation; or, The Body of the French Protestants, and the Honest Proselytes, Vindicated from the Calumnies Cast on them by one Malard and his Associates.* 1718.

[Dugard, Samuel.] περὶ πολυπαιδίης; *or, A Discourse Concerning the Having Many Children. In which the Prejudices against a Numerous Offspring are Removed. And the Objections Answered.* 1695.

[DuMoulin, Louis.] *A True Report of a Discourse between Monsieur de l'Angle, Canon of Canterbury, and Minister of the French Church in the Savoy, and Lewis du Moulin.* 1679.

[Durie, John.] *A Case of Conscience; whether it be Lawful to Admit Jews into a Christian Common-Wealth.* 1656.

An Elegy on the Death of Trade. 1698. In *Harl. Misc.*, 10:357–58.

England's Interest Asserted. 1667.

England's Wants; or, Several Proposals Probably Beneficial to England. 1685. In *Somer's Tracts*, 9.

The English Lady's Complete Catechism. Setting Forth the Pride and Vanity of the English Quality, in Relieving Foreigners before their own Country-Folks. [c. 1690.]

An Enquiry into the Causes of the Increase and Miseries of the Poor of England. 1738.

An Essay on the Naturalization of Foreigners. 2d ed. 1762.

An Essay on Ways and Means for the Advancement of Trade, and for Paying off in Few Years, the Debts of the Nation, without Laying any Additional Burden on Land. 1726.

An Essay or Modest Proposal of a Way to Increase the Number of People, and Consequently the Strength of this Kingdom. [c. 1693.]

The Expediency of a General Naturalization of Foreign Protestants and Others. 1751.

A Farther Argument against Ennobling Foreigners, in Answer to the Two Parts of the State Anatomy: With a Short Account of the Anatomizer. 1717.

Fielding, Henry. *An Enquiry into the Causes of the Late Increase of Robbers, &c. with Some Proposals for Remedying this Growing Evil.* 1751.

Fontaine, Jacques. *Memoirs, in Memoirs of a Huguenot Family.* Edited by Ann Maury. New York: 1853.

Foster, Richard. "A Letter." *Philosophical Transactions* 50 (1758): 464.

Fortrey, Samuel. *England's Interest and Improvement. Consisting in the Increase of the Store, and Trade of this Kingdom.* 2d ed. 1673. In McCulloch, *Tracts*.

Franklin, Benjamin. *Observations Concerning the Increase of Mankind, Peopling of Countries.* 1751. In *The Complete Works*, 3 vols., 2, (1806): 383–91.

French Snakes in British Clover; or, A Discourse Shewing that the Swarms of Frenchmen in the Service of the Families of Great Britain are Inconsistent with the Love of our Religion and Country, and Destructive of their Interests. 1744.

Gee, Joshua. *The Trade and Navigation of Great Britain Considered.* New edition. 1767. [1st. ed., 1729.]

Gentleman's Magazine

[Georgirenes, Joseph.] *From the Archbishop of the Isle of Samos in Greece. An Account of his Building the Grecian Church in So-hoe Fields, and the Disposal thereof by the Masters of the parish of St. Martins in the Fields.* 1682.

Glyn, Mayor, At a Court of Aldermen Held on Tuesday the 13th. Day of February 1759. 1759.

The Grand Concern of England Explained, in Several Proposals Offered to the Consideration of Parliament. 1673. In *Harl. Misc.*, 8:13–61.

Graunt, John. *Natural and Political Observations . . . Made upon the Bills of Mortality.* 1662.

[Gray, Charles.] *Considerations on Several Proposals, Lately Made for the Better Maintenance of the Poor.* 2d ed. 1752.

Gray, Robert. *A Good Speed to Virginia.* 1609. In Thirsk and Cooper, *Documents*, 757–58.

The Great Evil of Naturalizing Aliens Discovered by the City's Reply to the Aliens' Petition. [c. 1660.]

Grosley, P. J. *A Tour to London; or, New Observations on England and its Inhabitants.* Translated by Thomas Nugent. 2 vols. 1772.

[Haines, Richard.] *The Prevention of Poverty; or, A Discourse of the Causes of the Decay of Trade, Fall of Lands, and Want of Money.* 1674.

Hale, Matthew. *A Discourse Touching Provision for the Poor.* 1673.

———. *The Original Institution, Power, and Jurisdiction of Parliaments.* 1707 ed.

Hale, Matthew, *On the Primitive Origination of Mankind.* 1677.

Halley, Edmond *Degrees of Mortality of Mankind.* 1693. In Hutchison, *Political Economy.* 46.

[Hanway, Jonas.] *A Review of the Proposed Naturalization of the Jews; being a Dispassionate Enquiry into the Present State of the Case.* 3d ed. 1753.

[Hare, Francis.] *The Reception of the Palatines Vindicated in a Fifth Letter to a Tory Member.* 1711.

[Harris, Joseph.] *An Essay upon Money and Coins.* 1757. In J. R. McCulloch, *Old and Scarce Tracts.* 2d ed. London: 1933.

[Harris, William.] *Remarks on the Affairs and Trade of England and Ireland.* 1691.

[Hay, William.] *Remarks on the Laws Relating to the Poor; with Proposals for their Better Relief and Employment.* 1735.

Hayne, Samuel. *An Abstract of all the Statutes made Concerning Aliens Trading in England.* 1685.

———. *The Manifesto of Near One Hundred and Fifty Knights and Eminent Merchants.* 1697.

[Henderson, Andrew.] *The Case of the Jews Considered, with Regard to Trade, Commerce, Manufactures and Religion.* 1753.

[Herbert, William.] *Considerations in the Behalf of Foreigners which Reside in England; and of the English, who are out of their own Country.* 1662.

Hickes, George. *The True Notion of Persecution Stated.* 1681.

A Historical and Law Treatise against the Jews. 1703.

The History of Naturalization, with Some Remarques upon the Effects thereof, in Respect to the Religion, Trade and Safety of His Majesty's Dominions. [c. 1680.]

[Houghton, John.] *England's Great Happiness; or, A Dialogue between Content and Complaint.* 1677. In McCulloch, *Tracts.*

Houghton, John. *A Collection for Improvement of Husbandry and Trade.* no. 23 (25 June 1692).

[Hughes, William.] *Anglo-Judaeus; or, The History of the Jews whilst here in England.* 1656.

An Humble Address to the Honourable House of Commons, on behalf of the Traders of England, against Naturalizing Aliens. 1699.

An Humble Address with some Proposals for the Future Preventing of the Decrease of the Inhabitants of this Realm. 1677.

Hume, David. *Essay of Populousness of Ancient Nations.* 1752. In *Essays Moral, Political, and Literary,* edited by T. H. Green and T. H. Grose. 2 vols. 1:384 London: 1882. 1, p. 384 *et seq.*

The Jews' Case. 1697.

The Jews' Charter; or, An Historical Account of the Privileges Granted them by the Several Kings and Parliaments of England. 1702.

Johnson, Samuel, Rector of Corringham. *Confutation of a Letter Balancing.* 1697. In *Works.* 1710. Pp. 323–38.

[Johnston, Nathaniel.] *The Dear Bargain; or, A True Representation of the State of the English Nation under the Dutch. In a Letter to a Friend.* [c.1692] In *Somers Tracts,* 5:349.

Johnston, Samuel. *The Advantages of Employing the Poor in Useful Labour.* 2d ed. 1726.

[Jones, Erasmus.] *A Ramble through London: Containing Observations on Men and Things.* 1738 ed.

The Justice and the Footmen: Being a True and Impartial State of the Case of the Livery Servants Intended Meeting, at Hickford's Room, in Panton Street. 1744.

King, Charles. *The British Merchant; or, Commerce Preserved.* 3 vols. 1721.

King, Gregory. *Natural and Political Observations and Conclusions upon the State and Condition of England.* [unpublished 1696.] Edited by G. E. Barnett. Baltimore: 1936.

Knight, John. *The Following Speech.* 1694. In *Parl. Hist.,* 5:849–57.

Kocherthal, Joshua de. *Ausführlich und Umständlicher Bericht von der Berühmten Landschaft Carolina in dem Engelländischen America.* 4th ed. Frankfurt: 1709.

Lau, Theodor Ludwig. *Aufrichtiger Vorschlag von Glücklicher, Vortheilhafftiger, Beständiger Einrichtung der Intraden und Einkünffte der Souverainen und Inrer Unterthanen.* Frankfurt am Main: 1719.

Lawson, John. *A New Voyage to Carolina* 1709. Edited by Hugh T. Lefler. Chapel Hill, N.C.: 1967.

LeBrun, Bonaventure. *A True and Exact Copy of the Several Articles Imposed upon the French Protestants.* Dublin: 1685.

A Letter to a Country Gentleman: Setting Forth the Cause of the Decay and Ruin of Trade. 1698.

A Letter to the French Refugees Concerning their Behaviour to the Government. Dublin: 1711.

The Living Elegy of Mr. John Thorp late of Spittlefields, Weaver, and now Resident at the Weavers Arms in the Mint. [c.1700.]

Locke, John. *Second Treatise of Government.* 1690.

———. *Some Considerations of the Consequences of the Lowering of Interest.* 1692.

London Gazette.

The London Magazine; or, Gentleman's Monthly Intelligencer.

The Loyal Protestant and True Domestick Intelligence.

Luttrell, Narcissus. *A Brief Historical Relation of State Affairs, from September 1678 to April 1714.* 6 vols. Oxford: 1856.

Macchiavelli, Niccolò. *The Discourses.* 1531; Penguin ed., Harmondsworth: 1983.

[Mackworth, Humphrey.] *England's Glory; or, The Great Improvement of Trade in General, by a Royal Bank.* 1694.

Maitland, William. *The History of London, from its Foundation by the Romans, to the Present Time.* 1739.

[Malard, Michel.] *The French Plot Found out against the English Church.* 1718.

Malard, Michel. *The Proselytish Hercules against the Mystery of Inquity; or, A True Light into the Plot of the French Committee and its League, against the Church of England.* 1700.

Malthus, T. R. *An Essay on the Principle of Population.* 1803; Everyman ed., London: 1982.

Manasseh ben Israel. *To his Highnesse the Lord Protector . . . the Humble Addresses of M. B. I.* [1655.]

[Mandeville, Bernard.] *The Mischiefs.* Edited by H. T. Dickinson. Los Angeles: 1975.

Mandeville, Bernard. *The Fable of the Bees.* 1729. Edited by F. B. Kaye. 2 vols. Oxford: 1924

Manley, Thomas. *Usury at Six Per Cent.* 1669.

Murphy, Arthur. *The Englishman from Paris* 1756. Edited by Simon Trefman. Los Angeles: 1969.

Mirabeau, Marquis de. *L'Ami des Hommes.* Paris: 1757.

Misson de Valbourg, Henri. *Memoirs and Observations in his Travels over England.* Trans. ed. London: 1719.

A Modest Apology for the Citizens and Merchants of London, who Petitioned the House of Commons against Naturalizing the Jews. 1753.

The Monsieur's Misfortunes; or, The Shammer Shammed. [c.1690.]

Mun, Thomas. *England's Treasure by Foreign Trade.* 1664. In McCulloch, *Tracts.*

N., N. *A Letter of Several French Ministers Fled into Germany upon the Account of the Persecution in France, to such of their Brethren in England as Approved the King's Declaration Touching Liberty of Conscience.* [c. 1687.]

The Natives: an Answer to the Foreigners. 1700.

North, Dudley. *Discourses upon Trade.* 1691.

North, Roger. *Autobiography.* In Roger North, *The Lives of the Norths*, edited by A. Jessop. 3 vols. 1890.

Notes and Queries (1855).

Observations both Historical and Moral upon the Burning of London. (n.d.), in *Harl. Misc.*, 7.

Oldmixon, John. *The History of England during the Reigns of William and Mary, Anne, and George I.* London: 1735.

[Owen, Charles.] *The Danger of the Church and Kingdom from Foreigners Considered.* 1721.

The Palatines Catechism; or, A True Description of their Camps at Blackheath and Camberwell. In a Pleasant Dialogue between an English Tradesman and a High-Dutchman (1709). In *Ecclesiastical Records*, edited by Hastings, 1817–20.

Paley, William. *The Principles of Moral and Political Philosophy.* 2 vols. Dublin: 1785.

[Parott, Richard.] *Reflections on Various Subjects Relating to Arts and Commerce: Particularly the Consequences of Admitting Foreign Artists on Easier Terms.* 1752.

Pepys, Samuel. *The Diary of Samuel Pepys.* Edited by R. Latham and W. Mathews. 11 vols. London. 1970–83.

[Pett, Peter.] *The Happy Future State of England.* 1688.

Petty, William. *A Treatise of Taxes and Contributions.* 1662. In Hull, *Writings*, 1:1–97.

———. *Another Essay in Political Arithmetic, Concerning the Growth of the City of London.* 1683. In Hull, *Writings*, 2:473–98.

———. *An Essay Concerning the Multiplication of Mankind.* 2d ed. 1686.

———. *A Treatise of Ireland.* 1687. In Hull, *Writings*, 2:545–621.

——. *Political Arithmetic*. 1690. In Hull, *Writings*, 1:233–313.

——. *The Political Anatomy of Ireland*. 1691. In Hull, *Writings*, 1:121–231.

——. *Verbum Sapienti*. 1691. In Hull, *Writings*, 1:99–120.

Petyt, William. *Brittania Languens*. 1680. In McCulloch, *Tracts*.

Philips, Erasmus. *An Appeal to Common Sense; or, Some Considerations Offered to Restore Public Credit*. 1720.

[Philips, Erasmus.] *The State of the Nation, in Respect to her Commerce, Debts, and Money*. 1725.

Philo-Patriae. *Further Considerations on the Act to Permit Persons Professing the Jewish Religion to be Naturalized by Parliament*. 1753.

——. *Considerations on the Bill to Permit Persons to be Naturalized by Parliament*. 1753.

The Piety and Bounty of the Queen of Great Britain: with the Charitable Benevolence of her Loving Subjects, toward the Support and Settlement of the Distressed Protestant Palatines. 1709.

Pollexfen, John. *A Discourse of Trade, Coin, and of Ways and Means to Gain, and Retain Riches*. 1697.

——. *A Vindication of Some Assertions Relating to Coin and Trade*. 1699.

——. *Of Trade. Also of Coin. Bullion*. 1700.

Postlethwayt, Malachy. *Britain's Commercial Interest*. 2 vols. London: 1757.

Povey, Charles. *The Unhappiness of England as to its Trade by Sea and Land*. 1701.

The Present State of England. Part III and Part IV. 1683.

Proposals Moderately Offered for the Full Peopling and Inhabiting the City of London, and to Restore the Same to her Ancient and Flowering Trade, which will Suit with her Splendid Structure. 1672.

Prynne, William. *A Short Demurrer to the Jews Long Discontinued Remitter into England*. 1655.

[Puckle, James.] *England's Path to Wealth and Honour, in a Dialogue between an Englishman and a Dutchman*. 1700.

Quesnay, François. *Tableau Economique*. 3d ed. 1759. Edited by R. L. Meek and M. Kuczynski. 1972.

R., H. *The Brief Observations of J. C. Concerning Trade and Interest of Money, Briefly Examined*. 1668.

Reasons against a General Naturalization. [1708.]

Reasons against Erecting a French Church, St. Martin Orgars. 1700.

Reasons against the General Naturalization of Aliens. [c.1685.]

Reasons for Adding a Proviso to the Bill for Naturalizing David le Grand and Others. 1689.

Reasons for Passing the Bill for the Better Preventing the Covering of Alien Goods Imported. 1714.

Reasons Humbly Offered against Passing the Bill, Entitled, An Act for Naturalization of [Foreigners]. [c.1685.]

Reasons Humbly Offered against Passing the Bill, Entitled, An Act for Naturalization of Adrian Lofland, and Others. [1685.]

Reasons Humbly Offered against the Bill, for the Better Preventing the Covering of Aliens' Goods Imported. 1714.

Reasons Humbly Offered against the Clause Intended in the Act for Establishing the Land-Bank for Denizing or Naturalizing of all Aliens that Shall Subscribe 500l. to the Said Bank. [1696.]

Reasons Humbly Offered against the Frequent Naturalization of Aliens. [c.1685.]

Reasons Humbly Offered by Several of the Principal Inhabitants of the Parish of St. Martins Orgars London, against the Passing an Ingrossed Bill (from the Lords) for Erecting a Church for the French in the Churchyard of that Parish. [c.1700.]

Reasons Humbly Offered by the Inhabitants of the City and Liberty of Westminster, and of Other Places within the Weekly Bills of Mortality, to the Knights, Citizens, and Burgesses in this Present Parliament Assembled, against the Passing of a Bill, Entitled, An Act for the Enabling of Protestant Strangers to Exercise their Trades in the Places in the Said Act Mentioned. [1685.]

Reasons Humbly Offered for the Passing the Bill for the Better Preventing the Covering Aliens' Goods Imported. 1714.

Reasons Humbly Offered to the Lord Mayor, and Aldermen, and Commons to the City of London, in Common-Council Assembled; as Motives to Oppose the Passing of Several Bills Now Depending in Parliament for Naturalizing of Aliens. [c.1697.]

Reasons Humbly Offered to the Parliament by the Free-born Merchants of England. [c. 1660.]

The Reception of the Palatines Vindicated in a Fifth Letter to a Tory Member 1711.

Reflections on Various Subjects Relating to Arts and Commerce. 1752.

Reflections upon Naturalization, Corporations, and Companies; Supported by the Authorities of both Ancient and Modern Writers. 1753.

Remarks on the Reverend Mr. Tucker's Letter on Naturalizations. 1753.

Reneu, Hilary. *The Preface to the Second English Translation of Jean Claude's Les Plaintes des Protestants.* 1707. In *The Torments of Protestant Slaves*, Edited by E. Arber, 413–31. 1907.

Rey, Claude. *An Account of the Cruel Persecutions Raised by the French Clergy since their Taking Sanctuary here, against Several Worthy Ministers, Gentlemen, Gentlewomen, and Tradesmen Dissenting from their Calvinistical Scheme.* 1718.

Reynell, Carew. *The True English Interest; or, An Account of the Chief Natural Improvements and Some Political Observations Demonstrating an Infallible Advance of this Nation.* 1674.

To the Right Honourable the Commons in Parliament Assembled: The Humble Petition of the Native Merchants of England. [c.1660.]

The Rights and Libeties of Englishmen Asserted. With a Collection of Statutes and Records of Parliament against Foreigners. 1701.

[Robinson, Henry.] *Certain Proposals in Order to the People's Freedom and Accomodation.* 1652.

Roe, Thomas. *His Speech in Parliament. Wherein he sheweth the Cause of the Decay of Coin and Trade in this Land, Especially of Merchants Trade.* 1641.

[Romaine, William.] *An Answer to a Pamphlet, Entitled, Considerations on the Bill to Permit Persons Professing the Jewish Religion to be Naturalized.* 3d ed. 1753.

Rousseau, Jean Jacques. *The Social Contract.* 1762. Everyman ed. London: 1977.

The Royal Fishing Revived. 1670. In *Harl. Misc.*, 7:403–8.

[Salmon, Thomas.] *Considerations on the Bill for a General Naturalization as it May conduce to the Improvement of our Manufactures and Traffic, and to the Strengthening or Endangering the Constitution.* 1748.

A Satyr against the French. 1690.

Seasonable Observations on the Naturalization Bill, now Depending in Parliament. 1748.

Seasonable Remarks on the Act Lately Passed in Favour of the Jews; Containing Divers Weighty Reasons for a Review of the Said Act. 1753.

Several Grievances of the English Merchants in their Trade into the Dominions of the King of Sweden. 1700.

Several Letters Written by Some French Protestants now Refuged in Germany, from the Tyrannical Persecution of France, Concerning the Unity of the Church. 1690.

Shaftesbury, Earl of. *Characteristics of Men, Manners, Opinions, Times, etc.* Edited by John M. Robertson. 2 vols. 1711; Gloucester, Mass.: 1963.

[Sheridan, Thomas.] *A Discourse of the Rise and Power of Parliaments.* 1677.

A Short and Easy Way for the Palatines to Learn English; oder, Eine Kurze Unleitung zur Armen Pfaeltzer nebst Angehaengten Englischen und Teutschen A B C. 1710.

Some Considerations on the Reasonableness and Necessity of Increasing and Encouraging Seamen. 1728.

Some Considerations upon Trade. 1715.

Some General Considerations Relating to Trade. 1698)

Some Seasonable Queries on the third Head, viz. A General Naturalization. [c. 1694.]

Some Thoughts upon a Bill for General Naturalization: Addressed to those of all Denominations who Act upon Whig Principles. 1751.

The Spectator, 1711–12.

Spitalfields and Shoreditch in an Uproar. The Devil to Pay with the English and Irish. 1736. Reprinted in H. J. Bradley, *The History of Shoreditch Church,* 28–31. 1914.

The State of the Palatines for 50 Years Past to this Present Time. 1710.

Stuvens, B. G. *Ausführlicher Bericht von der Pfälzischen Kirchen-Historie.* Frankfurt, 1721.

Strype, John, and John Stow. *A Survey of the Cities of London and Westminster.* 1720.

Sundry Considerations Touching Naturalization of Aliens: whereby the Alleged Advantages thereby are Confuted, and the Contrary Mischiefs thereof Detected and Discovered. [c.1695.]

A Supplement to His Majesty's Speech. 1693.

A Supplement to Sundry Reasons against a General Naturalization of Aliens. [c. 1697.]

T., T. *Some General Considerations Offered, Relating to our Present Trade.* 1698.

The Tatler.

[Temple, William.] *Observations upon the United Provinces of the Netherlands.* 2d ed. 1673.

———. *An Essay upon the Advancement of Trade in Ireland.* 1673. In *Miscellanea.* 1680.

[Temple, William, of Trowbridge.] *A Vindication of Commerce and the Arts; Proving that they are the Source of the Greatness, Power, Riches, and Populousness of a State.* 1758.

Theatri Europaei, Achtzehnder Theil; oder, Ausführlich Fortgeführte Friedens-und Kriegs-Beschreibung. Frankfurt-am-Main: 1720.

Thomas, Dalby. *An Historical Account of the Rise and Growth of the West-India Colonies, and of the Great Advantages they are to England, in Respect to Trade.* 1690.

Thomson, James. *Liberty.* 1735–36.

[Tindal, Matthew.] *An Essay Concerning the Power of the Magistrate, and the Rights of Mankind in Matters of Religion.* 1697.

Tindal, N. *The Continuation of Mr. Rapin de Thoyras's History of England from the Revolution to the Accession of King George III.* 2 vols. Ed. of 1751.

To the Right Honourable the Commons in Parliament Assembled: the Humble Petition of the Native Merchants of England. [1660.]

[Toland, John.] *Reasons for Naturalizing the Jews in Great Britain and Ireland.* 1714.

———. *The Second Part of the State Anatomy.* 1717.

———. *The State Anatomy of Great Britain.* 5th ed. 1717.

Torism and Trade can never Agree. To which is Added an Account and Character of the Mercator and his Writings. 1713.

Tovey, D'Blossiers. *Anglia-Judaica; or, The History and Antiquities of the Jews in England.* Oxford: 1738.

The Town Spy; or, A View of London and Westminster. Gloucester, 1729.

The Trade of England Revived: and the Abuses thereof Rectified. 1681.

A True and Faithful Account of the . . . Late Dreadful Burning of the City of London. 1667. In *Somer's Tracts*, 7.

Tucker, Josiah. *Reflections on the Expediency of a Law for the Naturalization of Foreign Protestants, In Two Parts, Part I, Containing Historical Remarks.* 1751.

———. *Reflections on the Expediency of a Law for the Naturalization of Foreign Protestants, In Two Parts, Part II, Containing Important Queries.* 1752.

———. *A Brief Essay on the Advantages and Disadvantages which Respectively Attend France and Great Britain, with Regard to Trade.* 3d ed. 1753.

———. *A Letter to a Friend Concerning Naturalizations.* 1753.

———. *A Second Letter to a Friend Concerning Naturalizations.* 1753.

[Tutchin, John.] *The Foreigners.* 1700.

———. *The Elements of Commerce and Theory of Taxes.* 1755. In *Josiah Tucker: A Selection from his Economic and Political Writings.* Edited by R.L. Schuyler. New York: 1931.

———. *Instructions for Travellers.* 1757.

V., A. *Description d'une Fête Célébré à Paddington, par Plusieurs François Protestants.* 1716.

Vanderlint, Jacob. *Money Answers all Things; or, An Essay to make Money Sufficiently Plentiful amongst all Ranks of People, and Increase our Foreign and Domestick Trade.* 1734.

Vauban, Sébastien le Prestre de. *An Essay for a General Tax; or, A Project for a Royal Tithe.* Trans., 1710.

A View of the Queen and Kingdom's Enemies, in the Case of the Poor Palatines: to which is Added a List of the Persons Appointed Commissioners and Trustees of the Charity by Her Majesty's Letters Patent. [c.1710.]

Violet, Thomas. *The Advancement of Merchandize; or, Certain Propositions for the Improvement of the Trade of this Commonwealth.* 1651.

———. *A Petition against the Jews, Presented to the King's Majesty and the Parliament.* 1661.

Von Hornick, Phillip. *Österreich über Alles, wann es nur Will.* Vienna: 1684.

W., T. *The Present Condition of Great Britain, in a Discourse upon Things that have not been Considered, though they are of the Greatest Consequence to her.* 1746.

————. *The Natural Interest of Great Britain, in its Present Circumstances, Demonstrated. In a Discourse in Two Parts.* 2d ed. 1748.

[Wagstaffe, Thomas.] *A Supplement to His Majesty's Most Gracious Speech.* [1693.]

[Wallace, Robert.] *A Dissertation on the Numbers of Mankind in Ancient and Modern Times: in which the Superior Populousness of Antiquity is Maintained.* Edinburgh: 1753.

The Weaver; or, The State of our Home Manufacture Considered. 8 numbers 1719–20.

[Webb, Philip Carteret.] *The Bill Permitting the Jews to be naturalized by Parliament.* 1753.

[Webb, Philip Carteret.] *The Question whether a Jew, Born within the British Dominions was before the Making the Late Act of Parliament, a Person Capable, by law to Purchase and Hold Lands.* 1753.

Wendeborn, Friedrich August. *A View of England towards the Close of the Eighteenth Century.* 2 vols. Dublin: 1791.

Whitworth, Charles. *The Political and Commercial Works of that Celebrated Writer Charles Davenant, L. L. D.* 5 vols. 1771.

A Winter Evening's Conversation in a Club of Jews, Dutchmen, French Refugees, and English Stock-Jobbers, at a Noted Coffee-House in Change Alley. 1748.

Wood, William. *A Survey of Trade.* 1718.

SECONDARY SOURCES

Books

Aitken, George A., ed. *Later Stuart Tracts.* London: 1903.

Appleby, Joyce Oldham. *Economic Thought and Ideology in Seventeenth-Century England.* Princeton, 1978.

Arbor, E., ed. *The Torments of the Protestant Slaves.* London, 1907.

Ashley, Maurice P. *Financial and Commercial Policy Under the Cromwellian Protectorate.* Oxford: 1934.

————. *England in the Seventeenth Century.* Harmondsworth: 1967.

Ashton, T. S. *Economic Fluctuations in England 1700–1800.* Oxford: 1959.

Atherton, Herbert M. *Political Prints in the Age of Hogart.* Oxford: 1974.

Aytoun, Ellis. *The Penny Universities: A History of the Coffee-Houses.* London: 1956.

Bailyn, Bernard. *Voyagers to the West: A Passage in the Peopling of America on the Eve of the Revolution.* New York: 1986.

Barnett, George E. *Two Tracts by Gregory King.* Baltimore: 1936.

Bayne-Powell, Rosamond. *Travellers in Eighteenth Century England.* London: 1951.

Beer, G. L. *The Old Colonial System, 1660–1754.* 2 vols. New York: 1912.

Beer, Max. *Early British Economics.* London: 1938.

Beloff, Max. *Public Order and Popular Disturbances, 1660–1714.* London: 1938.

Biographia Britannia. 6 vols. London: 1747–66.

Birch, William de Gray, ed. *The Historical Charters and Constitutional Documents of the City of London*. Revised ed. London: 1887.

Blackstone, William. *Commentaries on the Laws of England*. 1765–69. Edited by Edward Christian. 4 vols. London: 1803.

Bonar, James. *Theories of Population from Raleigh to Arthur Young*. London: 1931; New York: 1966.

Bradley, H. J. *The History of Shoreditch Church*. London: 1914.

Brewer, John. *Party Ideology and Popular Politics*. Cambridge: 1976.

———. *The Sinews of Power: War, Money, and the English State, 1688–1783*. Cambridge, Mass.: 1990.

Bromley, J. S., ed. *The New Cambridge Modern History*. Vol. 6. Cambridge: 1971.

Brown, B. C. *The Letters and Diplomatic Instructions of Queen Anne*. London: 1935.

Browning, A., ed. *The Memoirs of Sir John Reresby*. Glasglow: 1936.

Buck, Philip W. *The Politics of Mercantilism* New York: 1942.

Burke, Peter. *Popular Culture in Early Modern Europe*. London: 1978.

Burnet, Gilbert. *The Life and Death of Sir Matthew Hale, to which are added Richard Baxter's Additional Notes on the Life and Death of Sir Matthew Hale*. London: 1805.

———. *Bishop Burnet's History of His Own Time*. Edited by M. J. Routh. 2d ed. 6 vols. Oxford: 1833.

Carlton, C. *The Court of Orphans*. Leicester: 1974.

Carsten, F. L., ed. *The New Cambridge Modern History*. Vol. 5. Cambridge: 1961.

Cartwright, J. J. *The Wentworth Papers 1705–1739. Selected from the Private and Family Correspondence of Thomas Wentworth, Lord Raby, Created Earl of Strafford*. London: 1883.

Chalmers, George. *Political Annals of the Present United Colonies, from their Settlement to the Peace of 1763*. Book 1. London: 1780.

Chandaman, C. D. *The English Public Revenue: 1660–1688*. Oxford: 1975.

Chandler, D. S. *The Art of War in the Age of Marlborough*. London: 1976.

Chandler, R. *The History of the Proceedings of the House of Commons . . . 1660 to . . . 1743*. 14 vols. London: 1741–44.

Clark, George. *The Later Stuarts, 1660–1714*. 2d ed. Oxford: 1956.

Clark, J. C. D. *English Society 1688–1832: Ideology, Social Structure and Political Practice during the Ancien Regime*. Cambridge: 1985.

Clark, Peter, and Paul Slack, eds. *Crisis and Order in English Towns, 1500–1700*. London: 1972.

Clark, W. E. *Josiah Tucker, Economist: A Study in the History of Economics*. New York: 1903.

Clarke, George, ed. *John Bellers: His Life, Times, and Writings*. London: 1987.

Clay, C. G. A. *Economic Expansion and Social Change: England 1500–1700*. 2 vols. Cambridge: 1984.

Cobb, S. H. *The Story of the Palatines: An Episode in Colonial History*. New York: 1897.

Cockburn, A. *Nationality; or, The Law Relating to Subjects and Aliens*. London: 1869.

Cole, Charles W. *Colbert and a Century of French Mercantilism*. 2 vols. New York: 1939.

Cole, G. D. H., ed. *A Tour through the Whole Island of Great Britain.* 2 vols. London: 1928.

Coleman, D. C., ed. *Revisions in Mercantilism.* London: 1969.

Colley, Linda. *In Defiance of Oligarchy: The Tory Party, 1714–60.* Cambridge: 1982.

———. *Britons: Forging the Nation 1707–1837.* New Haven: 1992.

Cooper, W. D., ed. *The Savile Correspondence: Letters to and from Henry Savile, Esq., Envoy at Paris.* London: 1858.

Corfield, P. J. *The Impact of English Towns: 1700–1800.* Oxford: 1982.

Cottrett, Bernard. *The Huguenots in England: Immigration and Settlement c. 1550–1700,* translated by Perigrin and Adriana Stevenson. Cambridge: 1991.

Coxe, W. *Memoirs of the Administration of the Right Honourable Henry Pelham.* London: 1829.

Cressy, David. *Coming Over: Migration and Communication between England and New England in the Seventeenth Century.* Cambridge: 1987.

Cunningham, W. *Alien Immigrants to England.* 2d ed. London: 1969.

Curtis, L. A., ed. *The Versatile Defoe. An Anthology of Uncollected Writings by Daniel Defoe.* London: 1979.

Davies, G., ed. *Bibliography of British History, Stuart Period, 1603–1714.* Oxford: 1970.

Davies, W. E. D. *The English Law Relating to Aliens.* London: 1931.

Davis, H., ed. *Prose Works of Swift,* 14 vols. Oxford, 1939–68.

Davis, Ralph. *A Commercial Revolution; English Overseas Trade in the Seventeenth and Eighteenth Centuries.* Historical Association Pamphlet, no. 64. London: 1967.

DeBeer, E. S., ed. *The Diary of John Evelyn.* 6 vols. Oxford: 1955.

DeKrey, Gary Stuart. *A Fractured Society: The Politics of London in the First Age of Party, 1688–1715.* Oxford: 1985.

Dickinson, H. T. *Liberty and Property: Political Ideology in Eighteenth-Century Britain.* London: 1977.

Dickson, P. G. M. *The Financial Revolution in England: A Study in the Development of Public Credit, 1688–1756.* London: 1967.

Doble, C. E., ed. *Remarks and Collections of Thomas Hearne.* 11 vols. Oxford, 1884–1918.

Downie, J. A. *Robert Harley and the Press.* Cambridge: 1979.

Duffy, Michael. *The Englishman and the Foreigner.* Cambridge: 1986.

Earle, Peter. *The World of Defoe.* London: 1972.

Edwards, John. *The Jews in Christian Europe.* London: 1988.

Ellis, F. H. *Swift vs. Mainwaring: "The Examiner" and "The Medley."* Oxford: 1985.

Endelman, T. M. *The Jews of Georgian England 1714–1830: Tradition and Change in a Liberal Society.* Philadelphia, 1979.

Fox-Genovese, Elizabeth. *The Origins of Physiocracy: Economic Revolution and Social Order in Eighteenth-Century France.* Ithaca, NY: 1976.

Fry, Anna Ruth. *John Bellers, 1654–1725, Quaker, Economist and Social Reformer. His Writings Reprinted with a Memoir.* London: 1935.

Furniss, E. S. *The Position of the Laborer in a System of Nationalism: A Study in the Labor Theories of the Later English Mercantilists.* Boston and New York: 1920.

Garraty, John A. *Unemployment in History: Economic Thought and Public Policy.* New York: 1978.

George, M. D. *London Life in the Eighteenth Century.* 3d ed. London: 1951.

————, *England in Transition: Life and Work in the Eighteenth Century.* Harmondsworth, 1953.

Glass, D. V. *Numbering the People: The Eighteenth-Century Population Controversy and the Development of Census and Vital Statistics in Britain.* Fainborough: 1973.

Glass, D. V., and D. E. C. Eversley, eds. *Population in History.* London: 1965.

Gonnard, René. *Histoire des Doctrines de la Population.* Paris: 1923.

Goubert, Pierre. *The Ancien Régime: French Society, 1600–1750.* 1969; New York: 1973.

Grell, Ole Peter, Jonathan I. Israel, and Nicholas Tyake, eds. *From Persecution to Toleration: The Glorious Revolution and England.* Oxford: 1991.

Grey, Anchitell, ed. *Debates of the House of Commons from the Year 1667 to the Year 1694.* 10 vols. London: 1763.

Gwynn, R. D. *Huguenot Heritage: The History and Contribution of the Huguenots in Britain.* London: 1985.

Häusser, L. *Geschichte der Rheinischen Pfalz nach ihren Politischen, Kirchlichen und Literarischen Verhältnissen.* 2d ed. 2 vols. Heidelberg: 1856.

Hagberg, L. *Djacob Serenius Kyrkliga Insats.* Stockholm: 1952.

Hanson, L. *Government and the Press, 1695–1763.* 1936; reprinted, London: 1967.

Hanson, L. W. *Contemporary Printed Sources for British and Irish Economic History, 1701–1750.* Cambridge: 1963.

The Harleian Miscellany. 12 vols. London, 1808–1811.

Harris, Tim. *London Crowds in the Reign of Charles II: Progaganda and Politics from the Restoration until the Exclusion Crisis.* Cambridge: 1987.

Harrison, William. *The Description of England.* Edited by Georges Edelen. Ithaca, N.Y.: 1968.

Hastings, H., ed. *Ecclesiastical Records: State of New York.* 7 vols. Albany, N.Y.: 1901–16.

Hay, Denys, ed. *The New Cambridge Modern History,* Vol. 1. Cambridge: 1957.

Hearsey, J. E. N. *London and the Great Fire.* London: 1965.

Heckscher, E. F. *Mercantilism,* 2 vols. London: 1934.

Henning, B. D., ed. *The Parliamentary Diary of Sir Edward Dering, 1670–1673.* New Haven: 1940.

————, ed. *The History of Parliament: The House of Commons, 1660–1690.* 3 vols. London: 1983.

Henriques, H. S. Q. *The Return of the Jews to England.* London: 1905.

————. *The Jews and the English Law.* London: 1908.

Hertz, F. *Nationality in History and Politics: A Study of the Psychology and Sociology of National Sentiment and Character.* London: 1944.

Hertz, G. B. *British Imperialism in the Eighteenth Century.* London: 1908.

Hessels, J. H., ed. *Register of the Attestations or Certificates of Membership, &c. Preserved in the Dutch Reformed Church, Austin Friars, London, 1568 to 1872.* London: 1892.

Heward, E. *Matthew Hale.* London: 1972.

Higgs, Henry, ed. *Bibliography of Economics: 1751–1775.* Cambridge: 1935.

Higgs, Henry. *The Physiocrats. Six Lectures on the French Economistes of the Eighteenth Century.* London: 1897.

Hill, Christopher. *Reformation to Industrial Revolution*. London: 1967.

——. *The World Turned Upside Down: Radical Ideas During the English Revolution*. London: 1972.

The History, Debates, and Proceedings of Both Houses of Parliament of Great Britain, from the Year 1743 to the Year 1774. 7 vols. London: 1792.

Holdsworth, William. *History of English Law*. 7th ed. 14 vols. London: 1956.

Holmes, C., ed. *Immigrants and Minorities in British Society*. London: 1978.

Holmes, Geoffrey. *British Politics in the Age of Anne*. London: 1967.

Holmes, Geoffrey. *The Trial of Doctor Sacheverell*. London: 1973.

Hont, Istvan, and Michael Ignatieff, eds. *Wealth and Virtue: The Shaping of Political Economy in the Scottish Enlightenment*. Cambridge: 1983.

Horwitz, Henry, ed. *The Parliamentary Diary of Narcissus Luttrell, 1691–93*. Oxford: 1972.

Horwitz, Henry. *Parliament, Policy and Politics in the Reign of William III*. Manchester: 1977.

Horwitz, Henry. *Revolution Politicks: The Career of Daniel Finch, Second Earl of Nottingham 1647–1730*. Cambridge: 1968.

Hoskins, W. G. *The Making of the English Landscape*. Harmondsworth, 1983.

Howell, T. B., ed. *A Complete Collection of State Trials*. London: 1816.

Les Huguenots: Exposition nationale organisée par la direction des Archives de France Ministère de la Culture a l'occasion du Tricentenaire de la Révocation de l'Edit de Nantes 1685–1985. Paris, 1985.

Hull, C. H., ed. *The Economic Writings of Sir William Petty*. 2 vols. Cambridge: 1899.

Jessop, A., ed. *The Lives of the Norths by Roger North*. 3 vols. London: 1890.

Johnson, E. A. J. *Predecessors of Adam Smith: the Growth of British Economic Thought*. New York: 1937.

Jones, J. M. *British Nationality Law*. Oxford: 1956.

Jones, J. R. *Country and Court: England, 1658–1714*. Cambridge, Mass.: 1979.

Katz, David S. *Philo-Semitism and the Readmission of the Jews to England, 1603–1655*. Oxford: 1982.

Kenyon, J. P., ed. *Halifax. Complete Works*. Harmondsworth, 1969.

Kenyon, J. P., ed. *The Stuart Constitution, 1603–1688: Documents and Commentary*. Cambridge: 1966.

Kippis, A. *Biographia Britannica; or, The Lives of the Most Eminent Persons who have Flourished in Great Britain and Ireland*. 5 vols. 2d ed. London, 1778–93.

Knittle, W. A. *The Early Eighteenth Century Palatine Emigration: A British Government Redemptioner Project to Manufacture Naval Stores*. Philadelphia, 1936.

Kohn, H. *Nationalism: Its Meaning and History*. Princeton, 1965.

Lacey, D. R. *Dissent and Parliamentary Politics in England, 1661–1689*. New Brunswick, New Jersey, 1969.

Lambert, Sheila. *Bills and Acts*. Cambridge: 1971.

Langford, Paul. *A Polite and Commercial People: England 1727–1783*. Oxford: 1989.

Lansdowne, Marquis of, ed. *The Petty Papers: Some Unpublished Writings of Sir William Petty*. 2 vols. London: 1927.

Lansdowne, Marquis of, ed. *The Petty-Southwell Correspondence 1676–1687*. London: 1928.

Latham, R., and W. Matthews, eds. *The Diary of Samuel Pepys*. 11 vols. London: 1970–83.

Lee, Jr., Maurice. *The Cabal*. Urbana, Ill.: 1965.

Lefler, Hugh T., and Albert Ray Newsome. *The History of a Southern State: North Carolina*. 3d ed. Chapel Hill, N.C.: 1973.

Lefler, Hugh T., and William S. Powell. *Colonial North Carolina: A History*. New York: 1973.

Letwin, William. *Sir Josiah Child: Merchant Economist*. Boston, 1959.

———. *The Origins of Scientific Economics: English Economic Thought 1660–1776*. London: 1963.

Lipman, V. D., ed. *Three Centuries of Anglo-Jewish History*. London: 1961.

Lipson, E. *The Economic History of England*. 4th ed. 3 vols. London: 1947.

Lillywhite, Bryant. *London Coffee Houses*. London: 1963.

Lovejoy, Arthur O. *The Great Chain of Being: A Study of the History of an Idea*. New York: 1936.

McCulloch, J. R. *Old and Scarce Tracts on Money*. 1856; London: 1933.

———. *The Literature of Political Economy*. 1854; London: 1938.

———. *Early English Tracts on Commerce*. 1856; Cambridge: 1970.

McKendrick, Neil, John Brewer, and J. H. Plumb. *The Birth of a Consumer Society: The Commercialization of Eighteenth-Century England*. London: 1982.

Mainsuch, H., ed. *John Toland, Gründe für die Einbürgerung der Juden in Grossbritannien und Irland*. Stuttgart: 1965.

Malcolm, J. P. *Anecdotes of the Manners and Customs of London during the Eighteenth Century*. London: 1808.

Marshall, Dorothy. *The English Poor in the Eighteenth Century: A Study in Social and Administrative History*. 1926; New York: 1969.

Maury, Ann, ed. *Jacques Fontaine, Memoirs of a Huguenot Family*. New York: 1853.

Meek, R. L. *The Economics of Physiocracy: Essays and Translations*. London: 1962.

Merton, Robert K. *Science, Technology, and Society in Seventeenth Century England*. 1938; New York: 1970.

Miller, John. *Popery and Politics in England. 1660–1688*. Cambridge: 1973.

Minet, W. *Notes on the Threadneedle Street Registers. HSQS*, 11. London: 1898.

Minet, W.& S. *A Supplement to Dr. Shaw's Letters of Denization and Acts of Naturalization. HSQS*, no. 35. Frome: 1932.

Moch, Leslie Page. *Moving Europeans: Migration Patterns in Western Europe since 1650*. Bloomington, Ind.: 1992.

Moens, W. J. C., ed. *The Marriage, Baptismal, and Burial Registers, 1571–1874, and Monumental Inscriptions, of the Dutch Reformed Church, Austin Friars, London*. London: 1884.

Monroe, A. E., ed. *Early Economic Thought: Selections from Economic Literature Prior to Adam Smith*. 8th ed. Cambridge, Mass.: 1965.

Moore, J. R. *A Checklist of the Writings of Daniel Defoe*. Bloomington, Ind.: 1960.

Murdoch, Tessa, ed. *The Quiet Conquest: The Huguenots 1685 to 1985*. London: 1985.

Namier, Lewis. *The Structure of Politics at the Accession of George III*. 2d ed. London: 1965.

Neale, J. E. *The Elizabethan House of Commons*. London: 1976.

Newman, Gerald. *The Rise of English Nationalism: A Cultural History, 1740–1830.* New York: 1987.

Nicholson, C. *Strangers to England: Immigration to England. 1100–1952.* London: 1974.

Novak, Maximilian E. *Economics and the Fiction of Daniel Defoe.* Berkeley, Calif.: 1962.

O'Callaghan, E. B., ed. *The Documentary History of the State of New York.* 4 vols. Albany, N. Y..: 1849–51.

———, ed. *Documents Relative to the Colonial History of the State of New York.* 10 vols. Albany, N. Y.: 1853–58.

Ogg, David. *England in the Reign of Charles II.* 2d ed. Oxford: 1956.

———. *England in the Reigns of James II and William III.* Oxford: 1969.

Papillion, A. F. W., ed. *Memoirs of Thomas Papillon, of London, Merchant (1623–1702).* Reading: 1887.

The Parliamentary History of England from the Earliest Period to the Year 1803. 36 vols. London: 1806–20.

Parker, Geoffrey. *The Military Revolution: Military Innovation and the Rise of the West, 1500–1800.* Cambridge: 1988.

Parry, Clive. *British Nationality Law and the History of Naturalisation.* Milan: 1954.

———. *Nationality and Citizenship Laws of the Commonwealth and of the Republic of Ireland.* London: 1957.

Payne, W. L., ed. *Index to Defoe's Review, 1704–13.* New York: 1948.

Pelling, H. *A History of British Trade Unionism.* 3d ed. London: 1976.

Perry, T. W. *Public Opinion, Propaganda and Politics in Eighteenth Century England: A Study of the Jew Bill of 1753.* Cambridge, Mass.: 1962.

Pettegree, Andrew. *Foreign Protestant Communities in Sixteenth Century London.* Oxford: 1986.

Piggott, F. *Nationality.* London: 1907.

Plumb, J. H. *The Growth of Political Stability in England 1675–1725.* London: 1967.

Plummer, Alfred. *The London Weavers' Company 1600–1970.* London: 1972.

Pocock, J. G. A. *The Macchiavellian Moment: Florentine Political Thought and the Atlantic Republican Tradition.* Princeton: 1975.

———. *Virtue, Commerce, and History: Essays on Political Thought and History, Chiefly in the Eighteenth Century.* Cambridge: 1985.

Pollins, H. *Economic History of the Jews in England.* East Brunswick, N. J.: 1982.

Poole, R. L. *A History of the Huguenots of the Dispersion at the Recall of the Edict of Nantes.* London: 1880.

Pibram, Karl. *A History of Economic Reasoning.* Baltimore: 1983.

Pulling, A. *A Practical Treatise on the Laws, Customs, and Regulations of the City and Part of London.* London: 1842.

Quarrell, W. H., and Margaret Mare, eds. *London in 1710: From the Travels of Zacharias Conrad von Uffenbach.* London: 1934.

Report of the Royal Commission for Inquiring into the Laws of Naturalization and Allegiance. London: 1869.

Report of the Royal Commission on Alien Immigration. London: 1903.

Robbins, Caroline, ed. *The Diary of John Milward.* Cambridge: 1938.

———. *The Eighteenth-Century Commonwealthman: Studies in the Transmission,*

Development and Circumstance of English Liberal Thought from the Restoration of Charles II until the War with the Thirteen Colonies. Cambridge, Mass.: 1959.

Robinson, Edward, The Early English Coffee House. 1893; Christchurch: 1972.

Roeber, A. G. *Palatines, Liberty, and Property.* Baltimore: 1993.

Roll, Eric. *A History of Economic Thought.* 4th. ed. London: 1973.

Roth, Cecil. *The Rise of Provincial Jewry. The Early History of the Jewish Communities in the English Countryside, 1740–1840.* London: 1950.

————. *A History of the Jews in England.* 3d ed. London: 1964.

Rotwein, Eugene, ed. *David Hume: Writings on Economics.* London: 1955.

Rudé, George. *The Crowd in History; A Study of Popular Disturbances in France and England 1730–1848.* New York: 1964.

————. *Hanoverian London 1714–1808.* London: 1971.

————. *Europe in the Eighteenth Century: Aristocracy and Bourgeois Challenge.* London: 1972.

————. *Paris and London in the Eighteenth Century.* London: 1972.

————. *Ideology and Popular Protest.* London: 1980.

Rymer, Thomas. *Foedera.* 2d ed. 20 vols. London: 1727.

Schmoller, G. *The Mercantile System and its Historical Significance.* New York: 1896.

Schumpeter, Joseph A. *History of Economic Analysis.* London: 1954.

Schuenemann, K. *Österreichs Bevölkerungspolitik unter Maria Theresia.* Band I. Berlin, 1935.

Schuyler, R. L., ed. *Josiah Tucker: A Selection from his Economic and Political Writings.* New York: 1931.

Schwartz, Hillel. *Knaves, Fools, Madmen, and that Subtile Effluvium: A Study of the Opposition to the French Prophets in England, 1706–1710.* Gainesville, Fl.: 1978.

————. *The French Prophets: The History of a Millenarian Group in Eighteenth-Century England.* Berkeley, Calif.: 1980.

Scott, Walter, ed. *Somers Tracts: A Collection of Scarce and Valuable Tracts, on the Most Interesting and Entertaining Subjects.* 2d ed. 13 vols. London, 1809–15.

Scott, Walter, *The Works of Jonathan Swift.* 19 vols. London: 1883.

Scott, W. R. *The Constitution and Finance of English, Scottish, and Irish Joint-Stock Companies to 1720.* 2 vols. Cambridge, 1910–12.

Scouloudi, I. *Returns of Strangers in the Metropolis, 1593, 1627, 1635, 1639: A Study of an Active Minority.* HSQS, no. 57 London: 1985.

Scouloudi, I., and A. P. Hands, *French Protestant Refugees Relieved through the Threadneedle Street Church, London, 1681–1687.* HSQS, no. 49. London: 1971.

Scoville, Warren C. *The Persecution of Huguenots and French Economic Development, 1680–1720.* Berkeley, Calif.: 1960.

Sedgwick, R., ed. *The History of Parliament: The House of Commons, 1715–54.* 2 vols. London: 1970.

Shaw, R. A., R. D. Gwynn, and P. Thomas. *Huguenots in Wandsworth.* London: 1985.

Shaw, W. A., ed. *Letters of Denization and Acts of Naturalization for Aliens in England and Ireland, 1603–1700.* HSQS, no. 17. Lymington: 1911.

————, ed. *Letters of Denization and Acts of Naturalization for Aliens in England and Ireland, 1701–1800.* HSQS, no. 27. Manchester: 1923.

Shelton, George. *Dean Tucker and Eighteenth-Century Economic and Political Thought*. London: 1981.

Slack, Paul. *The Impact of Plague in Tudor and Stuart England*. London: 1985.

Smiles, Samuel. *Huguenots: their Settlements, Churches, and Industries in England and Ireland*. 6th ed. London: 1889.

Smith, Adam. *The Wealth of Nations*. Edited by William Letwin. 1776; London: 1981.

Smith, E. *Foreign Visitors in England*. London: 1889.

Snyder, H. L., ed. *The Marlborough-Godolphin Correspondence*. 3 vols. Oxford: 1975.

Sommerville, R. *The Savoy Manor: Hospital: Chapel*. London: 1960.

Speck, W. A. *Stability and Strife: England, 1714–1760*. Cambridge, Mass.: 1979.

Spengler, Joseph John. *French Predecessors of Malthus*. Durham, N. C.: 1942.

Spufford, *Small Books and Pleasant Histories: Popular Fiction and its Readership in Seventeenth-Century England*. London: 1981.

Steele, I. K. *Politics of Colonial Policy: The Board of Trade in Colonial Administration 1696–1720*. Oxford: 1968.

Steele, R., ed. *Tudor and Stuart Proclamations: 1485–1714*. 2 vols. Oxford: 1910.

Stern, W. M. *The Porters of London*. London: 1960.

Stevenson, John. *Popular Disturbances in England, 1700–1870*. London: 1979.

Strangeland, Charles Emil. *Pre-Malthusian Doctrines of Population*. 1904; New York: 1966.

Strateman, C., ed. *The Liverpool Tractate: An Eighteenth-Century Manual on the Procedure of the House of Commons*. New York: 1937.

Sumner, W. G. *Folkways*. New York: 1906.

Supple, B. E. *Commercial Crisis and Change in England 1600–1642: A Study in the Instability of a Mercantile Economy*. Cambridge: 1959.

Suviranta, B. *The Theory of the Balance of Trade in England*. Helsinfors: 1923.

Tawney, R. H. *Religion and the Rise of Capitalism*. Harmondsworth: 1980.

Thirsk, Joan, ed. *The Agrarian History of England and Wales*. Vol. 5, ii. Cambridge: 1985.

Thirsk, Joan. *Economic Policy and Projects: The Development of a Consumer Society in Early Modern England*. Oxford: 1978.

Thirsk, J. and J. P. Cooper, eds. *Seventeenth-Century Economic Documents*. Oxford: 1972.

Thomas, P. D. G. *The House of Commons in the Eighteenth Century*. Oxford: 1971.

Thomas, P. J. *Mercantilism and the East India Trade*. London: 1965.

Thompson, E. P. *The Making of the English Working Class*. London: 1963.

Tillyard, E. M. W. *The Elizabethan World Picture*. London: 1943.

Tirel, Jean. *Lettres Fraternelles de un prisonnier publiées par Eva Avigdor en collaboration avec Elizabeth Labrousse*. Paris: 1986.

Todd, Vincent H., ed. *Christoph von Graffenreid's Account of the Founding of New Bern*. Raleigh, N. C.: 1920.

Traill, H. D., and J.S. Mann, eds. *Social England*. 6 vols. London, 1901–04.

Trevelyan, G. M. *England under Queen Anne*. 3 vols. London, 1930–34.

Tribe, Keith. *Land, Labour, and Economic Discourse*. London: 1978.

Turner, W., ed. *The Aufrère Papers: Calendar and Selections. HSQS*, no. 40. Frome: 1940.

Vaggi, Gianni. *The Economics of François Quesnay.* London: 1988.

Van Deursen, A. T. *Plain Lives in a Golden Age: Popular Culture, Religion, and Society in Seventeenth-Century Holland.* Translated by Maarten Ultee. Cambridge: 1991.

Van Muyden, Madame, ed. *A Foreign View of England in the Reigns of George I and George II: The Letters of Monsieur Cesar de Saussure to his Family.* London: 1902.

Vaughn, Karen Iverson. *John Locke: Economist and Social Scientist.* Chicago: 1980.

Viner, Jacob. *Studies in the Theory of International Trade.* London: 1937.

Waller, W., ed. *Extracts from the Court Books of the Weavers' Company of London 1610–1730. HSQS*, no. 33. Frome: 1931.

Walvin, James. *The Black Presence: A Documentary History of the Negro in England, 1555–1860.* New York: 1972.

Warner, F. *The Silk Industry of the U.K.* London: 1921.

Webster, Charles. *The Great Instauration: Science, Medicine, and Reform, 1626–1660.* New York: 1975.

Weisskopf, W. A. *The Psychology of Economics.* London: 1955.

Williams, Basil. *Stanhope: A Study in Eighteenth-Century Diplomacy.* Oxford: 1932.

Williams, E. Neville. *The Eighteenth-Century Constitution 1688–1715.* Cambridge: 1960.

Williams, O. C. *The Historical Development of Private Bill Procedure.* 2 vols. London: 1948.

———. *The Clerical Organization of the House of Commons 1661–1850.* Oxford: 1954.

Wilson, Charles. *Profit and Power: A Study of England and the Dutch Wars.* London: 1957.

———. *The Dutch Republic and the Civilisation of the Seventeenth Century.* New York: 1968.

———. *England's Apprenticeship: 1603–1763.* 2d ed. London: 1984.

Wing, D. G. *Short-Title Catalogue of Books Printed in England, Scotland, Ireland, Wales, and British America, and of English Books Printed in Other Countries, 1641–1700.* 3 vols. New York, 1945–51.

Wood, M. M. *The Stranger: A Study in Social Relationships.* New York: 1934.

Wrightson, Keith. *English Society, 1580–1680.* London: 1982.

Wrigley, E. A., and R. S. Schofield. *The Population History of England, 1541–1871.* Cambridge: 1981.

Articles

Abrahams, I. "Passes Issued to Jews in the Period 1689 to 1696." *Miscellanies of the Jewish Historical Society of England* 1 (1925): 24–33.

Allport, F. H. "Towards a Science of Public Opinion." *Public Opinion Quarterly* 1 (1937): 7–23.

Appleby, A. "Grain Prices and Subsistence Crises in England and France, 1590–1740." *Journal of Economic History* 39 (1979): 865–87.

Baugh, Daniel A. "Poverty, Protestantism, and Political Economy: English Attitudes toward the Poor, 1660–1800." In *England's Rise to Greatness, 1660–1763,* edited by Stephen B. Baxter. Berkeley, Calif.: 1983, 63–197.

Black, Jeremy. "The Print-Run of an Eighteenth-Century Pamphlet." *Notes and Queries,* new ser., 34 (1987): 345.

Black, Jeremy. "Ideology, History, Xenophobia and the World of Print in Eighteenth-Century England." In *Culture, Politics, and Society in Britain 1660–1800,* edited by Jeremy Black and Jeremy Gregory. Manchester: 1991, 184–216.

Blaug, Mark. "Economic Theory and Economic History in Great Britain, 1650–1776." *P & P* 28 (1964): 111–16.

Bog, Ingomar. "Mercantilism in Germany." In *Revisions,* edited by D. C. Coleman, 1969.

Bonacich, Edna. "A Theory of Ethnic Antagonism: The Split Labor Market." *American Sociological Review* 37 (1972): 547–59.

Bonacich, Edna. "A Theory of Middleman Minorities." *American Sociological Review* 38 (1973): 583–94.

Brooks, C. "Projecting, Political Arithmetic and the Act of 1695." *English Historical Review* 97 (1982): 31–53.

Buck, Peter. "Seventeenth-Century Political Arithmetic: Civil Strife and Vital Statistics." *Isis* 68 (1977): 67–84.

Burke, Peter. "Popular Culture in Seventeenth Century London." *London Journal* 3 (1977): 143–62.

Campbell, Mildred. "Of People Either Too Few or Too Many: The Conflict of Opinion on Population and its Relation to Emigration." In *Conflict in Stuart England,* edited by William Appleton Aiken and Basil Cuke Henning, 169–201. London: 1960.

Carpenter, A. H. "Naturalization in England and the American Colonies." *American Historical Review* 9 (1904): 288–303.

Carter, A. C. "The Huguenot Contribution to the Early Years of the Funded Debt, 1694–1714." *PHSL* 19 (1952–58): 21–33.

Chitty, C. W. "Aliens in England in the Sixteenth Century." *Race* 8 (1966): 129–45.

———. "Aliens in England in the Seventeenth Century to 1660." *Race* 11 (1969): 189–201.

Churchill, E. F. "The Crown and the Alien: A Review of the Crown's Protection of the Alien . . . to 1689." *Law Quarterly Review* 36 (1920): 402–28.

Clay, C. "The Price of Freehold Land in the Late Seventeenth and Eighteenth Centuries." *EcHR,* 2nd. ser., 27 (1974): 173–89.

Coats, A. W. "Changing Attitudes to Labour in the Mid-Eighteenth Century." *EcHR,* 2nd. ser., 11 (1958): 35–51.

———. "Economic Thought and Poor Law Policy in the Eighteenth Century." *EcHR,* 2nd. ser., 13 (1960): 39–51.

Coleman, D.C. "Labour in the English Economy of the Seventeenth Century." *EcHR,* 2nd. series, 8 (1956): 280–95.

———. "Politics and Economics in the Age of Anne: the Case of the Anglo-French Trade Treaty of 1713." In *Trade, Government and Economy in Pre-Industrial England: Essays Presented to F.J. Fisher,* edited by D. C. Coleman and A. H. John, 187–211. London: 1976.

———. "Mercantilism Revisited." *Historical Journal* 23 (1980): 773–91.

Colley, Linda. "The Apotheosis of George III: Loyalty, Royalty, and the British Nation 1760–1820." *P & P* 102 (1984): 94–129.

Craies, W. F. "The Right of Aliens to Enter British Territory." *Law Quarterly Review* 6 (1890): 27–41.

Cummingham, Hugh. "The Language of Patriotism." *History Workshop Journal* 12 (1981): 8–33.

DeBeer, E. S. "The Revocation of the Edict of Nantes and English Public Opinion." *PHSL* 18 (1947–52): 292–310.

Dickinson, H. T. "The Poor Palatines and the Parties." *English Historical Review* 82 (1967): 464–85.

———. "The Tory Party's Attitude to Foreigners: A Note on Party Principles in the Age of Anne." *BIHR* 40 (1967): 153–65.

Doolittle, I. G. "The City of London's Debt to its Orphans, 1694–1767." *BIHR* 56 (1983): 46–59.

Dunn, R. M. "The London Weavers' Riot of 1675." *Guildhall Studies in London History* 1 (1973): 13–23.

Dunn, Richard S. "William Penn and the Selling of Pennsylvania, 1681–1685." *Proceedings of the American Philosophical Society* 127 (1983): 322–29.

Earle, Peter. "The Economics of Stability: The Views of Daniel Defoe." In *Trade, Government and Economy in Pre-Industrial England: Essays Presented to F.J. Fisher,* edited by D. C. Coleman and A. H. John, 274–92. London: 1976.

Faust, A. B. "Übersicht über die Geschichte der Deutschen in Amerika". In *Das Buch der Deutschen in Amerika,* edited by M. Heinrici, 49–82. Philadelphia: 1909.

Fenske, Hans. "International Migration: Germany in the Eighteenth Century." *Central European History* 3 (1980): 332–47.

Fernsemer, O. F. W. "Daniel Defoe and the Palatine Emigration of 1709: A View of the Origin of Robinson Crusoe." *Journal of English and Germanic Philology* 19 (1920): 94–124.

Fiering, Norman S. "Irresistible Compassion: An Aspect of Eighteenth Century Sympathy and Humanitarianism." *Journal of the History of Ideas* 37 (1976): 195–218.

George, M. Dorothy. "London and the Life of the Town." In *Johnson's England,* 2 vols., edited by A. S. Turberville. Oxford: 1933, 1: 160–96.

George, R. H. "A Mercantilist Episode." *Journal of English Business History* 3 (1930–31).

Gibbs, C. G. "The Reception of the Huguenots in England and the Dutch Republic, 1680–1690." In *From Persecution to Toleration,* edited by Grell et al., 1991, 275–306.

Goebel, J. "Briefe Deutscher Auswanderer aus dem Jahre 1709." *Deutsch-Amerikanische Geschichtsblätter, Jahrbuch der Deutsch-Amerikanische Historien Gesellschaft von Illinois.* 12 (Chicago: 1912), 126–89.

———. "Neue Dokumente zur Geschichte der Massenauswanderung um Jahre 1709." *Jahrbuch der Deutsch-Amerikanische Historien Gesellschaft von Illinois* 13 (Chicago: 1913), 181–201.

Goldie, Mark. "The Theory of Religious Intolerance in Restoration England." In *From Persecution to Toleration,* edited by Grell et al., 1991, 331–68.

Goose, Nigel. "The Dutch in Colchester: The Economic Influence of an Immigrant Community in the Sixteenth and Seventeenth Centuries." *Immigrants and Minorities* 1 (1982): 261–80.

Goring, J. "Social Change and Military Decline in Mid-Tudor England." *History* 60 (1975): 185–97.

Grampp, W. D. "The Liberal Elements in English Mercantilism." *Quarterly Journal of Economics* 66 (1952): 465–501.

Gregory, T. E. "The Economics of Employment in England, 1660–1713." *Economica* 1 (1921): 37–51.

Grell, Ole Peter. "From Persecution to Integration: The Decline of the Anglo-Dutch Communities in England, 1648–1702." In Grell et al., eds., *From Persecution to Toleration*, 97–128.

Gwynn, R. D. "The Arrival of Huguenot Refugees in England 1680–1705." *PHSL* 21 (1965–70): 366–73.

———. "The Distribution of Huguenot Refugees in England." *PHSL* 21 (1965–70): 404–36.

———. "The Distribution of Huguenot Refugees in England, II: London and its Environs." *PHSL* 22 (1970–76): 509–68.

———. "James II in Light of his Treatment of Huguenot Refugees in England, 1685–86." *English Historical Review* 92 (1977): 820–33.

———. "The Number of Huguenot Immigrants in England in the Late Seventeenth Century." *Journal of Historical Geography* 9 (1983): 384–95.

Haycroft, T. W. "Alien Legislation and the Prerogative of the Crown." *Law Quarterly Review* 13 (1897): 165–86.

Helleiner, K. F. "The Vital Revolution Reconsidered." In *Population in History*, edited by D. V. Glass and D. E. C. Eversley, 79–86. London: 1965.

Hoch, P. K. "No Utopia: Refugee Scholars in Britain." *History Today* 35 (1985): 53–56.

Holmes, Geoffrey. "The Sacheverell Riots: The Crowd and the Church in Early Eighteenth Century London." *P & P* 72 (1976): 55–85.

Holmes, Geoffrey. "Gregory King and the Social Structure of Pre-Industrial England." *TRHS*, 5th ser., 27 (1977): 41–68.

Horwitz, Henry. "The Structure of Parliamentary Politics." In *Britain after the Glorious Revolution*, edited by Geoffrey Holmes, 96–114. New York: 1969.

Hoskins, W. G. "Harvest Fluctuations and English Economic History, 1620–1759." *Agricultural History Review* 16 (1968): 15–31.

Hutchison, T. W. "Berkeley's "Querist" and its Place in the Economic Thought of the Eighteenth Century." *British Journal for the Philosophy of Science* 4 (1953): 52–77.

Jones, D.W. "London Merchants and the Crisis of the 1690s." In *Crisis and Order in English Towns, 1500–1700*, edited by Peter Clark and Paul Slack. London: 1972.

Jubb, Michael. "Economic Policy and Economic Development." In *Britain in the Age of Walpole*, edited by Jeremy Black, 121–44. London: 1984.

Kellett, J. R. "The Breakdown of Gild and Corporation Control over the Handicraft and Retail Trade in London." *EcHR*, 2d ser., 10 (1958): 381–94.

Kellett, J. R. "The Financial Crisis of the Corporation of London and the Orphans' Act, 1694." *Guildhall Miscellany* 2 (1963): 220–27.

Kreager, Philip. "New Light on Graunt." *Population Studies* 42 (1988): 129–40.

Lart, C. E. "The Huguenot Settlements and Churches in the West of England." *PHSL* 7 (1901–4): 286–98.

Laslett, Peter. "John Locke, the Great Recoinage, and the Origins of the Board of Trade: 1695–1698." In *John Locke: Problems and Perspectives: A Collection of New Essays*, edited by John W. Yolton, 137–64. Cambridge: 1969.

Le Roy Ladurie, E. "Histoire et Climat." *Annales* 14 (1959): 3–34.

Levy, F. J. "How Information Spread among the Gentry, 1550–1640." *Journal of British Studies* 21 (1982): 11–34.

Luehrs, Robert B. "Population and Utopia in the Thought of Robert Wallace." *Eighteenth-Century Studies* 20 (1987): 313–35.

Lunn, K. "Immigrants and British Labour's Response, 1870–1950." *History Today* 35 (1985): 48–52.

Macaulay, T. B. "Sir William Temple." In *Critical and Historical Essays.* 2 vols. 1:195–272. Everyman ed. London: 1941.

Moore, J. R. "Introduction." *A Brief History of the Poor Palatine Refugees,* by Daniel Defoe. Los Angeles: 1964, vii.

———. "Defoe's *Some Seasonable Queries:* A Chapter Concerning the Humanities." *Newberry Library Bulletin* 6 (1965): 179–86.

Mullett, Michael. "Popular Culture and Popular Politics: Some Regional Case Studies." In *Britain in the First Age of Party,* edited by Clyve Jones. London: 1987, 129–50.

Nusteling, H. P. N. "The Netherlands and the Huguenot Emigrés." In *La Révocation de l'Édit de Nantes,* edited by J. A. H. Bots and G. H. M. Posthumus Meyjes, 17–34. Amsterdam: 1986.

Pascal, C. "Secours distribués aux refugiés Protestants Français par le gouvernment Anglais." *BSHPF* 44 (1895): 264–67.

Pearl, Valerie. "Change and Stability in Seventeenth-Century London." *London Journal* 5 (1979): 3–34.

Pinnington, J. E. "Anglican Openness to Foreign Protestant Churches in the Eighteenth Century." *Anglican Theological Review* 51 (1969): 133–48.

Porter, Roy. "Seeing the Past." *P&P* 118 (1988): 186–205.

Priestly, M. "Anglo-French Trade and the 'Unfavourable Balance' Controversy, 1660–1685." *EcHR*, 2d series, 4 (1951): 37–52.

Radner, John B. "The Art of Sympathy in Eighteenth Century British Moral Thought." *Studies in Eighteenth Century Culture* 99 (1979): 189–210.

Redstone, V. B. "The Dutch and Huguenot Settlements of Ipswich." *PHSL* 12 (1919–24): 183–204.

Resnick, David. "John Locke and the Problem of Naturalization." *Review of Politics* 49 (1987): 368–88.

Robbins, Caroline. "A Note on General Naturalization under the Later Stuarts and a Speech in the House of Commons on the Subject in 1664." *Journal of Modern History* 24 (1962): 168–77.

Rogers, Nicholas. "Popular Politics in Early Hanoverian London." *P&P* 79 (1978): 70–100.

———. "Popular Jacobitism in Provincial Context: Eighteenth-Century Bristol and Norwich." In *The Jacobie Challenge,* edited by Eveline Cruickshanks and Jeremy Black. Edinburgh: 1988, 123–41.

Roth, Cecil. "The Resettlement of the Jews in England." In *Three Centuries of Anglo-Jewish History,* edited by V. D. Lipman, pp. 1–25. Cambridge: 1961.

Rudé, George. "'Mother Gin' and the London Riots of 1736." *Guildhall Miscellany* 10 (1959): 53–63.

Scoville, W. C. "The Huguenots and the Diffusion of Technology." *Journal of Political Economy* 60 (1952), in two parts, pp. 294–311, and 392–411.

Selig, Robert A. "Emigration, Fraud, Humanitarianism, and the Founding of Londonderry, South Carolina, 1763–1765." *Eighteenth-Century Studies* 23 (1989): 1–23.

Shaw, W. A. "The English Government and the Relief of Protestant Refugees." *English Historical Review* 9 (1894): 662–83.

Smith, R. "Financial Aid to French Protestant Refugees, 1681–1727: Briefs and the Royal Bounty." *PHSL* 22 (1970–76): 248–56.

Speck, W. A. "Conflict in Society." In *Britain after the Glorious Revolution, 1689–1714*, edited by Geoffrey Holmes, 135–54. London: 1969..

———. "Political Propaganda in Augustan England." *TRHS*, 5th ser., 22 (1972): 17–32.

Statt, Daniel. "The City of London and the Controversy over Immigration, 1660–1722." *Historical Journal* 33 (1990): 45–61.

———. "The Birthright of an Englishman: The Practice of Naturalization and Denization of Immigrants under the Later Stuarts and Early Hanoverians." *PHSL,* 25 (1984): 61–74.

———. "Daniel Defoe and Immigration." *Eighteenth-Century Studies,* 24 (1991): 293–313.

Sundstrom, R. A. "French Huguenots and the Civil List, 1696–1727: A Study of Alien Assimilation in England." *Albion* 8 (1976): 219–35.

Sutherland, T. "Thomas Papillon, Merchant." *PHSL* 15 (1939): 290–309.

Thomas, Keith. "The Meaning of Literacy in Early Modern England." In *The Written Word: Literacy in Transition,* edited by Gerd Baumann, 97–131. Oxford: 1986.

Thomas Roger. "Comprehension and Indulgence." In *From Uniformity to Unity, 1662–1962,* edited by Geoffrey F. Nuttall and Owen Chadwick. London: 1962, 191–253.

Thompson, E. P. "Time, Work-Discipline, and Industrial Capitalism." In *P&P* 38 (1967): 38–72.

Thompson, [E.P.]. "The Moral Economy of the English Crowd in the Eighteenth Century." *P&P* 50 (1971): 76–136.

Thornton, P., and N. Rothstein. "The Importance of the Huguenots in the London Silk Industry." *PHSL* 20 (1958–64): 60–88.

Thorp, M. R. "The Anti-Huguenot Undercurrent in Late-Seventeenth Century England." *PHSL* 22 (1970–76): 569–80.

Trevor-Roper, Hugh. "Toleration and Religion after 1688." In *From Persecution to Toleration,* edited by Grell et al., 389–408, 1991.

Viner, Jacob. "English Theories of Foreign Trade before Adam Smith." *Journal of Political Economy* 38 (1930), in two parts, 249–301, 404–57.

Viner, Jacob. "Power versus Plenty as Objectives of Foreign Policy in the Seventeenth and Eighteenth Centuries." In *Revisions in Mercantilism,* edited by D. C. Coleman, 1969.

Waddell, D. "Charles Davenant (1656–1714): A Biographical Sketch", *EcHR,* 2d ser., 2 (1958): 279–88.

Wiles, R. C. "The Theory of Wages in Later English Mercantilism." *EcHR,* 2nd. ser., 21 (1968): 113–26.

Wilson, Charles. "Cloth Production and International Competition in the Seventeenth Century", *EcHR,* 2d series, 13 (1960): 209–21.

Wilson, Charles. "The Immigrant in English History." In *Economic Issues in Immigration,* edited by Sir Arnold Plant, 1–16. London: 1970.

Wrigley, E. A. "The Growth of Population in Eighteenth Century England: A Conundrum Resolved." *P & P* 98 (1983): 121–50.

Unpublished Sources

Grauman, R. A. "Methods of Studying the Cultural Assimilation of Immigrants." M.Sc. (Econ.) thesis, London School of Economics, 1951.

Gwynn, R. D. "The Ecclesiastical Organization of French Protestants in England in the later Seventeeth Century, with Special Reference to London." Ph.D. thesis, University of London: 1976.

Harris, T. J. G. "Politics of the London Crowd in the Reign of Charles II." Ph.D. thesis, University of Cambridge: 1984.

Jubb, M. J. "Fiscal Policy in England in the 1720s and 1730s." Ph.D. thesis, University of Cambridge: 1977.

Julian, M. R. "English Economic Legislation, 1660–1714." M.Phil. thesis, London School of Economics, University of London: 1979.

Mayo, R. "Les Huguenots à Bristol, 1681–1791." 2 parts. Thesis, University of Lille, 1966.

Thorp, M. R. "The English Government and the Huguenot Settlement, 1680–1702." Ph.D. thesis, University of Wisconsin, 1972.

Walker, Michael John. "The Extent of Guild Control of Trades in London, c. 1660–1820; A Study Based on a Sample of Provincial Towns and London Companies." Unpublished Ph.D. thesis. Cambridge: 1985.

Index